Tradition & Progress:
Southern Idaho's Growth Since 1990

Cedar Draw Bluffs/Vincent Andrew Hartgen, 1983

Tradition & Progress:

Southern Idaho's Growth Since 1990

9/3/19
To Terry and Judy McCurdy — thanks for all you do for the community and for your help with this book — Stephen and Linda Hartgen

Stephen Hartgen

Ridenbaugh Press
Carlton, Oregon
2019

Tradition & Progress: Southern Idaho's Growth Since 1990

For more information, contact Ridenbaugh Press, P.O. Box 834, Carlton OR 97111.

Printed and bound in the United States of America.

First edition July 2019

10 9 8 7 6 5 4 3 2 1

Library of Congress Cataloging in Publication Data

Stephen Hartgen

Tradition & Progress: Southern Idaho's Growth Since 1990

Bibliography

1. Idaho. 2. Idaho Economy.

I. Hartgen, Stephen. II. Title.

ISBN 978-0-945648-47-5 (softbound)

Ridenbaugh Press

P.O. Box 834, Carlton OR 97111

Phone (503) 852-0010

www.ridenbaugh.com

stapilus@ridenbaugh.com

Front Cover:

Thomas Moran (1837-1926)

Shoshone Falls on the Snake River, 1900. Oil on canvas. Overall (Image): 71 × 144 1/2 × 4 3/4 in. (180.3 × 367 × 12.1 cm). GM 0126.2339. Gilcrease Museum, Tulsa, Oklahoma

Back Cover:

Rep. Stephen Hartgen

Idaho House of Representatives

Drew Nash/*Times-News* photo © 2017.

Acknowledgements

First, to my family members, for both suggestions and gentle commentary which have kept me from many errors of both fact and tone. My spouse, Linda, a Southern Idaho native, longtime state trial court administrator and now a legislator in the Idaho House of Representatives, read many chapters at various stages and inspired many insights on the region's history and culture. I am honored to have her and Rep. Maxine Bell, (ret.) write forewords to this book. *Tradition & Progress* is mine, as are any regrettable errors, but they and others have prevented me, as Handel's Messiah says, from being a sheep gone too far astray.

My daughter Tiffany Paisley and her husband Joseph, both librarians in Colorado, used their sharp editing skills throughout, chapter by chapter. Joe's a former journalist at the Colorado Springs Gazette and he helped greatly in keeping my writing direct and clear. Ernest Hemingway once said his goal as a novelist was to write at least one perfect sentence. I doubt I come anywhere close to that standard, but Joe has kept me focused on it by his sharp editing. Tiffany offered a number of suggestions, including where to place different chapters, which have made this a better book.

My brother, David Hartgen, made many helpful suggestions on the Transportation and Growth chapters from his perspective as a national policy expert on these topics. My stepson, Trent Wright, executive director of the Idaho Bankers Association, steered me to some federal regulatory websites showing the importance of capital investment in the region's financial changes.

He and other family members Tara Wright Beck and Todd Wright and his spouse Kay, encouraged me to "push ahead" with the book, essentially giving me permission to reinvent myself yet again as a community historian after years in media management and public service. And a special thanks to my youngest daughter, Rachel, who has shown me by her example how to keep an open mind to this vast and changing world.

An additional special thanks to Ridenbaugh Press and its publisher, Randy Stapilus, who has helped many authors tell the "Idaho story" in various ways for many years. Thanks for your encouragement and confidence.

Longtime friends Sen. Lee Heider, Dr. Gary Walker and Terry McCurdy gave me additional perspectives on various chapters. Many other Southern Idaho citizens gave of their time and expertise in ferreting out specific information on a wide range of topics. They include:

Vince Alberdi, Neil Anderson, Shawn Barigar, Melissa Barry, Tara Bartley, Michelle Bartlome, Scott Bedke, Maxine Bell, Sharon Breshears, Michael Brown, Balthasar "Sonny" Buhidar, Vicky Calderon, Bill Carberry, Bruce Christensen, Tim Coles, Eva Craner, Brady Dickinson, Bobby Dye, Curtis Eaton, Mike Fenello, Eric Forsch, Jeff Fox, Alan Gerratt, Jim Gentry, Erin Giesler, Don Hall, Ann Joslin, Janet Matsuoka Keegan, Dennis Maughan, Doug Maughan, Gerald Martens, Bryan Matsuoka, David McClusky, Mike McDonald, Jason Meyerhoeffer, Jerry Meyers, Mary Lou Molitor, Bob Naerebout, Rick Naerebout, Drew Nash, Carl Nellis, Brian Olmstead, Dan Olmstead, Josh Palmer, Brian Patton, Andrew Paz, Jan Roeser, Janis Rogers, Travis Rothweiler, Donna Scott, Carl Snow, Rich Stivers, Beverly Stone, Gary Stone, Jody Tremblay, Doug Vollmer, Loren Ward, Carolyn White, Craig White, Eric Wildman, Rebecca Wildman, Debra Wilson, Sean Woodhead.

Many have given generously of their time and wisdom and have made this book better than I alone could have done. My thanks to all.

Twin Falls, Idaho
March, 2019

Contents

Foreword

By Rep. Maxine Bell, ret.
Idaho House of Representatives

When spring comes to the valley, you can take any road in any direction and the sky will be full of seemingly endless fountains moving steadily round and round over the emerald landscape.

This scene would be a wonderment to those sturdy souls who first looked on a bleak and arid land. Though few in number, they came with purpose and determination. Hours of back-breaking labor behind a team of stalwart horses provided the beginning of what would become a massive life-giving irrigation system.

Over time, horses have been replaced by computer-driven giants that roar through the night. Wise investment and time have continued to make changes beyond those envisioned by the first settlers. Milk leaves the valley in golden bricks of cheese, and the signature Idaho potato can be found as an almost necessary companion to millions of famous hamburgers.

Stephen Hartgen takes us beyond the obvious changes. We wonder if that strong spirit of cooperation is still a part of our communities. Do our citizens continue to practice self-reliance? As the area becomes the home for more people from different backgrounds and experiences, will these new pioneers be as welcome as those who came earlier?

It has been said that the more things change, the more they remain the same. For those readers who enjoy a look back in time, the author provides the opportunity through the eyes of a practiced researcher and teacher of history. But even more intriguing is his love and understanding of the human experience gained as the editor and publisher of *The Times-News*. For those of us proud to call the Magic Valley home, Hartgen provides a thoughtful look, and perhaps a view of what could be a new and exciting future.

By Rep. Linda Wright Hartgen
Idaho House of Representatives

I can think of no one better than Stephen to write a book on the recent changes of Southern Idaho. He has been a part of this valley for almost forty years and during that time he has learned and observed the community and its values.

In his 23 years as editor and then publisher of The *Times-News*, people would often stop him on the street to give him a story or to share something they wanted him to know. He learned the heartbeat of our community and the entire Southern Idaho area. He knew everyone and usually their children and where they were going to school. He would work with young people in choosing a college or university and always encouraged them to make the most of themselves in this world.

Stephen was part of the first regional economic development group that helped bring businesses to the area, not just to Twin Falls. As an economic development consultant, he has worked with many businesses to help them tell their stories better. He's worked with many politicians in helping them with their elections. He has served on many statewide projects and boards, including the Idaho Capitol Commission, which oversaw the restoration of our wonderful Statehouse. It is one of the projects of which he is most proud.

Stephen has reinvented himself several times in his life: college teacher, journalist, editor, publisher, business consultant, public official and now, community historian. Since retiring from the Legislature, he's returning to an early passion, the love of history, community and the American West of Southern Idaho.

He is a wonderful spouse, father, stepfather and grand-papa. His encouragement knows no boundaries and his love is huge. His tenacity seems to be endless, even in the face of adversity. Through an illness, he has grown, even though he is often physically tested. Through all of this, he has gained wisdom and acceptance, and he has supported and encouraged me as I try new things, just as he has our children. He is a strong, conservative and trustworthy person who answers to God and his conscience. I am honored to be his spouse.

In addition to his personal characteristics, Stephen has a broad background which has helped him write this book. He's a former college professor (Ohio State University, University of Minnesota) where he earned a Ph.D. in American History. He almost never mentions his academics; he just uses insights from that experience to inform his daily endeavors. He is as comfortable at a country café as he is on a college campus.

He's a been a business consultant and community leader, and a ten-year (five-term) elected public official in the Idaho House of Representatives. Although we differ on some issues, he encouraged me to run for the House seat from which he retired for health reasons in 2018. I am honored, as he was, to represent our community in the Legislature.

He's an avid fly fisherman and a person much in love with the West and its vistas. Often, he remarks on the beauty of our special Magic Valley, its landscapes, breadth and open space. In that, he's taught me to appreciate it even more; it's an appreciation which is evident throughout this book.

For *Tradition & Progress*, he has researched many topics, interviewed dozens of people and has written often late into the night and again early in the mornings. It is rewarding indeed to see him as an historian at work, capturing our valley's history and culture, its past and its unfolding future.

Best of luck with this publication, Sweetheart. God Bless You.

Introduction

How has Southern Idaho changed in recent years? What is new, different, remarkable? What's stayed the same? How is the region evolving? Where are we going in economic growth, infrastructure, political life, social and personal values?

If Southern Idaho was once considered part of an "empty quarter"[1] of the nation, we are now filling up, with people, businesses, prosperity. As that happens, what is the impact on our evolving ideas, our history, our models for the future? Are we leaving behind the conservatism of our ancestors and becoming another – perish the thought – California? What former patterns of life here remain vibrant in this new century?

It seems we're too busy in our daily lives to look much back or ahead. Maybe that's the reason there haven't been many historical overviews of the Southern Idaho region. Professor James Gentry's book, *In The Middle and on the Edge: The Twin Falls Region of Idaho*, covers the region's history to about 1990.[2] It is a story of eons of geologic time, then sparse settlement by Native Americans, then mostly an unappreciated region for fur traders and settlers heading West on the Oregon and California trails. It was virtually uninhabited until the early 20th century, when the vision of I.B. Perrine and federal lands expansion through the Carey Act brought settlers in significant numbers

---

1 Garreau, Joel. *The Nine Nations of North America*, Houghton-Mifflin, 1981. Garreau places much of the Intermountain West in what demographers call the "empty quarter" of the nation, where there are long distances between communities and local economies rely on extractive industries, including agriculture.

2 Gentry, James. *In The Middle and on The Edge: The Twin Falls Region of Idaho*, College of Southern Idaho, 2003.

to grub out the sagebrush and plant crops on minimal farms. We were then, and remain, a farming valley. Yet, we are changing too.

This book begins where Gentry's leaves off. I see that year, 1990, which marks Idaho's Centennial, as a demarcation line where Idaho's formative years slip behind us and a modern, thriving state in the Intermountain West begins to take shape. This book traces that recent development. It's a narrative that is part history, part journalism and part essays from a conservative perspective. It looks at our main cultural values today, how they came from our past, and how they seem to fit the Idaho many of us want to maintain and foster.

When I first thought about this book and its structure several years ago, a chapter on growth seemed the obvious way to begin. The Southern Idaho economy has been booming for nearly 30 years now, what former Gov. C.L. "Butch" Otter called the "Magic Valley Miracle." It's the driving dynamic in recent Southern Idaho history.

But while the growth is evident everywhere, in itself growth is not the only consideration. The underlying question was: How has the growth affected the cultural values of the region, and how have those values changed and remained constant pillars of our ways of life here?

Thus, the Growth chapter is in the book's first section, followed by chapters on such topics as Individualism, Conservative Roots, Faith and Entrepreneurship. In the final passage of *A River Runs Through It*, (1976) the narrator tells his father that the river's water comes before the words and that the words are borne along by the river's flow. No, the father says, "If you listen carefully you will hear that the words are underneath the water."[3] It seems that the values we all cherish are the words and that the growth phenomenon is perhaps just today's water, flowing over our bedrock of values.

People sometime say that when you come to Idaho, you are entering a place from out of the past, particularly in cultural values. Well, yea, OK. We've even been called the most boring state in the union, not that there's anything wrong with that.[4]

---

3 MacLean, Norman. *A River Runs Through It*, University of Chicago Press, 1976.

4 www.areavibes.com website, May 12, 2017. "Welcome to Snoozeville, America. The data has spoken, and it looks like Idaho is the most boring state in our great nation. Is that a shocker? What makes this such a boring place? First off, more than half of the population is married, and at 55%, Idaho has the 2nd highest rate of hitched individuals in the nation. As we all know, married people are far less exciting than single people are. It's just a fact. On top of that, more than a third of the population has kids at home. That means an exciting night for many Idaho families is trying to figure out who broke the iPad. Finally, there are only 19 people per square mile in Idaho. There's a great benefit to having wide open spaces, but let's be honest - solitude and excitement are practically opposites. But

Southern Idaho represents a good example of both how America was, remains and may yet continue to be. It embodies both the freshest trends in fields like agribusiness and economic development, as well as patterns of life which seem backward and traditional, perhaps even archaic.

Other parts of rural America may also seem like this. The national and sometimes local media portray rural Americans as little more than "Deliverance" folks, rednecks living in "Sticksville" or "West Buggywhip" with our backwater prejudices and ignorance.[5]

But a closer look shows us to be forward thinking, experimental and innovative, if overlooked. We're both progressive and conservative, picking and choosing. We're conservative on social values and public fiscal policies, yet forward thinking when it comes to practical applications in agriculture and research. There's a strong strain of anti-federalism in our political and social speech, yet we're surrounded by millions of acres of federal lands, mostly open to public use. Our love of Idaho is strong, but our love of country is stronger still and unshaken.

Our business institutions are becoming more corporate and owned by out-of-state interests, yet entrepreneurship and opportunity are highly prized assets locally. Start-ups can be found everywhere, many thriving with a growing population and increased investment.

Demographically, we're mostly a homogeneous white population, but recent influxes of immigrants and refugees, as well as a rapidly growing Hispanic population, have opened wide-ranging debates on what it means to be an Idahoan and an American. We welcome and defend our constitutional freedoms, yet we may seem parochial and isolated to casual observers and critics.

We defend individual freedoms and prize a light hand of government. Yet we accept government benefits and fiscal support as legitimate if unwelcomed intrusions.

We are a "neighborly" community of recent immigrants, as virtually none of us have local ancestries back more than four or five generations.[6]

---

we're sure that Idahoans will probably agree that things might be boring where they live, but they like it just the way it is, thank you very much." The next two "most boring" states: Utah and Kansas.

5 Presidential candidate Barack Obama once described rural America as a place where "It's not surprising then they get bitter, they cling to guns or religion or antipathy toward people who aren't like them or anti-immigrant sentiment or anti-trade sentiment as a way to explain their frustrations." Politico, April 11, 2008. In the 2016 presidential campaign, Democrat Hillary Clinton referred to half of Donald Trump's supporters as a "basket of deplorables." *Time*, Sept. 16, 2016.

6 The Twin Falls City Council passed a "neighborly community" resolution in 2017, on a 5-2 vote. Some saw it as a watered- down version of the "welcoming city" movement and

There's almost no "old money" here, but new, and sizeable wealth is being generated every day. We are all newcomers to this place and we welcome others who will work hard and thereby succeed. Yet quite a few of us are suspicious of strangers from other lands, particularly when they have different customs, ethnicity, race, language and religion.

We volunteer a lot and help those less fortunate. As a community, we're generous within our means. We have little time for sloth. Hard work is an accepted norm and indeed a cultural value. We attend a wide range of churches, or none at all. Religious affiliation makes little difference in our acquaintances and associates, although like people everywhere, we sometimes favor those most like us.

It is said that America is slowly coming apart, with people divided by income, ethnicity, politics and cultural values. Yet, Southern Idaho seems less divided and relatively more cohesive than many other regions of the nation.[7] In a world defined by polarization, it seems less of that is generally a good thing.

Who are we then, we inhabitants of Southern Idaho? One might say first that we are creatures of the land, which was here long before us. It seems bleak and forlorn in winter months, snowbound and wind-blasted plains stretching into the distance. In the spring, the narrow strips of riparian vegetation turn pale green with the sun's warmth. Birch, cottonwoods and sage then fade to muted golds and tans in the witherings of late summer and autumn.

Irrigated farmlands flourish. Villages, small towns and numerous farms, dairies and ranches dot the landscape. Through all of Southern Idaho, the dominant landscape traits are the land's immensity, breadth and scale.

These three – immensity, breadth and scale – still shape us in the American West. Some historians say the West is THE essential American story, the national conversation of our character embodying the nation's past, present and future. Of these, the present unfolds daily and the future is always, to some degree, unknown. But the past, ah, the past, is always with us. As the novelist William Faulkner puts it, "the past is never dead. It isn't even past."[8]

How can that be? How can the past be always with us? It is because we bring forward, in each new generation, both direct memory and patterns of

---

feared it would lead to a "sanctuary city" designation. Supporters saw it as a statement of the community's openness. See Brown, Nathan. "Twin Council Passes 'Neighborly Community' Resolution, *Times-News*, May 9, 2017.

7 Murray, Charles. *Coming Apart: The State of White America*, 1960-2010, Random House, (2013).

8 Faulkner, William. *Requiem For A Nun*, 1951.

life. The West certainly has been ingrained in our collective mind, from the Manifest Destiny of the 19th century, to Horace Greeley's exhortation, "Go West, young man, and grow up with the country," to Frederick Jackson Turner's essay in the 1890s on the closing of the frontier, to the surge of Western films in the 1960s, to the "Lonesome Dove" mini-series, to the modern struggle over how to best manage public lands. Southern Idaho's settlement and now vibrant growth seems to reinforce, yet again, that unfolding sense of the West as region and space.

This book sees Southern Idaho as an extensive expanse of farm land and high desert range in which a few smaller towns and one city, Twin Falls, are strewn about as if by the magic wand of agriculture. Put simply, we grow and raise food products and ship them to a nation and a hungry world. That is part of who we are and are likely to remain so into the future.

Until barely more than a century ago, there were almost no settlements here except at river crossings, stagecoach roads and way stations. Yet now, the region is filling up and the pace of that development is more hurried.

This is not to everyone's liking. You can find expressions of concern frequently in the *Times-News* comments section, often anonymous remarks about what is lost. Or listen to conversations at the Twin Falls Senior Center, or the chats at Bridgeview, or at The Depot Grill or Idaho Joe's, where "old-timers" often gather for coffee, memories and reminiscences. Or read the "You Might Be From Twin Falls, Idaho" postings on Facebook. Reminiscence is part of life here, and not a small part.

The land stretched out before the early homesteaders and settlers from one rolling ridge to the next, horizon to horizon. They wrote about it as if it were an animate, beautiful object. "Never a day passed," wrote settler Annie Pike Greenwood, "that I was not thrilled with the changing beauty of the vast cloud-filled skies, the purple and gold sunsets, the blue and white mountains, our gray and green valley, our own lovely, undulating farm, with its ivory wheat-fields, its green beet-fields, its purple-blooming alfalfa. I loved to go to sleep to the chorus of the crickets in the grass just outside my window, with its thorough-bass of the frogs down along the canal. The cool, delightful summer nights; the limitless stretches of clean, white winter snow."[9]

More than a century after Greenwood and her family settled in Minidoka County, the dominant features are still readily identifiable in the landscapes. The Magic Valley consists of more than a million acres of some of the most diversified irrigated farmland in the United States.[10] Gigantic food processing

9 Greenwood, Annie Pike. *We Sagebrush Folks*, Appleton-Century, 1934.

10 USDA Census of Agriculture, Idaho, 2012. Irrigated lands by county: Blaine, 42,000 acres; Camas, 20,000 acres; Cassia, 237,000 acres; Gooding, 175,000 acres; Jerome, 149,000 acres; Lincoln, 71,000 acres; Minidoka, 205,000 acres; and Twin Falls, 257,000

plants have sprung up and unemployment has dropped below three percent. Twin Falls pushes outward into what was once a sagebrush plain and then farmland, but now city and suburb.[11]

The region has attracted both labor and capital from the start. In a sense, it is like colonial America, a productive strip of food processing land, the products then shipped, sometimes after value adding, to distant markets. As in colonial America then, a major economic development challenge today is the availability of labor and a skilled workforce. There is opportunity for anyone who will come, work hard and thereby prosper. Just as in colonial America. It is another chapter in that great American story.

The Magic Valley name, as it is known locally, derives from the area's fertile volcanic soil and the abundant sunlight from which the region's crops seem to jump from the ground as soon as water is applied. "Just add water, to make the desert bloom," as a 2004 local song goes, to celebrate the region's first century. "Come on out West, there's room."[12]

And so they did. It was one of the great land rushes of the early 1900s, so much so that in just 15 years, from 1904 down to about 1920, some 65,000 people settled in this broad valley. Think about that. In just 15 years, the valley population went from virtually zero to 65,000. "We there abide," as the Colonial settlement saying goes.

As America has "filled up" in population over the decades, there have been many instances in which once modest towns have burgeoned into sizeable communities and then to substantial cities. The past quarter-century of Southern Idaho reflects some of those trends, but with singular variations and nuances as befits its physical location, history, setting, influences and social and economic conditions.[13]

It is said that all history begins with geography. Hence, the first section of this book deals with the dominant and constant natural forces of Southern Idaho: earth, climate, fire and water. It then takes a look at the booming

---

acres.

11 Farmer, Liz. "Idaho's Magic Valley: Miracle or Magic Trick,?" *Governing*, April 16, 2014. See also Fick, Bob. "Idaho's March Jobless Rate Hits 5-Year Low," Idaho Department of Labor, April 18, 2014. Twin Falls County was the third fastest growing county in the state in 2013, at 1.8 percent, to a population of close to 80,000. Department of Labor news release, March 28, 2014. It has since grown by another 5,000 residents in four years. Idaho's Department of Labor, May 31, 2017, estimates the South Central region of the state will grow at about 1 percent per year through 2025, twice the national average, pushing the region's population to 212,000 in 2025, up from 192,000 in 2016.

12 Scott, Donna . "Just Add Water," Twin Falls Centennial song, 2004. See also, Hutchins, Virginia. "Blog: Twin Falls Tune Shows up at the Campfire," *Times-News*, May 29, 2013.

13 Garreau, Joel. *Nine Nations*. Garreau notes how the region is dominated by vast expanses of public lands, mixed agricultural and natural resource activities, small communities and modest cities.

growth in the region in the past 25 years or so. From there, we analyze the rural values found here, and how they are changing: a broadly-held sense of conservatism, a homogeneous population, modest land holdings by many but without large concentrations in the hands of the few; an egalitarian social network and a socially-conservative political and religious culture.

The book then moves to individual chapters on topics which explore changes over the past quarter century, from our structures of government, to environmentalism to energy development, demographics and education, to media and politics.

Readers will notice that I view Southern Idaho mostly through a conservative lens. As a former newspaper publisher and journalist, I've been exposed to the fast pace of change in modern America. That's the nature of daily newspapering. But I've also retained an appreciation of valued patterns in past American life, deriving in part from my study of American history, my early years in rural Maine and now, from almost four decades in this city in the Intermountain West. I wrote about that background in a personal memoir, published in 2014, and in more detail.[14] This book isn't a sequel exactly, but the lens through which I see things echoes that continuity.

Finally, there are some predictions about where Southern Idaho is headed and what it may look like in decades to come. I have some projections in most of the chapters, as well as at the end of the book, in a final chapter called "The Spirit of Place – Revisited."

Instead of a bibliographic section on sources, I include running footnotes through the text for those who like to read them. I'm a big fan of these, as they often provide detail which doesn't fit the narrative but which provides context and background. Where I can, I use commonly-available media sources rather than academic journals, as the former are more readily available for readers. I use traditional sources such as historical records, books, interviews, newspaper accounts, government documents, power-points and such modern communications as Facebook posts and media comment sections and blogs. Some of these latter citations are anonymous, as they reflect the modern demand for personal privacy. I use them nonetheless and indicate when they're from unnamed parties. Readers can judge their value for themselves.

Overall, my goal has been to produce a comprehensive, readable and accessible source for both casual readers and those who want more detail. My hope is to provide a reference book on what Southern Idaho is like today, and how it got that way. It is hoped that future residents and the curious will use it to help understand this dramatic time in Southern Idaho's history.

---

14 Hartgen, Stephen. *Journey West: A Memoir of Journalism and Politics*, Ridenbaugh Press, Carlton, Or., 2014.

It's not an exact model, but I have long admired Thomas Jefferson's *Notes on the State of Virginia* (1785), in which he outlined to a French diplomat the nature of that state and its characteristics. Jefferson, inquiring individual that he was, dealt with Virginia's geography and economy, but also delved into its social and political institutions, including freedom of religion and slavery.

I don't pretend to be as insightful as he was. Unlike Jefferson, who was a Virginian by birth, I am not a native Idahoan. But I have lived here many years and consider this my adopted and beloved home. No place has fit me as well as this one.

My time here has afforded me the opportunity to consider many pros and cons of Southern Idaho life. I've been a journalist and editor; a college history and journalism professor; then a community newspaper publisher, then a business and economic development consultant, and a ten-year elected public official as a member of the Idaho House of Representatives. I've served on numerous civic boards and commissions, visited schools and ranchland, shopped both locally and online, raised children and helped aging in-laws navigate the challenges of advancing years. I've had health issues of my own, and I continue in my seventies with as much grace, forbearance and resolve as I can daily muster. God willing, I shall yet visit nearby trout waters, sparkling and clear, in the years ahead.

Like many other places, there are both enormous benefits and some downsides to life in this somewhat isolated region. I try to analyze both the pros and cons, chapter by chapter. I hope readers will find this book at once generous, fair and considerate, yet straightforward and truthful. If I can accomplish that, if it rings with authenticity, I will have succeeded as a public official, historian, journalist and community observer of what I consider to be a blessed land.

Stephen Hartgen
Twin Falls, Idaho 2019

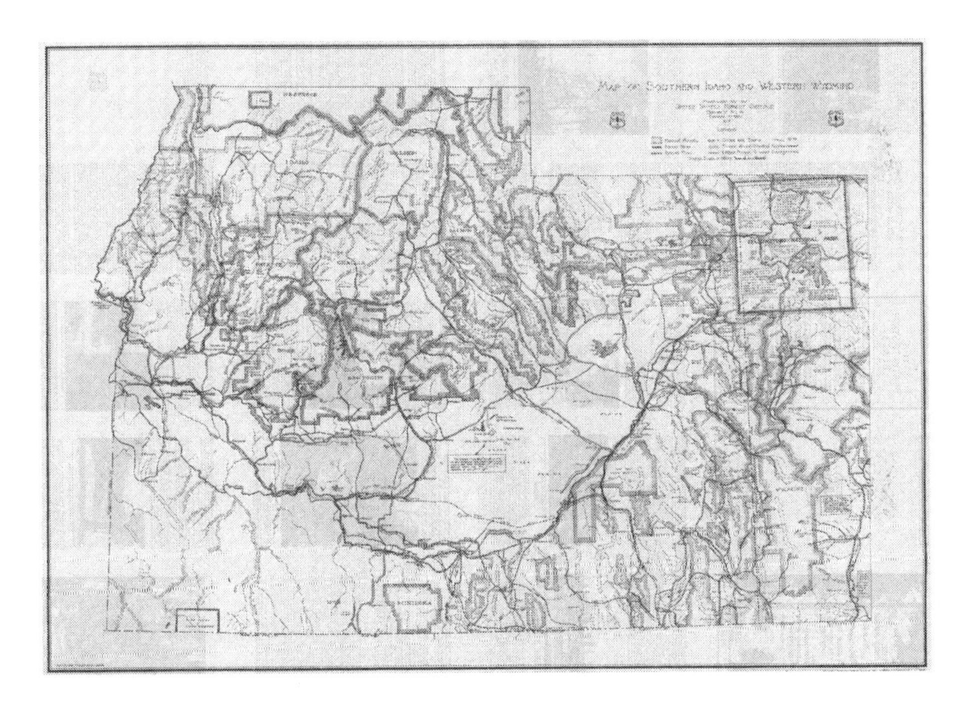

Map of Southern Idaho and Western Wyoming, United States Forest Service, 1926. Map courtesy of Idaho State Historical Society

Part I:
Time & Progress

Western Trees/Vincent Andrew Hartgen, 1983

1. Constants: Earth, Climate, Fire, Water

Earth

The first modern explorers in Southern Idaho found what seemed a desolate plain of grasses and sagebrush. Conditions were so harsh that they thought the region was only a pass-through place, essentially uninhabitable.[15] It must have been bleak indeed, even to the tough Hunt Party explorers of the region in 1811. Two generations later, the geologist and explorer John Wesley Powell thought the whole of the West beyond the 100th Meridian in central Nebraska received too little rain to be farmable. Unlike the Midwest, Powell thought, with its rich soils and abundant rainfall, the West's aridity of less than 20 inches of annual rainfall made the area unlikely to be developed without irrigation.[16]

---

15 Irving, Washington. *Astoria. Anecdotes of an Enterprise Beyond the Rocky Mountains*, Putnam, 1868. "In abandoning the river, (at Cauldron Linn) they (the Wilson Price Hunt party) would have to launch forth upon vast trackless plains destitute of all means of subsistence, where they might perish of hunger and thirst. A dreary desert of sand and gravel extends from Snake River to the Columbia. Here and there is a thin herbage, insufficient for pasturage of horse or buffalo. Indeed, these treeless wastes between the Rocky Mountains and the Pacific are even more desolate and barren'."

16 Stegner, Wallace. *Beyond the Hundredth Meridian: John Wesley Powell and the Second Opening of the West*, Penguin, 1992. See also Seager, Richard, et. al. "Whither the 100th Meridian? The Once and Future Human Geography of

Ah, yes, irrigation. I.B. Perrine's vision was of an irrigated landscape across Southern Idaho, a modest and then prosperous agricultural valley emerging from the volcanic soil. Long growing seasons, warm days and cool evenings led to vigorous fields, particularly of root crops like potatoes and sugar beets and grains like wheat and barley.

But first, there was the land itself. Eons of geologic time had left a rough landscape of lava flows, lava-flow basalt and beneath that, volcanic rhyolite. Soils were often less than a foot thick and contained little humus, decayed plant life or resulting acidity. A dry surface climate belied the potential productivity of the alkali soil for crop productivity. A flood of almost unimaginable proportions had transformed a quiet, lazy East to West river into a huge cataract of perhaps 20 million cubic feet per second about 15,000 years ago, tearing rock from canyon walls and scouring the landscape of its thin topsoil.[17] A narrow canyon of almost 500 feet was left in its wake before it widened out downstream into a wider valley with numerous ground-round boulders strewn about the landscape.[18]

Soils ripped from the land were deposited in "eddy" and "washbowl" locations, such as the early I.B. Perrine ranch in the Snake River Canyon, from which he was able to grow impressive fruits and vegetables. He followed those horticultural achievements within a vision to turn the plain into an irrigated tract of hundreds of thousands of acres.[19]

Back from the river's cliffs, where the Bonneville Flood didn't reach, Southern Idaho has significant acreages of high quality soils, characterized as "prime" in a federal nationwide standard. About 611,000 acres in Twin Falls and Jerome counties (approximately 40 percent) was in this "prime" category, but not all was available due to irrigation limits.

America's Humid Divide. Part I: The Story So Far," American Meteorological Society, Mar. 21, 2018.

17 Willsey, Shawn. *Geology Underfoot in Southern Idaho*, Mountain Press Publishing Company, Missoula, Mt., 2017

18 Geologists estimate the ancient (13,000 BC) Lake Bonneville flood at about 15-20 million cubic feet per second, or about a cubic mile of water per hour for a year, leaving today's Great Salt Lake behind. As a contrast, today's high water flows on the Snake rarely top 25,000 cfs. The Bonneville Flood is thought to have been 800,000 times today's high floods. See Friends of the Pleistocene, "The Bonneville Flood Revisited," Sept. 21-25. 2011, Central Washington University, Centralia, Wa.

19 Gentry, James. *In the Middle and on the Edge: The Twin Falls Region of Southern Idaho*, College of Southern Idaho, Twin Falls, 2003. See also Nokkentved, Niels. *A Forest of Wormwood*, Caxton Printers, Caldwell, Id., 2008, and Fiege, Mark. *Irrigated Eden: The Making of an Agricultural Landscape in the American West*, University of Washington Press, Seattle, 1999.

Additionally, farmland conversion to residential and urban uses has led over the decades to more marginal lands being farmed and used for pasture.[20] Many soils in Southern Idaho are on the high side of pH measurement, ranging to over 8.5 pH, more alkaline than acidic,[21] and are thus well suited for diverse crops.

Soil erosion from wind, water, excessive tilling and other factors has long been an issue in Southern Idaho. Modern soils preservation practices were introduced in recent years, including settling ponds and catch basins at the tail ends of fields, as well as soil binders to prevent or diminish erosion.[22] These improvements, as well as pivot irrigation systems which reduce runoff, have helped preserve Southern Idaho's soils and farmlands.[23]

Idaho has a history well before statehood in 1890 of soil conservation and farmland preservation. There are about 50 local soil conservation districts in the state, many in Southern Idaho, as well as a statewide coordinating commission. These groups work on sustainability with both federal partners as well as regional non-profits.[24]

---

20 US Department of Agriculture, Soil Survey of Jerome and part of Twin Falls County, Idaho, 1991.

21 DigitalAtlasIdaho, 1983: "Much of the area of the Snake River Plain is covered with a naturally dry, limy soil. This is found in a very thin layer less than six inches thick. It is made up of a mixture of wind-blown soil and volcanic ash. Most of the 3.5 million acres of irrigated land in Idaho is of this type and more than half of the field crops produced in Idaho are from this soil. The ash from volcanic explosions over millions of years has mixed with the soil to produce a soil well-suited for crops such as potatoes, wheat, corn, barley, sugar beets and alfalfa."

22 Sojka, R.E. and Lentz, R.D. "PAM in Furrow Irrigation: An Erosion Control Breakthrough," Northwest Irrigation and Soils Research," Kimberly, Id., 1996. See also, Snyder, Cindy. "No Till Gains Ground," *Times-News*, Oct. 24, 2016.

23 Twin Falls Canal Company website. "Water Quality,"2018.

24 Snyder, Cindy. "Soil Conservation Districts Celebrate Long History," *Times-News*, April 25, 2016.

Climate

Southern Idaho's climate patterns are characterized by moderate temperatures, low to moderate humidity, ample sunshine, limited rainfall, considerable windy conditions and persistent dryness, sometimes interspersed by fast-moving storms and snow squalls. These conditions give the region a harsh reputation, accentuated by the open expanse of the landscape. This Intermountain region is at the northern edge of the "Great Basin," which extends south, covering much of Nevada and parts of Western Utah, Northern Arizona and Eastern California.

The region is not as dry as the California deserts, but with less than 10 annual average inches of rainfall, Southern Idaho has a "high desert" environment. Mountain ranges to the north and south act as funneling "sideboards" which channel wind currents from west to east across the open landscape. For early travelers, Southern Idaho was not a place to linger.[25]

Temperatures vary greatly by altitude. On the Snake River Plain, they range from an average high of 62.1 degrees Fahrenheit to 36.5 degrees for the average low, with an overall average of 49.3 degrees. January's averages range from a high of 37 to an average low of 20. July is the warmest month, with an average high of 88 and an average low of 56. There are occasional 24-hour temperature swings of more than 40 degrees from overnight lows to next-day highs. Only a few hundred miles from the Pacific time zone and located along the 42nd parallel, Southern Idaho often has sunlight well into the winter evenings, with early summer daylight lasting until after 10 p.m.

Winter gives way, sometimes as early as February, as new green shoots rise from the soil and roadside rock chucks (Western yellow-bellied marmots) emerge from estivation to feast on the new plants; in many country café conversations, their emergence signals that field preparations will soon be underway. Long days, cool nights and abundant sunlight make for early planting, sometimes in March, and the first of several cuts of alfalfa are harvested by early May, sometimes monthly after that.

Because of a long growing season, it's not unusual for fields to be "double cropped," say from peas and then to alfalfa. Irrigation control using modern geo-positioned pivot water systems, allows for optimal application of water,

25 Goltra, Elizabeth. *Oregon Trail Journal* (1853). "Monday August 1st. Drove 7 miles this morning and came to Snake River again. No feed again here, nothing but sage covers the face of this Broad Plain. We watered here and started again and of all the rock roads, this day's travel is the worst and dust too dense to speak of, for our stock and ourselves are choked almost to suffocation. We followed down the river for 12 miles and came to Rock creek, where we found some good spring water (a luxury) and camped, grass very scarce. Drove 19 miles." See also McPhee, John. *Basin and Range*, 1982.

herbicides and pesticides to maximize crop production. Visitors often marvel at how such innovations work to produce such vibrant fields of grains, potatoes and alfalfa.

Idaho participates in many ongoing snowpack and water measurement surveys, as accumulated snow volume and water content are good predictors of available water supplies. Snotel sites at many locations provide ongoing data for many users, including recreation, sports, agriculture, forest and range productivity, as well as providing the basis for future economic development projections. An army of researchers and agencies work year-round on these data points, which are often then converted to ongoing news reports and estimates.[26]

Southern Idaho's climate varies considerably due to an altitude varying from more than 3,000 feet to more than 8,000 feet. Winter blizzards are regular occurrences, particularly at higher elevations and over mountain passes.

Blustery winds, west to east, are common in Southern Idaho. In winter, it's not unusual for north-south roads to be drifted shut as the snow flies horizontal to the open fields. Summers often bring squally gusts, sometimes in excess of 60 miles per hour, which can take down older trees, thinly rooted as they often are in the shallow soil.[27]

While climate change is discussed both nationally and locally, there is a spirited debate as to its cause and little political or scientific consensus, particularly with how it might affect Idaho.[28] Many scientists attribute the changes to human activity, while others point to centuries-long and sometimes eons-long patterns. There is little doubt that changes in the intermountain climate over time will likely prompt changes, particularly to agricultural practices and crop selection.[29]

---

26 National Weather Service, Boise, Idaho. "Idaho Spring Flood and Water Resources Outlook," March 9. 2018. An overview of the coming year's potential impacts.

27 USA.com. Idaho Average Wind Speed County Rank. Weatherspark.com at "Average Wind in Twin Falls, Idaho" lists Twin Falls' windiest months from Nov. 2 to May 23, with an average wind speed of 8.7 mph.

28 Bunch, Riley. "Climate Change Hearing Shows Lack of Data on Potential Impacts on Idaho," *Idaho Press*, March 6, 2019.

29 US Environmental Protection Agency. "What Climate Change Means for Idaho," August, 2016.

Fire

July 2007 was the hottest in almost 40 years, and the weathered grass out on the 71 Livestock Association range to the west of Rogerson was plenty dry. Across what has been called "God's Country for grazing cows,"[30] plant life shriveled and water holes dried to caked mud.

As ranchers expected, the humidity dropped and the heat increased. In the second week of July, temperatures spiked daily at over 96 degrees. Frowning thunderheads boiled up over the Jarbidge Range just across the Nevada border and along the East-West ridge of hills from Elk Mountain east to China Mountain and Brown's Bench. There were more than 30 separate lightning strike fires in three days, July 16-18. Afternoon winds picked up daily and with the approaching fronts came waves of pressure variants. There wasn't much rain, mostly just wind and lightning.[31]

Lightning strikes lit up the range during the hot evenings, pressing ranchers and BLM officials into action. But by the time sufficient resources could be mustered, the small fires had melded into the huge Murphy Complex Fire which consumed more than 650,000 acres of grasslands and range, an area not much smaller than the state of Rhode Island.

Beyond the loss of rangeland, on which ranchers depend to feed their cows, was the loss of the cattle themselves. Panicked by the storm-driven flames, the beasts stampeded to the fence lines where they were trapped. Dozens died in the smoke and flames. A week later, Three Creek rancher Bert Brackett, his head down disconsolately, kicked the ash and dirt at his feet. Behind him was burned up rangeland as far as the eye could see; a burned and bloated dead cow lay in the near background.[32]

Rangeland fires have shaped the Southern Idaho landscape and ecosystem for centuries. Early settlers were struck by the ferocity of wind-driven flames devastating summer ranges. Prior to settlement, Western fires were generally less intense, but of more frequent duration. With settlement came longer intervals between fires, but they were more intense.[33]

---

30 The description of the rangeland as where "God would run cows," is attributed to an early developer of the livestock industry in the West, Joseph Scott, in the 1870s. See Brackett, Gus and Kimberly, et. al. The 71: A Century of Bettering Conditions on the Range," *The 71 Livestock Association*, 2017.

31 Brown, Nathan. "Murphy Complex Fire: By the Numbers," *Times-News*, July 9, 2017.

32 Brown, Nathan. "10 Years Later: The Legacy of Idaho's Murphy Complex Fire," *Times-News*, July 10, 2017.

33 Miller, Rick, et. al, "Pre- and Post-Settlement Fire Regimes in Mountain Big Sagebrush Steppe and Aspen," National Interagency Fire Center, *The Northwestern Great Basin Final Report*, 2001.

While rangeland fires of more than 100,000 acres were regular occurrences, it was the enormous Murphy Complex Fire which got ranchers and the BLM thinking that no-graze policies needed revision. But the agency was slow to change. In 2012, the BLM ticketed a rancher who tried to put out a range fire on his own. The agency cited safety concerns with no apparent consideration to the rancher's loss.

The ticketing was seen as a direct slap to land users trying to protect their allotments from devastation.[34] Yet, pro-active management of fire-prone rangeland began to get a more intensive look in the 2010s. New Rangeland Protection Associations, including both ranchers and government crews, formed and began to halt the spread of small blazes before they became conflagrations.[35]

It remains to be seen if the BLM will actually shift policies to recognize that grazing is an important proactive tool in managing wildfires before they start. There are some hopeful signs, including major BLM staffing changes in the new administration.[36] It would be positive indeed to see a policy shift that reflects the importance of multiple uses, including range grazing and other economic benefits, rather than the lock-it-up and keep-people-out emphasis of the past.

Locally, BLM district manager and Southern Idaho native Michael Courtney says "livestock are probably our cheapest and most effective tool to manage (wildfire) fuels out here. If we're not using livestock, we've got to do it chemically or mechanically, and that's very expensive."[37]

Hot summers, dry conditions, winds driven by pressure variants and lightning strikes seem like permanent conditions in Southern Idaho. No one expects a complete end to fires in the West. Climate changes and expanding dry lands could affect the entire region.[38] Still, recent changes in land management practices seem headed in the right direction from the perspective of Southern Idaho ranchers and cattlemen.[39]

---

34 Welch, Laurie. "On Public Land, the Fire Still Burns," *Times-News*, Oct. 7, 2012. See also, Cheers and Jeers, "Jeers to the BLM for ticketing ranchers for fighting fires on federal lands," *Times-News*, July 21, 2012.

35 Smith, Brian. "Ranchers Serve as First Line of Fire Defense," *Times-News*, April 23, 2014.

36 Eilperin, Juliet and Rein, Lisa. "Zinke Moving Dozens of Senior Interior Department Officials in Shakeup," *The Washington Post*, June 16, 2017.

37 National Cattlemen's Beef Association, Facebook post, May 22, 2017.

38 Chambers, Jeanne C. "Climate Change and the Great Basin," US Department of Agriculture, Forest Service, General Technical Report, RMRS-GTR-204, 2008. See also, Ridler, Keith. "Great Basin Rangeland facing challenges with Climate Change," Associated Press, Dec. 27, 2015.

39 Halofsky, Jessica E. et. al., eds. "Climate change vulnerability and adaptation in the Northern Rocky Mountains," Part 1, Gen. Tech. Rep. RMRS-GTR-374. Fort Collins, CO: U.S. Department of Agriculture, Forest Service, Rocky Mountain Research Station, 2018.

Beginning in the 2010s new federal forestlands and rangelands policies gave Idaho additional tools to better manage both grazing and timber allotments. The change allowed state land managers, in cooperation with federal land owners, to form joint management districts for environmentally-protected parcels for both timber harvest and range grazing. Both goals should help reduce fire destructiveness, as well as allow for better detailed management for multiple use.[40]

Water

A Western expression goes that, "Whiskey is for drinking: Water is for fighting." It's often attributed to Mark Twain, who spent quite a bit of time in the Old West almost 150 years ago. The phrase has the ring of authenticity when it comes to describing Southern Idaho water issues.[41]

Idaho case law is filled with statutes, court rulings, interpretations, briefs, public pronouncements and arguments over how water is to be owned and used. Today, water law conflicts are more likely to be worked out in the courtroom than over a closed headgate on an irrigation canal. Because "billable hours" are the coin of modern legal practice and hydrology research, it's not surprising that disputes over "first in time, first in right" or the "prior appropriation" of water rights are mostly now before robed judges and "special courts water masters."[42]

Southern Idaho's water allocation began with the first uses to which water was put. We might think of water as the original renewable resource: Moisture accumulates in the higher elevations of the West mostly in the form of winter snows. The runoffs are then captured in a series of impoundments along the Upper Snake River, where it is then allocated for "beneficial" uses.

Borrowed from water allocation laws and practices elsewhere, Idaho evolved a "first in time, first in right" standard, or "prior appropriation" doctrine for water allocation. The earlier a beneficial use is claimed, the

---

40 Idaho Department of Lands. "Idaho doubles effort to increase federal land Management, expands 'Good Neighbor Authority' to federal rangelands," June 28, 2018. The new cooperative agreements are set out in Idaho Legislature, Senate Concurrent Resolution 126, 2015 Legislative Session.

41 Quote Investigator. "Whiskey is for Drinking; Water is for Fighting Over," June 3, 2013.

42 Hill, Peter J. "Old West Violence Mostly Myth," PERC (Property and Environmental Research Center), Bozeman, Mt., July 17, 2005.

higher its "first in time" status.[43] A beneficial use may be of several types, but agriculture has consistently been included.

In Southern Idaho's early agricultural development, water prioritization was almost constantly being litigated but until the 1960s, there was enough water that new filings were routinely approved. It was not until the water supply in storage and the Eastern Snake River Plain Aquifer began to decline that legal disputes increased markedly.

Water law disputes culminated in the 1980s, when the Idaho Supreme Court effectively gave Idaho Power Company control of the Snake River water.[44] The immediate results included several mid-1980s wranglings between the power company and the state, resulting in the "Swan Falls Agreement." The agreement included provisions by the Legislature establishing an adjudication process and court procedures for determining prioritization of water rights in the Snake River Basin.[45]

It took until 2014, some three decades after the Court's ruling, for the basin's water allocations to be completed. One apparent result is the legal clarity the process has brought to both the "first in right" doctrine and the meaning of "beneficial use." Without the agreement and the subsequent adjudication process, water disputes in Idaho would likely still be much in turmoil.

There's also been a "cultural shift" in how Idahoans look at water, says former Twin Falls Canal Company general manager Vince Alberdi, who serves on the state's Board of Water Resources. Twin Falls has led the way in converting lawn sprinkling systems from city potable water to surface irrigation supplies, thus extending supplies of the first.[46] While storage

---

43 The National Agricultural Law Center. "Water Law: An Overview," Fayetteville, Ar. n.d. and Getches, David H. *Water Law*, 1997.

44 Idaho Supreme Court, *Idaho Power Co. v. State of Idaho*, 104 Idaho 575 (1983)

45 Jones, Jim. *A Little Dam Problem*, Caxton Press, Caldwell, Id., 2016. Jones was Idaho's Attorney General when the court's ruling came down and was one of Idaho's key leaders in putting the adjudication process in motion. along with then-Governor John Evans and state Sen. Laird Noh, R-Kimberly. Jones' book unspools the dispute well for today's Idahoans, who may only know vaguely of the agreement and how, through it, Idaho retained control of the state's water.

46 The city of Twin Falls has made significant progress at reducing use of potable water by converting lawn and parks use to surface irrigation water from its own canal company rights. The program, in place since 2003, is ongoing. As new plats are brought onto city water, developers build in separate watering from irrigation supplies for lawns, parks, etc., parallel to the potable water connections. Peak per capita consumption in 2003 was 911 g/d on a population then of 36,747; in 2017, consumption had dropped to 511 g/d, on a higher population of over 47,000. Put another way, potable water in the city peaked in 2003; if it had continued at the same rate as population growth, consumption would have been over 43 mg/d in 2017 instead of the peak use of 24 mg/d. Email from Twin Falls City Manager Travis Rothweiler, July 27, 2018.

capacity hasn't expanded significantly in recent decades, improved conservation measures, more accurate metering of usage and purchase of potable spring supplies have helped meet current demand, despite growing populations.[47]

This process, along with progress on disputes between so-called "surface users" and "groundwater" pumpers, has given Idaho a solid foundation of water law in the Snake River and other basins.[48] More water disputes are likely, given the state's population growth and the competing uses to which water can be put.[49]

Nonetheless, the decades of intense legal disputes seem to be fading.

A major player in that effort has been Clear Springs Foods, the Buhl-based commercial trout company, which put its own resources into efforts to clarify the prior appropriation doctrine. Seeing its spring flows declining, Clear Springs and its tireless leader, Larry Cope, led legal efforts to bring water law cases forward. These decisions led to cooperative conclusions to numerous disputes.[50]

Recharging the aquifer is an important issue, as are groundwater contamination and adequacy of supply. As Idaho approaches 130 years of statehood and has burgeoned into one of the nation's fastest growing states,[51] questions certainly abound as to water adequacy and quality.

Yet, it seems a relatively more peaceful era of water use and allocation is emerging.

Important changes in water conservation, combined with good water/snowpack years at higher elevations, have positioned Southern Idaho better on the water front than it's been in many decades. Since the 1950s, the aquifer was being drawn down by about 200,000 acre feet per year. Although

47 Alberdi, Vince. Interview, July 24., 2018. Twin Falls city water usage peaked in 2003 at 30-32 million gallons/day; since then, it has declined. The 2015 peak was 25 mg/d. The city estimates water usage will climb at about 2 percent/year to about 38 mg/d by 2063. See Kennison, Heather. "Driving Growth: A Look at Water in 9 Magic Valley Cities," *Times-News*, July 10, 2016.

48 Snake River Adjudication Judge Eric Wildman in 2014 estimated the record of final decrees was more than 275,000 pages, involving some 43,822 claims, resulting in 36 additional Idaho Supreme Court basin opinions and one US Supreme Court ruling. Cited in Jones, p. 353.

49 Fereday, Jeffery C., et al. *Idaho Water Law Handbook*, Givens Pursley LLP, Boise, Id., May 8, 2018.

50 Dumas, Carol Ryan. "Fish Farm Transfer Settles Idaho Water Rights Dispute," *Capital Press*, Dec. 20, 2012. Full disclosure: The author served as a business consultant to Clear Springs Foods from 2005-2007.

51 Idaho Department of Labor. "Idaho's April Unemployment Rate Unchanged at 2. Percent," May, 2018. The department put Idaho's workforce at 821,875, up 25,619 over the previous year of 796,256.

thought to be the size of Lake Erie (115 cubic miles of water, covering nearly 10,000 square miles), the Snake River Plain Aquifer nonetheless showed signs of over-appropriation and overuse.

Recharge efforts have been ongoing for years, but secure state funding, plus agreements across water districts and among both surface and groundwater users, brought recharge volumes to over 500,000 acre feet in 2017, more than twice the original estimates.[52]

The recharge efforts, led by House Speaker Scott Bedke and others, have placed Idaho on an even more secure path for water sustainability, measurement and use.[53]

New Constants

For a high and often dry mountain state, there's good news on all these "constant" conditions which Idaho will face in the years ahead.

Soil stability and erosion prevention remain key parts of land use models. Climate conditions are mostly known and quantifiable.

Fires, which once devastated Southern Idaho rangelands, are now being attacked by both ranchers and government officials; there appears to be an evolving recognition of the importance of grazing and other multiple uses in proactive fire suppression and control.

And on the water front, better practices and management are stretching out supplies, despite a rapidly growing population. By 2018, about 98 percent of wells were being monitored and outflows being measured. Agricultural water use averaged about 7.5 million acre feet annually from 1980 to 2015. Since then, recharge has added back about 2.3million acre feet in the two years, 2016-2017.[54]

They're all part of the background "constants" which shape life in the Magic Valley now and in the future. Decades from now, Southern Idahoans will undoubtedly be concerned with each of these constants, but the management of each has improved appreciably in our time.

52 Matthews, Mychel. "Wildly Successful Recharge Program Surpasses Annual Goal," *Times-News*, April 21, 2018.

53 Russell, Betsy. "Eastern Snake River Plain Aquifer Sees Largest Annual Increase in Water Volume in 80+ Years," *Idaho Press*, Nampa, Id., July 18, 2018.

54 Patton, Brian. Idaho Department of Water Resources, "Eastern Snake River Plain Aquifer Recharge and Management," Twin Falls Kiwanis, power point presentation, Dec. 6, 2018.

2. Growth

Growth has been the norm of the past quarter century for most everywhere in Southern Idaho. A few economic sectors have grown very little, or not at all, But not very many. Most sectors grew extensively. In a 2017 report, the city of Twin Falls laid out some recent statistics of the city:

- Taxable value: $2.659 billion, up more than $500 million in just five years, since 2013.
- Major investments in food processing new plants: Chobani, $580 million, for a yogurt processing plant employing over 1,000 workers; Clif Bar, an energy bar company, $90 million investment with more than 250 new jobs; Glanbia milk, new downtown headquarters and research center, $20 million.
- Commute time: 14 minutes, still one of the lowest in the nation.
- Permanent Twin Falls population: 47,500, and 75,500 during the workday.[55]
- Housing prices: midrange average of $141,000.
- Urban renewal: over $13 million in downtown improvements; $3.2 million in parks, $4.3 million in airport terminal expansion.
- Population growth: up more than 30 percent in twenty years.[56]

---

55 Rothweiler, Travis." City of Twin Falls: Creating Sustained Excellence," Zions Bank 20th Anniversary, July 21, 2017. US Census data shows Twin Falls County growing by more than 30,000 people since 1990, 53,817 residents to 85,124; Jerome County, from 15,216 in 1990 to 23,627 in 2017; and Cassia County, from 19,601 to 23,664.

56 Rothweiler, City Report, 2017.

It's widely known that the whole state of Idaho has had exponential growth overall, with much of it coming in the state's larger communities, including Twin Falls. Overall, the state's population was 1.683 million in 2016, a net migration increase of almost 19,000 in just one year, on top of the natural increase of over 10,000. Idaho is one of the fastest growing states in the country; a quarter century ago, it stood at just over 1 million people; the 25-year gain is close to 70 percent. Put another way, almost one of every two Idahoans is new to Idaho in less than the past 30 years.

In 20 years, from 1997, more than 200,000 jobs were created statewide, with the workforce now over 708,000, with major increases in construction, transportation, financial services, health care, leisure and hospitality.[57]

In Southern Idaho, the base growth is coming from in-migration, natural increases (ie, birth/death ratios), as well as retention of people who were born and raised here. The impact of this overall population growth can hardly be overestimated, with almost every sector of the economy and social service structure showing the growth pressure, from school enrollments to court filings, transportation congestion to delivery of social services, building permits to labor shortages.[58]

We think of America as a transient nation in which people move at the drop of a hat, but studies show large numbers of people stay close to where they were born and raised. Almost four in ten Americans live in the same community where they were born; another 10 percent have moved but still live in the same state.[59]

That's particularly true when job opportunities abound locally. When job creation stagnates or declines, people pick up and move to follow the work. The better times of recent years has lessened migration out of Idaho and other rural states.

We see the same pattern within Southern Idaho.

---

57 Spendlove, Robert. Idaho Economic Snapshot, Zions Bank, July 21, 2017.

58 Wootton, Julie. "Schools Brace for More Students in Classrooms," *Times-News*, July 27, 2017. Twin Falls has added a second high school and is looking at needing a third within ten years. A new school, and three new elementary schools have been built in the past few years. The 2017 projected enrollment was 9,595, up almost 300 students in one year.

59 Cohen, D'Vera and Morin, Rich. "Who Moves? Who Stays Put? Where's Home,?" Pew Research Center, Dec. 17, 2008. Almost four in ten Americans (37 percent) have lived in the same community all their lives; another 10 percent have moved, but are still in the same state. Westerners have moved more often than Midwesterners. Not surprisingly, the people who have stayed put have closer ties to other family members in the immediate area; those who have left have tended to do so for economic opportunities elsewhere. Some recent research suggests that willingness to relocate for employment is declining somewhat as work availability expands with the economy and people's family considerations take higher priority. See Feintzeig, Rachel and Weber, Lauren. "Fewer Americans Uproot Themselves for a New Job," *Wall Street Journal*, Aug. 20, 2018.

The more rural counties, such as Gooding, Lincoln and Camas, show slower population growth. More urbanized counties, including Twin Falls, show higher proportions of people who have come in from 2011 to 2015. Twin Falls and Jerome counties have led the local workforce growth since 2000, up close to 25 percent; the Mini-Cassia area lagged in the first decade, but has responded nicely since 2013.[60]

In the sub-categories, manufacturing jobs have seen the most growth, much of it in the food processing industry, at about 27 percent growth from 2007 to 2017. Hospitality/leisure and health care employment aren't far behind, as more motels and restaurants have sprouted in the Twin Falls area during that span and Twin Falls develops as a regional health care center.[61] That's a similar pattern across much of the small-city, urbanized West.[62]

There are some seemingly contradictory patterns for Southern Idaho communities. Population growth is strong in urban centers, but "stay put" patterns are seen in more rural, outlying areas. Overall, the South Central region is projected to grow at about one percent per year, more than twice the national average.[63]

As unemployment rates tick down below 2.5 percent, the demands for increased services employment also continues to increase.[64] Help wanted signs are ubiquitous in front of many businesses. No employer, it seems, can find enough qualified workers. The College of Southern Idaho is adding new programs annually in an effort to help area businesses find the qualified people they need, but in some cases, it can barely keep up.

A special need noted by many is the increase in demand for services for senior citizens, who seem to have discovered the Magic Valley, its relatively low cost of housing, lower living expenses, crime rates and ease of car

---

60 Roeser, Jan. Siedo Annual Summit, Sept. 25, 20128. slide 6.

61 Roeser, Jan. Siedo Annual Summit, Sept. 25, 2018, slide 10. The uptick in manufacturing employment is particularly welcome, as this category has been slow to recover across the country following the Recession of 2008-2013. See Kennison, Heather. "News bite: Manufacturing Job Growth in South Central Idaho is Fastest in the State," *Times-News*, Feb. 14, 2018. Manufacturing jobs reached 10,000 in the first half of 2017, a 4.2 percent gain from the prior year.

62 Adamy, Janet and Overberg, Paul. "Struggling Americans Once Sought Greener Pastures – Now They're Stuck," *Wall Street Journal*, Aug. 2, 2017. Twin Falls County showed more than 18 percent of the population had moved in within the immediate past five years, 2011-2015. Cassia County was over 16 percent. Other, more rural counties in the state show much lower "move in" rates.

63 Idaho Department of Labor, "Idaho Population Projected to Increase 21.3 % By 2025," May 31, 2017.

64 Matthews, Mychel. "Growing Up: Magic Valley – How Did we Get Here,?" *Times-News*, July 12, 2018. The newspaper launched a series of articles in 2018 on various aspects of Magic Valley growth. This is the first installment.

transportation, if not mass transit. Across Idaho, the seniors' population jumped five percent from 2015 to 2016 in just one year.[65]

At this point, there's no sign of let-up. Recent data puts Southern Idaho among Idaho's fastest growing regions, with Twin Falls County at 85,124, Jerome County at 23,627 and Cassia County at 23,506, all new records. Additionally, Twin Falls and Jerome were also recently designated as a new micropolitan urban area in U.S. Census data. Idaho's population growth continues to outpace the nation as a whole, with an estimated rate of 2.2 percent, three times the national pace.[66]

Close analysis shows that Idaho's growth patterns are indeed divided among urban and rural counties. Southern Idaho has one urbanized county, Twin Falls, and one commuting county, Jerome. Three other counties – Cassia, Blaine and Minidoka – are considered "rural center" counties and three more counties – Camas, Gooding and Lincoln – are considered "open rural." Twin Falls County is showing the most growth, up 1.9 percent in one year. Nearby counties, called "commuting" counties, show the next most rapid gains.[67]

"Rural center" counties (those predominately rural but with one or more "center" towns), show more modest growth. And in more outlying directions, the "open rural" areas are pretty much stagnant on growth as young people leave for jobs and amenities in bigger places.

From 1990 on, urban growth is close to 100 percent and commuting distance counties show about 60 percent. Both "rural center" counties and "open rural" counties have lagged, with the "open rural" counties showing gains of only about 25 percent over almost 30 years.[68]

More of these patterns are visible in sub-groups, including income sources and industry sectors. As Idaho's population ages, reliance on retirement income sources has increased as well. In 2005, less than 15 years ago, only 21 of Idaho's 44 counties showed high reliance on retirement incomes,

---

65 Idaho Department of Labor, "Idaho Population Aging Faster Than the Nation's," June 27, 2017. Here are some general population increases for the South Central region: Twin Falls County, from 53,817 in 1990, to 63,894 in 2000, to 77,539 in 2010 and 83,514 in 2016, a gain of almost 30,000 in 25 years or more than 55 percent. In the South Central region, the population has jumped from 137,563 in 1990, to 162,679 in 2000, to 186,286 in 2010 to 193,947 in 2016, a gain of more than 56,000 or about 41 percent.

66 Idaho Department of Labor, Census data, March 23, 2018.

67 Manufacturing jobs continue to be added in the region's food processing industry in 2018. A summary of eight expansions in manufacturing shows seven of the eight expansions listed are in the food processing sector, projected to add hundreds more jobs. See Kennison, Heather. "8 Manufacturing Expansions Underway in the Magic Valley," *Times-News*, Oct. 4, 2018.

68 Wolkenhauser, Sam. "The Future of Rural Idaho," Idaho Department of Labor, July, 2018. Comprehensive report on Idaho's demographics and growth patterns back to the 1990s.

mostly Social Security and some with investment income. By 2016, that number had climbed to 35 of the state's counties, including most of the Magic Valley.[69] A similar pattern can be seen in the expanding benefits paid to retired state workers, which grew statewide from $168 million in 1997 to $836 million 20 years later. In Twin Falls County, these payments grew from $24 million in 2012 to $32 million in 2017, paid to 1,905 retirees.[70]

School enrollments are another area in which growth is evident. The Twin Falls district, for example, has seen enrollment jump from 7,777 students in 2010 to over 9,600 in 2017, a 23 percent increase.

The same growth pattern is evident for Jerome School District which is up nearly 500 students since 2010; up 7 percent in two years and closing in on 2,000 students in 2017.[71] Farther out districts are mostly flat. This seems to be similar to the population growth pattern generally, which is rapid in larger communities, but stagnant or more measured in more remote areas.

Growth in student enrollment puts school administrators in a quandary. In the near term, schools see growth, which is also reflected in assessed valuations of land. Since Idaho relies on local bond issues for new school construction, such levies are easier to pass in growing communities than in stagnant ones. If a levy fails, it's usually because it's too much for taxpayers to absorb; second or third tries, with less money sought, are almost always successful.[72]

Bond debt for Idaho schools generally needs a two-thirds majority from local voters, but supplemental levies for year-to-year changes can be passed with simple majorities. Some emergency levies, which sometimes come after enrollment growth, can be approved by local school boards without a public vote.

Critics of bonding limits argue that public education costs should be borne by the state as a whole, but Idaho's system of funding seems generally fair to school needs while remaining cognizant of local voter input. As Idaho continues to grow in population and school enrollment, how to pay for schools will likely be a continuing discussion for years to come.

The same pattern is reflected in the range of available housing. Rural counties have fewer available rental homes, where most young people first

---

69 Wolkenhauser.

70 Email from Drum, Don, executive director of Public Employees Retirement System of Idaho (PERSI), Aug. 2, 2018

71 Wootton-Greener, Julie. "Magic Valley Schools Weigh Option to Deal with Enrollment Growth," *Times-News*, Aug. 2, 2018.

72 Wright, Samantha. "What It Takes to Pass a School Bond and What It Could Mean to Your Taxes," IdahoEdNews, Mar. 2, 2017.

reside. Without affordable housing these younger Idahoans migrate to larger communities, thus adding to the percentage of seniors in more rural areas.[73]

Idaho does not show complete data for house prices to income ratios. But what is shown gives housing prices of three to four times incomes, comparable to much of the country, except in California, coastal Washington and East Coast metropolitan areas.[74] Similar data shows fewer than one-fourth of Idaho wage earners can afford a home mortgage in either Boise or Twin Falls, but that disparity could help nearby smaller commuter towns grow by offering lower-priced housing.[75]

Any discussion of growth should contain some cautions about how a fervent pace of economic dynamism can be followed by years of stagnation. In the 1980s, Idaho grew very little in population and business development after the more robust 1970s. Flat growth, high interest rates, what then-President Jimmy Carter called a period of national malaise all translated to widespread stagnation. More than one wag said, "If you're the last one leaving Southern Idaho, turn out the lights."

In the 2008-2011 period, Idaho again suffered significant contractions in many fields, including housing and construction, from which the state has since recovered. Legislators had to restrain spending as state revenue declined hundreds of millions of dollars, only partly covered by reserve "rainy day" funds. A 2018 report shows Idaho among the top states in the nation in reserves to expenses, yet another example of Idaho's fiscally responsible approach to government funding.[76] We pride ourselves in Southern Idaho with robust growth in virtually every sector, and the outgoing governor, C.L. "Butch" Otter, left office having handled both recession and now, a substantive recovery. He says: "It's up to all of us who hope to encourage continued sustainable growth to help instill in more Idaho employers the confidence to invest in their own future, and the future of our state."[77]

There is never time for a let-up, because that often leads to a downward spiral of stagnation, population decline and so on. You don't have to look hard around America to see the devastation left by negative change and failed

73 Wolkenhauser.

74 Forsch, Eric, Idaho Department of Commerce, "Homes Prices to Incomes Ratio, 2017," Power Point presentation to the Southern Idaho Economic Development Organization, Annual Summit, Sept. 25, 2018, slide 11.

75 Forsch, "Share of Homes Affordable to Potential Buyers Varies Widely," slides-11-12.

76 Pew Center of the States Report. "States Make Progress Rebuilding Rainy Day Funds," Aug. 29, 2018.

77 Otter, C.L. "Butch." Idaho in "State of the State," *Site Selection*, Jan. 2017. Idaho ranked 20th in business tax climate, 21st in electric rates, and 12th in state fiscal stability, but 46th in higher education expenditures and 50th in career readiness certificates.

government meddling. A shuttered pulp/paper mill in Maine. An empty mall in the Midwest. A closed union hall in Ohio. An abandoned mine in Minnesota or Montana. A weather-beaten, abandoned farmstead in the Dakotas.

There are often specific reasons for each of these: product supply changes, world trade patterns, excessive union demands, marketing failures, inadequate workforce, falling capital investment, civic stubbornness, on and on.

Southern Idaho is enjoying a period of outstanding growth, but there is never a guaranteed future. Like the townsfolk in the Pieter Bruegel painting "Winter Landscape With A Bird Trap," (1565), we blissfully skate over a pond of unknown depth on ice of undetermined thickness. The future is promised to no one, nor to any human enterprise. It's something we all need to constantly work for.

Decline is not inevitable, but growth is fed by continued vigilance and adaptability. Communities which are constantly trying to reinvent themselves have the best prospects.

Often, local boosterism for present successes may cloud long-term judgments. The focus on today's growth may be a dark glass through which we do not see the future clearly.

So what to do? Diversify, diversify, diversify might be a good first mantra; the more dependent a community is on one industry, the higher the long-term risks.

Then, build the local employment base. Many economic development efforts focus on finding new, outside "buffaloes" to shoot and bring back to camp; the "big kills" so to speak. But studies show much long-term growth comes from retention and internal expansion.

These often need nurturing which they may not always get, particularly in smaller communities where retention isn't always a top priority and which newly-minted economic development "specialists" have little workforce experience or regard for this "meat and potatoes" task.[78]

Third, get the basics right: Low taxes, sound local and state fiscal policies, polite politics, safe and effective schools, low crime, clean environments, and low living costs.

---

78 Sometimes, lower profile companies are below the local radar for retention efforts, even though their economic contributions are substantial. See Weeks, Andrew. "Twin Falls Meat Company Gears up for the Holidays," *Times-News*, Nov. 6, 2012; Kennison, Heather. "Seastrom Manufacturing Ships Small Parts to Thousands of Customers World Wide," *Times-News*, Feb, 18, 2018; Glazar, Ed. "Solo Cups Made in Twin Falls," *Times-News*, Oct. 5, 2014.

Keep expectations reasonable, in line with resources. Don't try to "shoot the moon." You can't change where you are, but you can change what you are.

Southern Idaho's growth, particularly in the food processing sector, has caught the attention of many in those industries and related fields. The right set of preliminary conditions have certainly helped the region position itself well for future growth, but important regional efforts have helped as well.

The Southern Idaho Economic Development Organization (SIEDO), headed by long-time executive director Jan Rogers, lassoed many an outside prospect.[79] So has a private sector initiative, Business Plus, which raises money that is used to "sweeten" proposals. These local "grass roots" efforts, combined with strong support from the Idaho Department of Commerce, have brought thousands of new jobs and millions of dollars in capital investment to the region which has spurred further growth in many satellite sectors and service industries.[80]

One key has been a regional approach to project siting.

Potential businesses do their own specific site selection based on their individual needs. The local communities offer their "best foot forward" appropriate "packages" of amenities, such as urban renewal incentives, tax increment financing, design and water/sewer capacity improvements to bring the prospects to fruition.[81]

---

79 From SIEDO's website, October, 2018: "Southern Idaho Economic Development Organization (SIEDO) is a joint venture of public and private sectors in the communities of Buhl, Burley, Camas County, Fairfield, Filer, Glenns Ferry, Gooding, Gooding County, Hansen, Heyburn, Jerome, Jerome County, Lincoln County, Murtaugh, Paul, Rupert, Shoshone, Twin Falls, and Wendell, formed to help diversify and strengthen the local economy by retaining and attracting business to the Southern Idaho region. SIEDO works closely with each of these communities to promote economic development through expansion of existing business and to implement a focused consistent program to attract new businesses to the region." SIEDO has shifted its focus somewhat to more individual talent attraction to the region and less emphasis on business recruitment. It's an open question as to whether this strategy will sustain the excellent pace of Southern Idaho's job creation. See Kennison, Heather. "What's in a Name? SIEDO Ends Pronunciation Debate with Name Change," Times-News, Jan. 15, 2019.

80 Business Plus website, October, 2018. Full disclosure: the author served on the SIEDO and Business Plus boards for many years and was the Business Plus executive director from 2006 to 2009, before his appointment to the Idaho House of Representatives. Business Plus, beginning in 1987 through 2018 has allocated over $2 million in specific industry grants and another $1.35 million in recruitment help through SIEDO. The efforts have brought over $1 billion in investments and expansions to Southern Idaho and over 2,000 new jobs. Email from Business Plus Executive Director Rebecca Wildman, Oct. 17, 2018.

81 Rogers, Janis., former executive director of SIEDO, Email, Feb. 27, 2019: "As I took the helm of the first regional economic development organization in 2001, I often heard from the "no growth" crowd who wanted things to stay the same. My response was always, "No

Beginning in the late 1980s, many sectors have brought new projects and expansions to the region. Companies looking to expand in the West have often given Southern Idaho a close look, and many have landed here. That list includes TrusJoist, building trusses; Clear Shield National (now Solo Cup) plastic utensils; Dell Computers, call center (now C3); Jayco and Dutchman, recreational vehicles; Rite-Stuff Foods, twice-baked potatoes; Bridon Cordage, plastic baling twine; Spears Manufacturing, plastic piping; Hilex Poly plastic bags; DOT Industries, transportation; Everton Mattress, institutional mattresses; and Seastrom, precision machine parts, mostly for the aircraft industry.[82]

These manufacturing businesses and others have broadened the base of Southern Idaho employment. While Southern Idaho is likely to remain an agriculture and food processing region, we can expect more non-agriculture business growth here as well.

As a state, Idaho does not offer much incentivization beyond urban renewal financing, and locally, the most successful projects have had a jobs creation focus, rather than blight mitigation and street improvements. In recent years, however, the blight side of urban renewal has gained more attention with a major revitalization project for downtown Twin Falls. It remains to be seen if this will only shuffle existing entertainment and recreation venues or actually create new, livable-wage jobs.[83]

To some degree, this shift represents an emphasis on making downtown Twin Falls more of an attractive center for entertainment and hospitality venues and events.[84] Entertainment and hospitality are good focuses for communities, but job creation, particularly in manufacturing, creates the base employment upon which the others depend.

Idaho already has a good reputation as a recreation state with numerous outdoors opportunities. The growth of the past couple of decades has been in employment sectors like health care, manufacturing and food processing. Employment in these areas should continue to be the primary emphasis of economic development.

---

worries, the only people that come and stay will be like-minded people. Rural life is not for everyone." Thankfully, the personality of the community and region has not fundamentally changed, even as the population has almost doubled. The foresight of business leaders to aggressively market and drive opportunity to the Magic Valley has paid off in spades over the last two decades. From a Dell Technical Support Center to Chobani and Clif Bar and beyond, the region has grown thousands of direct jobs and opportunities while continuing to maintain and enhance its character."

82 Business Plus website, Oct., 2018.

83 Idaho Statutes, Title 50, Chapter 20.

84 Twin Falls City Comprehensive Plan, 2016.

The region has seen some dramatic growth in employment particularly in health care, as well as in manufacturing and in agriculture. Over 20 years, from 1997-2017, employment in the South Central region increased from 65,456 to 88,726, a 28 percent gain. Agricultural employment grew from 6,026 to 10,620, a 76 percent increase; manufacturing gained from 6,026 to 10,252, a 27.5 percent increase; health care grew from 5,778 to 10,191, also a 76 percent gain.

Each sector now represents about 10-12 percent of local jobs, a nice balance in a period when manufacturing has declined generally across many states.[85] There are dozens of communities all over the country which would love to have these kinds of gains and valuations over the same 20 years, through two recessions and still expanding.[86]

Is there a downside to growth?

To be sure. You can read critiques of modern farming and business growth on almost any nostalgic reminiscence site on the "way things used to be." Every new subdivision, particularly on what was once farm ground, seems to reflect both change and "progress" as the land use goes from corn and wheat fields and gated pipe to housing lots, then to the houses themselves, then to lawns, trees and outside decorations, neighborhood by neighborhood, until really old-timers say they don't recognize the place any more.

Well, why should they? It's been transformed to new uses, more profitability, more growth.[87] Some will decry this as a false progress. We've seen a number of these critics of modernization through Idaho's recent past, but they seem to have mostly given way now to economic growth supporters.[88]

---

85 For 2018, Southern Idaho Regional Gross Product shows manufacturing, dominated by the food processing industry, as the leading sector at $1.242b, about 15 percent of market share; agriculture at $1.006b, or 12 percent of market share; and health care at $584m, about 8 percent of market share. Government and trade, both retail and wholesale, were also major sectors. Hotels and restaurants were less than $400m, and recreation, arts & entertainment, barely at $100m. Email from Roeser, Jan., regional economist, Idaho Department of Labor, Jan. 31, 2019.

86 Idaho Department of Labor, South-Central region, 1997-2017. Email from Roeser, Jan. Department of Labor regional economist, Jan. 22, 2019.

87 Willams, Carter. "The Rise of Rural America: Opportunity in Agtech," ISelectfund website, Nov 17, 2016.

88 Among these critics are Bill Chisholm, Ed Smith, Lee Halper, Max Hatfield and, more recently, recreationist and so-called "conservation" groups. All can be found in the *Times-News* archives from the 1980s to about 2015. An example: Bill Chisholm, Sept. 24, 2010:

"Keeping up with the Jones" has its proponents in the real estate, retail and home improvement sectors; the advent of big-box stores in the local retail economy suggests a continued emphasis on consumerism. Since the shoppers are here, they deserve the opportunity to buy what they want. There's a reason people flock to these stores: they carry what people want and can afford.

Idaho may seem a more material culture than 50 years ago, but the same can be said for all of America, and for earlier periods of American history. "Times were great back then" thinking is at least as old as the Colonial period; more than one historian has noted that the Revolutionary War was really a conflict by the colonists who wanted to preserve their rights as English subjects, freeborn and of free will, which they saw threatened by Parliament, an uncaring sovereign and biased trade patterns.

That push-pull of American culture, from paucity of material goods to prosperity and now abundance, is played out in many places. For decades, Southern Idaho was a decidedly innocuous place when it came to material wealth. Now, that's changing. It's doubtful many would want to go back to that wash-board and kerosene lamp era, or earlier. We just need to manage the growth well while retaining the freedoms of choice we all treasure.

It's a harder task than it seems.

"Our problems are self-imposed. We have abandoned in large measure the ideals this country was founded on. We have taken on the colonial arrogance that we fought to free ourselves of. Greed and the quick buck have been made virtues. Hard work, once a valued currency, is looked down on and avoided at all cost. Self and selfish interest plays above the common good. Less government can only come about through more personal responsibility."

Part II: Enduring Values

South Hills Meadow/Vincent Andrew Hartgen, 1983.

3. The Spirit of Place

Anyone brought up in the West knows the song "Don't Fence Me In," made famous in the 1940s by The Andrews Sisters, Bing Crosby and Roy Rogers:

Oh, give me land, lots of land under starry skies above
Don't fence me in
Let me ride through the wide open country that I love
Don't fence me in
Let me be by myself in the evenin' breeze
And listen to the murmur of the cottonwood trees
Send me off forever but I ask you please
Don't fence me in
Just turn me loose, let me straddle my old saddle
Underneath the Western skies
On my cayuse, let me wander over yonder
Till I see the mountains rise
I want to ride to the ridge where the West commences
And gaze at the moon till I lose my senses
I can't look at hovels and I can't stand fences
Don't fence me in[89]

89 "Don't Fence Me In" was first written in 1934 and has been recorded and performed by many artists. It has been used as recently as 2013 in a Nevada state tourism promotion. The tune has often been listed on the top 100 best Western songs. See "Don't Fence Me In," Wikipedia, Aug. 6, 2017.

Every line seems to capture that expansive quality of the West: "land, lots of land," "wide open country," "I want to ride to the ridge where the West commences," "I can't stand fences."

Yearning to be free of constraints has been a dominant American desire since our founding, and perhaps no more evident than in the patterns of Western immigration and settlement. By the time the Magic Valley was transformed into farms and towns, much of the arable land elsewhere in the West had been taken up. Any place which could be watered through irrigation was either being farmed or was surveyed for farming.

The abundance of unbroken land in America brought in homesteaders from across the country and across the oceans in a Westward push to fill up a continent.

Here, out of a rugged and forbidding landscape of sagebrush, lava rock and arid soil, these immigrants and their successive generations created a fertile land, first of adequate return and then of today's abundance.

"Every continent has its own great spirit of place," writes the English novelist D.H. Lawrence, "Every people is polarized in some particular locality, which is home, the homeland. Different places on the face of the earth have different vital effluence, different vibration, different chemical exhalation, different polarity with different stars: call it what you like. But the spirit of place is a great reality."[90]

It has been that way with the West. As they travelled farther and farther across the northern plains and then into Idaho, the American explorers Meriwether Lewis and William Clark often remarked on the beauty of the landscape, the majesty of the mountains and the long distances they had both travelled and still had to traverse.

They kept accurate records of the distances, the flora and fauna, the potential for settlement, water supplies, mineral deposits, timber availability and arable land.

Like the president who sent them, Thomas Jefferson, the new homesteaders thought it would be many decades, perhaps centuries, before the country would be "filled up." They would surely marvel today to visit Southern Idaho with its endless fields, its bustling city, its quiet towns.

Consider this.

You come north up on Hwy. 93 from a desolate Nevada of sagebrush plains and there, just north of Jackpot, the land is suddenly verdant with irrigated fields, the golden wheat and barley waving in the late light of an August evening. The farm homes neat and tidy if not ostentatious. As the highway unspools ahead, there's a gradual sense of entering a broad valley,

90 Lawrence, D.H. "The Spirit of Place," *Studies In Classic American Literature*, 1923.

lower in altitude. You can see across to the mountains, seemingly close but miles away. The population density increases; the farms are closer together, the fencerows closer still. A bit farther on is the town (or city if you will) of Twin Falls, with a compact industrial center and steam emanating from the food processing plants, the spread-out retailing, side streets of prairie-style architecture homes, a few churches and, just beyond, this huge looming canyon of the Snake River.

If you're from California or anywhere more urban and used to congestion and crowding and have never been here before, you're probably thinking, "How did I not know about this place?" It may remind you of an America left behind in the crush of big cities like Los Angeles, San Francisco or Las Vegas.

And so it is. There are no obvious slums, no rundown schools, no abandoned churches and only a few fading neighborhoods. The traffic is modest. Commute times are low, under 16 minutes.[91]

Southern Idaho seems almost idyllic, as if from a sepia tone photograph in which the family members lounge under a fruit-bearing tree on a languid evening.

The ladies in the photograph wear broad brimmed, flowered hats and white, frilly dresses, the fellows in their straw hats and suspendered trousers. Across the front of one is written "Me, Mommy and Daddy at City Park." Her mother appears to be holding a book of poems. Here are some words of verse:

> "I spun, I wove, I kept the house, I nursed the sick,
> I made the garden, and for holiday
> Rambled over the fields where sang the larks,
> Gathering many a flower and medicinal weed
> Shouting to the wooded hills, singing to the green valleys.
> At ninety-six I had lived enough, that is all,
> And passed to a sweet repose.
> What is this I hear of sorrow and weariness,
> Anger, discontent and drooping hopes?
> Sons and daughters,
> Life is too strong for you "
> It takes life to live life."[92]

91 DataUSA website, Twin Falls, Idaho, 2016.

92 Masters, Edgar Lee. From "Lucinda Matlock," *Spoon River Anthology*, 1916.

Memory is the residue of childhood, carried later in life from a far-back place and remembrance. It is also so with villages which then grow into towns and cities. They change, but they remain in memory changeless and enduring. As Faulkner says, “The past is never dead. It isn’t even past.”[93]

93 Faulkner, William. *Requiem For A Nun*, 1952.

4. Individualism & Common Endeavor

The Idaho writer Vardis Fisher is best known for his novel *Mountain Man* (1965), a fictional tale of the old West and its fur trade years and its adapted film, *Jeremiah Johnson* (1972), an account of perseverance and individual self-sufficiency in an extreme mountain climate.

Fisher lived in the Hagerman valley of Southern Idaho in his final years and the ruins of his now-derelict stone house can still be seen. His extensive book series on the evolution of humans, *Testament of Man*, is mostly unread.[94] Although a prolific writer, he is forgotten as an American literary figure.

Yet, his novel and the film starring Robert Redford have had a wide audience, as the movie seems a quintessential exemplar of the traits many Americans associate with the 19th Century West: solitude, self-reliance, adaptability, courage and fearlessness in confronting both the elements and human dangers, and cooperation with others when the need arises.[95]

The landscapes of the novel and the film are more mountainous than the Southern Idaho plains, with a harsher winter than is found on the high desert. Yet the vistas evoke the "man against the elements" theme to which almost every rural American can relate. It is part of our national character, displayed in books, films, songs, on television and in

---

94 Fisher, Vardis. *Testament of Man*, 1934-1940.

95 Woodward, Tim. *Tiger on the Road: The Life of Vardis Fisher*, Caxton Press, Caldwell, Id., 1989.

numerous other aspects of our modern culture. And for some of us, the really lucky ones, we get to live it.

Southern Idaho residents often recall the sideways blasts of winter blizzards, the closed county section roads blown over with drifted snow. Weather forecasting and winter snow plowing have improved, but there are still plenty of times when the elements take over. When that happens, it brings back memories of past winters, spring flooding, livestock rescues or a few nights in an abandoned, isolated ranch or line-shack on a hunting trip. It's then when personal independence and survival become paramount.[96]

Every winter, it seems, brings at least one memorable weather event in Southern Idaho, and people then recall how they coped, were stranded or had to hike to a nearby farmhouse.[97] Death by exposure is always a possibility. There's a reason weather and road reports advise people not to travel in such conditions and to stay with the vehicle if stranded.

The backcountry of Southern Idaho is still remote in the extreme and survival may depend as much on luck as on skill. Even a routine walk out back to the shed can end desperately, much more likely so if one takes an unintended wrong turn in the mountain vastness.[98]

If the region inspires a "man against the elements" theme, it also inspires respect for nature's power. It's that power we hear in the whistling wind at the farmhouse window pane, the rattle of the shed door, the "witch of November come stealing."[99] That is why people from other states, who live in more settled places, get nervous when we take a two-track desert lane which heads out among the rocks, sagebrush and canyonlands, a path seemingly endless, to a destination unknown. They will anxiously say something like, "Are you sure you know where we're going?" Not entirely.

Mountain man re-enactments can be found almost any year in Southern Idaho,[100] focusing on traded "old West" goods and such social activities as whiskey drinking, shooting muzzle-loading firearms, animal hide curing and knife and ax throwing contests. They're usually set in some rural location, reminiscent of the landscapes of the fur trade era. The people involved say

---

96 Kennison, Heather. "16 Big-Water Battles: Flood, Snowstorm Recovery is Far from Over," *Times-News*, April 30, 2017.

97 Matthews, Mychel. "Hidden History: Winter of 1948-49 Was Beautiful and Treacherous," *Times-News*, Jan. 5, 2017.

98 In 2011, a Canadian couple became stranded in the Owyhee region of Northern Nevada and Southern Idaho in late winter, relying on a false GPS reading. The woman survived weeks in the mountains; her husband perished going for help. Their story was on world-wide news. *Daily Mail Reporter* (UK). "Woman Found Alive After 7 Weeks in Nevada had Blindly Followed GPS into the Wilderness," May 12, 2011.

99 Lightfoot, Gordon. "The Wreck of the Edmund FitzGerald," 1975.

100 Welch, Laurie. "Mountain Man Rendezvous," *Times-News*. June 24, 2017.

they participate to keep alive the "old ways" of the West. Even if that's not literally so, these modern Rendezvous-goers have a comfortable air to them, along with the costumes, the camping out and the Great West settings.

The fur trade records of those 19th Century years are well documented, as are the financial records of the companies which brought manufactured goods like firearms, metal kettles and woolen blankets to the Indians in exchange for skins and beaver pelts.[101]

Not everyone participates in Rendezvous, but if you listen carefully to local people in Southern Idaho today, you can sense a spirited individualism in their modern life patterns. It is in the cultural air we breathe in the West. There's the appreciation of solitude through a long day on a tractor, readying a field for planting. Perhaps this is why young people often raised on farms and ranches decide to settle back into their comfortable rural settings where they can get up each morning to a brilliant sunrise and irrigate a thirsty field. For them, it is a perfect life.

There's an "I can do it myself" attitude often found in agricultural work, whether it be setting irrigation pipe, fixing a fence or repairing a combine; the willingness to "try it differently" if the repair doesn't hold, through the ingenious use of those three essentials, baling twine, duct tape and a larger hammer.

These young people sometimes don't fit well in the traditional schooling models of desk-bound education, but you can find them frequently at field-man seminars, agricultural extension classes and in vocational programs in high schools and colleges. They learn by doing, working with their hands as well as their minds. They're the salt of our valley, its constants.

Often, they take over a family farm or ranch, nestling into its routines, slowly changing some, as the parents age. They learn the financials from their elders and their lenders, then begin to make decisions on their own, for better or sometimes for worse, to which any agricultural lender can attest.

If they're making a land payment and prices turn down substantially, they may lose it all. They learn livestock management, irrigation, crop rotation, when and where to make an offer on an adjoining piece of farm ground. They do most of these tasks independently, although they may ask parents and knowing uncles and aunts for advice on various topics. Sometimes, if not often, they may even consult their elders on the choice of a spouse.

---

101 DeVoto, Bernard. *Across the Wide Missouri*, Houghton-Mifflin, 1947. DeVoto's book, based on fur trade documents and reminiscences is one of the best accounts of life in the mountains in the 1830s before the Oregon Trail travelers arrived. The book included watercolors by the artist Alfred Jacob Miller, among the earliest visual images we have of that "mountain man" era.

Cooperation and common endeavor may seem counterpoints to this individualism, but they are part and parcel of it. There are many aspects of rural life where cooperative effort is needed, and in Southern Idaho, these group endeavors date back to the earliest settlements. Canal building, dam and diversion construction, rural road development and tasks like barn-raising, school construction and church functions all pay tribute to the community spirit with which this land was settled.

Today we see cooperation in the gatherings of local highway districts that manage the section line roads on which dairy feed is brought in and milk taken out. Without the commonly-maintained road, the farm economy would collapse. We see the same in school and community functions, from school board meetings and bonding votes, from volunteer Meals-on-Wheels and social action networks, to ladies' PEO chapters which raise money for the education of young women, to civic clubs and groups like the West End Men's Club, which meets bi-weekly in the Buhl area. It's also evident in the number and focus of many social service networks which help people when they need it.[102]

Partly, it derives from the region's rural heritage, from the farm families who arrived here more than a century ago from both Midwest and Utah. You can see it in the many family and class reunions in which groups show off their common roots, their heritage, their pasts; they all serve as a form of generalized common social support.[103]

There's often an easy division of household work on a farm, with Mom getting the kids ready for school and Dad up and out early to swath an alfalfa field's cut. A landowner speaking out at a school board meeting, offering an opinion on both the needs of the elementary school and the seemingly ever-rising taxes. An elderly couple wants to stay in their own rural home as long as they can, despite their infirmities and declining health. "Don't worry about us," they tell their worried, furrowed children, "We're ok."

And you know, they are. The cooperative life is all around us, despite our children's departure for work, college, missions, life's great challenges. We love them as they go, brag on them to our friends, and pray for their safe returns, the rush of memory at the Thanksgiving door, the hugs all around. "Two roads diverged in a yellow wood," the poet Robert Frost tells us, "and I took the one less travelled by."[104]

---

102 The South Central Community Action Partnership, led by longtime director Ken Robinette, helps people in need across the valley with transportation, home weatherization, food services, counseling and life improvement skills See SCCAP website, 2018.

103 Wikipedia. "Relief Society," updated May 17, 2018.

104 Frost, Robert. "Two Roads Diverged In A Yellow Wood," 1916.

No matter where they go in this wide world, they are part of our collective memory, with us always.

And perseverance. Stay with a task til it's completed. Don't start something you can't finish. The task isn't done 'til it's done. "Stick-to-it-tive-ness," as it was called by our parents and grandparents. "You cannot push anyone up a ladder," writes the philanthropist Andrew Carnegie, "unless he be willing to climb himself."[105] Perhaps that's why we often see such confidence and faith in those who have worked hard and thereby succeeded.

Individualism is so ingrained in our Western way of life that it is often overlooked. If you live and work in a big city, or even a suburb, people are everywhere. It's partly a result of sheer numbers. Whether it's in Interstate traffic zooming by, or the roar and blare of city streets, one encounters other humans relentlessly, all the time.

But in Southern Idaho as elsewhere in the West, it is the space and land which dominate. You can take almost any mountain two-track road and not see another person until you come back to the place you turned. You are part of humanity to be sure, but you are also an individual, tall and proud, confident and firm.

You are mostly on your own. It is a form of pure "Protestantism" as it were, in which each individual has a direct relationship with the Creator, this bountiful land and the opportunities it offers. The American experience writ on each individual.

Many earlier writers on America noted how the breadth of land opened the way for individual accomplishment, freedom and self-sufficiency. Hector St. John de Crevecoeur, a French observer of America in the Revolutionary War period, asks a basic question: What is this American?

He writes, "Here the rewards of his industry follow with equal steps the progress of his labour; his labour is founded on the basis of self-interest: can it want for a stronger allurement? Wives and children, who before in vain demanded of him a morsel of bread, now, fat and frolicsome, gladly help their father to clear those fields whence exuberant crops are to arise to feed and to clothe them all; without any part being claimed, either by a despotic prince, a rich abbot, or a mighty lord. The American is a new man, who acts upon new principles; he must therefore entertain new ideas, and form new opinions. From involuntary idleness, servile dependence, penury and useless labor, he has passed to toils of a very different nature, rewarded by ample subsistence."[106]

---

105 Carnegie, Andrew. *Autobiography of Andrew Carnegie*, 1920.

106 De Crevecoeur, Hector St. John. *Letters from an American Farmer*, Letter 3, 1782.

If this French observer could come back today and visit Southern Idaho, he would see echoes of the same American spirit, a blend of individual self-sufficiency, combined with a cooperative spirit of common endeavor. We are both our separate selves against all forces and yet of common linkage to our heritage and to each other. That Southern Idaho has these shared traits is a blessing indeed.

5. Diversity & Isolation

Many social scientists identify increasing diversity in communities as a dominant and constant feature of American life. They usually see increasing diversity in mostly positive terms, with its broad results of improving community creativity, cross-cultural awareness, economic equality and increased opportunity for all.[107]

But others have also identified significant downsides to community diversity, including a resulting tendency for people to splinter into "tribes" with similar interests and persuasions, and mistrust between ethnic and multi-cultural groups.[108] This polarization is often seen as breaking down our common American history, a broad sense of who we are as Americans, and leading to a growing fragmentation and "siloing" of interests, values and perspectives.

---

107 Weiner, Joann. "Diversity is good. Why doesn't everyone agree?" *The Washington Post*, Nov. 26, 2014.See also Phillips, Katherine. "How Diversity Makes Us Smarter," *Scientific American*, Oct. 1, 2014. She writes "Members of a homogeneous group rest somewhat assured that they will agree with one another; that they will understand one another's perspectives and beliefs; that they will be able to easily come to a consensus. But when members of a group notice that they are socially different from one another, they change their expectations. They anticipate differences of opinion and perspective. They assume they will need to work harder to come to a consensus. This logic helps to explain both the upside and the downside of social diversity: people work harder in diverse environments both cognitively and socially. They might not like it, but the hard work can lead to better outcomes."

108 Putnam, Robert D. "E Pluribus Unum: Diversity and Community in the Twenty First Century," *Scandinavian Political Studies*, Vol 30, no. 2 (2007). See also Putnam's *Bowling Alone*, (Simon & Schuster, 2000) which outlines how cultural and ethnic isolation has eroded America's sense of common values and "melting pot" common identity and left us with heightened, all-pervasive "identity politics."

A major feature of the Southern Idaho region is that it has delayed and perhaps permanently blunted this fragmentation. That may be due to two dominant features of life here, our homogeneity and our relative isolation or insularity.

Southern Idaho is perhaps one of the most homogeneous areas of its population size, nearly 200,000 people, in the United States.[109] It has been that way since settlement in the early 1900s. Various census data put Twin Falls County today at above 90 percent white, including Hispanics. There are small numbers of Asian- and African-Americans, the latter group at less than one percent of the population. Other counties in the Magic Valley area have higher percentages of Hispanics but remain predominately white with even fewer African- and Asian-Americans.

In addition to being mostly homogeneous in ethnicity, the Magic Valley is also relatively isolated, both from the rest of Idaho as well as from the nation. We're in what some might call "the middle of nowhere." It is a broad swatch of mostly farms and open rangeland, stretching across the Snake River plain along the Nevada border, a region of small communities and really only one larger one: Twin Falls. The region is 120 miles or so east of Boise and some 180 miles from the Salt Lake City area. To get here from anywhere in the West, one needs to cross a vast sagebrush and lava-field plain, arid and mostly treeless.

This isolation from larger and more diverse communities gives Southern Idaho an insular quality which parallels the homogeneous demographics. Only half-jokingly, people say that when you leave Boise on the Interstate 84 and drive up Micron Hill to the East, you are entering a "no-man's land" of farms, small towns and Republican politics, a land of conservative "dinosaurs."

Among residents and those returning after a time away, it's common to hear about these traits as part of the reason people are moving here, and sometimes why they left. People cite family ties, the smaller manageable communities, shared values, good public schools, low costs of living and outdoor recreation as among the reasons they settled here or returned.

Sometimes also cited, although more carefully stated in today's politically-charged conversations, are such factors in their prior communities as crime, neighborhood racial divisions, lack of discipline in schools, contentious community debates which often break along racial, ethnic and political lines, and such simple matters as retail and customer service, vandalism and gang violence.

---

109 US Census estimates the Twin Falls County population at 80,955 in 2016, with another increase in 2017 to over 85,000. US Census, 2018.

You hear the same things from outsiders moving into the area from more urbanized places like coastal California, Oregon and Washington. They say they wanted to escape the crowding, as well as a broad liberalism of values which they reject and sometimes deplore. They also say they are seeking cleaner, safer and more family-oriented environments in which to raise their children, lower costs of living and a freedom of personal action and responsibility which they sense is in the Idaho cultural air.

By moving here, they know they are leaving amenities behind, such as major league sports, "name" entertainment, a long list of four-star and five-star restaurants, and the multi-ethnic mix of academic settings. But they are willing to trade these for other values and lifestyles.[110]

This self-selection of people into communities of selected self-interest has also been widely noticed in scholarly and popular literature.[111] People, it seems, often prefer to live around those most like themselves.

This sorting by region, community and neighborhood is often described as a negative consequence of the polarization of America. But it has also been cited as a community plus, resulting in more polite community debates, more consensus on civic projects and less-testy discussions in community forums such as newspaper anonymous blogs, opinion pages and Facebook give-and-takes.

Not surprisingly, views about diversity fall along political lines. Liberals often see diversity as a positive trait, particularly as it relates to race, gender, ethnicity, religion and sometimes marital status and family structure. Conservatives see downsides.[112] It's a common theme in "diversity writing" for diversity supporters to cite shared cultural values on these traits but to overlook other manifestations of diversity which don't "fit" common diversity norms, particularly diversity of political and social views.

Some scholars cite this "leveling" effect on many aspects of American life. "Greater diversity means inevitably that we have less in common," writes Edward J. Erler, a professor emeritus at California State University, San Bernadino, "and the more we encourage diversity the less we honor the common good. Any honest and clear-sighted observer should be able to see that diversity is a solvent that dissolves the unity and cohesiveness of a nation

110 This attraction of a more homogeneous environment has long been seen as one of the pluses of a move to the Intermountain West, particularly to Idaho. See Sigler, Kirk. "Leaving Urban Areas for the Political Homogeneity of Rural Towns," National Public Radio, Feb, 14, 2017.

111 Bishop, Bill. *The Big Sort*, Mariner Books, 2009. See also, Murray, Charles. *Coming Apart: The State of White America, 1960-2010*, Crown Forum, 2012.

112 Goldberg, Jonah. "What If Diversity Isn't America's Strength?", *Los Angeles Times*, Jan. 15, 2018. See also Dreher, Rod. "What If Diversity Is Our Weakness?" *The American Conservative*, March 15, 2016.

and we should not be deceived into believing that its proponents do not understand the full impact of their advocacy! Diversity, of course, marches under the banner of tolerance, but is a bastion of intolerance. It enforces its ideological liberalism with an iron fist that is driven by political correctness, the most ingenious (and insidious) device for suppressing freedom of speech and political dissent ever invented."[113]

Local people sometimes cite the homogeneity of the Southern Idaho region as a unique and mostly positive trait. It may not be as diverse here as elsewhere, but that seems to suit people here just fine. Not everyone wants to live in a more diverse community. The bigger prejudice sometimes is seen in diverse communities such as a college campus where conservative views are often dismissed. Disrespect is routinely shown to others from rural backgrounds and more conservative traditions.[114]

These differing perspectives are often evident in the anonymous comments on variously reported clash points in the Magic Valley. In a recent effort by one individual to get the Twin Falls City Council to pass a resolution in support of Central American children being united with their border-crossing adults, the council turned down the proposal on a 5 to 2 vote.

The sponsoring individual, a refugee herself, then tried to bring the issue back. When that was denied, she attacked the council verbally and was escorted from the chamber by security. The following news story resulted in a heated, back-and-forth exchange among the resolution's supporters and opponents, carried out mostly anonymously on the newspaper's blog website and on Facebook posts.[115]

---

113 Erler, Edward J. "Does Diversity Really Unite Us? Citizenship and Immigration," *Imprimis*, Hillsdale College, July/August 2018.

114 In a thoughtful essay on how diversity plays out on liberal college campuses, researchers found admission prejudice was common against applicants with so-called "conservative" backgrounds. Diversity usually meant racial diversity, but not diversity of thought. See Nieli, Russell K. "How Diversity Punishes Asians, Poor Whites and Lots of Others," Minding the Campus website, July 12, 2010. Nieli, a Princeton University professor, writes, "Most elite universities seem to have little interest in diversifying their student bodies when it comes to the numbers of born-again Christians from the Bible belt, students from Appalachia and other rural and small-town areas, people who have served in the U.S. military, those who have grown up on farms or ranches, Mormons, Pentecostals, Jehovah's Witnesses, lower-middle-class Catholics, working class "white ethnics," social and political conservatives, wheelchair users, married students, married students with children, or older students first starting out in college after raising children or spending several years in the workforce. Students in these categories are often very rare at the more competitive colleges, especially the Ivy League. While these kinds of people would surely add to the diverse viewpoints and life-experiences represented on college campuses, in practice "diversity" on campus is largely a code word for the presence of a substantial proportion of those in the "underrepresented" racial minority groups."

The running commentary intensified when resolution proponents returned to the council and asked for a "diversity commission" of interested citizens to explore such issues.[116]

As in much of America, discussions on such topics often break along predictable lines, although it seems that in Southern Idaho, the back-and-forths are usually more muted. This isn't the same in much of America, where press scrutiny and long-standing social divisions infect many civic debates. Southern Idaho has seen little of the raucous confrontations which are often portrayed in the news; it seems there is yet enough self-control in public discussions in Southern Idaho to impose a sort of informal "check" on letting these disputes rise from too much calumny and name-calling.[117] Angry, back-and-forth, street corner sloganeering and public forum shout-outs are rare locally.

Why is this so? Is there a social "check" on debate in Southern Idaho which reduces their intensity and thus ameliorates the outbursts? If more homogeneity lessens "tribal" divisions in public discussions, it would seem logical that Southern Idaho's homogeneous population and relative isolation from other places help create these calmer social waters.

The diversity mantra is usually expanded from race to include liberal progressive politics and social issues, such as respect for gay and lesbian rights, a pro-choice abortion perspective, a pro-gun control viewpoint and an emphasis on non-manufacturing economic sectors, like recreation. This latter element also places an emphasis on leisure time activities and a social scene created to attract young people through a vibrant night life of bars, dance venues and other social settings.

---

115 Kauffman, Gretel. "Update: Twin Falls City Council will not Reconsider Family Separation Resolution," *Times-News*, July 23. 2018.

116 Kauffman, Gretel. "Residents ask Twin Falls City Council to Form Diversity Advisory Commission," *Times-News*, Aug. 7, 2018. Here's a sampling of some of the Facebook comments, pro and con: Jason Cook: "This just in, the city council wants to waste more money addressing non- issues or issues that twin falls can do nothing about." Kathleen Levy: "It's the job of the white people in power to stop abusing and profiting from white privilege. We need to change our communities and stop the violence, physical and verbal, against people of color. We need to stop shielding ourselves with white fragility and own up to our wrongdoings and make changes." Joshua Warwick: "Must have wasted my white male privilege working at Staples. Can't believe I did that." Jason Cook: "Wow, you're a moron. I'm sorry but it's so very true. White privilege in our local politics? Nothing is stopping other ethnicities to run for office. It's the evil white man's fault. Jesus Christ, listen to yourself. The United states allows minorities to thrive in comparison to other countries. Why do you think so many Mexicans come here illegally?"

117 Fox News. "Portland Police in Riot Gear called in to clear Clashes Between Right-wing and Antifa Protestors," Aug. 4, 2018.

Implicit is the underlying principle that anything opposite to these standards is old-fashioned and vaguely pernicious. We see this all over the United States, reflected in partisan politics, changing social values, and rural versus urban living. Young people often see the world in this way. This kind of social hedonism is widely, if silently, rejected in many smaller communities To these folks, the libertine life has little or no appeal.

Local high school graduates often flee areas like this for college and the world's vast horizons, vowing never to return to the staid, dull, stultifying hometowns of their childhoods. They convey this in many ways about their left-behind communities, in phrasing like, "I just had to get away," "I wanted to see the world," or "Magic Valley? Just bunch of old folks and rednecks." Is there a military recruiter in any small community who hasn't heard these comments in talks with young military aspirants? Sometimes, it takes years for those now-older escapees to see that little ole' Southern Idaho wasn't so bad after all.[118]

It's been said that all of us carry the memories of our familiar former settings with us into adulthood. That's perhaps why those who leave a place, particularly a place of pleasant memories, often carry those positive remembrances all of their lives, which they may try to replicate or recapture in their new settings.

This is evident in the comments section of an ongoing Twin Falls Facebook page, which has almost 5,700 followers and often features nostalgic comments by "old Twin Fallsians" living elsewhere who remember growing up here, a town with minor league night baseball, soda shops, cruising Main Street and other youth activities of an idyllic past.[119]

In those memories, the isolation of the Southern Idaho area is an occasional topic. Diversity of the community, not so much. The memories which remain are pretty much positive, and the small-town character in those years is much appreciated. "This will be mainly for those of you that were born early enough, '30s and '40s to attend the Idaho Theater (on) Saturday mornings during the fall and winter months or however long they did this for the kids," writes Facebook poster Irvin Rile. "Usually a Western movie, anywhere from six to eight cartoons, and a running serial. At times, ticket numbers were called and if you were lucky, you got to go on stage and answer questions and win a silver dollar."

"There wasn't much paper money back then. They had specials for Halloween, and you got to up and bobbed for apples and such as that. Hey, we had a lot of fun! Was not much else to do on Saturdays during the winter

118 Simon, Paul and Garfunkel, Art. "Nothing but the dead and dying back in my little town," My Little Town, 1975.

119 Facebook page. "You Might Be From Twin Falls, Idaho," 2018.

months and it was so nice for the theater and whoever else made it all possible. I for one feel so blessed to be born and raised in Twin Falls, Idaho, God's country, my home town. I would not trade my growing up in Twin for any time since then. I wish all kids could have had the experience of growing up during the era that I have had."[120]

Comments like these suggest that the isolation of the region and its homogeneous profile should be prized. This puts residents in sometimes awkward conversations when they travel to more diverse and less insular places. They find they need to be less descriptive of why they like Southern Idaho as it is, and they're often enthusiastic to return to their comfortable settings.

It's a love of the place they carry always.

120 Rile, Irvin. "You Might Be From Twin Falls, Idaho," Facebook page, Aug. 7, 2018.

6. Conservative Roots

If you were to wander up a residential street in Boise's North End, and ask people randomly what single word came to mind when they thought about rural Southern Idaho, the word "conservative" probably would get a mention. You might also hear "Republican," "farm country," or having a "hot and dry" climate.

From the less kind or more partisan, you might hear "backward" or perhaps even "Deliverance" from someone who had seen that classic film set in the rural South. There might have been a reference to the Mormon Church, or to Hispanic labor in the Southern Idaho workforce. Probably not on that list would be "progressive," "liberal," "innovative" "cultural" or "Democratic."

Fixed negative opinions about rural places have been part of the American verbal landscape for generations, at least since H.L. Mencken's sharp barbs a century ago, or the legions of journalists who covered "the South" in the 1960s and deemed the "Ma and Pa Kettle" people there as emblematic of the region. Today, you can hear this disdain on any college campus, in every newspaper, in many "progressive" churches, as well as in college faculty lounges and in the demeaning chit-chat of the news.

But is it true? Is Southern Idaho as conservative as such comments imply? Are we – perish the thought – "conservative" in our values and way of life, and if so, what are the implications of being so? The answer is a "yes," with a qualifying "but."[121] The "but" is that

121 Blanchard, Nicole. "Bright Red Idaho has Always Been Conservative. Now Comes Growth and Californians," *Idaho Statesman*, July 22, 2018. Idaho historians regularly describe the state as conservative, although it was more mixed politically over past time. Democrats held public office in territorial Idaho, as well as in the

conservative values are potentially open to change given the right mix of issues, changing times and generational shifts.

Where did this "conservative" tilt on values come from? It appears to have been part of the Southern Idaho social landscape from the start, since the first settlements more than a century ago. The first settlers were from two major immigration strains, one deriving chiefly from Midwesterners and the other from Mormon farmers moving up from Utah. Both groups had conservative political histories; the first votes in Twin Falls County showed a conservative lean, with a mix of "Bull Moose" Party independence support for Teddy Roosevelt. Except for occasional short deviations, that's been the political and social profile of Southern Idaho ever since, right down to the modern era.

Writing in the first edition of the *North Side News* in Jerome County in 1908, publisher John Nims declared that the newspaper would generally follow conservative principles. "As a general proposition," he wrote, "we believe these principles right and best for the people who live in this country."[122]

Boise State University has conducted public policy surveys of Idahoans since 1990, and while not as comprehensive as they might be, nor broken down by region, the surveys provide a good overview of how Idahoans view their state and its issues.[123]

The 2018 survey shows education and economic development as top priority issues, with health care an important topic as well. About 60 percent think the state is generally going in the right direction and a similar percent think taxes overall are about right, with an additional 24 percent thinking they're too high; fewer than 9 percent thought taxes were too low.[124] Although they may seem to get lots of media attention, issues like public lands management, environmental protection, federal regulations, immigration and firearms regulations each polled below five percent in importance.

The 2016 survey, for example, found 48 percent consider themselves conservative, compared with 21 percent liberal; almost two-thirds were married (64 percent); and almost 60 percent were comfortable with the overall direction of the state. On specific issues, education and economic development rated the highest priorities, with social issues at less than six percent; almost 60 percent favored a "light touch" government in which

---

1930s and in the 1970s and 1980s with Governors Cecil Andrus and John Evans.

122 Brackett, Kimberly Williams. *Keepers of the Record: Pioneer Newspaper of Great North Side Tract*, Twelve Baskets Book Publishing, Three Creek, Id., 2019.

123 Boise State University. Scholar Works, Annual Idaho Public Policy Surveys, 1990-2018.

124 BSU Public Policy Survey, 2018.

individuals would rise on their own "merit" (57). Half thought taxes should be lower.

Over 71 percent thought wolves should be hunted; 56 percent thought federal lands should be transferred to the state; and that economic development should generally take precedence over environmental protection (68 percent to 25 percent.)[125]

Across the years, there are mostly similarities in the survey responses. In 2006, for example, 48 percent described themselves as conservative, with 15 percent saying they were "liberal"; 64 percent thought the overall direction of the state was about right; 57 percent supported a ballot initiative to limit property taxes (It passed that fall with over 72 percent of the vote, carrying every precinct in the state.[126]); 50 percent favored a state Constitutional provision banning same-sex marriages (31 percent opposed).[127]

In 2000, 51 percent described themselves as conservative, compared with 13 percent liberal;" satisfaction with Idaho's quality of life was high, 93 percent. Three-quarters (74 percent) thought Idaho should do more to encourage career-specific courses in high schools. On the environmental issue of breaching lower Snake River dams for salmon recovery, 40 percent in the Southern Idaho region opposed it, perhaps reflecting the importance of irrigation to the region.[128]

The first survey in 1990 didn't ask about people's ideological leanings or political affiliation, although legislative partisan divisions between the parties were less pronounced then.[129] In general, satisfaction with life in Idaho stood at 94 percent, with 95 percent satisfaction in the Magic Valley; as in later years, education, transportation and economic development were among Idahoans' top concerns, with 72 percent saying the state should focus on current needs rather than finding new areas for funding; state and local government scored the highest in level of confidence by citizens at 34 percent each, with confidence in the federal government at only 13 percent, even a generation ago.

---

125 BSU Public Policy Survey, 2016.

126 Idaho Secretary of State, Election Results, 2006. The initiative carried in every county in Idaho, including Ada and Blaine. In Twin Falls County, the margin was better than 2 to 1.

127 BSU Public Policy Survey, 2006.

128 BSU Public Policy Survey, 2000.

129 In 1990, there were 23 Republicans and 19 Democrats in the Idaho Senate; in the House, the makeup was 64 Republicans and 20 Democrats. Totals declined following the 1990 reapportionment, to 35 Senate seats and 70 House seats. By 2000, Republican strength had increased, with 31 GOP seats and 4 Democrats in the Senate, and 58 Republican seats in the House with 12 Democrats. See Wikipedia. "Political Party Strength In Idaho," 1990, 2000.

On social issues, 80 percent thought the state needed to regulate day care centers better; 91 percent wanted to see stronger child support enforcement; 46 percent thought government should be the primary entity to help the poor, with 41 percent of those saying the national government should take the lead role. Only seven percent thought charities could handle the need and only six percent thought helping the poor should be left to churches alone.[130]

Other recent research shows similar conservative leanings and how values structures also break along party lines. Idaho Republicans have a stronger "belief in God" (76 percent) versus 47 percent among Idaho Democrats; 63 percent of Republicans say religion is important in their daily lives versus 37 percent of Democrats; 72 percent of Republicans say they go to church regularly, compared with 54 percent of Democrats; 82 percent of Republicans say they pray regularly, compared to 49 percent of Democrats; 92 percent of Republicans say they rely on religious teachings for guidance, compared with 28 percent of Democrats, where 57 percent say they rely on "common sense."

On policy issues, 87 percent of Republicans prefer smaller government, compared to 34 percent of Democrats; 66 percent of Republicans think aid to the poor "hurts as much as helps," compared with 26 percent of Democrats who feel that way.

On abortion, 66 percent of Republicans think it should be illegal under most circumstances, compared with 29 percent of Democrats. (68 percent of Democrats think abortion should be generally legal and available.) Southern Idaho has a pro-choice Planned Parenthood clinic, as well as a pro-life Stanton Healthcare Pregnancy Resource Center, which offers abortion alternative services, pregnancy testing, options counseling and support.[131] The Planned Parenthood center experienced some protests when it first opened and the issue, as we all know, remains a flash-point for many people today. Local active Democrats, liberals and media have generally sided with Planned Parenthood, with conservatives and Republicans generally taking pro-life perspectives.[132]

The Department of Health & Welfare reported 258 abortions in Southern Idaho in 2017; the number has been over 200 annually since 2012. Of the 258 abortions, all but 14 were to residents of Idaho. Of the total 1,285 abortions in Idaho in 2017, more than 70 percent were to women 20 to 34; another 11

130 BSU Public Policy Survey, 1990.

131 Stanton Healthcare Magic Valley, website, 2019.

132 Brown, Nathan. "Blog: Planned Parenthood Only Federally-Funded Family Planning in Magic Valley," *Times-News*, Oct. 9, 2015. See also Alexander, Jon. "When Men Talk Vaginas," *Times-News*, Feb. 24, 2015, and Thompson, Paul. "Open Shame Belongs to Us," *Times-News*, Aug. 1, 2015, and Kauffman, Gretel. "Local Lawmakers Talk Abortion, Suicide, Drugs at Town Hall," *Times-News*, March 2, 2019.

percent were to women ages 15-19 and another 11 percent to women 35-39. An estimated 80 percent were unmarried.[133]

On how the earth evolved (a question which goes to the teaching of Creationism in public schools) 25 percent thought evolution was a "natural process;" another 29 percent thought the earth was formed "by God;" and 35 percent thought evolution had always been "in existence."

On demographic traits, Republicans are also more likely to be married (68 percent) than Democrats (56 percent), who are more likely to be single or never married (18 percent). Republicans skew more to higher incomes, but not substantially so (20 percent of Republicans have annual incomes below $30,000 while 30 percent of Democrats do). Both groups have about the same level of education (74 percent of Republicans have at least some college, as do 68 percent of Democrats.)[134]

These surveys suggest that Idahoans have retained a skeptical view of government and that conservative opinions from the past pretty much are carried into the present. Some issues may change or even fade from active consideration, but the overall perspectives of Idaho citizens remain remarkably constant, practical and common-sense oriented.

The 2019 survey continues many of these patterns. Education remains a top issue (24.7 percent), followed by the economy and health care. Despite the media attention they get, environment, taxes and immigration each was under five percent as a top issue. About 60 percent of respondents thought the state was going in the right direction with under 30 percent saying "wrong direction." About 22 percent thought of themselves as liberal, while 54 percent said conservative; 25 percent were Democrats, 47 percent Republican.[135]

It's a general principle of social science research that, if not immutable, social value positions remain more or less consistent over time. Thus, we shouldn't be surprised to see attitudes of Idahoans today – like elsewhere in the nation – are similar to what they were in the 2000s and 1990s and probably earlier.[136]

---

133 Idaho Department of Health & Welfare, Division of Public Health, website, "2017 Induced Abortion, Idaho Vital Statistics."

134 Pew Research Center. "Political Affiliations Among Adults in Idaho," website, 2018.

135 Boise State University Public Policy Survey, 2019.

136 Interestingly, some recent research suggests people may shift their views on various social issues over time to better align with their political views. See Bacon, Jr., Percy. "Americans Are Shifting the Rest of Their Identity to Match Their Politics," Fivethirtyeight website, Sept. 13, 2018. and Margolis, Michele. *From Politics to the Pews*, University of Chicago Press, 2018.

What's different today across America is that many people move and change communities to be closer to people like themselves.[137] For Idaho, that's both good and bad, a plus that it creates shared bases of community, a minus in that it can lead to increased "tribalism" and lack of understanding and tolerance.

These patterns show up as well in studies of political prejudice, which seek to measure how people on one side of the political aisle see others of the opposite persuasion. A recent Predictwise study ranked every county in the country on political bias, with some interesting results. Counties with more mixed populations were generally less prejudiced than ones with homogeneous traits, either on the left or right politically.

In Southern Idaho, for example, the least prejudiced counties were Cassia, Minidoka, Camas, and Jerome, followed by Gooding, Lincoln, and then Twin Falls. Blaine County ranked highest in political prejudice, presumably against more conservative Americans; Idaho's most populous area and trending "blue" in elections, Ada County had considerably more prejudice from Democrats toward Republicans than visa-versa.[138]

Although uncommon, fundamental changes can occur in people's values. On gay rights, for example, Idahoans voted in 2006 to add language to the state's constitution saying marriage was only between a man and a woman. Yet, as the national discussion has changed, so have attitudes in Idaho. The 2015 US Supreme Court ruling, *Obergefell v. Hodges*, 135 S. Ct. 2584, essentially overrode Idaho's constitutional language, but didn't place any new "Add the Words" language to Idaho's anti-discrimination statute.

The survey shows some that Idahoans are now generally more accepting of gay relationships (59 percent), but 37 percent still think they should be "strongly discouraged." On same-sex marriages, about 49 percent are okay with it, but 39 percent "strongly disapprove."

A generation ago, it would have been rash indeed to say that by 2015, gay marriages would be sanctioned nationwide by the courts, much less move from illegal to acceptable. But that's what happened to Idaho opinions as the courts defined new interpretations of constitutional protections. Idahoans seem to saying that, yes, they can accept gay relationships, and many accept that gay marriages are legal, even if they don't agree with them.

---

137 Bishop, Bill. *The Big Sort: Why the Clustering of Like-Minded America Is Tearing Us Apart*. Houghton-Mifflin, 2008.

138 Ripley, Amanda, et al. "The Geography of Partisan Prejudice," *The Atlantic*, March 4, 2019: "In general, the most politically intolerant Americans, according to the analysis, tend to be whiter, more highly educated, older, more urban, and more partisan themselves."

As gay rights emerged in the 1980s and 1990s as a social issue, practical considerations overrode past patterns. Newspapers in Idaho at that time followed the same trend, although some readers objected. By 2003, the Associated Press writing style manual said the term "gay" was acceptable, but that the term "homosexual" should be avoided.[139]

Another example of changing attitudes is the public acceptance of marijuana legalization and medical use of marijuana derivatives. In states like Idaho, which border other states where marijuana use is legal or widely available, media reporting of marijuana has changed from coverage of it as a criminal activity to coverage of marijuana use as a medical issue for pain relief. The change has been driven by newspaper coverage which favors more availability and which has led the public on reframing the issue.

There are still some sharp differences on attitudes on this topic, which may delay Idaho falling into the "pro-legalization" camp. Democrats favor legalization by 20 points higher than Republicans (67 percent v. 47 percent), but as well known, Idaho is more of a Republican state, by roughly a 2 to 1 margin. Also, people who think the criminal justice system is too harsh are more likely to favor legalization. In Idaho, that's likely to include both liberals and some arch-conservative, libertarian-leaning Republicans. So while the issue of legalization hasn't yet reached full-force in Idaho, it's apparent that attitudes are indeed changing nationally and could lead to changes here as well.[140]

When it comes to values then, Idahoan's views reflect both past attitudes as well as adjustments, incorporating changing norms which are driven, at least in part, by broader outside forces. Idaho as a relatively small state in population and remote geographically, may not be first on the list of states to address gay rights or marijuana legalization, but the issues are likely to come to the state regardless.

These shifting views reflect how attitudes changed on other social issues, like women's suffrage, where Idaho was an early state to enact women's right

---

139 Associated Press, 2003 AP Stylebook, p. 103.

140 Adamczyk, Amy, et al. "This Is The Surprising Reason Why Americans Have Dramatically Shifted Their Views on Legalizing Pot," *Market Watch, Wall Street Journal*, Feb. 9, 2019. The authors write: "Gradually, the stereotypical persona of the marijuana user shifted from the stoned slacker wanting to get high to the aging boomer seeking pain relief. Of course, many Americans do not read The New York Times. But analysis of newspapers of record, like this one, provide insight into how the news media has changed its framing of marijuana, especially during an era when newspapers were still a primary news source. The cause and effect is clearer with respect to the media framing of marijuana. The news media's portrayal of marijuana began to change shortly before the public did, suggesting that the media influenced support for the legalization of marijuana." See also The Conversation website, "Why Do So Many Americans Now Support Legalizing Marijuana?," Feb. 5, 2019.

to vote, in a state constitutional amendment approved in 1896. That issue had a lengthy history going back to the Founding Fathers' time. ("I desire you would Remember the Ladies," Abigail Adams wrote to her husband John in the spring of 1776, "and be more generous and favourable to them than your ancestors. Do not put such unlimited power into the hands of the Husbands. Remember all Men would be tyrants if they could. If perticuliar care and attention is not paid to the Laidies, we are determined to foment a Rebelion, and will not hold ourselves bound by any Laws in which we have no voice, or Representation.")[141] What was once deemed the "values" position of the past was set aside and replaced by another point of view.

Whether that will happen in Idaho with respect to the "Add The Words" movement or marijuana legalization is still undecided. Following defeat of "Add The Words" bill in 2015, it hasn't been reintroduced, and some legislators' views undoubtedly are unchanged. But with normal seat turnover, "values" reflect changing positions of constituents back home. That's one great truth about values: they are deeply anchored in their communities, subject mostly to retention and occasionally to change.

Property Rights

A final issue having to do with Idaho values is the strong adherence many Idahoans feel toward the sanctity of private property rights. Since two-thirds of Idaho's 83,000 square miles are public lands, residents often bristle at the perceived power of government land management policies and the not-infrequent attempts by government to restrict private land uses. We see this in suspicion of any land use "inspection" authority, whether it be in zoning, sewage waste disposal systems, surveying disputes and many more.

Following the 2005 Supreme Court decision (*Kelo v. City of New London*, 545 U.S. 469), affirming the right of government to take private property for another private party's economic use under eminent domain, Idaho and a number of other states passed laws restricting the "takings" process.[142] In 2006, Idaho voters turned down a Kelo-inspired restriction proposal on eminent domain. Idaho has been judged harshly for this vote, but apparent confusion as to the effects was cited as a reason for the rejection. The state

141 Adams, Abigail to Adams, John, Letter of March 31, 1776. Adams Family Papers, Massachusetts Historical Society website, 2018.

142 Utt, Ronald. "States Vote to Strengthen Property Rights," The Heritage Foundation, Feb. 1, 2007.

has passed some additional statutory language restricting takings, but these have also been criticized as inadequate.[143]

Rejecting the proposed "fix" to eminent domain was apparently widely seen as the more conservative position. In any case, the proposition was defeated by a 76 to 24 percent vote after being opposed by then Gov. James Risch, many Idaho mayors and the associations of both Idaho cities and counties.[144]

Property rights issues continue to surface in the state from time to time. A 2018 legislative proposal to rewrite Idaho's trespass laws passed by wide margins, despite being opposed by outdoor enthusiasts. The issue pitted land owners, agricultural interests and other conservative groups against recreational and outdoors enthusiasts. The proposal passed the House first on a 45-22 vote, with wide GOP support and Democratic opposition in which some Republicans joined. The Senate passed a revised version 29-6, with unanimous GOP support and unanimous Democratic opposition. It then returned to the House for a concurrence vote, which passed 51 to 18. Gov. C.L. "Butch" Otter let the measure become law without his signature, again reflecting the disparate differences of opinion; another attempt at clarifying trespass law seemed likely as the 2019 session approached,[145] so the issue is hardly resolved.

Another example illustrates the importance Idahoans place on property rights, but also on access to lands which may "look" public but which are actually private. In 2016, two Texas oilmen purchased 172,000 acres of land in Idaho in a private party transaction with the prior owner, a timber company. They then closed the land to the public, which had been previously allowed. The purchase set off a debate in Idaho as how property rights may collide; it was softened a bit when the oilmen later put 54,000 acres up for sale.[146]

---

143 Powers, Matt. "2007 Eminent Domain Report Card: Idaho Gets a D+." Institute for Justice, website, June 6, 2007. See also Solomon, Mark. "Idaho Prop 2: Property Wrongs," New West website, Sept. 7, 2006, and comments.

144 Idaho Secretary of State, election returns, 2006.

145 Idaho Legislature, 2018 Session, HB 658. Groups in support of the bill included the Farm Bureau, Idaho Freedom Foundation, Food Producers of Idaho, Idaho Realtors, Property Rights Coalition and Gem State Patriot News. Opponents were led by the Idaho Recreation Council and some sporting groups. The *Times-News* opposed the bill, "Our View: Idaho Outdoorsmen Deserve Better Than Trespassing Bill," March 16, 2018.

146 Landers, Rich. "Texas Billionaires Bar Hunters from Former Potlatch Land," *Spokesman-Review*, Sept. 29, 2016. See also, Barker, Rocky. "Texas Billionaires put 54,000 acres of Idaho Land Up for Sale," *Idaho Statesman*, March 2, 2018. As with many issues, this one became politicized, with the Idaho Democratic Party saying the sale was an example of Idaho public lands being sold to "folks who can afford them," but not mentioning that the sale was a private party to private party transaction which didn't involve public lands at

Idahoans generally lean right on conservative issues like property rights. While many enjoy access to the state's "great outdoors," when property rights are perceived to be at stake, there's little doubt that the more conservative values position will prevail.

Idahoans are likely to face recurring examples of such conflicts in many quarters in the years ahead. But it's hard to see how a legislative vote on this issue 30 years in the future would turn out much differently, at least when conservative values are perceived to be at stake.

---

all. See Idaho Democratic Party website, "No Place to Hunt," Jan. 19, 2016.

7. Faith & Tolerance

When people look at the Magic Valley in religious terms, they often think of it as broadly Christian, including The Church of Jesus Christ of Latter-day Saints (Mormons) and a wide variety of non-Mormon and other Christian denominations. Church membership is often reported as the number of adherents to a particular denomination. By that measure, the total adherents in Twin Falls County in 2010 was listed at about 50 percent of the population (38,700 out of about 77,000).

The Church of Jesus Christ of Latter-day Saints adherents was the largest single denomination, at about 19,000, roughly 25 percent of the county population,[147] followed by Catholics (about 5,800) or 7.5 percent of the total population. Several denominations had about 1,000 members each: American Baptists, 824; Assemblies of God, 991; Nazarenes, 1,100; Lutheran Church-Missouri Synod, 1,666; Evangelical Protestant, 1,905; Reformed Church, 1,633; and United Methodist, 981.

The number of Muslim adherents was listed at about 100, with other world-wide religions at even lesser numbers.[148] Muslims are about .13 percent of the Twin Falls County population. Although serving few in number, the valley's Main Islamic Center in Twin Falls was vandalized in 2015; many citizens came to the denomination's defense and urged tolerance and respect for their beliefs.[149]

---

147 Church of Jesus Christ of Latter Day Saints reports membership in 2018, by county as follows: Blaine, 1,965; Camas, 142; Cassia, 11,265; Gooding, 2,815; Jerome, 4,598; Lincoln, 1,178; Minidoka, 7, 025; Twin Falls, 18, 963. .

148 Association of Religious Data Archives, Twin Falls County, 2010.

149 Dunlap, Tetonia. "Twin Falls Islamic Center Vandalized," *Times-News*, Dec. 10, 2015.

The overall adherent numbers showed some change from prior religious census counts. Gains were concentrated in just a few denominations, including Mormons, up 74 percent and Catholics, up 60 percent.[150] But, as seen elsewhere in America, there have been significant declines in some local mainstream Protestant memberships. Both the Presbyterian Church and the United Methodist Church have smaller active memberships than they did 50 years ago. Of the Twin Falls downtown churches, only St. Edwards Catholic Church is showing significant growth, with about 2,000 congregants spread across five Sunday services, three of which are in Spanish.[151]

Declines in national memberships have been widely reported, with almost countless reasons cited. Some blame broad changing social patterns; less intensive parenting and a lessening of home environments; declining "authority" institutions; a breakdown of doctrinal Scriptural principles. And then there are the hot button social issues like gay pastors, LGBT (Lesbian, Gay, Bisexual, Transgender) marriage, female pastors, abortion, and a long list of other "social justice" causes.[152]

One can hardly read a magazine or a general website without encountering articles on these topics and their link to church attendance. People seem less forgiving of variations on these themes; if they don't hear what they like in a Sunday sermon, they're "outta there," along with their wallets.[153]

A 2014 comprehensive study by the Pew Research explored these issues in great detail. Here are some points that are particularly relevant to the Magic Valley:

Eighty-two percent of Mormons who are married or living with a partner have a mate who shares their religion, as do 75 percent of Catholics and evangelical Protestants.

Mormons are more likely to be married than other churchgoers, and have larger families, an average of 3.4 children among Mormons ages 40-59, way more than the national average of 2.1 children. They also have more children still in the household (1.1).

---

150 Ibid, 1990-2010 change.

151 Wootton-Greener, Julie. "Times Have Changed: How 5 of Twin Falls' Historic Downtown Churches Are Trying to Adapt to a New Era," *Times-News*, Jan. 21, 2018.

152 Lovett, Ian. "Methodist Church Faces Possible Schism Over Gay Rights," *The Wall Street Journal*, Fe. 21, 2019: "The United Methodist Church isn't the first mainline Protestant denomination to reach a breaking point over LGBT rights. Over the past two decades, hundreds of congregations left Presbyterian, Lutheran, and Episcopal denominations after they began ordaining gay clergy. Fights over who got to keep the church buildings have dragged through court for years."

153 "Religious Congregations In 21st Century America," University of Chicago, National Congregations Study, 2015.

Both Hispanic Catholics and Mormons are concentrated in the West and Southwest United States. Their combined numbers contribute to a higher number of churchgoers in Southern Idaho than would be found otherwise.

Both Mormon and Evangelical churchgoers report low participation by gays in their congregations. Among Mormons, it's less than 1 percent, although that percent may be low due to wider acceptance and more people disclosing; among Evangelicals, it's 13 percent.[154]

Judging from the Pew study, there are several trends concerning religion in Southern Idaho that will likely continue well into the future:

First, Southern Idaho is like the rest of the country, with growing unaffiliated or unchurched populations, particularly among young adults.

Second, mainstream Protestant denominations are falling in number locally, as they are nationally.

Third, the number of Mormons and Catholics are increasing, partly due to higher birth rates, proselyting efforts and, in the case of Hispanics, an influx into the area.

Fourth, Evangelical denominations also are rising in numbers, but not all. The ones with strong financial underpinnings are doing better than others.

Fifth, because of some shared beliefs, many denominations reinforce each other in the teaching of moral values, the sanctity of marriage and opposition to abortion and sex before marriage. Although these moral suasions may be stronger in some denominations than others, their commonly-shared bases across Southern Idaho may give the region a stronger religiously-inspired set of common life lessons, particularly for young adults. Unlike the pulling apart often seen in larger communities, the "shared values" base of faith groups seems to be another way in which life in Southern Idaho seems distinctive.

It seems likely that expressions of faith in Southern Idaho will continue to evolve as well. A general pattern of American life is the breaking down of cohesive, cross-group experiences and a resulting isolation of one group from another. People mix less often with others who are different than they did a generation or two ago, whether in social contacts, politics or on social media.[155]

This "pigeon-holing" may well apply to religion, even in a homogeneous area like Southern Idaho, where commonly-held traditions and principles

154 Pew Research Center: Religion in Public Life, "America's Changing Religious Landscape," May 12, 2015.

155 Putnam, Robert D. *Bowling Alone: The Collapse and Revival of American Community*, Simon & Shuster, 2000, reviews how Americans have become more disconnected from each other and how that breakdown affects communities and the social capital on which representative government and civic life depend.

seem to abound. That's caught the attention of Andrew Paz, pastor of the First Baptist Church of Filer, who's been there more than a half-dozen years and has witnessed changes in the Filer Ministerial Association, where churches in the community once worked closely together on projects.

Community work by the combined churches is not as common as it used to be, he says. The group formerly sponsored a prayer breakfast during the Twin Falls County Fair in September, but that event broke up over the division of work involved and how to make up for lost offering donations at the individual churches. Local churches now "distance themselves from overall community involvement," he says.

His own church sponsors an after-school Kid Zone for youngsters, but while parents have their children attend, almost none of the parents get involved in the church itself. It's become more of an inexpensive child care service. Churches, he says, have become more of a place people turn when they need help, but not something in which they are willing to fully participate. There's less individual responsibility than a generation or two ago. "People are more willing to ask for help when they should be doing it for themselves."[156]

There's a strong sense in people that they just want to be left alone, he says, and simply "not bothered" by community involvements in many regards. That's noticeable when it comes to proselytizing faith to others. There seems to be a "systematic withdrawal" from such outreach in these times, he says, referring to the period before Martin Luther's renewal of faith through Europe in the 1500s.

American Protestantism, he thinks, seems adrift in these currents of change, with no clear path forward, even in insular Southern Idaho. Once previously-held standards are abandoned, they are left behind for good, and once left behind, they are soon deemed irrelevant, like the churches of the European Reformation, now vacant across Germany, much of Europe and in some of America as well.[157]

No pastor wants to preside over such a slow descent as engulfed European Christianity for hundreds of years and may now be in motion in today's Western civilization. By nature, Paz is an optimist about modern Protestant faith, relying as it does on the individual and collective holy spirit to inspire and lead. It pains him to see a diminishing of that in the spiritual life of communities. There are no easy answers.

---

156 Paz, Andrew. Interview, Feb. 18, 2029. Full disclosure: The author attends the Filer First Baptist Church.

157 Paz, Interview, Feb. 18, 2019.

Mormons and Non-Mormons

As homogeneous as the Magic Valley is, religion is one area where there are significant differences. Although the valley is heavily Christian, part of that group is the Mormon faith, estimated at up to 35 percent of the population. Settlement patterns for Southern Idaho have been pretty much established for many years, indeed for generations, and these settlement patterns have helped shape the valley's religions, demographics and by extension, its values.

Mormon pioneers first settled Cassia County, including the Oakley area in the 1880s then pushed further West into what is now Twin Falls County beginning in the early 1900s. Today, Mormons make up about 50 percent of Cassia County's population, and about 30 percent in Twin Falls County.[158] Prior to the 1990s, Mormons attended more distant temples in Logan, Utah and Boise and Idaho Falls, Idaho. In the 1990s, local stake leaders asked for a temple in the Magic Valley, and it opened in 2008.[159] The new facility, a prominent landmark on the East side of town, gave Southern Idaho Mormons their own, more-convenient church "home."

If we want to understand Southern Idaho's culture and values, a good place to start is by asking how Mormonism affects Southern Idaho. The mix of population is certainly part of the equation, but so are other, less formal features of Mormon life. Because of the settlement patterns and the growth of the Mormon faith in Southern Idaho, it's useful to think of the region as a sort of cross-boundary extension of Utah, where the Mormon faith is dominant, and with it, cultural patterns which may not be easily transferred to other regions of the country.

One recent observer, writing in Bloomberg View, explored the cultural aspects of Mormonism and how they might point to a better America. Among the patterns are childbearing only within marriage, an efficient helping-hand welfare system which assists people but also emphasizes self-sufficiency, and, as in the case of Southern Idaho, a relatively homogeneous population of

---

158 AncestryDNA website, July, 2017. Ancestry.com has DNA sampling from almost 800,000 Americans, which shows the previous patterns of migration and settlement of Mormons from upstate New York, to the Midwest, and then to Utah, from which further migration led to numerous settlements north into Idaho and northwest into Cassia and Twin Falls counties. Genetic data mapping is a new application of DNA analysis which is increasingly useful in tracing genetic heritage back many generations.

159 There's an extended unofficial history of the LDS faith's growth in Southern Idaho at www.ldschurchtemples.org/twinfalls/. The Twin Falls temple serves 15 stakes in the region.

shared values of less government, conservative politics and higher economic mobility.

These conditions aren't found in all parts of the country and "this does raise some questions about the viability of Utah's (or Idaho's) "compassionate conservative" model outside the state," writes Megan McCardle. "The vast welfare infrastructure from the Mormon church naturally makes it easier to have smaller government. Perhaps that could be replicated by other communities. But the values of the Mormon church may create a public that simply needs less help. That's harder for another community to imitate. I'm not sure this key ingredient is available in a secular version; I think religion might only come in religion flavor."[160]

This "compassionate conservative" model in Utah seems to be replicated in Southern Idaho, where social mobility, especially when compared to areas beyond the Intermountain West, is also more widespread. Mormon and non-Mormon young people go to school together, play sports, participate in community activities like Fourth of July parades, community projects and generally interact in common activities. They positively associate with each other, despite their religious differences.

As they get older though, subtle pressures intrude. Mormon young people attend longer weekly church services, recently changed to two hours of Sunday worship, and Monday family nights restrict their time even further. After high school, many go on missions in other parts of the world to advance their faith.[161] They often return from those experiences with an appreciation of people elsewhere who are different. With those experiences of tolerance, they then focus on furthering their education, and not incidentally, on finding a suitable marriage partner within the faith.

Thus, by the time they are in their mid-twenties, many Mormons are securely anchored in their faith's norms and values, often with a life partner already paired unto and sealed for eternity in temple ceremonies.

By the time Mormon community members engage fully in the world of work and faith around them, they have already mostly learned how to navigate an environment in the Magic Valley which has elements of both their faith's norms, as well as those of others.

It is rare in Southern Idaho today to hear a public "anti-Mormon" comment, or the reverse. Yes, there's a history of prejudice in the state going back decades, but it seems less evident today. One can attend dozens of

160 McCardle, Megan. "How Utah keeps the American Dream Alive," Bloomberg View, Mar. 28, 2017.

161 Newsroom, The Church of Jesus Christ of Latter-Day Saints. "Church Lowers Mission Service Age," Oct. 6, 2012. Mission ages were lowered from 19 to 18 for men and from 21 to 19 for women, resulting in more flexibility for missionary service.

government meetings, civic clubs, business associations and class reunions without hearing any such remarks. It is as if all have learned to acknowledge their respective faiths without the contentiousness seen elsewhere.

As homogeneous as the Magic Valley is, the Mormon/non-Mormon division has traditionally been the most significant divergence in the valley. The Mormon/non-Mormon local divisions aren't singularly intense, nor even noticeable in most situations. There isn't any perceptible split, for example, in political offices; both Mormons and non-Mormons hold political office at all levels and from both parties, although Mormon Democrats seem less common today than in earlier generations.[162] In Idaho as a whole, about a third of the Legislature in 2013 were LDS, with strong representation in Southern Idaho seats.[163]

The same pattern can be seen in local school boards, city council seats and county office holders. One former Twin Falls school superintendent, Carl Snow, recalls that it was understood that Mormon and non-Mormon seats were to be more or less equally divided on his local school board, but that there wasn't any discernible conflict among the board members.[164]

School "released time," in which young people are allowed to take religious class study off campus during school hours, usually in a facility near to a school or campus, is another feature of Mormon life. Released time seminaries and institutes are common in the region, as they are in Utah. There is little conflict over the practice; it's been in place regionally for many decades and appears to be widely accepted in the community.[165]

Part of these patterns of mutual tolerance may be a result of how Mormon congregations are established, by geographic area. If a Mormon moves into a new community, he/she is assigned to the church ward of their location and thus lives adjacent to other Mormons and non-Mormons from the same neighborhood. Unlike other religions, Mormons don't get to choose their ward, or "church shop," although some do go so far as to decide to live in a certain location because of the ward it is in, but that doesn't seem to be a common pattern, at least in Southern Idaho.

And because they are set down in often diverse neighborhoods, they come in contact frequently with people of other faiths. The result is a broader perspective of tolerance than might be seen elsewhere, perhaps more like the "melting pot" America of past decades which many people nostalgically

---

162 Pew Research Center "Religion & Public Life" (2014) found about 70 percent of Mormons are Republicans, with about 20 percent Democrat.

163 Saunders, Emilie. "Who Are Idaho's Legislators? A Demographic Breakdown of the 2013 Legislature," State impact (Boise State National Public Radio), Jan. 7, 2013.

164 Snow, Carl. Jan. 6, 2019.

165 Anonymous. "Released Time," Wikipedia, last updated, July 6, 2016.

recall. One recent article by a Mormon writer, Jana Reiss, describes it this way:

"Mormons attend church based on geography, plain and simple. You don't get to congregation-shop based on which ward has the hippest bishop or the largest youth group (though some Mormons will actually hunt around in different wards *before* buying a house, knowing that once they move, they'll be locked in to those ward boundaries). And you certainly don't get to choose where to go to church based on your political tendencies.

"I used to rail against this policy," she says, "especially when I moved to a rural area where I knew no one and had little in common with the long-term residents of that ward. They were Kentuckians born and bred, and I was a carpetbagger, just passing through; many hadn't finished college, and I'd just gotten my PhD. I was the only one with a John Kerry sticker on my car in the parking lot."

Reiss goes on with an observation seemingly applicable to much of the world beyond: "Back in those days, my Mormon ward was not the only place in my life where I regularly encountered – and loved – people whose views were diametrically opposed to mine. But I would say it is now. The worlds I swim in at work are primarily academia and journalism, both of which have a particular political persuasion, and as a rule our nation has moved deeper into our own silos. Our online interactions nowadays tend to merely reinforce our thinking. If they don't, we all-too-quickly unfriend one another, often in ugly ways."[166]

It is almost as if this region of Southern Idaho has struck a good balance in this regard. In smaller, outlying communities where the Mormon faith dominates, one hears occasional complaints of how the "deck is stacked" in social interactions, awards and other school activities. But these incidents don't seem very common, and they often have more than one side to the story, pro and con responses from observers and participants.[167]

While such underlying social patterns as religion aren't likely to forever be completely smooth, the dominant trend among Mormons and non-Mormons in Southern Idaho is one of civility and personal accord. It's a distinguishing feature of our social landscape. America would indeed be a better place if this were true everywhere.

166 Reiss, Jana. "How Mormonism Can Save America," Religion News Service, Aug. 3, 2018.

167 Norman, Sierra. "I did what I had to do," Her Campus at Bryn Mawr, Nov. 3, 2016. See also, "ACLU, Cassia County Schools Settle Discrimination Suit," *Times-News*, Oct. 19, 2016, and the comments following.

The Unaffiliateds and Spiritualists

One observant individual who has lived in both Idaho and Wyoming, has a quip about the differences between the two states in terms of religion. In Wyoming, he says, there are larger bars and smaller churches. In Idaho, the bars are smaller, but the churches are larger. While amusing, it isn't accurate.

The religious affiliation studies for the two states show little difference. About 51 percent of Idaho citizens report being "highly religious;" in Wyoming, it's 54 percent. Both states fall in the middle nationally. We're not as deeply religious as the South, nor as unreligious as New England.

Both Idaho and Wyoming fall more or less in line with their neighbors (Montana, 48 percent "highly religious,") but less so than neighboring Utah (64 percent).[168] This percentage (51 for Idaho) matches almost exactly with data collected by the Association of Religious Data Archives, 50 percent "unclaimed" in 2010. Other Magic Valley counties show predictable patterns. In nearby Jerome County, about 40 percent are unaffiliated (9,000); in more-heavily Mormon Cassia County, the unaffiliated group is smaller, about 28 percent; and much lower in recreation-oriented Blaine County, where the unaffiliated group is much larger, over 71 percent, approaching three-fourths of the population.[169]

But for the rest of Southern Idaho, there are significant numbers of people who are unaffiliated or, as some of the research calls them, "unchurched." But that doesn't mean they've given up on religion. Indeed, many say they are spiritualists in faith, if not attending a particular denomination on a regular basis.

A recent study found that the unaffiliated group sometimes had once attended church more often but no longer did so, for a variety of reasons. Some simply had moved and were still looking for a spiritual "home." Others could no longer abide doctrinal changes or interpretations they disliked, or practices in the liturgy and music they found grating or unfamiliar.

Others simply married someone of another faith, had gone through a divorce or lost a spouse and didn't feel comfortable in their previous religious setting. And some found they were just too busy to get the kids up and ready for church every week.[170]

---

168 Lipka, Michael and Wormald, Benjamin. "How Religious Is Your State?" Pew Research Center, Feb. 29, 2016.

169 Association of Religious Data Archives, Idaho reports for Twin Falls, Jerome, Cassia and Blaine Counties, 2010.

170 Pew Research Center, "Choosing a New Church or House of Worship," Aug. 23, 2016.

It's tempting to see the unaffiliateds in Southern Idaho as a singular group, made up mostly of agnostics and atheists. However, these two categories represent only about five percent of the population. The rest of the unaffiliateds are in some sense, religious participants in suspended states of participation due to other circumstances.

They may be more recreation-oriented, as the Blaine County group seems to be, or simply individuals in transition, having left one faith but not yet settled into another. America has long witnessed changes in how people choose religious identity and it may well be premature to declare that faith in a general sense is dead in America. It certainly doesn't seem that way in Southern Idaho now, or in the past, or in the future.

Another factor may be the beauty all around us. The Northwest, with its high bluffs, open vistas, snow-capped peaks, scenes of forests, lakes of pure waters and rough-tumble rivers rushing to a distant sea, has long inspired a nature-based spirituality appreciative of "Mother Earth," "Gaia," and other philosophic considerations. In that way, we may have a regional "religion" of natural beauty.

When Lewis and Clark crested the Continental Divide into Idaho they paused, looking farther on, and remarked on the seemingly endless rows of mountain ranges yet ahead.[171] It was both a physical world and a mythic one which lay before them, a new world which F. Scott Fitzgerald later described where man must have "held his breath in the presence of this continent face to face for the last time in history with something commensurate to his capacity for wonder."[172] How could they not have seen the wonder and majesty of Creation? Observations like this abound throughout American literature; they're not even limited to America, but go back in writing hundreds of years, as generations, each in their own time, discover the Earth's grandeur.

We fish not only for the health of our bodies, but "for the health of our souls," writes Dame Juilana Berners in *A Treatyse on Fysshynge Wyth An Angle*, one of the first books in the English language written by a woman (1496), for the solitude, peace and serenity the outdoors brings. Who can doubt that in this vast Intermountain West, a religious faith is often imparted by the natural world?[173]

---

171 Lewis, Meriwether and Clark, William. The party crossed the Continental Divide on Aug. 12, 1805, looking farther at the "immense ranges of high mountains still to the West of us with their tops partially covered with snow." *Journals of Lewis and Clark*, Aug. 12, 1805.

172 Fitzgerald, F. Scott. *The Great Gatsby* (1925).

173 Binder, Melissa. "Where the Religious Nones Roam: Does Nature Religion Explain Pacific Northwest Spirituality,?" *The Oregonian*, Aug. 14, 2015.

Perhaps this explains why Blaine County, with its peaks, ranges, forests and rangeland, shows the highest proportion of unaffiliateds of any county in Southern Idaho. In geography, it is where the great Idaho mountainous and forested batholith begins which then stretches hundreds of miles north. In a sense, Blaine County seems the southern-most portion of "Cascadia," a name given to the whole Northwest region.

When we think about faith in the Southern Idaho social landscape, perhaps we should see it as stretching beyond the confines of Scripture and formalism to include this broad reach of the natural world. That is the doorway by which the natural world opens onto reverence. We are put here for, oh, so brief a moment of time, and in that moment, privileged to see God's beauty and creation, if we will only open our eyes to it.

8. Entrepreneurship & Opportunity

Who runs the Magic Valley? Who owns it?

Thirty or more years ago, say in the mid-1980s, if you'd asked that question, you'd have gotten an array of answers. Some would have said the Mormon church, with its growing population. Others might have cited local banks, with their dominant lending positions, including First Federal Savings Bank, Twin Falls Bank & Trust, and Farmers National Bank, all with prominent downtown presences. Or the medical community, with a then-county-owned hospital and a separate, doctor-owned facility, the Twin Falls Clinic, adjacent to City Park.

Some might have mentioned Idaho Power Company, with its series of dams along the Snake River. There might have been a nod or two to The *Times-News*, whose editor and family publisher were both well known in town. Or local civic clubs, which then had a combined membership of several hundred community members, all men, including many major local businesses owners.

Within their various spheres of influence, there likely would have been mention of food processing plants, an emerging dairy industry and a growing College of Southern Idaho. Local politicians, such as Speaker of the Idaho House, T. W. Stivers, probably would have made the list of the "most powerful," as would have state Sen. Laird Noh, CSI president Jerry Meyerhoeffer, banker Curtis T. Eaton, auto dealers Bob Latham and Emmett Harrison, and retailers John Roper and Earl Faulkner.

A perceptive individual might have thought for a bit about the question and then said, "No One," reflecting the egalitarian nature of the place and its anyone-can-make-it-here with entrepreneurship and opportunity.[174] It would have been hard indeed to come up with a very long list, there being little "old money" in the valley tied to agriculture or manufacturing.

Smaller regional communities reflected similar patterns. In adjacent Cassia and Minidoka counties, the Mormon church was more dominant with its larger proportion of church goers, as was a small regional newspaper, the South Idaho Press, as well as a couple of sizeable food processing employers, Kraft Foods and Amalgamated Sugar. To the south in Jackpot, Nevada, two casinos provided gambling, drinks, restaurants and floor shows. A multi-story hotel, Cactus Pete's, then locally owned, dominated the outpost's skyline. In nearby Buhl, major employers included a growing commercial trout industry, a fresh vegetable plant, and a viable array of Main Street businesses.

Across the Snake River in Jerome and Gooding counties, a modern dairy industry was taking shape, supplying milk and cheese products for export to a wider American market, but not yet a world-wide one. Further still to the north, in the Wood River Valley, the Sun Valley Company dominated ski-season tourism. Forest management then was still focused on multiple use, including light timbering and ranching with many grazing leases on public lands.

In 2018, much of this economic and social landscape has changed, yet important entities retain their major presences. The dominant themes in the intervening years have been growth, outside ownership (often from afar) and resulting expansion of consumer choices. Yet we remain an agricultural valley with many farms, a few small towns, and lots of wide, open spaces. Now as then, no single entity strides over the whole.

So, who runs the Magic Valley today? Who owns it? Is it still "No One?" In a sense, yes. The Southern Idaho area offers opportunity to anyone willing to seize it. "Achieve. Achieve. Achieve" writes American entrepreneur and later philanthropist, Andrew Carnegie. Southern Idaho still reflects that great continuing American story of burgeoning promise and success.[175]

As elsewhere in America, many formerly-local businesses have changed hands, usually to out-of-town ownership. Smaller start-ups develop in many fields and some expand significantly. Some businesses have shrunk markedly in the past decades, notably the *Times-News*, now a minor division of an out-of-state company.[176]

---

174 Hartgen, Stephen. "Twin Falls: The Town," *Journey West: A Memoir of Journalism and Politics*, Ridenbaugh Press, Carlton, Or., 2014.

175 Carnegie, Andrew. *Autobiography of Andrew Carnegie*, 1920.

Other once-prominent employers were sold to regional or national corporations, including banks, auto dealerships, and implement companies. Chamber of Commerce leadership has changed as well. Thirty years ago, leading business owners were the active chamber leaders. Now, it's the local general manager, or a substitute. Big decisions about company expansion and growth are now made mostly elsewhere.

With less local ownership comes less local leadership. Non-profits scramble for annual fund-raising events, and even though out-of-area companies contribute, their "donations" budgets are likely to be more limited than previously. It's the rare non-profit which hasn't seen at least some of this fragmentation or shifts in donor profiles or amounts.

The same is true for continuity of leadership. Many businesses have seen three to five "top manager" turnovers in less than twenty years. For example, the local hospital, St. Luke's Regional Medical Center, has had five chief executives since 2004; the *Times-News*, seven publishers and an equal number of editors since it was sold in 2002; KMVT, the local television station, has had three different owners in 15 years, and an equal number of general managers. At least two businesses, Lytle Signs and Clear Springs Foods, have been sold internally to ESOP ownership (Employee Stock Ownership Plans) which often results in new management.

Thirty years ago, the Magic Valley had what can be fairly called a mostly-staid retailing profile. Sure, there was the Paris, a women's apparel store owned by Earl Faulkner, which showed off his merchandising touch by having a pink Paris card in the purse of many local female shoppers. He did more than $6 million in sales out of a 10,000-foot store on Main Avenue. It closed when he retired.[177] Elsewhere in town, it was mostly smaller malls (Woolworths, The Lynwood, Sears and Kmart) and many free-standing small merchants.

Today, that's mostly been transformed. Local retailing has been supplemented by behemoth "big box" outlets. There's Costco, three Walmarts in the valley, a Fred Meyer, Winco, Pier One, Barnes & Noble. Kmart is still in town, but the Bon Marche, Shopko and Macy's are gone, as is Sears. A wide range of fast-food restaurants line local streets; there are at least 10 McDonalds across the valley. Every week, it seems, marks a new restaurant opening. Most are franchises of regional and national entities.

---

176 The *Times-News* sold to Lee Enterprises in 2002 as part of a 16-newspaper buyout from Howard Publications for $694 million. Lee press release, Feb. 12, 2002. The *Times-News* valuation was about $55 million from the payment rate of about 14.5 times ebidta earnings.

177 Hartgen, Stephen. "Earl Faulkner: He's An Ordinary Person on Main Street," *Times-News*, Dec. 28, 1983.

New to the local retailing scene are such familiar American outlets as Old Navy, Michaels, Sportsman's Warehouse, Dick's Sporting Goods and Ulta, a cosmetics specialty store, Men's Wearhouse and various others. Many of these operations are franchises as well.

As the valley has grown in population to nearly 200,000, the "jump in" factor has increased. We've got a leafy Olive Garden[178] and a crafty Hobby Lobby. A Red Lobster franchise is said to be crawling our way on its gnarly, boiled claws. With more population growth, we can expect yet more expansion in the retailing sector in the years ahead.

Yet, there are quite a few holdovers, often under the same or family leadership. Con Paulos Chevrolet, Wills Toyota and Middlekauff Ford have important auto sector positions, as does Vicker's Western Wear in western clothing. So does Wilson-Bates in furniture and appliances. They've all grown with the valley, as have many service industries, including Brizee Heating, Oasis convenience stores, Mr. Gas fuels and others. Entrepreneurship here means scouting out opportunities and crafting businesses to fill emerging niches.

What follows are examples of Southern Idaho entrepreneurs. They have different accounts of how they got where they are and where they are going. But they share some common threads:

Perseverance. In each case, the individual refused to give up a dream despite the hurdles. If one way doesn't work out, they try another, keeping an eye on long-range objectives.

Leveraging. In each case, the individual leveraged what he or she already knew into something else. They were able to look ahead, see what might be, and strive for it. Each was also able to identify suitable partners at the right time, although each also relied on his own instincts repeatedly. Each was a "lone wolf" in that respect.

It's the size of the fight in the dog. Fortitude, stick-to-it-tive-ness and concentrated effort carried the day. Each of these individuals had an idea and followed it, thus being in on the ground floor of their respective endeavors.

Youth's a plus, but only that. They may have had more energy then, but each now has more knowledge on how to overcome setbacks. None of them lingered or lounged around in their 20s and 30s.

Being in an isolated valley didn't matter to them. Each saw a niche and moved to fill it. In each case, they worked both alone and in common endeavor with others. Working in isolation at least in part proved to be a successful, if unexplored, path. It gave each better insight on how to advance.

---

178 Kennison, Heather. "Olive Garden Buys Liquor License, Plans to Hire At Least 150 in Twin Falls," *Times-News*, Dec. 19, 20, 2018.

Each is gregarious, but in their own way. They're not introverts, but each seems to like time alone to reflect, re-energize, rethink. Each seems more comfortable among peers, family and close social networks like church than among those they don't know.

Each is press-shy, except when it suits them, which isn't often, which is good. Publicity usually has limited value, but many downsides, only a few of which are obvious at the time. One is an almost invisible agri-business operator; the other two are more visible, but not publicity hungry. A fourth was a high-profile community leader and elected official, frequently in the news in her long career. Privacy once lost is very hard to regain. They use social media sparingly, if at all.

Personal serenity. Sure, each is driven, to succeed, but each seems content with how their lives are unfolding in Southern Idaho. There's no evident restlessness in any of them. They could probably be successful anywhere, but each chose this place and figured out how to grow along with it.

Melni Connectors / Mark Melni. You can see the entrepreneur in Mark Melni almost immediately. A bit disheveled in appearance, pork pie hat, left-leaning politics. A sometime musician, which seems appropriate for a man who listens to his own tune. Melni grew up in an entrepreneurial home in California where his father owned and ran a charter bus company. "The entrepreneurial drive was hereditary in my case," he says. But California wasn't a place he wanted to be in the 1980s, where, he says, people were too complacent, too reliant on government, less ambitious. He started looking around.[179]

Melni knew Twin Falls from driving charter bus trips through the area back and forth from California to Sun Valley; his wife was from Buhl, although she wasn't particularly keen on a move back. Nonetheless, they took the plunge and moved here in 1989, to a place he felt they could raise their children in safety.

It wasn't long before he opened a computer repair service, Microchips. There wasn't a computer repair service quite like it in the area then, Melni says, and it fulfilled his "geek" instincts. But his real break came when, in a flash of insight, he saw in his mind's eye how to devise an entirely new product. The Melni Connector, as he named it, seemed simple at first, a hard plastic tube into which electric cable ends could be inserted, given a twist to tighten them down in a Chinese finger trap mechanism, and voila, connection complete. No tools needed. No crimping. Whenever he showed it to someone he trusted, the response was the same: "That's a really good idea, Mark." He knew then he was onto something.

179 Melni, Mark. Interview, Twin Falls, Idaho, Sept. 11, 2018.

And so Melni Connectors was born, an example of which its inventor keeps on his desk at his Twin Falls office. The hard part, says Melni, was taking it to market, but he's had some significant breaks, including an appearance on the entrepreneurial television show, "Shark Tank" where venture capitalist and Dallas Mavericks owner Mark Cuban said he would put in $500,000 for a 12 percent stake in the company.[180] Melni has been boosted additionally by other investors, including some local Kiwanians, where Melni is a club member. His local associations have been enormous help, something he didn't think he would have found in California. It's as if his local friends shared his dream from the start, and put money in to help him get started.

He's also been helped by a recent decision by Home Depot to carry Melni Connectors on its website listings.[181] He's opened production facilities in both Meridian and Burley; the support he's received from the state and local business communities has been outstanding. Southern Idaho may not seem like an entrepreneurial hothouse, but Melni says he's more than comfortable with the range of talent locally and the willingness of parties like the Chamber of Commerce and the state Department of Commerce to help as he's needed it.

He has some advice for out-of-the-box thinkers: "Follow your bliss. You need to figure out what makes you happiest and when you do, it's rewarding. Find what it is and immerse yourself in it. When I started Melni Connectors, many said it would never work, but I kept at it and look where we are now."[182]

EHM Engineers, Inc. / Gerald Martens. Gerald Martens says his best personal strength when it comes to looking at a potential development is that he can "envision things." He offers an example, such as a planned housing and neighborhood development in a mountain resort town setting. He says he'll look at the ground, and he can see the infrastructure, such as roads and bridges, some of the amenities, like walking paths and strategically-placed or diverted streams or a scooped-out pond. He can see, in his mind's eye, the layout of the housing, commercial entities, parking, lighting, access, on and on.[183]

---

180 Bade, Gavin. "Utility Cable Connector Startup Cashes In Big on Shark Tank," Utility Dive website, April 20, 2015.

181 Melni Interview, Sept. 11, 2018, and Melni Connectors website, Melniconnectors.com.

182 Merlino, Rob. "Melni Connectors Update," Shark Tank Blog website, Feb. 9, 2018. See also Kennison, Heather. "Melni Connectors Gets Much-Needed Certification to Tap into Vast Market," *Times-News*, Feb. 18, 2018.

183 Martens, Gerald. Interview, Sept. 17, 2018.

Partly, it's a trait he has cultivated his whole professional life in the Magic Valley, beginning in 1972. As his work has varied across Idaho and close to 30 other states, he says he always tries to look at the final product and the big picture, not at tiny details like the color of the facing brick on a building. Rather: "It's the ability to visualize the final product" that interests him the most. The project "has to interest you," he says.

Over the years, Martens initiated or worked on a wide range of projects, including high-end residential developments, specific client commercial buildings, as well as large projects, like the million-square-foot Chobani yogurt plant south of Twin Falls, completed in less than a year. That project brought him and his team to the office many days at 4 a.m. to finish the $450 million plant ahead of schedule.

Other projects included the St. Luke's Medical Center on Pole Line Road, the Home Depot store, First Federal Savings Bank downtown office, as well as projects in the Boise area. "You have to be committed to the vision" of each project to be successful, says Martens, and "you need to fight for it," the vision, of what each project can be.

In a sense, Martens' approach is an adaptation of the old mantra in business of "getting to yes" but without giving up essentials. It may be something he learned at home, where his father, Waldo Martens, was also someone who looked for solutions. Rep. Waldo Martens served in the Idaho House for two terms (1985-1988) and Gerald says he had thought from time to time about running for the Legislature, but it didn't materialize. He's content now to continue doing projects, large and small, in the development arena.

His company, EHM Engineers, Inc.[184] occupies a modern office on College Road, as part of an office complex he designed and built across Fillmore Avenue from the U.S. Post Office. The buildings are all one-story structures with parking directly in front, a quirk of local business preferences. In the Boise area, he says, two-story and higher buildings are acceptable, but in the Magic Valley, people prefer getting out of their cars and walking in, not up. So that's what he designs and builds.

Martens has grown the business to about 25 people over the years, offering services in engineering, design, hydraulics, materials, GPS mapping, environmental issues, planning and zoning considerations and construction management. With the local area growing rapidly, he says, the Magic Valley has offered many opportunities for him and his company. "You need to understand the nature of who you're working with," he says.

Developing a level of trust is important, he says, particularly with government officials who learn that when he says he will do something, he

184 EHM Engineers, Inc. website, 2018.

will do it. That trust level, cultivated over the years, often gives him the ability to advance a project's financial needs with lenders who also know he'll deliver. That is a feature of local entrepreneurship, one built over time. Entrepreneurship always involves risk, he says.[185]

Martens keeps his hand in local development affairs in other ways as well. He chairs the local Greater Twin Falls Transportation Committee, which meets monthly and reviews upcoming highway projects and long-term needs. Growth in the area is continuing apace and new growth is always just over the horizon. He has no plans to slow down.

Midway Dairy / Alan Gerratt. It isn't easy to find Alan Gerratt. He's not on Facebook, doesn't have a website for Midway Dairy. His office is in a nondescript strip mall in Burley. There's a sign on the front window, but nothing else. No brochure about the business, no self-promotion. He's not in the phone book except a one-line business listing. He drives a practical pickup truck. Nothing fancy.

He stays out of the media. The operation has never been profiled in the *Times-News*. There's almost nothing about him in Google. Without a personal referral from a fellow dairy industry leader, it seems doubtful he would have agreed to an interview or a tour at all. At the end he asked to keep some details vague, or not use them at all.

Yet, Gerratt runs what is arguably one of the more innovative dairy operations in Southern Idaho, a several-generation dairy and farming operation in, we'll just say, rural Cassia County. It's a remote site, one of two dairies the Gerratt family operates. There are about 4,500 cows on this site, averaging about 28,000 pounds of milk a year; the combined herds produce over 500,000 pounds of milk daily, most of which goes to local processors. He raises replacement calves on the site and has about 70 full pivots of irrigated farmland, most of it nearby, for feed for the animals.[186]

The sites have their own labor crews, many of whom are foreign-born; all have work permits and quite a few are American citizens. Gerratt says it's impossible to find Americans who will do such hard work. Eighty percent of the crews have been with him for years; many own their own homes in town, and he provides some on-site housing as well. He has helped some with personal loans to buy homes. He says he's never been stiffed. He feels the longevity of his crew is due to how they're treated. He carries health insurance for them, provides for flexible scheduling when they need it, offers vacation time and pays a fair wage.

185 Martens Interview, Sept. 17, 2018.

186 Gerratt, Alan. Interview, Dec. 3, 2018.

The milking is three times a day. Cows enter the milking stations on their own and computer-driven milking robots do the rest, giving the animal an underside wash, attaching laser-guided suction cups to the cow's teats, and disconnecting the cups when done. Each animal has a chip which links to a computer to monitor its production and health.

The investment in technology is expensive, but it's needed to stay current in a rapidly evolving industry. Some industry observers think that 40 to 50 percent of dairy milking in America will be automated in five to seven years; today, it's about 2 percent.[187] Gerratt is on the front edge of the change for an operation his size.[188]

Gerratt is reserved at first, almost suspicious of the interview idea. He values his privacy and admits he's not a fan of media. Partly, it's just his way, but he's also aware that media exposure leads to attention and attention means scrutiny and, potentially, harassment or vandalism by anti-agriculture or eco-extremist groups.

Yet, as the tour of the dairy progresses, he opens up and is rightly proud of the operation. It's a family business with multiple participants; a son is now involved, the fourth generation. Like many family businesses throughout the Magic Valley, it's taken decades to build it from, well, plain hard work.

Gerratt's grandfather came to Idaho in the 1930s during the Great Depression and worked as a "hired man." He started by raising hogs with his son, Gerratt's father; then switched to calves in the 1950s. In the 1960s and 1970s, they went into the dairy business, milking 200-300 cows twice a day. It was as natural a fit for himself, Gerratt says, as he loved working with the animals and growing the business. That dairy has been in the family now more than 50 years; it's closer to his office, but smaller in scale, at 2,200 cows.[189]

Gerratt says they've doubled station milking since the 1990s, and he keeps an eye for innovation, cost savings and improving productivity. The new robotic milking equipment will take years to pay for itself, but there are numerous pluses, including better cow health monitoring, some labor savings and better herd diet management. The animals get mostly corn silage and other components, such as cottonseed, which he gets by rail from southern states.[190] He says they're better fed than some humans. Cow waste is cleaned out daily from the sheds; he uses settling ponds to separate the solids. Some

187 Varinsky, Dana. "These Robots are Milking Cows Without Any Humans Involved, and the Cows Seem To Like It, Business Insider, June 3, 2017.

188 Millenkamp Cattle milks close to 28,000 cows twice daily at a dairy also in Cassia County. It too uses robotics to handle most of the milking process, on rotary platforms. That dairy produces over 1 million pounds of milk daily, filling some 15-20 tanker trucks a day. See Millenkamp Cattle, LLC website, 2018.

189 Garrett Interview, Dec. 3, 2018.

is then used as an on-field fertilizer; the operations compost additional manure for sale. He says everything is recycled.

Gerratt is on the board of the Dairy Farmers of America and he travels frequently on behalf of the industry. It gives him the opportunity to see what the industry trends are all over the country. Major issues facing American dairies include labor supply and foreign investment and competition. The issues "come up all the time," he says. The dairies themselves, family time, church activities and the industry activities keep him plenty busy. For a Southern Idaho agricultural entrepreneur, that seems like a full plate.

Women Leaders / Maxine Bell. She's not the head of a major Southern Idaho company, but there's no one in public life in this region of the state who's been a more committed public servant than Rep. Maxine Bell, R-Jerome.

She retired in 2018 from the Idaho House as its senior member after 30 years, 20 of which she's been the co-chair of the Joint Finance & Appropriations Committee. More than any other person, except perhaps her Senate co-chairs over time, she's set the tone and dollar amounts of most of Idaho's state budget, amounting to billions of dollars.

She's done so with a sharp pencil and an even sharper mind, good humor, and a keen eye for Idaho's future needs. She has the respect, admiration and love of those who have worked with her. She listens to others, but people also listen to her, an inspiring public speaker who can put complex budget discussions into common terms.

She's a person of and in her community, like the people of Southern Idaho who are just like her and her husband Jack, who have to pay their bills on time and save for a rainy day.

In short, she was the most powerful woman in Idaho, on a par with the state's top political leaders and ahead of many business CEOs.[191] Even in retirement, she's not really retired. Though in her mid-80s, she's got plenty to do. She'll serve next on the College of Southern Idaho Foundation board, an institution she's always seen as one of the community's best assets.[192]

What Bell has done also exemplifies a path upward which many Southern Idaho women have taken, and are taking, through public service and civic involvement, community leadership and an abiding effort to make this valley

---

190 Feeding Whole Cottonseed," Hi-Pro Feeds website, 2018 and "Whole Cottonseed is Super Feed for Dairy Cows," Cotton Incorporated website, 2018.

191 Bell, Rep. Maxine. Interview, Jan. 30, 2019. See Also Kauffman, Gretel. "Maxine Bell: The Most Powerful Woman in Idaho," *Times-News*, March 31, 2018.

192 College of Southern Idaho, CSI Foundation website, 2019.

a better place for their own generation, and the next, and the next. It's a form of community building sometimes not as widely appreciated as it should be.

The list of people who admire Maxine Bell is endless. "Creative," "astute," says CSI Foundation director Debra J. Wilson. "She's opened other avenues for women."[193] Those roles have often been in community and public service rather than in traditional businesses. Wilson says. "It's all about the betterment of the community. How can I make it better?"

It appears to be a leading trait in Southern Idaho female leaders, says Wilson. "They're often from the region. Many grew up on a farm or ranch where there's a respect for hard work. I was taught that no work was beneath you. It was just work that had to be done," she says.

Wilson fits the pattern herself some. She grew up in the Bliss area on a ranch, then attended the College of Idaho. When a marriage ended, she came home and applied for a secretarial job at CSI. One step after another, she has worked her way into her current post. She's had mentors, people like Curtis Eaton, her immediate predecessor, and Joan Edwards, the Foundation's first director.

That skill of knowing the community and working on its behalf is what many also admire most in Bell. She and her husband Jack have been longtime farmers in Jerome County; she served as a school librarian for a time and got involved in Jerome County politics in the 1980s. In 1990, she won a seat in the Idaho House, serving since then with several House Speakers and co-chairing the Finance & Appropriations committee.

She has some observations as to why Southern Idaho has avoided the intense right-wing libertarianism found elsewhere in state Republican politics. "We're neighbors here," she says. Area legislators understand the region and "we're close to the voters" whom we know. The alt-right movement, she thinks, arose in other parts of the state where voters "felt they didn't have a voice."[194]

Bell has never lost her "down home" touch. Asked to identify what others coming along should learn, she says, it's the ability to listen to others. She's as genuine as a cool breeze on an Idaho spring morning, enthusiastic as ever, despite her advancing years. Put simply, she loves the people of Southern Idaho and it shines in her in every regard. A grand legacy indeed.

Entrepreneurship isn't an exclusive American trait; it's found in many places today and has been evolving for centuries, as the silk traders in Marco Polo's time would attest. The history of commerce and trade has involved

193 Wilson, Debra J., Interview, Jan. 30. 2019.

194 Bell, Maxine. Interview, Jan. 25, 2019.

risk taking since the Greeks first brought Aegean wines to Lebanon in Phoenician ships. and English merchants founded the Hudson Bay Company in 1690 to bring back beaver pelts from the New World.[195]

Yet, we think of entrepreneurship as a decidedly American trait, born of the open door of opportunity found widely in American life. But it seems more of the economic landscape here in Southern Idaho, where a stable and low tax environment, combined with business-friendly politics, opens the doors for many opportunities.

Some things may change in Southern Idaho, but these conditions seem pretty well rooted in the conservative business climate. Thirty years from now, there will be new industries, new opportunities and new innovations in a host of fields. And yes, there will be entrepreneurs throughout the Southern Idaho landscape, in many endeavors.

---

195 Braudel, Fernand. *The Wheels of Commerce*, Harper & Row, 1979.

9. Egalitarian Culture

Land for the man of small means

One of the characteristics of Southern Idaho has been relative equality among economic groups. There's no upper class in economic terms, nor any captains of industry, because there aren't many ways for high-level wealth to develop locally. The pervasive quality of early agriculture didn't create farming overlords, nor was there high-value manufacturing with factories.

It's not easy to visualize how limited the first developments were compared to today's consolidated mega-farms. Under the 1894 Carey Act, each state was allotted up to a million acres for agricultural development, of which Idaho ultimately used about 850,000 acres, much of that in Southern Idaho. Allotments were limited to 160 acres per farm, a standard in place since before the Civil War, as it was thought that was all an individual farmer could handle.[196]

---

196 Bunderson, Harold, ed. "Twin Falls County, Twin Falls," *Idaho's 200 Cities: The Southwest*, Ridenbaugh Press, 2017, pps. 17-18, 511. By 1914, ten years after the Twin Falls tract opened, the 23 Idaho completed Carey Act tracts had about 850,000 acres under irrigation with $100 million in outside private investment, and about 50,000 people, the early settlers and our ancestors. The 1920 U.S. Census gives the following populations for Southern Idaho counties: Blaine, 4,473; Camas, 1,730; Cassia, 15,659; Gooding, 7,518; Jerome, 5,729; Lincoln, 3,496; Minidoka, 9,035; and Twin Falls, 28,398. Twin Falls and Cassia counties, with 8,324 and Burley with 5,408, were the only settlements with "urban" areas of more than 2,500 people each.

Federal laws from the 1850s allowed married couples to purchase an additional 160 acres, thus giving couples the chance to buy 320 acres they could work together. The result, as one might expect, increased both the number of purchases, as well as the number of marriages.

Recipients had to make improvements and live on the land for four consecutive years before they received title. One source says dryly that "this law influenced many marriages,"[197] but had the benefit of helping to create real equality in this decidedly rustic place. Combined with a woman's right to vote, established in Idaho in 1896, the land development pattern helped create an egalitarian quality of life on this new frontier. Right from the start, people could vote and own land, regardless of gender. In that sense, we were one of the first genuine "equality" states.

The acreage limit and farming technology meant that early Southern Idaho was dotted by smaller farm operations from the beginning. Even today when farm ground is sold, it's often in these 160-acre parcels, or variations of that: 40, 80, 320 and full sections of 640 acres.

The 1910 Census of Agriculture provides an early look at farm operations in Southern Idaho when the land was first being broken from sagebrush, irrigated and farmed. "The great majority of farms in the state," says the report, "have been acquired by their owners or operators from the government or from private corporations in the form of homesteads, Carey Act entries, desert-land entries or irrigated farms. Most of these have been acquired at a small price, or on long time or favorable terms, making ownership possible to the man of small means."[198]

Almost 90 percent of all farmers in Idaho owned the land they worked; tenant farming wasn't common in Idaho, a factor which also contributed to the egalitarian rural feature of the state. Unlike the South, for example, there weren't land overlords who owned land while thousands worked it, often for pittances.[199]

Idaho was a rapidly growing farm state at the time and the local statistics then show both the investments being made and the then-modest scale of most operations. In 1910, the population of Twin Falls County was 13,543, in the first census to report the county separately. There were almost 1,300 farms counted, of which about 1,140 were owned by white Americans and 148 owned by foreign-born white farmers, with only five farms in non-white hands.

Most of the foreign born came from Europe, including Germany, Sweden and England. Acreages were small, ranging from 310 operations of 20-49

---

197 Bunderson, pp. 15-16.

198 U.S. Department of Agriculture, Census of Agriculture website, 1910, Idaho, p. 379.

199 Census of Agriculture, 1910, Idaho, p. 382.

acres, 347 of 50-100 acres, 367 from 100-250 acres, and 81 farms of less than 250 acres, with 64 of these under 500 acres.[200] There were only 16 farms in Twin Falls County over 500 acres in this first census.

The total value of the farmland in Twin Falls County was just shy of $16 million, with $12.7 million in land and $1 million in buildings, consisting of cobbled together prove-up shacks, some modest homes and out-buildings, or about $12,000 total value per farm, $10,600 of which was in land. All crop value in the county (mostly oats, wheat and barley) totaled just $1.7 million. Potatoes were a "specialty crop" using only 2,100 acres.

A total of 1,614 dairy cows were counted in the county, mostly on individual farms producing milk for the family; but also $75,000 in sales of off-farm milk, probably to townsfolk. Cheese production was too small to be enumerated. The main livestock animals in the county were 63,000 sheep valued at $341,000 in meat. There were about 6,000 horses listed, mostly draft animals, but only three jackasses, a number which has surely increased.[201]

It may be a stretch to visualize how physically difficult life was for those early settlers. The prove-up shacks were small, many of no more than 200 or 300 square feet into which were crammed a family and their worldly goods, living and cooking space and whatever small amenities could be kept and treasured. Quite a few of these shacks are on Southern Idaho farmsteads still, serving as modest out-buildings, tool sheds, wood sheds, canning centers and general storage. They're good reminders of what life was like on this arid and dusty plain.[202]

Tasks were divided on many early farms, with the men working the land, crops, livestock and water distribution and the women responsible for the home, child care and food preparation. Women also often enhanced the meager money supply through the sale of vegetables, canned goods, clothing items and handmade household items. Children often took care of sheep, goats, chickens and eggs, and helped with gardening and household chores. Thus, the early farm was a true egalitarian common endeavor in which all participated and benefited.[203]

---

200 Census of Agriculture, 1910, Idaho, p. 392.

201 Census of Agriculture, 1910, pps. 392, 395, 398.

202 Ramseyer, Duane. "Sucker Flat - A Small Capsule of History," (2016) in Matthews, Mychel. "Filer Man Pens History of Sucker Flat," *Times-News*, Sept. 20, 2016. The Ramseyer farm reached Century Farm status in 2017. On how women contributed to the region's early formation, see Keys, Scott. "Economics and Work," *The World of the American West*, Greenwood, 2017. Keys estimates that up to 10 percent of the "prove up" land filings were to single women, although that topic has not been researched for Idaho filings to the author's knowledge.

203 Keys, *World of the American West*, p. 125 ff.

Much has changed in Southern Idaho agriculture since those formative decades, but this leveled farming profile has shaped our local culture today. The wide land ownership pattern reinforced the common belief in economic fairness.

Coming as it did in the Progressive Era of American history and deriving inspiration from that movement, Southern Idaho's roots were thus practical, broad-based, but also idealistic. Success in life depended on hard work, some good luck and development of institutions, social and economic patterns which fostered family, faith and fortitude.

Communities of farm families, small nearby trading towns, one-room schoolhouses, modest places of worship and the economics of small-scale farming all contributed to the sense of equality, further enhanced by the area's homogeneity and isolation.

We also see this egalitarian trait in the lack of manufacturing in Southern Idaho and how, as a result, there were no local barons of industry. Almost from the start, manufacturing centered around food processing and related industries. A sugar beet processing plant was established early on with the investors from Utah,[204] and other food value-adding facilities dotted the landscape. But there were no local manufacturing employers in non-agricultural ownership and hence, no "baron class." No Carnegies, no Rockefellers, no J.P. Morgans, no Pullmans, no McCormacks, no Weyerhausers, no Pillsburys. no James Hills, no Leland Stanfords.

I.B. Perrine had to find investors from "out East" to create the irrigation network he envisioned; the investors themselves visited the area and gave its towns their names (Buhl, Filer, Kimberly), but didn't live here. In general, the economic landscape was more like the agrarian farm lands envisioned by President Thomas Jefferson a century before than the textile, manufacturing and lumber towns of New England or the cotton mill towns of the South.

The lack of an ownership class had many other results. There was no "mansion" section of town, no carriage houses, no footmen, maids or other positions reflecting the trappings of wealth earned by others. Off-farm jobs were limited to construction crews, merchants and their sales people, plus a few government positions once Twin Falls County and city were established. These positions added some stable positions to an up-and-down farming economy.

Finished luxury goods like feathered hats and fancy dresses could be ordered, but few people could afford these items. Social events revolved around community and church picnics, dances and occasional staged shows.

---

204 Wikipedia. "Amalgamated Sugar Company website, Updated Sept. 5, 2018. The Twin Falls plant dates from 1915, but earlier plants were established in Idaho and Utah in the 1890s."

Schools were modestly staffed; as children grew and learned, they helped teach their younger schoolmates. Few young people went on to college, and of those, a good number went to institutions which trained teachers. Albion State Normal School served Southern Idaho until the late 1940s; it opened in 1893, offering two-year degrees. Promising young women had to be at least 14 to enroll; boys could enroll at 15.[205]

About 80 years later, changing land ownership patterns in the 1970s and 1980s changed this broad egalitarianism. High operating loans, with rising interest rates and the general malaise of the times stressed many farms, leading to bankruptcies. As operations grew larger and efficiencies increased through technologies like pivot irrigation and larger equipment, economic gaps widened between the larger farms and their more modest neighbors.

A sense of declining equality emerged in political debates over water quality, field runoff, feedlot nutrient loading, confined animal feeding operations (CAFOs) locations and the rapid growth of the dairy and cheese industries. Egalitarian patterns seemed to be slipping way. Critics bemoaned these changes, but couldn't stop them.

The underlying economics encouraged growth as dairy expansion took hold and many farmers shifted more land into grain production or feed storage and alfalfa hay to supply that expanding industry.[206] There was a modicum of competition as to where one could sell farm products, but many preferred the relative certainty of growing on contract. This, in turn, resembled tenant farming in terms of independence and freedom of economic choice.

Some local "populist" political candidates spoke out against these trends in the 1980s and 1990s, but they were rarely heeded. Most left the political arena after a failed try or two, but one in particular, Buhl area activist Bill Chisholm, had his name on the ballot in virtually every election over four decades, though he was never elected to any position.[207]

By the early 1990s, Southern Idaho agriculture had evolved to reflect changing economics, work patterns, farm consolidations and other factors over the 80 years. In Twin Falls County, there were 1,457 farms, with an average size of 336 acres, and an estimated land and buildings value at over $338,000 each. Farm sizes remained relatively modest, with 493 farms of less than 50 acres, 762 farms between 50 and 500 acres, but now with 197 farms of over 500 acres, 76 of which topped 1,000 acres each. Primary crops

---

205 Wikipedia website. "Albion State Normal School," Updated Jan. 22, 2018.

206 Hatfield, Max. "Research Center Is Snake Oil for Residents," *Times-News*, March 28, 2008. See also, Matthews, Mychel. "Officer Hears Testimony in Hafliger Water Transfers," *Times-News*, May 20, 2015.

207 Hartgen, Stephen. "Bill Chisholm: Roots in the Valley," *Times-News*, Feb. 1, 1984.

continued to include wheat and barley, but also potatoes, beans and sugar beets. Hay for livestock amounted to 51,000 acres, producing 257,000 tons, mostly for local milk cow and beef production.

The average market value of crops and livestock was put at $169,000, with a net farm annual average revenue of $38,000. There were almost 1,000 primary occupation farmers, but almost 500 others worked off the farm for their primary income, reflecting the growing diversity of employment opportunities. Sheep and hog numbers had languished, but milk cows and cattle had grown; still, in 1992, there were just over 18,000 milk cows in the county, nothing like the enormous growth in the dairy industry yet to come.[208]

Twenty years later, in 2012, some of these trends were even more evident. The number of farms in Twin Falls County declined to 1,294, not much different from where it had been in 1910, and the average farm size was 374 acres, up from the early years, but perhaps mostly attributable to using larger equipment. Farm values in the county totaled almost $600 million, of which $216 million was in crops and $383 million in livestock, reflecting the concentrations of beef cattle and dairy cows.

Farm sizes were still modest, but there were more "hobby" operations, 273 farms of under 10 acres, 282 farms of 10 to 50 acres, 305 farms of 50 to 180 acres, 260 farms of 180-500 acres, and 174 farms of over 500 acres, 76 of which were larger than 1,000 acres. Of the operators, 715 were fulltime, while 579 were part time, deriving at least some of their income from off-farm sources.[209]

Further changes are likely in the 2017 agriculture data, a five-year report due out this year. We shouldn't be surprised to see farm sizes again increase as modern agricultural technologies like geo-positioning become more common. Consolidated farm operations are likely to be even larger, and more expensive to maintain. Self-operating equipment is also on the horizon, which is likely to further reduce farm labor needs and costs. Crop yields are also likely to increase with new varieties being tested and readied for use.[210]

In the 2010s, the development of specialized agriculture sectors has continued apace. Dairy cows in Twin Falls County totaled almost 64,000 in 2012, more than triple the number 20 years earlier, as Idaho continued to become a major milk-products state, trailing only California, New York and Wisconsin. Silage corn production surpassed 33,000 acres in Twin Falls

---

208 Census of Agriculture, Idaho, Twin Falls County, 1992, p. 167.

209 Census of Agriculture, Idaho, Twin Falls County, 2012.

210 O'Connell, John. "Newly released barley variety geared toward craft brewing industry," *Idaho Farm Bureau Producer*, Sept. 2018.

County alone, with barley, alfalfa, beans, sugar beets and wheat all adding to farm crop values.[211]

As these shifts occur, we can expect to see changes in other measures of life in Southern Idaho. Church membership at the Twin Falls Reformed Church, widely thought to be a result of support from Dutch dairy families migrating to the area, has gone from 380 to almost 2,000 since the late 1980s under Pastor Brian Vriesman's leadership.[212] It's another example of how social changes are driven by underlying economic ones.

The same has been happening with home values, which have shot up in recent years. A 2015 list of ten highest valued homes in Twin Falls County showed valuations ranging from $865,000 up to $1.174 million, with home sizes ranging from 5,500 to 8,500 square feet, quite a change from the 200-300 square foot "prove-up" shacks of a hundred years ago. Today, values are likely to be higher still on what one wag refers to as "starter castles." The owners include such professionals as developer, doctor, attorney, securities broker, and dairy owner.[213]

One indicator of the egalitarian equality of Southern Idaho life is the lack of elitism in where young Idahoans choose to attend college. Sure, there are some high school graduates who go to out-of-state, so-called "elite" schools, but not many. Except for those attending LDS schools at Brigham Young University-Idaho, and Brigham Young University in Provo, Utah, it's more common for local high school graduates to choose a college either closer to home, a less expensive school, or one more in tune with their religious and family circumstances.

In Southern Idaho, for example, popular choices include the state's four-year public colleges, some private schools and quite a few choices, among Mormon young people, for BYU and BYU-Idaho in Rexburg, Some may pick a close-to-home community college, or a private school focused on professional training.

Surveys of Idaho young people show attendance at 450 schools in some 49 states, but not surprisingly, in-state Boise State University topped the list with just over 1,000 new Idaho enrollees from the class of 2012.[214]

The usual approach is for the youngster to look close to home, if not on the doorstep. Idaho has a relatively low "go on" rate to colleges of any description, and both educators and policy makers would like to see that improved.[215] In Twin Falls, it was 47 percent in 2017, up from 43 percent in

---

211 Census of Agriculture, Idaho, Twin Falls County, 2012.

212 "Pastor Brian Vriesman Retires," *Times-News*, Aug. 25, 2018.

213 "Gallery: 10 Highest Valued Homes in Twin Falls County," *Times-News*, July 9, 2015.

214 Richert, Kevin. "Idahoan's Many Paths to College," IdahoEdNews.org, Sept. 24, 2013.

2016; other larger school districts were similar, smaller ones typically lower, on intent to "go on."

Twin Falls has a highly-regarded community college in the College of Southern Idaho and the state's four-year schools offer a mix of degree programs, so it's relatively easy for a young person to further his or her education nearby at relatively low cost.[216] It's not surprising that CSI is an attractive option for young people since the campus is familiar to many already as a center for arts, sports and other activities. Thus, yet another example of egalitarian values is reinforced locally by the accessibility to many who might not "go on" otherwise.

CSI is also attractive to non-traditional and adult students who are living in the region, many of whom are already working and whose circumstances preclude them going further away for more education. That fits other patterns of life here, the up-by-your-own-bootstraps individualism and self-reliance we proudly see in so many of our young people.

The college thus reflects how life in Southern Idaho has been, and continues to be, infused with egalitarian elements. People here tend to look at the value of what they have rather than bemoan what they don't.

Residents often take out-of-town visitors through the CSI campus and point out its diverse offerings. It's a way of demonstrating the community pride and egalitarian roots which so many here feel.

---

215 Richert, Kevin. "'Go-on Rate Is Stuck in Neutral," IdahoEdNews website, March 15, 2018. See also, Richert, Kevin, "Life After High School," four-part series, IdahoEdNews website, Dec. 11, 2017.

216 College of Southern Idaho website, "Tuition and Fees" lists tuition at $3,880 annually in 2018. Dual credit programs with area high schools and a "deep pockets" scholarship program also help reduce student costs.

10. Federalism & Anti-Federalism

The Gadsden Flag, now known as the "Don't Tread On Me," flag, dates from the Revolutionary War where it was used as the colors of naval ships intercepting British supply vessels on coastal waterways and the high seas. It's renewed use today is more as a symbol of an anti-federalism strain in both American history and that of the various states.

Its unusual image, of a coiled rattlesnake ready to strike, on a distinctive yellow background, has endeared it to modern challenges to the federalist structure of the U.S. Constitution by groups like the Tea Party movement following the 2008 election cycle.[217]

Its message of resistance to federal authority and defense of individual rights serve as a poignant reminder in states like Idaho where resistance messages have long had expression. The Ruby Ridge incident in 1992 in a remote corner of Northern Idaho is said to have effectively launched a militia and political movement which can be found today in pockets all across Idaho, including the southern part of the state, although not with the same virulence as "up North."[218] Anti-federal rhetoric was also fueled later that year by the presidential election of Democrat Bill Clinton, whose environmental policies and anti-gun rhetoric caused some to think the federal government had, indeed, become the West's adversary.

---

217 Wikipedia. "Gadsden Flag," updated Aug. 28, 2018.

218 Wilson Jason. "Ruby Ridge, 1992: The Day the American Militia Movement Was Born," *The Guardian*, Aug. 26, 2017.

This anti-federal movement has found expression in a variety of ways: the election of a small cadre of legislators from across the state and their subsequent promotion of anti-federal legislation; the spinning off of various militia and anti-federal splinter groups, which often have narrow agendas like positions on the rights to own, carry and use firearms; a virulent strain of anti-federalism laws which purport to assert states' rights and the nullification of federal laws which are perceived to negatively affect Idahoans, and the asserted rights of states to abrogate federal compacts with other countries.[219]

Given the press attention these various movements and issues have raised and the conservative nature of people here, one might expect these anti-federal sentiments to have wide currency locally.

But that isn't the case in Southern Idaho. Local groups espousing such extremist rhetoric are small in numbers, albeit loud in public forums. But when they run candidates for public office, those are roundly defeated by more traditional, common-sense Republicans. They do try, from time to time, to take over local forums like the Twin Falls County GOP Central Committee, but again, these efforts are roundly rejected.[220] Nonetheless, groups like the John Birch Society, We The People and further-right groups like the III Percenters, continue to protest against what they see as creeping federalism in Idaho life.

These organizations and others like them seem more powerful today than in the past, but they have been part of the American political landscape for decades, indeed centuries. One of George Washington's early successes as

---

219 The new "stand your ground" personal defense law, IC 18-4009, outlines how deadly use of force may be claimed. Proponents of the "stand your ground" position, led by arch-conservative Rep. Christy Zito, preferred another version which disallowed prosecution under such circumstances, but that did not pass. See also Peterson, Chuck. "Stand Your Ground: When, Where and Who," Idaho Criminal Defense Blog, July 18 2,018. In 2015, the House Judiciary Committee members voted 9-8 to kill legislation which would have updated Idaho's child support laws, thus forcing a special session in May to fix the issue. Opponents, led by North Idaho conservative firebrand Rep. Heather Scott, saw it as giving away Idaho's sovereignty to foreign courts in child support cases, and thus opening the door to foreign Sharia Law rulings affecting Idaho. Supporters said Idaho laws wouldn't be overridden. The House then passed the measure on a 49-21 vote. See Prentice, George. "Update: Idaho House and Senate Approve Child Support Measure, Sending Bill to the Governor," *Boise Weekly*, May 18, 2015. The pro-nullification bill, HB461, was defeated in the House on a 40-29 vote. The bill's author, Rep. Paul Shepard, gave an impassioned litany on how federal laws directives and court orders had negatively impacted Idaho and her people, but opponents, including myself, asserted how Idaho should work within the federal U.S. Constitution rather than seek to overturn it. See Hartgen, Stephen. "Nullification: An Old Debate Resurfaces in Idaho", *Times-News*, Feb. 26, 2018.

220 A Twin Falls GOP Central Committee meeting on May 23, 2016 was disrupted when a John Birch Society member from Boise accused local legislators of being "terrorists" in the halls of the Capitol. He was asked to leave, and did.

president was to put down Shay's Rebellion and the Whiskey Rebellion, both threats to the young nation.[221]

In North Idaho, the rhetoric of nullification and secession is more common, but it's almost unheard in the arid, unreceptive political soil of Southern Idaho. Why is that? "North Idahoans will tell you that Southern Idaho is where the potatoes grow," writes Anne Helen Petersen. "It's where the Mormons rule. It's where the land is flat. The winters and living are easier, the land is less beautiful, the people less fun. North Idaho, by contrast, is filled with mountains and sprawling lakes, with people who minded their own business and liked you to mind yours, with hardworking loggers and miners, with hunters and fishermen and land."[222]

This comment seems to pinpoint several cultural or philosophical differences between North Idaho and the state's southern reaches. Yes, Southern Idaho is more agricultural, has a higher Mormon population, a milder winter, and arguably, isn't as much fun. We shouldn't be surprised to see wide differences across a state seemingly cobbled together from land no other state really wanted, hundreds of miles across corner to corner, with widely varying natural and human topographies. Yet, we share similar suspicion of over-arching federal power and the far-away national capitol's ability to impact our daily lives, if not at the same intensity.

Take tax protests, for example. It's not uncommon to read about some North Idaho tax protester, such as former Rep. Phil Hart, whose running tax complications with the Internal Revenue Service were seen as a quixotic parry driven by constitutionally-flawed logic. Hart was elected to several terms in the Idaho House, but his I-won't-pay-em logic on taxes lost resonance with voters when it was reported he built a home out of logs taken illegally from state public lands, claiming he had a right to them as a citizen. He lost a 2018 bid in the GOP primary to return to the House.[223]

This kind of windmill tilting seems more common north of Idaho's Salmon River and in Idaho's remote back-country towns and counties where

---

221 The *Federalist Papers*, written by John Jay, Alexander Hamilton and James Madison, make the cogent case for a stronger federal government governing with the people in their respective states. The less-well-known *The Anti-Federalist Papers*, 1986, taps much of the concern among Constitutional Convention delegates at the time that the proposed new structure would create too strong a federal, overarching governing body. Many anti-federalists today refer back to those arguments in opposition to concentrated federal power at the expense of the states.

222 Petersen, Anne Helen. "Welcome to Idaho. Now Go Home," Buzzfeed News, Oct. 22, 2017.

223 Idaho Secretary of State, election returns, May, 2018 GOP primary. See also Russell, Betsy. "Ex-Idaho Rep. Phil Hart settles Federal Tax Dispute," *Spokesman-Review*, July 26. 2015.

individualism runs high and the willingness to confront authority seems more in the cultural air.

It is hard to imagine as go-it-alone an individual as Hart being elected in Southern Idaho's more centrist political districts. There don't seem to be any Southern Idaho community leaders or figures who would fit this mold. We've got plenty of individualism and tenacity here, but we don't tilt windmills much, tempting as it sometimes is.

Take My Guns? Never.

One issue in which Southern Idaho may be infused with more anti-federalism is the endless clarification of the meaning of the Second Amendment, assuring citizens of the right to own and carry firearms. Idaho has long had a strong gun rights and National Rifle Association lobby, active back into the 1980s when gun rights advocates sided with Congressman Steve Symms in his successful challenge to Democratic Senator Frank Church.[224] Strong support for gun rights has long been a given for successful Idaho political candidates and any shortcoming on this issue has been something of a litmus test for GOP candidates, no matter where their districts are.

The Democratic Party platform, by way of contrast, supports the "full text" of the Second Amendment, as well as "universal criminal background checks," prohibition of gun sales to domestic abusers and "scientific research on gun violence."[225] While parsed in language designed not to further alienate potential supporters, the Democratic Party statement gives plenty of wiggle room to people who would like to see more gun control. And its "full text" language allows room for gun control advocates to argue the Second Amendment was written to apply only to formal militias, and not to individual ownership.

Idaho allows both purchase and carrying of firearms in most circumstances, with some restrictions on age of purchase and some exclusions for jails, lockups, courthouses, schools and juvenile detention facilities. Concealed weapons carrying in general has had fulsome debate in

---

224 Benenson, Frank K. "Frank Church and the Politics of Guns," Christian Science Monitor, April 9, 1980.

225 Idaho State Republican Party Platform, Article XIV, Idaho GOP website, 2018 and Idaho Democratic Party platform, Sect. 14, website, 2018.

the Legislature. As of July 1, 2018, a firearm may be carried concealed in Idaho in most circumstances.[226]

In 2014, the Legislature approved allowing the carrying of firearms on state college campuses, including the College of Southern Idaho, with some restrictions. There were concerns at the time about the measure and the CSI Board opposed the proposal, but once the law passed, schools soon developed policies to follow the new legislation. There haven't been any problems with the new law locally and the issue seems to have faded from public view.[227] That same year, gun rights advocates showed Twin Falls County Commissioners where an older county ordinance ran counter to open-carry, and the commissioners quickly repealed the prior ordinance.[228]

Idaho has long allowed general gun purchase, ownership and carry. In 2008, for example, the state passed a law prohibiting municipalities from enacting laws any stricter than the state's relatively permissive purchase statutes. The re-election of President Barack Obama in 2012 prompted a run on firearms purchases locally. People said they were concerned the federal government would soon pass registration laws and move toward confiscation.[229] Except for Democratic legislators from District 26, all of Southern Idaho's political leadership have strong ratings from the NRA; anything less wouldn't be acceptable in Idaho's overall conservative circles.

Overall, if anti-federalism sentiment is less charged in Southern Idaho, there are still plenty of issues into which federal power and overreach can be felt. Home schooling of children, the heavy hand of federal education directives, inadequate payments to local governments in lieu of taxes, as well as criminal court rulings which frequently seem to favor guilty defendants are only some of these additional flash-point issues. The litany of anti-federal rhetoric also includes complaints against the Environmental Protection Agency (EPA) and the Occupational Safety and Health Administration.

Yet, these and other conflicts don't seem to have led to a ground-swell sentiment for nullification of the U.S. Constitution, much less secession, or really anything more than an occasional rally, letter to the editor against federal intrusion or small-group protest over a specific issue.

Protests against federal authority do come up from time to time and may erupt into media-savvy flash-points. The "Sagebrush Rebellion," for

---

226 National Rifle Association. "Idaho Gun Laws," NRA-ILA website, April 11, 2017, and updates.

227 Wootton, Julie. "CSI Gears Up for New Guns on Campus Law," *Times-News*, June 8, 2014.

228 Brown, Nathan. "Twin Falls County Oks New Gun Law," *Times-News*, Aug. 30, 2014.

229 Smith, Alison Gene. "Idaho Gun Sales Increase as Laws Are Questioned," *Times-News*, Dec. 21, 2012.

example, grew out of changes in federal land management policies in the 1970s and 1980s and gained considerable attention in the national press through the involvement of Utah Sen. Orrin Hatch and others.[230]

A resurgence of this anti-federal sentiment broke out again in the 1990s with federal efforts to close an Elko County stream-side road near Jarbidge, Nevada, a remote high-desert and mountain village just south of the Idaho-Nevada border. The so-called "Shovel Brigade" raised continuing resentment over federal land-management policies and considerable media attention.[231]

The Sagebrush Rebellion is now a distant memory if it is remembered at all. A more recent confrontation at an Oregon wildlife refuge office resulted in the shooting death of one protestor, but even that tragic death didn't lead to a broad anti-federal uprising.[232]

This "don't trust the feds" is evident in a recent survey of Idahoans' attitude toward the federal government despite a strong economy, booming state population growth and record low unemployment. The survey found only a third of Idahoans thought the federal government did a "good job" in its various tasks; half said they didn't trust federal elected officials.

But over 85 percent of Idahoans felt the state was doing a good or fair job on the state's economic development.[233] Southern Idaho may be a less-confrontational landscape and the heavy hand of federal regulation may be less weighty, but there's no love lost from Idahoans to the feds.

Nonetheless, the region doesn't feel like a place a very deep rebellion would start. That may be attributed to the essential love of country which most citizens appreciate, despite the frequent debates over the direction of the country and its leadership.

In Southern Idaho, the rule of law seems a widely regarded principle of civic discourse and the ballot box seems to remain the primary change vehicle. The right of assembly and protest of grievances is well regarded, but seldom used, even on electric-fence issues like federal lands management.

Jefferson may have mused about the need for the occasional shedding of blood by patriots and tyrants,[234] but few Southern Idahoans seem to think that

---

230 Cawley, R, McGregor. *Federal Land and Western Anger: The Sagebrush Rebellion and Environmental Politics*, University Press of Kansas, 1993.

231 Chereb, Sandra. "Nevada's Sagebrush Rebels Fight Feds Over Roads; U.S. Control Over Public Lands Angers Residents," *Deseret News*, Oct. 14, 1999.

232 Sottile, Leah. "Malheur Wildlife Refuge Occupation Still Reverberating as FBI Agent Goes On Trial," *The Washington Post*, June 25, 2018. See also Maughan, Ralph. "The Malheur Occupation and its Aftermath," *Idaho State Journal*, April 6, 2016.

233 Bernick, Bob. "Survey Shows Idahoans Aren't Big Fans of the Federal Government," Idaho Politics Weekly, Nov. 25. 2018.

234 Jefferson, Thomas to William Stephens Smith, Paris, Nov. 13, 1787: "The people cannot be all, & always, well informed. The part which is wrong [. . .] will be discontented in

should be the current course. Debates over such matters don't take the same tack as in North Idaho. America may be experiencing a "culture war" or civic fragmentation, but in this part of the state, we think of our country as "One Nation, Under God, Indivisible, With Liberty And Justice For All." What part of Indivisible isn't clear?

---

proportion to the importance of the facts they misconceive. If they remain quiet under such misconceptions it is a lethargy, the forerunner of death to the public liberty. We have had 13 states, independent 11 years. There has been one rebellion. That comes to one rebellion in a century & a half for each state. What country before ever existed a century & half without a rebellion? & what country can preserve its liberties if their rulers are not warned from time to time that their people preserve the spirit of resistance? Let them take arms. The remedy is to set them right as to facts, pardon & pacify them. What signify a few lives lost in a century or two? The tree of liberty must be refreshed from time to time with the blood of patriots & tyrants. It is it's natural manure."

11. Multiple Use of Public Lands: Use It or Burn It

Speaker of the Idaho House Scott Bedke, who in private life is a cattle rancher south of Oakley, tells a story about how a fire was getting started on a nearby public lands allotment and the ranchers went out to put it out. There, they were confronted by a federal rangeland agent who told them they couldn't take their bulldozer off a flatbed trailer and start a fire control strip until higher-ups had arrived to give permission. They also told the ranchers that a field natural "historian" would need to walk slowly ahead of the bulldozer to identify and save any endangered species or historical artifacts in its path.[235]

---

235 Bedke, Scott. Speaker of the Idaho House of Representatives, Testimony before the (U.S. Congress) House Committee on Natural Resources, Oct. 25, 2017. "This past summer, my family witnessed first-hand how good intentions and a total lack of practical knowledge can backfire. Lightning started a range fire on one of our grazing allotments on the Nevada-Idaho border. The fire burned approximately 500 acres and was declared out and contained, and the fire crews left. The next day, the fire started again and burned approximately another 20,000 acres, all of which was in sage grouse habitat. As the fire began to build again, the hard-working firefighters showed up with their fire-fighting equipment. To our surprise, most of the heavy equipment sat unused for hours. The fire continued to grow and get more out of control. Why? Because federal regulations prevented the use of fire-fighting equipment since a "cat tender" had not shown up. A "cat tender" is a person who walks in front a bulldozer as the fire line is created, in order to assure that no historical artifacts are disturbed. However, most of the time the fire line is laid down in areas that have already been disturbed, such as an existing road or fence line, as it was in this case – thus obviating the need for archaeological clearance or cat tending. So instead of extinguishing the fire, thousands of acres of prime sage grouse habitat burned. In fact, essentially the entire winter unit of our allotment was consumed in one large catastrophic wildfire."

The delay and restrictions struck the ranchers as illogical. Burn up public lands because of a bureaucratic delay when equipment was on the scene? The ranchers didn't wait for the bureaucrats; the dozer came off the flatbed, and went to work.

Back in the 1980s and 1990s, there were numerous confrontations between ranchers and federal managers over multiple use of public lands in Southern Idaho. Ranching interests were being portrayed as "welfare cowboys" on their leases and recreational users were teaming up with environmentalists and some agency officials and going to court.

A generation of range managers saw their job as protecting the land first, not in working with traditional users like ranchers, timber interests and mining claimants. There's some indications this has since moved back to a more practical approach in which federal land managers say they want to work with permittees and establish better relations.[236]

In the 1990s, one no-nonsense lands ranger, Don Oman, butted heads with area cattlemen in Southern Idaho over allotments and grazing rights. An equally stubborn aging rancher named Winslow Whitely went so far as to say Oman could wind up with his throat cut if he wasn't transferred. The remark was reported in *The New York Times*, and was seen by environmentalists as yet another example of how Western cattle interests ran roughshod over public property.

The ranchers saw it differently, as an example of how haughty range managers were imposing unfair orders on land users who had held permits for decades.[237] While Southern Idahoans might have supported Whitley in private, he got little public support for a remark widely considered intemperate and inappropriate.

Today, the multiple use/public lands disputes across Southern Idaho and much of the West continue in much the same way: a series of running skirmishes among various special interest groups to which there is no discernable end or outcome. The rhetoric may not be as sharp, but almost every party involved has a position to protect and an agenda to advance. That's because, for many, the "War For The West" is never over.

---

236 Welch, Laurie. "Changing: Q & A with BLM's New District Manager," *Times-News*, May 14, 2015.

237 Egan, Tim. "Trouble on the Range as Cattlemen Try to Throw Off Forest Boss' Reins," *New York Times*, Aug. 19, 1990. Whitley's comment, down the article, was reported as: "'Either Oman is gone or he's going to have an accident,'' said Winslow Whitely, who has one of the biggest herds in the district. ''Myself and every other one of the permit holders would cut his throat if we could get him alone.'' Asked if he was making a specific threat on the life of the district ranger, Mr. Whitely said, ''Yes, it's intentional. If they don't move him out of this district, we will.'

Environmental groups, emboldened by court victories, the continual finding of new or threatened species, and fueled by rafts of money from urban and foundation sources, press every seeming advantage.[238] In this, they are often allied with recreational users who want to see de facto wilderness lands and watercourses fixed in time, preserved even as humans press more into nearby open space with growing communities, human population and profit-minded equipment suppliers.[239]

Ranchers, grazers, timber operators, energy developers, and mining claimants push back, often with industry support, arguing that multiple users can now be done safely and that the abuses of the past are just that, in the past.[240] American energy independence compels public lands use to remain "multiple use" in fact as well as in theory.[241]

Agency district staffs, many with backgrounds in environmental studies and parks and recreation management, mostly align with their friends in the environmental community. Some are urbanites by upbringing who lost their direct land connections at least a generation ago. They lean toward the protectionist role against multiple-use, which they tend to see as another example of the pillagers and land despoilers of the distant past. They usually take an anti-development approach, which may dovetail with their own walk-about, do-some-fishing-and-hiking personal use of the lands.[242]

Despite past histories and suspect motives, groups like the Western Watersheds Project continue to protest virtually every land use beyond light

---

238 Long, Katherine. "A Tiny Snail's Bug Impact – The Endangered Species Act – Little Black Dots In the Water are Symbols of Trouble in Idaho," *Seattle Times*, July 17, 1995.

239 The Wilderness Society website. "Special Interests Aim for Idaho's Wildlands –7 Reasons to Fight Back," n.d.

240 Southern Idaho isn't thought of as hard-rock mining country, but there's a sizeable "Oakley Stone" quarrying site on Middle Mountain near Oakley, from which several companies extract the building stone used all over the country in both decorative and structural applications. The companies operate under BLM permits and land restoration is as important today in modern mining as extraction. The industry's value is estimated at $90 million annually. See Welch, Laurie. "The Big Story: Oakley Stone: How Middle Mountain Yields Its Treasure," *Times-News*, June 18, 2017 and other articles in the same presentation. See also Kent Hale obituary, *Times-News*, Sept. 26, 2012. Hale was one of the stone industry's pioneers beginning in the 1940s.

241 Midas Gold. News Release. "Idaho Lawmakers Encourage President & Federal Officials To Move Stibnite Gold Project Forward," Feb. 22, 2018. Full disclosure: as a member of the Idaho House, the author voted with the majority to support this joint memorial.

242 Poppino, Nate. "A Day in the Field," *Times-News*, June 19, 2008. Full disclosure: The author, who is quoted in this article, served as a consultant to a wind farm developer from 2006 to 2008 before becoming an Idaho legislator later that year. During the 2008 tour, BLM agency staffers said they didn't want to see additional human presence in the area, as that was where they liked to recreate and hunt themselves. See also Brown, Nathan. "Decades-old Lands Debate Flares Up In the West," *Times-News*, May 1, 2016.

recreation. The founder, Jon Marvel, brought many suits and protests against rangeland cattle grazing,[243] His efforts, lasting for more than 20 years, were joined by others, who have turned the issue more political by openly opposing at least one Idaho Republican legislator running for reelection in 2018.[244]

Turnover of Federal Lands to the States? Unlikely.

One particularly sharp flashpoint has been the proposal, advanced in neighboring Utah and other Western states, is finding a way for the states to be given control of federal lands within their boundaries. The proposal stems from the long history of federal lands ownership of huge tracts of federal lands which go back to when Western states entered the Union in the late 1800s.

As part of their admittance enabling acts, states including Idaho, generally disavowed future claims to the federal lands, in Idaho's case, an estimated 32 million acres or roughly 60 percent of the state's landmass. Advocates of turning over federal title to the states point to the potential for better management, "equal footing" with other states, and a general sense equity and fairness.[245] Opponents of the idea cite increased costs which they say the

---

243 *Times-News*. "Marvel's Rangeland 'Stunt' Simply An Attack On Livestock," Jan. 12, 1993. See also DeSilver, Drew. "Cattle Foe Marvel No Steward Of His Own Land," *Times-News*, Jan. 6, 1993. Marvel continued to be a sharp critic of Western ranching and grazing, bringing many lawsuits and generally attacking public lands multiple use. Some writers painted him as a crusader against so-called ranching abuses on public lands. See Gibson, Lydialyle. "True Grit," *University of Chicago Magazine*, Jan.-Feb., 2010 . Others saw Marvel as an obsessed anti-range activist. See Findley, Tim. "A Mad Tea Party," *Range Magazine*, Spring, 2004 See also Dorinson, Patrick. "The Western Watershed's Assault on Family Ranchers," PJ Media, June 6, 2010. El Paso Pipeline announced they had helped fund Western Watershed's buyouts of Idaho ranching leases as part of a deal to head off a lawsuit by Western Watersheds, which would have tied up the pipeline project. An Idaho legislator, Rep. Scott Bedke, called the payment by El Paso nothing short of "blood money." See Hurst, Dustin. "Gas Pipeline Company Blasted for its Role in Purchasing Idaho Grazing Leases," Idaho Reporter.com., March 24, 2011.

244 Conservation Voters of Idaho, website, 2018. The effort was successful and the Republican incumbent was defeated in heavily-Democratic Blaine County.

245 Fretwell, Holly and Regan, Shawn. "Divided Lands: State v. Federal Management in the West," PERC Report (Property and Environment Research Center, Bozeman, Mt.), 2015.

states can't afford, as well as concerns that any such lands would soon be sold to private owners and public access lost.[246]

Idaho undertook a study of the issue in 2014 and held hearings around the state. The committee's report did not support the transfer of title proposal, but rather encouraged the state to expand and improve access and to find ways work with federal land agencies to improve land management. These conclusions were approved as a joint resolution in the 2015 Legislative Session.[247]

Since then, the Idaho Department of Lands has created a working division within the agency to work out details with their federal counterparts. There are no transfers of title involved and all timber and other operations must comply with federal EPA and other environmental requirements.[248]

Agency officials and others hope these kinds of new models of Western federal lands management will open the way for future cooperative efforts. Although doubts remain as to the success of the program, interested parties in Washington and other Western states are looking at the Good Neighbor Authority as a way to improve forest health, reduce fires and improve the economic strength of timber-dependent communities throughout the Northwest.[249]

There are additional discussions on how the Bureau of Land Management might be better included in the concept as well, beyond the timber harvest model. The Good Neighbor Authority concept, as demonstrated already in the Idaho projects, is likely to be used more extensively in the coming years and may be a compelling tool for decades from now for Western lands management.[250]

It strikes many as wishful thinking that the federal government would simply turn over titles to thc states; politically, that seems unrealistic. But new cooperative models to increase access, reduce overgrowth of woodlands, while complying with modern environmental standards, seem to be

---

246 Nie, Martin. "Transferring Federal Lands to the States: Unanswered Questions," Wildlife Society Annual Meeting, Helena, Mt. March 17, 2017.

247 Idaho Senate Concurrent Resolution 126, 2015 Session. Full disclosure: The author served on this study committee and voted for the resolution on the House floor.

248 Idaho Department of Lands, Good Neighbor Authority Update, March 21, 2018. The cooperative projects, authorized in the 2014 Farm Bill, have 29 projects under study, totaling 22,000 acres across four national forests with an estimated cut on the first 12 projects of nearly 70 million board feet valued at over $16 million.

249 Nadvornick, Doug. "Washington, Idaho Embrace Change to Help Manage Federal Forests," Spokane Public Radio, April 19, 2018.

250 Ward, Xavier. "State and Federal Partnership to ramp up for Forest Management…," *Idaho Press*, Dec. 18, 2018.

emerging. If so, it would represent a true national breakthrough for federal lands management and fire suppression.[251]

Increased human activity, along with lightning strikes, fuels buildup and a general drying trend of Western lands all contribute to wildfire occurrence and intensity. A recent summary for Idaho projected that by 2050, wildfires will be two to five times larger. In 2017, some 686,000 acres burned in Idaho alone, twice the size of Teton National Park. Across the United States, but mainly in the West, wildfires consumed more than 10 million acres at a cost of $3 billion in federal suppression funds.

Wildfires in the country have cost more than $1 billion in 13 of the past 17 years since 2000, in suppression costs alone, not including private structures and the toll in human lives lost or displaced, as well as in lost economic activity in recreation and timber harvest.[252] The 2016 Pioneer Fire in the Boise National Forest consumed about 188,000 acres at a suppression cost of over $94 million, one of the ten most expensive fires in Western history.[253]

Numbers like these drive the search for better suppression methods, forest thinning and more conscientious human recreational use. There's no single cause and no single solution, but many are recognizing how careful multiple use policies can play an important positive role.[254] Fire costs on Idaho's state land in 2018 totaled $17 million, about 80 percent of the 20-year average; 183 of 236 blazes were human caused.[255]

Where to Recreate? On Public Lands, of course.

More than a century ago, a frail New York boy, a Harvard graduate, used some of his inherited fortune to buy a cattle ranch in Western North Dakota. A hunter and sometime tourist, he roamed the Badlands country in the 1880s, hunting antelope, bighorns and deer. He even claimed to have killed a cougar

---

251 Northwest Fire Science Consortium. "Rangeland Fire Protection Associations: An Alternative Model for Wildfire Response," website, 2012-2018.

252 Cooper, Leigh. "Wildfire in the West," University of Idaho News, June, 2018.

253 Berry, Harrison. "Pioneer Fire Makes List of Top – 10 Western Wildfires," *Boise Weekly*, Oc. 6, 2016.

254 Part I of this book, "Fire."

255 Russell, Betsy. "Idaho's fire-season bills come to just over $17 million," *Idaho Press*, Sept. 18, 2018.

with a hunting knife and his bare hands. This, some said, gave him good training when later in life, fate made him President of the United States.[256]

Teddy Roosevelt is one of the four presidents on Mount Rushmore in South Dakota, a fitting location to the president who almost by himself launched the appeal of being fit, on the trail, the outdoors enthusiast, the sportsman, the hunter, an American icon. He and a few others essentially created the American recreation movement.[257]

Is there any outdoor enthusiast today who isn't familiar with John Muir's wilderness advocacy, Rachel Carlson's *Silent Spring*, or Ernest Thompson Seton's *Wild Animals I Have Known* or turned the pages of Roger Tory Peterson's *Field Guide to the Birds*? Today, millions of recreationalists prowl the American West exploring every corner of the country, recording every sparrow in an outdoor journal, taking its picture on a cell phone camera to be spread worldwide.

Every rivulet and stream is a candidate for inclusion in the "navigable waters" list, having been thoroughly mapped, GPSed, camped on and usually had the trash and human waste taken out, leaving nothing but the footprints of boaters and kayakers.

And where do they go to recreate? To public lands, of course, particularly if they're nearby and accessible as Southern Idaho's lands generally are. Wild destinations are all around us; that is part of why we are settled here but heavy use of Western lands has added both conflict and cooperation to the term "multiple use."

An army of people trek about, from rock climbing at City of Rocks, to snowmobiling in the South Hills in winter, to a June morning on Silver Creek with the trout sipping tiny trichos in lazy rings, to the thrill of jumping off a perfectly good I.B. Perrine bridge in a sport known as BASE Jumping, (Building, Antenna, Span, Earth) or taking hikes on a Blaine County trail to Pioneer Cabin.

This expansion of recreational activity in the West underlies much of the conflict Idahoans find on public lands, because people's definition of "multiple use" vary and each wants his or her primary use to be first. Recreation isn't always compatible with agriculture, ranching, timber harvest or mining, all human endeavors focused on production uses and often with heavy equipment.

Ask any permitted rancher in Southern Idaho about how his operation is affected by recreational uses and be prepared for an earful on tree lots cut

---

256 Theodore Roosevelt National Park website, Medora, North Dakota, "Theodore Roosevelt The Rancher," Updated, 2015.

257 After becoming President in 1901, Roosevelt created the Forest Service as well as dozens of national monuments, parks, wildlife refuges and other set-aside preserves.

away for firewood, gates left open allowing livestock to wander, impromptu campsites set up near water, littered with trash, bark stripped from trees by hungry pack animals, line shacks and cabins broken into and ransacked to the point many ranchers and owners today don't even try to maintain such structures.

Add in people who, if confronted, may well be carrying a firearm and some alcohol-fueled lack of judgment, resulting in an argument. And that's just the top of the list, which may also include careless fire control and huge campers and recreational vehicles brought in for "camping" in the outdoors. It's no wonder land owners and permittees wince when the topic of multiple use comes up. Yea, they say, multiple use is often someone's disregard for others' traditional uses.

Many recreational users of public lands are indeed respectful of where they are and leave nothing but their footprints. Southern Idaho is no different in that regard; most people make a conscious effort to practice good conservation ethics. But there just enough of those who don't to raise ongoing ire among landowners and land managers who are stuck with the cleanup.

As human populations increase across Idaho and land uses get more intense, it's likely that recreational uses will continue to compete with other activities on public lands. Educating the public will take even more effort than it does today, and may not be successful in every case, particularly for lands close to population centers.[258] We all know the phrases, "pack it in, pack it out," and "leave the land better than you found it." We just have to practice what we know.[259] All of us.

---

258 Bureau of Land Management, Twin Falls District Office. "2018 Spring Cleanup Planned for Snake River Canyon North Rim," May 14, 2018.

259 Leave No Trace Center for Outdoor Ethics website, "The Leave No Trace Seven Principles," n.d.

12. Agriculture

Is there a more iconic image of Idaho farmland than the vast expanses of potatoes, wheat and other crops ripening in the late summer heat and sunshine? On a late July day, it would seem, every combine in Southern Idaho is out working a field as another harvest begins. In the pasture lands, cattle graze in small groups, up to their chins in the grass and alfalfa stubble aftermath.

In the past quarter century, Idaho agriculture has come into its own. A leader in potatoes for many decades, it joined the top ranks of states in a wide range of other commodities in 2016:

- Potatoes: No.1 state, 139 million hundred weight, on 324,000 acres, valued at $926 million;[260]
- Barley: No.1 state, 62 million bushels on 580,000 acres. valued at $313 million;
- Milk: No. 4, with close to 600,000 milk cows, valued at $2.36 billion;
- Cheese: No. 3 with 871 million lbs., behind only Wisconsin and California;

---

260 US Department of Agriculture, Statistics by State, 2016. Statistics for Idaho agriculture in 2017 show gains in many commodities and livestock production, up about 3 percent overall from 2016, with 2018 statistics expected to show continuing gains. Ag production total for 2017 is $7.49b, with crop production at $3.06b and livestock at $4.43b, both up from 2016 numbers. See Ellis, Sean. "Idaho Ag Production Value increased 3 percent in 2017," *Gem State Producer*, Dec., 2018. Updated figures from 2018 show milk sales at $2.359b; hay, $883m; wheat, $490m; potatoes, $864m; and cattle $1.6b. See Eborn, Ben and Taylor, Garth. "The Financial Condition of Idaho Agriculture - 2018," University of Idaho, College of Agriculture & Life Sciences, Jan. 9, 2019.

- Hay: No.10, with 5.126 million tons, on 1.33 million acres, valued at $678 million;
- Sugar beets: No. 2 with 7 million tons on 170,000 acres, valued at $300 million;
- Beef cattle: 500,000 head plus another 120,000 replacements, valued at $392 million;
- Beans: No. 6 with 2.6 million cwt on 137,000 acres, valued at $69 million;
- Silage Corn: No.6 state with 6.9 million tons, on 235,000 acres.

Idaho's agricultural sector has more than doubled from $4.4 billion in 2004 cash receipts to close to $9 billion in 2014. Nine of the 11 years set annual records. Processed foods and beverage sales totaled another $8 billion; combined, food production and processing counted for over 20 percent of the state's economic output and more than 15 percent of state gross domestic product.[261]

Idaho agricultural products are sold worldwide. Canada and Mexico are the state's leading agricultural export buyers at over 45 percent; another almost 30 percent goes to Asia. Exports totaled almost $1.9 billion in 2015.

Milk products ($3.2 billion) and cattle ($1.27 billion) are the state's leading agricultural products, but potatoes, hay, wheat, sugar beets and barley each contribute hundreds of millions of dollars to the agricultural sector profile. Potatoes alone were valued at over $1.2 billion in 2017, a more than 20 percent annual increase.[262]

This agricultural bounty is concentrated in Southern Idaho. Four area counties are in the state's top 10 (Cassia, Gooding, Jerome and Twin Falls), joined by two adjacent counties (Elmore and Owyhee). Each of the six has thousands of acres dedicated to agricultural production. Combined, the six of 44 state counties produce almost half of Idaho's total agricultural value.

The diversity of Idaho's agricultural sector may surprise some. In addition to the crops and livestock listed above, the state is the nation's No. 1 producer of commercial trout, farm-raised in Southern Idaho; 6th in sheep and lambs; 8th in wool production; 13th in honey; 3rd in hops, 3rd in mint and 4th in onions. A good share of this output is concentrated locally as well.

261 Idaho Department of Agriculture, Agriculture Facts, 2016. "Idaho agriculture is diverse, abundant and rooted in our history. The state has nearly 25,000 farms and ranches which produce more than 185 different commodities and the state ranks in the top ten in the nation in 30 of those commodities. Idaho is the third-largest agricultural state in the West and second in net farm income."

262 Koger, Chris. "Idaho Potato Crop Value Hits $1.2 Billion High", *The Packer*, March 5, 2018.

New crops, such as mint and industrial hemp, may add to this agricultural diversity in the future.[263]

Looking at individual counties, the cash receipts for crops and livestock for several Southern Idaho counties in 2014 were: Cassia, $1.57 billion; Gooding, $1.2 billion; Jerome, $758 million; Twin Falls, $699 million and Minidoka, $401 million.[264] Compare that to the about $184 million in recreation/tourism revenue. Several individual crops bring in more, let alone the combined revenue generated by agriculture.

Many factors help make Southern Idaho an agriculture-friendly area: Weather patterns including warm sunny days and cool evenings. Good soil conditions. Measured and controlled irrigation.[265] Modern, labor-saving equipment and techniques hold down costs. Relative closeness of processing plants and direct shipping to markets, primarily in the West but also increasingly abroad. Relatively low land and labor costs when compared to elsewhere in the nation.[266] Innovative thinking on the part of local owners, farmer entrepreneurs, willing to create practical solutions to ongoing issues of farm management and profitability.[267]

Then there are the less-tangible factors: local communities with relatively low taxes including an agricultural sales tax exemption on purchases,[268] and common-sense state laws on such matters as property rights versus eminent domain, trespass and "Right to Farm;"[269] large farm organizations like the Idaho Farm Bureau and various commodity groups; a cultural setting in which quality agriculture is respected and admired in policy decisions and legislation.

A common thread in American history is the underlying belief that a nation of farmers was preferred to urban crowding; that being "close to

---

263 Ellis, Sean. "New Farm Bill Allows for Production of Hemp," *Idaho Farm Bureau Quarterly*, Winter, 2019.

264 University of Idaho Extension, "Economic Contribution of Idaho Agribusiness, 2016" (2014 data).

265 Kennison, Heather. "Ag-Tech Company CropLogic to open sales office at CSI," *Times-News*, Oct. 26, 2018.

266 Ellis, Sean. "Northwest Farmland Values Continue to Increase," *Capital Press*, Sept. 7, 2017. National Agriculture Statistics service, Idaho land values put 2017 Idaho farmland values at $5,150/acre for irrigated land and $1,460/acre for non-irrigated land. Magic Valley farmland prices have generally been below the $8,000 to $10,000 range. In recent years, sales have been reported up to $14,000/acre.

267 Standlee Hay Company. Eden, website, 2018. Standlee is a good example of agricultural entrepreneurship, specializing in high-quality hay and pelletized feeds for shipment all over the country and overseas.

268 Idaho Tax Commission, "Production Exemption Guide", May 10, 2018.

269 Russell, Betsy. "Right to Farm Bill Passes House, 57-11," *Spokesman-Review*, March 10, 2011. See Idaho Session Laws, 2011, HB 210.

nature" led to a higher moral plain of life. Thomas Jefferson frequently extolled the virtues he thought came from agricultural effort, balanced though it was with both the development of commerce and the benefits of manufacturing.[270] The purity of the rural life wasn't new with our third president; it stretches back at least to Greek and Roman philosophy where Virgil in his poem *Georgics* contrasts the virtues of the Roman citizen/farmer with the depravity of the Roman Senate.[271]

But it was Jefferson and his notion of ethical goodness rooted in agricultural living, who gave an American voice to the moral implications of rural life. He notes in Query XIX of his *Notes on the State of Virginia*, (1785) "Those who labor the earth are the chosen people of God, if ever he had a chosen people, whose breasts he has made his peculiar deposit for substantial and genuine virtue;'' a sentiment he repeats in Query XXII: "No age of history has ever recorded corruption in the mass of cultivators." To James Madison, he writes, "I think our government will remain virtuous for many centuries as long as they are chiefly agricultural; and this will be as long as there shall be vacant lands in any part of America. When they get piled upon one another in large cities, as in Europe, they will become corrupt as in Europe."[272]

Jefferson died on July 4, 1826, fifty years to the day of the Declaration of Independence, and thus didn't live to see the development of western farmlands. He might be surprised by the scale of agriculture today, the millions of irrigated acres, the variety of crops, the productivity of livestock operations, but it's easy to see how the agriculture of the farm country of Southern Idaho would win his praise.

Southern Idaho was settled in the heyday of the Progressive Era, at a time when moral virtue and the benefits of republican and representative government were widely appreciated in social and political thought.[273] Idaho's early adoption of women's suffrage (1896) and alcohol prohibition (1916) fit in well with early elected leaders like Fred Dubois, who served in the US Senate as a "bi-metalism" proponent of silver currency against the gold standard.

---

270 Holowchak, M. Andrew. "Jefferson's Moral Agrarianism: Poetic Fiction or Normative Vision," Springer Science and Business Media, Sept. 2010.

271 The Roman historian Livy writes of the noble civic virtue of the patrician Lucius Cincinnatus, who left his farm to lead the Roman state and army and then returned to his farm in 458 B.C., leaving the trappings of power aside. President George Washington, who is often compared with his Roman predecessor, greatly admired the Roman general. Cincinnati, Ohio is named after him. It was common in America's formative years for place names to be taken from admired leaders of ancient history.

272 Quoted in Holowchak, 2010.

273 Hofstader, Richard. *The Progressive Movement 1900-1915*, Prentice-Hall, 1963.

These positions dovetailed with the rural populism of those early 20th century decades, overlapping with Southern Idaho's settlement and offering an inherent belief in the moral and ethical superiority of rural, agricultural life and values. These features of Southern Idaho life would also have pleased Jefferson, arguably our first president of the common man.

It shouldn't be surprising then to see these values of self-sufficiency, individualism and common endeavor bound to the way Southern Idaho developed in those early years. Hard work, practical neighborly relations with others, empathy in social relations, an appreciation for heritage are all traits we associate with farming communities. They seem to have been present from the first settlement days, and are evident today in many aspects of agriculture.

Stroll through any Southern Idaho county summer fair, with its quilting displays; garden and canned vegetable awards; the wafting, sweet smell of a Dutch Apple homemade pie; the wash-and-brush preparation of the 4-H livestock; the saw-wa-wah, saw-wa-wah, sputters of single-cycle engines. Or stop by the craft booths with their wheat-straw dolls and Christmas wreaths; or the pavilion building with displays of the newest product lines and brochures; or a community meal at the Filer First Baptist Church with the can't-put-down scrumptious Brownies; or the everyone-stands crowd at the Rodeo arena, hands over hearts singing along with a pint-sized soloist the Star-Spangled Banner; or the prayers before the start of the weekly Kiwanis or Rotary meetings which often thank Providence for the beauty, glory and bounty of our Earth. They all say this is our heritage, our bequeathed inheritance, our ancestry and our future, our common values.

Groups like the Idaho Farm Bureau continue these traditions in their many membership meetings. The group has thousands of participating farm families in the Magic Valley and their annual policy booklet reflects the broad outline of supported values and positions.[274] The Magic Valley Farm Managers & Rural Appraisers group provides a monthly meeting for trends in agriculture and agricultural finance on which the valley depends, with discussions on water supply, farmland pricing and a fair mix of county, state and federal politics and policy.

It wouldn't be a surprise to see these examples and others of our agricultural culture still vibrant decades from now. Crops may change, and so may farming practices. The landscape of community, field and town may look different, but it will still be a predominantly farming valley, as we have been from the start. It is easy to overlook such continuity, an enduring

274 Idaho Farm Bureau website, Policies for 2019, Dec., 2018.

cultural trait, in the rush of daily events. But it is part of us nonetheless. "The past," says Faulkner, "is never dead. It isn't even past."[275]

Here are short descriptions of some leading Southern Idaho agricultural commodities:

Alfalfa – Alfalfa hay is a major feed component for the area livestock industries. Fast growing and often yielding multiple cuts in a growing season, alfalfa production in South Central Idaho totaled almost 1.5 million tons on 310,000 acres in 2016. Twin Falls County led the valley production with 330,000 tons, followed by Cassia County at 265,000 tons, Minidoka County at 202,000 tons and Jerome County at 197,000 tons. Yields were generally between 5.2 and 5.6 tons/acre.[276]

Barley – Idaho planted over 500,000 acres in 2017, with 206,000 acres harvested with an average yield of 95 bushels/acre, about 1 million metric tons. Idaho grows about a third of American barley, most of which (85 percent) goes to malting and the rest for livestock feed.[277]

Beans – Dry edible beans are a common crop in Southern Idaho, on about 180,000 acres, producing about 1,600 lbs/acre, with an estimated value of $83 million in 2017.[278] A good share is exported.

Corn – Southern Idaho produces feed and silage corn for nearby livestock yards and dairies. Grain corn production in 2017 was about 115,000 acres with an estimated value of $99 million. Silage corn was grown on about 220,000 acres, producing 6.6 million tons.[279]

Potatoes – Idaho is the nation's leader with almost 140 million hundred weight (ctw) grown annually on about 325,000 acres. Much of the product goes into frozen French Fries and similar potato products.[280] Another large Southern Idaho potato processor, McCain Foods, is building a $200 million expansion at its Burley plant, expected to add almost 200 jobs with an average wage of $44,200, bringing employment to about 600 workers in 2019.[281]

Expansion of processing cascades quickly to other manufacturing and handling. The McCain expansion in Burley is being quickly followed by a

---

275 Faulkner, William. *Requiem For A Nun*, 1952.

276 USDA, National Agricultural Statistics Service, Idaho, 2015-2016.

277 Idaho Barley Commission, website, updated, July, 2018.

278 USDA, National Agricultural Statistics Service, 2018.

279 USDA, National Agricultural Statistics Service, 2018.

280 Lamb-Weston website, Oct. 2, 2018. The company (NYSE:LW) was spun off from Con-Agra in 2016. It reported lst Q 2019 net sales of $915 million, up 12 percent from 2018.

281 Kennison, Heather. "McCain Foods Plans $200 Million, 180 job Expansion of Burley Plant," *Times-News*, May 3, 2017.

new 180,000-square foot NewCold storage plant, dedicated to McCain. Automated cold storage of food products is a hot satellite opportunity, say food processing experts.[282] Henningsen Cold Storage operates a 12-million cubic foot facility in Twin Falls,[283] adjacent to Lamb-Weston.

Growth has also come in the transportation and redistribution sides of food processing and handling, with national companies like DOT establishing distribution centers in the valley.[284] Specialty companies like Rite Stuff Foods have added to the mix of product lines and offer attractive wages of more than $20/hour. Job vacancies in their workforce are rare.[285]

Sugar Beets – Beet production in Idaho was 6.5 million tons in 2017, on 167,000 acres, virtually all of it in Southern and Eastern Idaho. Beet production has been a dominant Idaho crop going back to the first settlements in the area. Amalgamated Sugar operates plants at Twin Falls and in Minidoka County and maintains numerous "beet dumps" throughout the valley where farmers weigh in their truckloads. Production is almost 40 tons/acre.[286] Sugar beets are mostly grown under contract. The two modernized Magic Valley plants date from the 1910s. Combined with a plant in Nampa, they produce over 1.6 billion pounds of sugar a year.[287]

Wheat – Idaho produced over 100 million bushels in 2018, half of which was exported. Winter wheat planted 720,000 acres and harvested 680,000 acres at more than 90 bu/acre. Spring wheat had 460,000 acres planted, 445,000 acres harvested, producing 42 million bushels at 95 bu/acre.[288]

Dairy – Among the biggest changes in Idaho agriculture has been the growth of the dairy sector. Today, Idaho is the No. 3 dairy state, producing milk and dairy products valued at over $2 billion. The industry is concentrated in Southern Idaho, where relatively mild winters, low humidity, lower costs of land and availability of feed supplies have all contributed to growth. There are an estimated 580,000 dairy cows in Idaho, with more than 416,000 alone in the Magic Valley on some 296 dairies, with about 1,400 cows each.[289]

Despite its recent growth, the state's dairy industry faces several challenges, says Bob Naerebout of the Idaho Dairymen's Association. Having

---

282 NewCold Logistics website, October, 2018.

283 Henningsen Cold Storage Co. website, 2018.

284 DOT Foods website, 2018.

285 Rite Stuff Foods website, October, 2018.

286 USDA, National Agricultural Statistics Service, 2018.

287 Amalgamated Sugar Company website, 2018.

288 Idaho Wheat Commission, website, 2018.

289 Idaho Dairymen's Association website, Industry Profile, 2017. The Magic Valley has about 60 percent of the state's dairy cows.

enough workers is an immediate concern, but broader immigration solutions seem intractable at the federal level. Unless they are resolved, he says, Idaho's dairy workforce isn't a sure thing and any slippage in labor availability would endanger milk production as well as further industry growth.[290]

One hopes the current back-and-forth arguments on immigration policy would, at some point, give way to practical solutions in which foreign workers could be admitted in agricultural sectors without their presence overwhelming local services such as schools, social services and health care. But given the long history of immigration debate in America, that goal of reasonable solutions seems far off indeed.

Perhaps just as pressing, although less visible, is foreign ownership of milk processing, which underlies some of Idaho's dairy expansion. Cows can be raised successfully in many locations worldwide, not just in Southern Idaho. The economics of geography for Southern Idaho agriculture depends on many intertwined factors; any major change in any one of these could affect the rates of financial return and thus slow further investment.

Cattle, Calves, Sheep, Trout and Hogs – While row crops and dairy farms are ubiquitous throughout Southern Idaho, cattle and calf production is also a major economic driver in the region. In 2012, for example, Idaho was the 10th largest cattle state with an estimated value of over $1.8 billion. Idaho cattle inventories were 2.4 million animals.[291]

In the past, Idaho has not been a major beef packing state, with most beef going out-of-state for processing. That's begun to change, however, with the opening of an Ida-Beef packing plant near Burley, which is handling about 100 culled dairy cows a day and designed to process up to 400.[292] A much larger beef plant opened in Kuna in 2017, handling about 1,700 animals daily. Both operations take culled cattle from beef and dairy herds which can account for a third of Idaho's milk producing cows annually. In both cases, the plants represent another example of how processing thrives close to production.

Sheep production has diminished markedly from the heyday of decades ago. There were over 63,000 sheep in Twin Falls County alone in 1910. The industry nonetheless maintains an inventory of about 230,000 animals with an estimated value of roughly $42 million, seventh in the nation.[293] Many Idaho sheep producers have been in the industry for decades, with the

---

290 Naerebout, Bob. Interview, Oct. 3, 2018.

291 USDA, National Agricultural Statistics Service, 2017 (2012 data).

292 Kennison, Heather. "New Beef Plant Near Burley Can Save Dairymen the Costs of Transporting Cull Cows," *East Idaho Business Journal*, May 14, 2018.

293 USDA, National Agricultural Statistics Service, 2018.

operations passed along, generation to generation in ranching families. In Southern Idaho, the industry uses foreign herders and Basque-Americans, whose ties to the industry go back generations.[294]

Aquaculture – The constant-temperature, fresh-water springs which spill into the Snake River Canyon from the Eastern Snake River Plain aquifer support the nation's largest commercial trout industry, valued at about $53 million.[295] The industry is concentrated in the Magic Valley and production in spring-fed raceways is often adjacent to processing for restaurant-ready fillets and specialty items. A leading local industry producer is Clear Springs Foods,[296] which ships product throughout the country. A main supplier is Rangen, a privately-held Southern Idaho company which specializes in aquaculture and other feeds.[297]

Hogs – Idaho is not a major hog raising state, with an annual value of just about $43 million,[298] yet the Southern Idaho region has a major hog processing facility in Independent Meat, a long-term, multi-generational family company. Product generally comes from Montana and other Intermountain locations. The company focuses on preferred, non-antibiotic pork products and has significant sales in the western United States and Asia.[299]

Food Processing: "Silicon Valley of Food"

When Hamdi Ulukaya, the CEO of Chobani Yogurt, talks about the decision to locate the company's one-million square-foot new plant in Twin Falls, he cites the usual promotional razzmatazz of pitchmen and economic development directors: a good, trainable and reliable workforce, strong local community ties and the usual round of state economic development incentives. But the decision also illustrates a principle as old as commerce itself: the processing plant is near the milk producers.[300]

---

294 The sheep industry in Southern Idaho participates, in a "Trailing of the Sheep" Festival each October, which celebrates the movement of herds out of the mountain high country. Many sheep operations use both deeded and public leased land for grazing. See Trailing of the sheep website, 2018.

295 USDA, National Agricultural Statistics Service, 2017 (2012 data).

296 Clear Springs Foods website, 2019.

297 Rangen , Inc. website, 2019.

298 USDA, National Agricultural Statistics Service, Quickstats website, 2017.

299 Independent Meat Company website, 2018.

300 Food Processing Technology, "Chobani Yogurt Plant, Twin Falls, Idaho." website. n.d.

Ulukaya often compares Southern Idaho to Silicon Valley, the California hub of high technology; Idaho's location makes it a "Silicon Valley of Food," says the affable Turkish entrepreneur who leads the company he founded.[301]

It's a leap of logic for some; Twin Falls, a small city in an agricultural state doesn't seem to compare at first to the Bay area with its high-technology companies and world-wide recognition. But both rely on the principle of economic geography: that is "value adding" generally locates close by the production of the product, as this embodies a significant reduction in costs by eliminating bulk transportation and thus maximizing the investment rate of return. In this case, the yogurt is made near the source of the milk, a dairy industry with about 415,000 cows within 50 miles of the plant.[302]

It's a simple principle. If you put the yogurt factory near the milk supply (i.e. the cows), you only have to transport the milk from the dairy, not the whole cow. Similarly, a Lamb-Weston potato processing plant for French fries and hash browns adds value to nearby potato production. A malting plant makes sense near barley fields. Frozen trout fillets are packaged near the trout-raising raceways of the Snake River Canyon. Sugar beet fields aren't usually far from an Amalgamated Sugar plant. A frozen vegetable plant isn't usually far from the field of peas. A box plant which makes shipping cartons isn't likely to be very far from the processing plants.[303]

So one feature of Southern Idaho agriculture is that value adding has come along side of production in a variety of agricultural commodities. A cup to hold Chobani yogurt is made in nearby Burley,; it's made from wheat-straw, another local product.[304] Would the cup manufacturer locate here if

---

301 Hughes, Trevor. "Yogurt Maker Chobani Expanding in Tiny Twin Falls, Idaho," *USA Today*, Nov. 9, 2017.

302 Wikipedia, "Economic Geography," updated Sept. 5, 2018. The field is described as "the study of the location, distribution and spatial organization of economic activities across the world. It represents a traditional subfield of the discipline of geography. However, many economists have also approached the field in ways more typical of the discipline of economics. Economic geography has taken a variety of approaches to many different subject matters, including the location of industries, economies of agglomeration (also known as linkages"), transportation, international trade, development, real estate, gentrification, ethnic economies, gendered economies, core-periphery theory, the economics of urban form, the relationship between the environment and the economy (tying into a long history of geographers studying culture-environment interaction), and globalization."

303 Kapstone Paper and Packaging Corporation website, 2018. Kapstone's Twin Falls box plant, formerly Longview Fiber, in 2018 added a $25 to $30 million upgrade in 2018 to accommodate growth. See Dahdah, Jeffery. "Kapstone planning nearly $30 million expansion to Twin Falls plant," KMVT, March 17, 2018.

304 Kennison, Heather. "Fabri-Kal will Nearly Double the Size of Its Burley Plant," *Times-News*, June 21, 2018.

Chobani was elsewhere? Another good example is WOW Logistics (Warehousing of Wisconsin) which has a warehousing facility of over 450,000 square feet adjacent to Jerome Cheese in Jerome. The company provides cool storage for cheese during the aging process. This is yet another niche in the Southern Idaho economy.[305]

About 85 percent of Idaho milk goes to cheese production, in a variety of uses, from pizza toppings to fast-food cheeseburgers. Values for most months are estimated at over $85 million per month; 2017 values totaled over $958 million, up from $178 million in 1990, $583 million in 2000, $850 million in 2010.[306]

In the future, it seems likely that Southern Idaho agriculture will expand in production, processing and research. Both Glanbia and Chobani are investing in milk product applications, including by-products like whey, proteins and other nutritional products.[307] The research is often done in Southern Idaho, giving creative push to the value-adding process. Companies like Glanbia are leading innovators in a wide variety of food products and have the deep pockets to make strategic investments to advance both their own product lines and spur overall industry growth.[308]

Production and processing are likely to expand together. In 2018, milk production in Southern Idaho was about 42 million pounds a day, but a good deal of the milk was going out of state for cheese production elsewhere in the West, including Colorado, Arizona and Utah. Additional capacity locally would be a plus, says Bob Naerebout with the Idaho Dairymen's Association, a need that may be somewhat addressed in 2019.[309]

---

305 Inbound Logistics, "Warehousing Aged to Perfection," July, 2009.

306 USDA, National Agricultural Statistics Service, Quickstats, 1990, 2000, 2010, 2017.

307 Glanbia Nutritionals website, "We offer a wide range of protein, clean label and functional ingredient solutions, including Grade A and rBST free options, for dairy products such as yogurts, and dairy beverages and desserts."

308 Glanbia's market capitalization as of Oct. 12, 2018 was $4.251 billion. Glanbia website. The company's new research center in Twin Falls is a leading site for product development: "Glanbia Nutritionals operates a total of three cheese plants, all in Idaho; and also commercializes all cheese on behalf of the Southwest Cheese joint venture in New Mexico. Including the joint venture, Glanbia Nutritionals sells a total of 400,000 tons of cheese per annum and are the leader in the American-style cheese market. Their business model is based on large-scale, low-cost manufacturing and a clear focus on operational excellence ensures Glanbia Nutritionals is among the most efficient operators in the sector. The cheese innovation center in Idaho facilitates an increased level of engagement with customers and further differentiates Glanbia from its competitors."

309 Kennison, Heather. "Milk Processor Wants to Build Plant on Washington St. South," *Times-News*, Dec. 15, 2018. The 200,000 square-foot plant is scheduled for 2020 and would employ about 100 workers. See "Milk Processor to build 200,000-square-foot plant, create 100-plus jobs in Twin Falls," *Times-News*, Feb. 26, 2019.

The number of dairies in the state has shrunk since 2000 with fewer than 500 now operating. But milk production per cow has increased sharply to over 24,000 pounds (12 tons per animal per year.)[310] Modern technologies like individual cow monitoring and "almost completely human hands free" milking on large rotary platforms or in animal "self-milk" walk-in stations have increased herds and allowed dairies to expand into more remote areas of Southern Idaho.[311]

Agricultural Research

Southern Idaho agriculture will likely change in the years ahead with additional innovation and research-based marketing. Some may be business-specific and proprietary; other projects may involve a nutrition and dairy research center located in the region, to be run by a consortium of the University of Idaho, the College of Southern Idaho, BYU-Idaho and other schools. The dramatic growth of that sector warrants such a development for both nutritional and waste management reasons.[312]

Individual companies, recognizing the importance of close-by research, have established research divisions as part of their Magic Valley operations, developing product lines to meet shifting consumer demands and opportunity.[313]

This may also develop as part of a larger trend to locate important university-based sectors closer to their "customer" commodities. In the next few decades, we should expect to see even more industry-driven development closely supported by research components.[314]

---

310 Naerebout, Bob. Idaho Dairymen's Association, Interview, Oct. 3, 2018.

311 Millenkamp Cattle, LLC website. updated 2018. Millenkamp raises feeder calves at its Jerome operation and has some 27,000 cows being milked twice a day at its East Valley dairy and farm in Cassia County. The company employs about 300 workers at an average salary of $45,000. The East Valley dairy produces about 1 million pounds of milk a day. Idaho Legislators Mini-Cassia Tour, Sept., 2017.

312 Dumas, Carol Ryan. "Research Center Would Support Agriculture, Idaho Economy," *Capital Press*, Jan. 30, 2018. See also, Kauffman, Gretel. "UI Outlines Plans for Magic Valley Ag Research Centers," *Times-News*, Jan.,24, 2019 and Brown, Nathan. "Dean Says MV Ag Research Facility Could Be World's Best," *Times-News*, June 6, 2017; Ellis, Sean. "Proposed $45 Million Livestock and Ag Center Picks Up Steam," *Idaho Farm Bureau Quarterly*, Winter, 2019.

313 Glanbia website, note 43. See also Haddon, Heather. "America Can't Move its Cheese," *The Wall Street Journal*, Dec. 17, 2018.

314 Ward, Loren. "Glanbia Nutritionals," Power point presentation, Twin Falls Kiwanis Club, Feb. 21, 2019. Ward is senior vice president for research and development at Glanbia

Additionally, Boise State University, the University of Idaho and Idaho State University collaborate with the National Science Foundation on many topics, including agriculture and genetics. The inquiries help shape these and many other fields.[315]

The University of Idaho Agricultural Research Center already has stations at Kimberly and Aberdeen[316] so adding others in Southern Idaho wouldn't be a stretch. It would further cement the Magic Valley as an agricultural research hub for the future. For example, the Aberdeen station was instrumental in developing new malting barley varieties, known as "Charles" and "Endeavor" which are particularly suited for Southern Idaho's climate and irrigated fields. These adaptable varieties have allowed winter malting barley to expand into Southern Idaho with exceptional yields of over 130 bu/acre.[317] By way of contrast, when Twin Falls County was first settled, barley production was only about 26 bushels/acre, four and five times less than today.[318] It's reasonable to expect such product-focused research to open the way for even more innovation in this "Silicon Valley of Food."

Nutritionals, Twin Falls. His presentation showed how by-product whey proteins are being used in medical research in helping hip replacement patients recover and regain fuller mobility.

315 University of Idaho, "$20 Million Idaho Research Award Focuses on Genetics of Rainbow Trout, Sagebrush," Sept. 18,2018. EPSCOR chairman Laird Noh, former Southern Idaho state senator, says, "It will continue to strengthen Idaho's scientific research excellence in areas of national importance and which are critical to achieving the goals of Idaho's science and technology strategic plan." See also EPSCOR Idaho website, 2018.

316 Windes, Juliet and Obert, Don. "Charles: Two Row Winter Malt Barley," University of Idaho Extension, website, 2009.

317 Snyder, Cindy. "Barley Industry Changing with New Varieties," *Times-News*, July 20, 2009. See also, "Idaho Barley Commission presents Hu with Barley Service Award," Gem State Producer, Dec., 2018. Gongshe Hu, based at the Aberdeen Research Station, has overseen the development of many new barley varieties appropriate for Southern Idaho.

318 Idaho Agricultural Statistics, Twin Falls County, 1910.

13. Capital, Labor & Costs of Living

One less appreciated aspect of change in Southern Idaho during the past several decades has been infusion of investment capital and the resulting development in both private and public infrastructure. Most has been in private industries, notably food processing. But there have also been significant investments in public projects, including schools, transportation and public and non-profits, such as health care.

On the private sector side, companies like Chobani have poured hundreds of millions of dollars into manufacturing and processing. Although not "high tech" in the Silicon Valley sense, the investments have often been cutting edge for the industries, resulting in improved earnings and profit margins.

The nearly million-square-foot Chobani plant is a good example. Chobani had an existing smaller facility in upstate New York, but the rapid growth of its sales quickly overwhelmed that capacity. The company conducted a wide search in the Intermountain West and settled on the Magic Valley because of its nearby milk supply, good transportation network and proximity to West Coast markets. Idaho being a Right to Work state was also a factor, as the ability to operate without required union membership is a consideration in many site selection decisions.

The new plant was built in less than a year in 2012 at a cost of $450 million, by far the largest capital investment ever made in Southern Idaho. Initial employment quickly expanded to 300 employees, and to over 1,000 by 2018.[319] Chobani went through some financial issues and had a $750 million loan from private equity firm, TPG. Those financial issues weren't widely reported at the time locally, but were outlined in some detail in a 2018 *New*

319 Strom, Stephanie. "U.S. Hunger for Yogurt Leads to Gigantic Factory," *The New York Times*, Dec. 16, 2012.

York Times article on the company's improved financial health.[320] The upshot is that Chobani remains a privately held company with a heavy commitment to its Twin Falls operation.

A similar infusion of investment seems to have paid off for St. Luke's Magic Valley Medical Center, which built a new hospital at a cost of $240 million on Pole Line Road, opening in 2011. The previous county-owned and aging hospital did about $160 million in revenue annually with several studies showing substantial leakage of patient care money going outside Southern Idaho. By 2017, St. Luke's Magic Valley total local sales impact had grown to $642 million, a three hundred percent increase from 2006, or nearly $500 million. The four Southern Idaho facilities of St Luke's (Twin Falls, Jerome, Wood River and Mountain Home) had combined total sales impacts in 2017 of over $800 million in the Southern Idaho region.[321]

Local economic growth in available capital can also be seen in bank deposit increases in the area. From 1997 to 2017, deposits at regulated banks more than doubled in Twin Falls County, from $684 million to $1.401 billion. In Cassia County, deposits similarly jumped from $234 million to $392 million. Jerome County also more than doubled, from $107 million to $227 million, while smaller and more remote Lincoln County was essentially flat in deposits, from $21.2 million to $21.8 million.[322]

In 2017, Twin Falls County ranked 5th statewide in bank deposits, behind Ada, Kootenai, Canyon and Bonneville counties. One local financial institution, First Federal Saving & Loan, jumped from deposits of $163 million in 1994 at five branches, to $550 million in 2018 through 11 branches, a 340 percent increase in 24 years.[323]

Idaho's property values have grown substantially since 1996, a trend mirrored in most regions of the state, including the Magic Valley. While these changes have resulted in higher tax bills for many properties, many of the bumps have come through increased values, as well as from increased bonding, particularly for schools.

The table below shows the changes for Magic Valley counties, as well for the state, in assessed valuations. Notice how Twin Falls added more than $1.1

---

320 Gelles, David. "Chobani, the Greek yogurt maker, reclaims control of its finances," *The New York Times*, June 28, 2018.

321 Peterson, Steven. "2017 Report on Local and Statewide Economic Impact of Idaho's Community Hospitals," March 27, 2018. The breakdown by facility was Magic Valley, $642m; Jerome, $30m; Wood River, $98m and Mountain Home, $42m. Data from 2006 is from county hospital information at the time. The author served as a private consultant to St. Luke's in advance of the 2006 public vote approval.

322 Federal Deposit Insurance Corporation (FDIC), "County Summaries Deposit Market Share Report, Idaho," June, 2017.

323 FDIC, "Institution Deposits Report," June, 2018.

billion in valuation from 2010-2017 after adding $1.26 billion from 2006 to 2010. The late 2000s growth was probably more due to increased valuations on existing property, while the growth since 2010 can partly be attributed to new construction:[324]

County	2006	2010	2017
Twin Falls	3.074b	4.337b	5.441b
Jerome	863m	1.117b	1.340b
Cassia	911m	1.129b	1.443b
Lincoln	259m	385m	360m
Gooding	671m	856m	1.074b
Blaine	11.780b	10.585b	9.447b
Camas	103m	151m	131m
Minidoka	775m	975m	1.331b
State of Idaho	107.23b	112.30b	138.51b

Other factors at work in the Twin Falls expansion include consolidation of larger, national banks, which spurred people to shift their banking to regional entities like First Federal, which has an all-local board and wide presence in the community, says Jason Meyerhoeffer, CEO. He adds that even during the housing/debt crisis in the late 2000s, First Federal kept its financial loan ratios for home loans-to-income at about the same at 36 percent. Despite upward pressure from rising prices, people throughout the 2000s didn't take on more debt than normal, reflecting the generally conservative principles of most local borrowers.[325]

Right to Work and Southern Idaho Labor

Idaho is one of 27 Right to Work states, which allow most workers in a wide range of industries to work without being required to join a union. The state law implementing the policy was passed in 1985 and confirmed in a referendum ballot vote in 1986, on a 54 percent vote.[326] The public vote followed a vigorous public debate, passage of the law by the Legislature and a veto by Democratic Gov. John Evans, which was then overturned.

---

324 Idaho Tax Commission. "Net Taxable Values by Major Category." Updated, 2017.

325 Meyerhoeffer, Jason. Interview, Oct. 19, 2018.

326 "Idaho Retention of Right to Work Law," Ballotpedia website, n.d.

Since then, union membership has declined in Idaho, as it has in other states which have implemented Right to Work legislation. Idaho's percentage of union representation is estimated at less than five percent,[327] one of three Western states below that level and one of the lowest in the nation.

In Southern Idaho, only a few manufacturing businesses have unions and efforts to expand local union representation have proved unsuccessful.[328] Indeed, this is a make-or-break issue for many businesses looking at Southern Idaho for possible expansion. Occasionally, local business and economic development professionals are called by people in other states and asked what have been our "success ingredients" here. Right To Work and unionization is always on the list, and usually a major consideration.[329]

Union membership in Southern Idaho has some private sector representation including Amalgamated Sugar and United Parcel Service, but is otherwise concentrated among public sector employees, such as city firefighters and teachers. Idaho Education Association union chapters have memberships estimated at 50 percent or less in most districts.

In the Twin Falls school district, for example, about half of the district's 500 eligible employees are paying members of the Twin Falls Education Association. That number was fewer during the recession, when the $60 per month dues were significant to many teachers, particularly beginning ones.[330] A recent U.S. Supreme Court decision limiting public employee unions from charging dues to non-members is likely to further depress public union representation across the country.[331]

Looking at the broader picture, Southern Idaho wages have generally lagged both the state and nation, although there has been marked improvement in the past decade. The region's per capita income has increased over 20 percent since 2007, from $31,183 to $38,225.

Agricultural and service sector employment still hold down overall per capita income averages, compared to both the state (a 3 percent difference),

---

327 U.S. Department of Labor, Bureau of Labor Statistics, "Union Members in Idaho - 2017," March 14, 2018.

328 Kennison, Heather. "No Union at Lamb Weston: With 92% turnout, 80% of Employees Voted No," *Times-News*, July 17. 2017. One employee, Lisa, wrote on the *Times-News* website, "Thank you for letting the community know how the vote turned out. As you can tell by the vote most of us like our jobs at Lamb Weston & we (are) well compensated for our work & we have received a 2-3% raise every year for the 18 years I have worked there."

329 Bosman, Tracey. "The Importance (Or Non-Importance?) of Right to Work in Relocation Decisions," *Industry Week*, June 28, 2012.

330 Estimates from Twin Falls School District, Aug. 3, 2018.

331 Wolfe, Richard and Korte, Gregory. "Supreme Court Deals Major Financial Blow to Nation's Public Employee unions ," *USA Today*, June 27, 2018.

and the nation (a 22 percent lag).[332] Labor analysts cite a number of underlying reasons for the wage lag, which also trails neighboring states.

The reasons cited include Idaho's minimum wage rate at $7.25 per hour is tied to the federal rate, while Idaho's neighbors have increased theirs independently; lack of a statewide community college system, which benefits wages in rural areas; lack of significant oil and gas development, a traditionally higher-paying industry; low union membership; and a relatively higher prison and former inmate population, a group which generally has difficulty finding higher-paying work upon release.[333] A less-quantifiable factor is the long history of non-unionization in rural America, particularly in agricultural sector employment and a general non-union and anti-union sentiment perhaps derived from the region's culture of independence.

Despite these factors, Southern Idaho's labor market in 2018 showed a very low unemployment rate of less than three percent. Wages have risen in several sectors, including health care, retailing and food service, where larger entities have boosted wages along national lines, including several large local employers such as Costco, Walmart and McDonalds.[334]

Liberal organizations and politicians occasionally cite Idaho's wage rates as something which need a governmental solution, but this has been rejected by the generally conservative Idaho Legislature.[335] There's a general belief in the Legislature that wage rates should be determined by the marketplace without governmental interference, a position widely supported among constituents.

In Southern Idaho, the early immigration and settlement patterns also contributed to holding down wages by putting other things first, like community. The region's waves of settlement from Midwestern, agricultural states reinforced a "work hard" ethic which placed work ahead of seeking personal gain.

That was also reinforced by the influx of Mormon settlers from Utah who were also used to working for community common good. Scriptural exhortations told people not to place undue influence on worldly goods: "Lay

332 Roeser, Jan. "South Central Idaho Workforce Trends," Idaho Department of Labor, June, 2018.

333 Regional economist Jan Roeser, quoted in Sowell, John. "Idaho's Workers' Wages Topped the Nation in 2017. Good News, You Say? Look Closely," *Idaho Statesman*, April 18, 2018.

334 Hanbury, Margaret. "Costco just Became an Even More Appealing Place to Work After Raising its Minimum Wage to $14 an Hour," *Business Insider*, June 1, 2018. Costco subsequently raised its minimum wage to $15/hour in March, 2019.

335 Idaho Code 44-1502, passed in 2016, prohibits political subdivisions of the state from enacting local minimum wage rate ordinances higher than what state law allows, at $7.25 per hour.

not up for yourselves treasures upon earth, where moth and rust doth corrupt, and where thieves break through and steal: But lay up for yourselves treasures in heaven, where neither moth nor rust doth corrupt, and where thieves do not break through nor steal."[336] Thus, it was considered more important to work first to make the land productive and then to benefit oneself.

The whole pattern of immigration to America, from the earliest Colonial days to modern migrations, has this strong element of work hard and thereby prosper. Southern Idaho fits this immigration pattern even today. When refugees from other lands are asked why they have come to America, they invariably say some version of this work-hard-rise-up American story in which they are eager to succeed.

Looking at several broad categories of employment, there have been substantial increases in wages from 2007 to 2017.[337] These patterns are likely to remain or perhaps accelerate, given the tightness of the labor supply and the rising demand by businesses for expansion, if they can find employees with the right skills and work habits:

Category	**2007**	**2017**
Agriculture	25,262	35,543
Construction	28,301	35,901
Manufacturing	34,124	47,417
Information	29,272	39,445
Financial	37,527	44,692
Edu/health	30,728	40,241
Govt	31,162	34,445

Other statistics show similar patterns. Across Southern Idaho in the 20 years from 1997 to 2017, all industry workforce employment has jumped from 65,456 to 88,725, a 35 percent gain; total wages have gone from \$1.387b to \$3.216b, a 132 percent gain; average wages have gone from \$21,183 to \$36,270, a 71 percent gain.

Agricultural employment has gone from 6,026 in 1997 to 10,620 in 2017, a 76 percent gain; agricultural workforce total wages have gone from \$107m to \$378m, a 254 percent gain; average agricultural wages have gone from \$17,808 to \$35,774, a gain of more than 100 percent in the 20 years.

In the health care sector, employment has gone from 5,778 in 1997 to 10,191 in 2917, a 76 percent gain; total wages have increased from \$134m to

336 Matthew 6: 19-21, King James Version.

337 Idaho Department of Labor, Workforce Trends, Twin Falls County, Aug. 2018.

$400m, a 199 percent gain, and the average wage has increased from $23,143 to $39,259, a 69 percent increase. The sector has risen from 9.6 percent of employment to 12.4 percent.

In the manufacturing sector, total employment has gone from 8,040 in 1997 to 10,242 in 2017; total wages from $206m to $484m, a 126 percent gain; Average wages have gone from $25,178 to $47,298, a gain of 85 percent. Manufacturing's share of share of employment has inched up from 14.8 percent to 15.1 percent, a gain nonetheless in 20 years.[338]

The Bureau of Labor Statistics, US Department of Labor, maintains extensive records of wages and salaries for a wide range of professions in Southern Idaho. Among the positions shown in 2017, and the mean wages, are: Overall Managers, $71,420; Human Resource Managers, $75,370; Education Managers, Secondary Schools, $76,549; Lawyers, $56,100; Dentists, $184,600; Physicians, $176,380, Reporters, $34,357; Insurance sales, $55,892; Transportation, including truck driving, $40,000. Food batch workers, $34, 121; Fast food workers, $18, 622; Tree Trimmers, $38,079; Retail sales, $30,363; Secondary school teachers, $56,711; Elementary School Teachers, $51,232; Tellers, $25,501; Construction labor, $30,048.[339] All of these categories are up substantially from 20 years ago.

An important workforce issue generally, which wasn't as common a generation ago, is the rise of drug use and, with it, more intensive screening of employees and pre-employment testing. Many businesses use pre-employment drug screening in positions like machinery operation and truck driving. Drug test failures are rising in Idaho, as in other states.[340] This factor has an influence on employment when a larger number of potential employees can't pass this screening process.

Costs of Living

Southern Idaho has lower costs of living than many places in the nation, but surveys suggest the benefit is mostly concentrated in housing pricing. In utilities and health care, for example, costs locally are pretty much in line with national averages (4 percent lower and 3 percent lower respectively.)

---

338 Data in the preceding sectors from Idaho Department of Labor, Roeser, Jan. regional economist, Email, Jan. 30, 2019.

339 US Department of Labor, Bureau of Labor Statistics, Occupational Employment Statistics, South Central Idaho, May, 2017.

340 Bennett, Dean. "Positive Drug Tests Among Employees Rising In Idaho," *Idaho Business Review*, Sept. 26, 2017.

Transportation costs tend to be close to national averages, with local gasoline prices often higher than other western locations. Idaho does not have any petroleum refineries, making for higher local pricing. Various investigations over the years have failed to show any distributor collusion or price spiking, despite popular misconceptions.

On other sectors in cost of living, Southern Idaho tends to be less than national markets, averaging 12 percent lower overall. The biggest savings areas are groceries (19 percent lower) and housing (27 percent lower). This overall advantage has been a feature of the local market for many years and is frequently cited to potential in-migrants. There is some concern that with housing costs rising across the West, Southern Idaho may see upward trends in this category.[341]

Another survey puts the Twin Falls area housing costs at $200,000 for 2,000 square feet of housing space, second lowest of the state's major cities. It also makes the case that, with lower costs of living, incomes may not need to be as high as elsewhere to maintain a standard of living. The spread of income levels for Twin Falls is three percent of wage earners more than $150,000, 17 percent from $75,000 to $150,000, 47 percent from $30,000 to $75,000, and 33 percent under $30,000.[342]

These numbers reflect the Idaho "wage gap" when compared to other states and are often cited by those on the left politically and in the media. But the critics usually don't mention the pairing of wages to the costs of living, which are also lower. Residents are well aware that it's cheaper to live in Idaho than many other places and thus are generally satisfied with their quality of life here.[343]

That seems to be particularly true in Southern Idaho where, despite wage differences, satisfaction scores are high. It is certainly part of the human condition to want to see one's circumstances improve over time, but people here seem to have an intuitive sense that the raw numbers don't tell the whole story.[344]

Even in stressed professions like teaching, recent efforts to boost wages seem to be paying off. Idaho, like many other states, has high teacher turnover, but overall working conditions put Idaho in the middle range of

---

341 Payscale website, "Cost of Living in Twin Falls, Idaho," 2018 survey. The same survey puts Boise at 8 percent less than overall national average and Idaho Falls at 18 percent lower. Spokane is 4 percent lower, but Portland (29 percent higher) and Seattle (49 percent higher) cost more.

342 Movoto.com website, Idaho, 2018 survey.

343 Boise State University. Scholar Works, Annual Idaho Public Policy Surveys, 1990-2018

344 BSU Public Policy Survey, 2000.

states, not at the bottom when just classroom spending is ranked.[345] Average teacher salaries in Idaho are close to or over $50,000 annually, although there are considerable differences across districts. Blaine County, for example, pays teachers an average of over $72,000 annually and Boise has relatively high numbers too, over $60,000.

Smaller districts usually pay less since they often have less property assessment values on which to raise taxes for teacher pay. Overall, teacher pay has increased in Idaho, particularly for new teachers, who now make almost $40,000 to start, on nine-month contracts. Since the recession ended in 2013, the Legislature has put almost $450 million in new money into the K-12 budget, mostly into the teacher career-ladder pay scales, with another $100 million or so anticipated in the 2019-2020 budget year.[346]

Given the relative cost of living advantage, the capital investment occurring in the region, the employment opportunities and rising wages, it's not a surprise that the Southern Idaho region looks attractive to outsiders as a place to settle. It's something the residents already know.

---

345 WalletHub website, "Best and Worst States for Teachers," 2018, ranks Idaho as 28th overall, but 22nd in competition and opportunity for advancement, and 28th for academic and work environment.

346 Idaho Legislative Service Office, 23017 Fiscal Facts, p. 38, shows k-12 budget increase of $443 million from 2013 to 2017, from $1.598 billion to $2.041 billion with another 6 percent increase anticipated.

Part III: Further Considerations

Mountain Stream/Vincent Andrew Hartgen, 1983

14. Transportation

Thirty years or so ago, you could drive out of Twin Falls going north on Blue Lakes Blvd., cross the bridge (It didn't have a formal name then, as it does now, named for I.B. Perrine.) and go several miles on Hwy. 93, turn easily onto Interstate 84, headed west to Boise and points beyond. Except for traffic at Blue Lakes and Pole Line Road, there weren't many intersections with much traffic. The average commute for Twin Falls workers was under 20 minutes, among the lowest in the country.[347] The Blue Lakes "rush hour," such as it was, lasted maybe 20 minutes, a "nano-second" compared to major cities.

Once on the Interstate, traffic was also light most of the time. Between the interchange and the first Jerome exit, traffic averaged 13,600 vehicles a day in 1990, barely more than 500 cars an hour, in both directions. It wasn't exactly snoozeville, but it wasn't a Los Angeles freeway either. At night, once you got beyond Jerome, you could go miles without seeing another vehicle. Traffic was heavier in the summer as tourists came to and from the Yellowstone and Grand Teton national parks. Some paused for gas and sundries in Twin Falls, took a quick look at the canyon and maybe Shoshone Falls and then hurried on. In 1990, except for the Interstate itself and the road from Twin Falls out to the interchange, there was hardly another four-lane road anywhere in the Magic Valley.

Traffic volumes at that same intersection have doubled to 26,500 vehicles daily in 2017. Increases have been steady through the years, except for a dip with the Recession in 2007-2009, and are projected to grow 1.5 to 2 percent per year going forward.[348]

---

347 U.S. Census Bureau, Twin Falls County, Idaho, 1990.

There was no development at the intersection itself. A sea of sagebrush stretched endlessly in every direction. No gas stations, no convenience stores, no hotels, no office complexes. Nothing. If you needed gas, you had to come into Twin Falls.

The 1960s decision to place the Interstate north of the canyon, running from Burley to King Hill and Glenns Ferry, essentially set the valley's vehicle transportation pattern. Placing the Interstate there had many practical advantages, including lower right-of-way purchase costs and maintenance, as it avoided the higher elevations to the south and associated weather patterns.[349]

But the route put the new highway on the opposite side of a 500-foot Snake River Canyon from Twin Falls, a proposal not readily accepted by local businesses. To improve access to Twin Falls from the north, a new bridge was constructed and opened in 1976.

The decision to locate the major east-west Interstate on the north side of the canyon reoriented Twin Falls' travel patterns. Previously, Twin Falls had been an "east-west" town through which Hwy. 30 passed along the Snake River's south side, traversing downtown directly. The new highway made the north entrance to the city the major one, effectively turning Blue Lakes Blvd. into a major commercial strip, where the heaviest traffic volumes are today.[350]

The decision also created a new, important commercial strip on South Lincoln St. in Jerome. Commercial development soon followed. This allowed for urban renewal districts to be created on South Lincoln St. as well as a narrow "spaghetti strip" of urban renewal land in Twin Falls to capture a commercial site along Blue Lakes Blvd.

Traffic counts in Southern Idaho have grown over the years with population increases. More people mean more vehicle registrations and more

---

348 Idaho Transportation Department, Road Data, Annual traffic counts statewide by year. District 4 Engineer Bruce Christensen writes that, "From 2000-2016 the average annual traffic volumes on Interstate 84 between Twin Falls and Jerome increased 23%. This amounts to a 1.344% yearly increase. Specific years of interest: 2000, 21,000 vpd; 2007, 22,500 vpd; 2012, 21,500 vpd; and 2016, 26,000 vehicles per day. As you can see, there was a significant downturn in traffic volumes around the time of the great recession. But I still would expect only around 1.5 to 2% growth per year going forward. This amounts to a lot over time." Email, Oct. 10, 2018.

349 Idaho Transportation Department, "Celebrating 50 Years of Idaho Interstates," Updated website, May 31, 2006. ITD's description of the route selection notes that, "In 1960, as the interstate route was being planned and selected, city leaders said the route would deal an "economic blow" to the region. Representing the Twin Falls Chamber of Commerce, John E. Hahn said Highway 30 had served the city well since the beginning of the paved roadway system and that the new route, "...called for a hard-selling job by the citizens to lure the tourist into the area."

350 Brackett, Kimberly Williams. "Following the Path of I-84," *Times-News*, July 1, 2014.

vehicles on the valley's roads and bridges. From 2005 to 2015, highway records show about a 9,000 vehicle increase in registered vehicles in the Southern Idaho region, 161,000 to 170,000. Half of the increase is in Twin Falls County alone, from 69,000 vehicles in 2005 to 74,000 in 2015.[351]

Building an Interstate highway across Southern Idaho also affected other commercial aspects of the region. One was the opening of markets in Portland, Seattle and Salt Lake City for Idaho commodities due to more direct routes and quick deliveries. A further development was the improvement of Hwy 93 south into Nevada where it connects with Interstate 80, which allowed better access to Reno and California. This too helped trade with both Mexico and Canada, two of Idaho's leading international trade partners.[352] The new trade agreements with these countries are likely to further boost Idaho's trade picture.[353]

The Greater Twin Falls Transportation Committee meets monthly to discuss local and regional transportation issues, usually attended by Idaho Transportation Department representatives, the Twin Falls city engineer, various local highway district board members, plus county officials, Idaho State Police and several legislators and business community members. The group works through a list of pending projects with updates on how they're doing, plus some discussion of long-range needs and plans. There are similar groups in other parts of of Southern Idaho, so among them all, there are ongoing discussions on everything from bridge capacity to in-town truck routes, public transit needs and bike lane configurations.[354]

As with many growing cities in the West, Southern Idaho is looking at new traffic corridors, by-pass and diversion routes. A Southeast corridor route connecting the Hansen Bridge around the south side of Twin Falls to link up with Highway 93 has been under some discussion for years, but no specifics have been designated.

The need for such a route is evident from the truck and travel patterns already in place, but as elsewhere, local NIMBY (Not In My Back Yard) opponents have raised concerns about the details. As Twin Falls is currently

---

351 Idaho Department of Transportation, Division of Motor Vehicles, Total Vehicle Registrations, by County and Calendar Year, ITD website, Sept., 2018.

352 Canada is Idaho's single largest export market at $842 million in 2017. Exports to Mexico are $234 million. Other major export purchasers are China, $353 million; Taiwan, $573 million; and Singapore, $459 million. Idaho exported nearly $3.9 billion to 180 countries in 2017, double the exports in 2003, just 15 years ago. See Idaho Department of Commerce, Top Export Destinations website, updated July 24, 2018.

353 Haddon, Heather. "U.S. Dairy Farmers Score Gains in New Trade Deal," *Wall Street Journal*, Oct. 1, 2018.

354 Kennison, Heather. "Twin Falls, Glanbia work on Truck Route, Council Asks State to Keep Heavier Trucks Off Blue Lakes," *Times-News*, Oct. 2, 2018.

jammed up against the 500-foot-deep Snake River Canyon, alternative transportation routes will surely be needed. Looking ahead 30 or 40 years, as the city grows outward, new alternatives will merit consideration; a Southeast corridor route will likely be in place by then, despite current opposition.[355]

Another topic has been the need for additional bridge capacity across the Snake River Canyon, now spanned by the I.B. Perrine Bridge at Twin Falls proper and the Hansen Bridge, several miles to the east. There's been periodic discussion of adding deck lanes to both structures, as well as looking at an additional bridge west of Twin Falls, which would follow 2400 Road North with a canyon crossing into Jerome County to hook up with Interstate 84 west of Jerome.[356] None of these plans are on the drawing board, state officials say, but they could be in 10 to 15 years if the area continues to grow. Thirty to 40 years from now, people can expect a broad discussion of this topic, and perhaps progress. A new crossing, rim to rim, is estimated to cost $200 million in 2019 dollars, a big-ticket item for which there has yet to be any concrete planning.

There are several other pieces of the transportation picture which merit brief discussions:

Rock Creek Bridge/Highway 93 North Bypass. Using federal stimulus money, the ITD in 2010 completed a 5.5 mile link on the north and west sides of Twin Falls with a new bridge over Rock Creek Canyon that links Hwy. 93 from Nevada to Pole Line Road and into Twin Falls. The new route improvement has already brought additional development along Pole Line Road near St. Luke's Magic Valley Medical Center and is likely to be the "jump off" point for a Snake River Canyon bridge in the future. Cost savings allowed for a fly-over bridge at 2400 Road where Hwy. 93 turns south. We're likely to see this open up further development on this northwest corridor in the coming decades, particularly if a third bridge river crossing gets new scrutiny.[357]

Public Transit. The 2020 US Census is likely to push Twin Falls' population to over 50,000, which will trigger a need for enhanced mass transit. The city has an "on call" van system now, but it is mostly used for calls for medical appointments and similar individual needs. A local study

355 Matthews, Mychel. "The Rural-Urban Divide: As Cities Expand, Rural Residents Feel the Squeeze of Population Growth," *Times-News*, Aug. 16, 2018.

356 Kennison, Heather. "Canyon crossings: Twin Falls' Bridges are in Good Shape, But Traffic Could Become an Issue," *Times-News*, Oct. 22, 2017. The issue may be moved up in discussions beginning in 2019; increased truck traffic through Twin Falls has raised concerns of Twin Falls officials and others and significant transportation improvements may be needed sooner rather than later.

357 Coltrain, Nick. "Bypass Opens Possibilities on Pole Line," *Times-News*, Dec.17, 2010.

committee is looking at various options, including a fixed-route system, but the costs are high and the potential usage likely to be low. The picture could change in 20 to 30 years, but it's hard to see how a high-cost, fixed-route system could be established in a cost-effective way.[358]

Bicycle Lanes. Federal support money is available for communities like Twin Falls to add bicycle lanes to highway corridors, and the city has used some of these funds in the past. But big questions remain as to the costs of such amenities which serve much smaller populations than vehicles; discussion on this subject is still in the early stages, but some expansion of the bike lane system in 20 to 30 years seems likely.[359]

Metropolitan Planning Organization. Rapid regional growth is also likely to trigger formation of a regional planning entity to weigh in on topics like regional transportation needs. As Twin Falls reaches 50,000 in population, discussion of this topic among city, Jerome County and nearby communities like Kimberly is likely to accelerate. The topic is likely to be on officials' radar well before 20 or 30 years from now.[360]

Highway Districts. Idaho has a broad assortment of local highway districts which carry tons of bulk items daily, such as feed going to farms and milk coming out. Most of these local "farm to market" roads were built decades ago and were not designed for the heavier loads they carry today. The districts, which rely partly on local taxes, typically don't have the resources for extensive improvements. How the state and districts will handle the needed upgrades is an open question and likely to be one in the decades ahead. Major flooding across the state in February, 2017, brought the issue to a head; the Legislature appropriated $50 million in repair monies, but local districts were still out-of-pocket on some costs.[361]

Highway Efficiency Report. Idaho has had a mixed picture when it comes to measuring highway effectiveness. In the 1990s, under the administration of then-governor Phil Batt, the state ranked 4th in the nation. It fell in the rankings after that, but has recently climbed back into the top ten. This year, it was 7th. The state's best categories are in urban congestion, rural pavement condition and administrative disbursements per mile. Attention is needed in other areas, but overall, the Idaho Department of Transportation ranks well against other states.[362]

---

358 Kennison, Heather. "Is Twin Falls set to install fixed-route Public Transportation? Not so fast, City Official Say," *Times-News*, Aug. 31, 2018.

359 Brown, Nathan. Where Should Twin Falls Bike Paths Go,?" *Times-News*, Apr. 19, 2017.

360 Kennison, Heather. "4 Things to Know about an MPO," *Times-News*, Feb. 23, 2018.

361 Idaho Association of Highway Districts, website, 2018. See Brown, Nathan, "After Disastrous Winter, Idaho Cities, Highway officials wait for Road Repair Help," *Times-News*, May 21, 2017.

Drone Package Delivery and Autonomous Vehicles. Delivery of packages by drone directly to the customers' front porch or driveway is likely to a major delivery method in the future. Expansion will depend on weight and distance ratios. We may not see whole tractors delivered to farms via high-lift drones, but delivery of innumerable small products, from veterinarian supplies to home goods to tractor parts is likely to be commonplace.[363] Similarly, autonomous vehicle deliveries are rapidly emerging as a viable technology, one in which Southern Idaho is well positioned by its flat, gridded terrain and road system. In 2018, the governor's office and the Legislature launched a study committee on autonomous vehicle technologies and their potential applications.[364]

Airports and Airline Service. A second key development with long-term impacts on Southern Idaho transportation was the decision not to build a new regional airport in Jerome County, near Hwy. 93/Interstate 84 interchange. Twin Falls had a city/county airport, Joslin Field, which dated back decades. In 1971, the Idaho Legislature approved a study of the need for a regional airport for Southern Idaho, which recommended a northside location. Resistance from Twin Falls ultimately scotched the project and Joslin Field, the Magic Valley Regional Airport, today remains the region's primary airfield south of the city.[365] Some civic "bad blood" flowed from this determination and it took a number of years before Twin Falls and their Jerome County neighbors put the issues aside.

The Magic Valley Regional Airport has had ups and downs in passenger boardings/arrivals over the years, but recent figures show a decided upward trend. Over the past 15 years, boardings/arrivals grew from 60,000 annually in 2003 to nearly 80,000 in 2011. With the recession, numbers fell back to barely above 50,000 in 2013, but have climbed again nicely since then, to over 85,000 in 2018, a record and up more than five percent from 2017.[366] Convenience to gates and free parking have helped keep the numbers growing compared to costs in and out of Boise. Service to and from Twin

---

362 Reason Foundation. "Idaho Ranks 7th Overall in Highway Performance and Cost-Effectiveness," 2018 report. Full disclosure: For much of its 23 years of reports, the Reason Highway Effectiveness Report was led by the author's brother, David T. Hartgen at the University of North Carolina, Charlotte. He has since retired from that role.

363 Regev, Amit. "Drone Deliveries Are No Longer Pie In The Sky," Forbes, Apr. 10, 2018.

364 Gov. C.L. Butch Otter, Executive Order 2018-01, Creating the Autonomous and Connected Vehicle Deployment Committee, Jan. 2, 2018.

365 US Department of Transportation, Federal Aviation Administration draft EIS Report, Proposed Southern Idaho Regional Airport, 1973.

366 Email from Bill Carberry, airport manager, Twin Falls Airport boardings/arrival statistics, Oct. 4, 2018. See also Kennison, Heather. "Twin Falls Airport Reports Fuller Planes, More Pounds of Freight," *Times-News*, Feb. 10, 2019.

Falls is through a Salt Lake City connection via Sky West/Delta; three daily flights offer dawn to dusk service on modern regional jets.[367]

The airport has adapted in various ways, including modernizing passenger services, gates, and luggage screening and handling. The 8,700-foot runway is used for "touch and go" military training flights, as well as a base for fire-fighting aircraft and handling diverted flights from the Sun Valley airport during inclement weather. A new terminal expansion was completed in 2017.[368]

As the Magic Valley grows and businesses expand and locate in Southern Idaho, it's probable that the airport will expand as well. Passengers 20 or 30 years from now are likely to have a wider range of flights, and perhaps new non-stop connections to Denver, Portland and other regional hubs. Around the country, smaller communities have sometimes struggled with holding onto their commercial air service as costly subsidies have been whittled away, but that does not seem to be the case locally. The market position of the Magic Valley Regional Airport seems stable, secure and improving over time.

Railroads. The Oregon Short Line Railroad began in the 1880s as a "short cut" from Wyoming to Oregon and the northern west coast. Sections of that original right-of-way can still be seen along Interstate 84 as it climbs out of the Snake River Canyon to the west of Glenns Ferry.[369] Union Pacific now operates a main line across Southern Idaho, passing from Pocatello to American Falls, where it crosses the river, then through Southern Idaho's Minidoka County to Shoshone, Gooding and Bliss where it skirts the Snake River near Glenns Ferry. This route is one of Union Pacific's main corridors and handles multiple trains a day in each direction.

Union Pacific's Idaho operations are regulated at several different levels, including federal authority over railroads generally, through the state, and with some impact from local government. Concerns at the local level include noise, crossings safety, train speeds and bridge overpasses and underpasses.

Union Pacific operates in more than 20 states and a large percent of its freight volume is passing through Idaho, and isn't loaded or unloaded here. Idaho, like other states, submits a regular railroad plan covering rail's impact on the economy and other issues. The 2013 Idaho plan covers a wide range of topics. An estimated 87 percent of freight is neither Idaho bound nor of Idaho origin.[370]

---

367 City of Twin Falls website, Oct. 4, 2018.

368 Kennison, Heather. "Airport Celebrates Terminal Project Completion," *Times-News*, Apr. 20, 2017.

369 Wikipedia. "Oregon Short Line Railroad," updated May 26, 2018.

370 Idaho Transportation Department, Idaho Statewide Rail Plan, Project Number 13304, June 21, 2013, p. 1-4.

In Southern Idaho, rail freight service handles mostly agricultural commodities, such as dairy feed, sugar beets, grains, potatoes and fertilizers. Eastern Idaho Railroad (EIRR) has about 150 miles of track, mostly in two segments. The first runs from Minidoka to Wendell on the north side of the Snake River Canyon; the other runs from Minidoka, crosses the river at Heyburn and continues west through Burley and on to Kimberly, Twin Falls, Filer and Buhl.

A good example of that which adds value to local agricultural production is Standlee Hay, based in the small town of Eden, but with both rail and truck/highway transportation access. Standlee manages over 30,000 acres for hays, alfalfas and other premium animal feeds, then compresses bulk volumes for shipment and store distribution. Over the years, the company has added international markets, which it supplies by shipboard containers moved to port by intermodal rail. Even small price adjustments in shipping costs can affect end-costs.[371]

A Northern division of EIRR also serves Idaho Falls and upper Snake River plain. Combined, the segments have about 265 miles of track and handled more than 48,000 carloads of freight in 2012.[372] Customers include major food processing plants and related industries. EIRR's parent company is Watco, which operates 39 short line railroads in America with about 5,100 miles of track.[373] In Southern Idaho, Watco operates out of Burley and focuses on agricultural products, including grains, sugar beets, agricultural chemicals and feeds. The state rail plan estimates modest growth in short line train counts by 2040.[374]

With many aspects of transportation expanding in Southern Idaho, it's likely these issues will be widely discussed for the foreseeable future. The specifics may change, but the topics are likely to be on many people's watch lists for years to come.

---

371 Standlee Hay Company website, Oct., 2018, and Matthews, Mychel. "Union Pacific Surcharge Puts Pressure on Ag Exports," *Times-News*, Oct. 15, 2014.

372 Idaho Statewide Rail Plan, p. 2-11.

373 Watco Companies website, 2018.

374 Idaho Statewide Rail Plan, p. 3-28.

An Eternal Landscape. A waterfall cascades over the canyon wall's stark winter landscape to the Snake River below at Thousand Springs. Sharon Breshears photo © 2019.

Fire's Destructive Power. Rogerson rancher and state Sen. Bert Brackett surveys a fire-scarred landscape following the Murphy Complex Fire in 2007. The fast-moving blaze claimed many cows, including the one in the background. Ashley Smith/*Times-News* photo © 2007.

Growth. Houses sprout on what was once farmland at the Grandview Estates subdivision in Northwest Twin Falls. Drew Nash/*Times-News* photo © 2016.

Commercial Expansion. A strip mall of offices and stores nears completion along W. Cheney Drive in Twin Falls' retail area. Drew Nash/*Times-News* photo © 2018.

Conservative Values. Stanton Healthcare offers abortion alternative services for the Magic Valley. Stanton Healthcare photo © 2019.

Faith. A new Mormon Temple for the Magic Valley, opened in 2008, has helped attract Mormon professional families to the area. Here, church volunteers help maintain the temple grounds. Ashley Smith photo/*Times-News*. © 2011.

Multiple Use. A lone cross-country skier descends the 500 Road in the South Hills. Outdoor recreation of all kinds on easily-accessible public lands is a popular activity in the region. Virginia Hutchins/*Times-News* photo © 2015.

Agriculture. The gigantic Chobani milk processing yogurt plant, at nearly a million-square feet, was completed in 2012. It employs hundreds of Magic Valley residents and adds millions of dollars to the local economy. Drew Nash/*Times-News* photo © 2018.

Agriculture. A spring freshet creek waters a pasture and hayfield in Camas County. Southern Idaho agriculture is known for its diversity of crops and variety of settings, many of them beautiful, as here. Bill Grange/Idaho State Department of Agriculture photo © 2019.

Transportation. It's early morning, and traffic is already crossing the I.B. Perrine bridge to and from Twin Falls. Local traffic volumes are increasing about 1-2 percent per year, says the Idaho Department of Transportation. Pat Sutphin/*Times-News* photo © 2018.

Politics. Although from different parties, state Sens. Michelle Stennett, D-Ketchum, and Lee Heider, R-Twin Falls, are both concerned with Idaho's education system, Here, they get a computers-in-the-classroom lesson from a student at Oregon Trail Elementary School. Pat Sutphin/*Times-News* © 2018.

Minorities. The Boise Oinkari Dancers perform the sagar dantza or apple dance at the annual Gooding Basque Picnic. Ed Glazer/Time-News photo (c) 2014.

Health Care. The opening of a new St. Luke's Magic Valley Medical Center in 2011 boosted both the quality of health care services and added thousands of jobs to the local economy. Michelle Bartlome/St. Luke's photo. © 2012.

Education. O'Leary Middle School students in Twin Falls pack a crowded lunchroom. The district has since opened a new middle school and two new elementary schools as school populations continue to swell. Eva Craner/Twin Falls School District photo. © 2014.

Diversity. Neema Niyu, Miss Burundi Idaho 2016, attends the World Refugee Day at Twin Falls City Park in a traditional dress. Expanding Magic Valley ethnic diversity adds to the area's array of cultures. Drew Nash/*Times-News* photo © 2018.

Education. The Collee of Southern Idaho campus, on the North side of Twin Falls, is a heavily-used community facility. Shown in this aerial shot are the Fine Arts Center, Taylor Administration Building, the Library and sports arena, as well as other structures arrayed around the campus circle. Doug Maughan/College of Southern Idaho photo © 2016.

Fauna & Flora. Southern Idaho wildlife populations adapt to human presence. Here, Mule Deer graze a Twin Falls neighborhood lawn on a late winter afternoon. Linda Wright Hartgen photo © 2019.

Environment. On a late fall's day, Mt. Harrison is clear as a bell, though some 50 miles away to the East of the I.B Perrine bridge in Twin Falls. Air quality here is among the best in the nation, say the Idaho Department of Environmental Quality. Drew Nash/*Times-News* photo © 2018.

Recreation & Tourism. Bike Path walkers on a 5K run/walk go past the I.B. Perrine Bridge on a March day. The Canyon Rim Trail skirts the canyon for 8.2 miles. Drew Nash/*Times-News* photo © 2019.

Arts & Entertainment. Public art is taking a more prominent place in Twin Falls' arts scene. This statue of pioneer surveyor John Hayes graces the plaza at Twin Falls' new downtown City Hall. Sculpture by David LaMure. Josh Palmer/City of Twin Falls photo 2018.

Arts & Entertainment. Twin Fall artist Gary Stone has been painting Magic Valley scenes for decades, including a multi-panel display at the Magic Valley Regional Airport. Stone photo, © 2019.

Evening Tunes. A band gets out a tune on Twin Falls' Main Avenue on a pleasant evening, part of the city's emerging night life. Josh Palmer/City of Twin Falls photo © 2018.

Sports. From its founding more than 50 years ago, the College of Southern Idaho has fielded quality sports teams. Here, elated fans react as CSI's Darius Smith runs out the clock in a double overtime win. Drew Nash/*Times-News* © 2019.

A Shared Love of Country. Scouts and veterans perform a flag retirement ceremony at a Memorial Day service at Buhl's West End Cemetery. Drew Nash/*Times-News* © 2017.

Local History. Community restoration projects, such as the Wilson Theater on Rupert's town square, show what can be done by groups with a dedicated love of local history. Drew Nash/Fly Photography © 2017.

Libraries & Broadband. The modern Southern Idaho library in Twin Falls is not just a "keeper of books" but a "Keeper of Discovery" in the internet age. Drew Nash /Times News photo © 2017.

Irrigated Landscape. A pivot waters a field of Idaho potatoes, just one of many crops grown in the region. Steve Stuebner/Idaho Water Resources Board photo © 2018.

The Spirit of Place – Revisited. An irrigation canal winds lazily through a Gooding farm under a classic Idaho sunset. Thousands of farms like this one have turned the Magic Valley into verdant fields and given the valley its sense of space and timeless endurance. Sharon Breshears photo © 2015.

15. Southern Idaho Republicans

Magic Valley politics has been dominated by the Republican Party all the way back to the valley's settlement, except for the Depression years of the 1930s and the Bull Moose era of Teddy Roosevelt and Woodrow Wilson, 1912 and 1916. GOP dominance is a a well-known feature of Southern Idaho public affairs, but what's lesser known are the reasons behind it.

The dominance is partly due to the settlement patterns of the valley. Twin Falls County was settled in a rush of land filings in the years from 1904; those first settlers generally came from the Midwest and Utah, both regions with well-established conservative politics at the time. The newcomers brought that political profile with them, which has varied little ever since. It's a pretty good bet that in any given election, Republicans will take or keep the seat.[375]

---

375 Here's how Wikipedia describes the politics of Cassia County: "At every level Cassia County is a Republican Party stronghold. All county-level offices are held by Republicans and have been for decades. Republican primaries are tantamount to election to office as Democrats rarely field challenges for county or state legislative office. Cassia County is one of the most consistently Republican counties in the state and in the gubernatorial election of 2010 Republican Butch Otter carried Cassia County with 76.54% to Democrat Keith Allred's 16.73%. In the presidential election of 2012 Mitt Romney, whose father lived for a few years in his youth in Oakley, carried Cassia County with 85.2% while Barack Obama received 13.1%. The last Democratic presidential candidate to carry Cassia County was Franklin D. Roosevelt in the election of 1940, edging out Wendell Willkie by about 100 votes. State legislators from Cassia County traditionally hold their seats for long periods of time. Two of the longest serving legislators in Idaho history were from Cassia County: Rep. Vard Chatburn of Albion (1957-86) and Sen. Denton Darrington

Another related reason is that the GOP's positions and overall philosophy dovetail closely with shared conservative values of the region's social norms, customs and culture. We all know that politics and values usually mirror each other. In Southern Idaho, this is not due to chance, but through the alignment of voters with conservative candidates for local, state, legislative and national offices. Citizens vote for candidates whom they see as best representing their core values.[376]

The voting margins tell the story. Except for 1932 and 1936, Republicans have carried Twin Falls County in almost every year since the city's first election in 1908, which the GOP carried at 55.6 percent, 1,757 votes to 1,051 Democratic votes. In the past seven elections back to 1992, the GOP margin has ranged from 44.9 percent (1992, when there was a third candidate, H. Ross Perot, in the race who got almost 30 percent of the vote.) to as high as 74.4 percent (2004). The most recent election years have each shown GOP margins of more than 66 percent.[377]

Other counties in Southern Idaho show a similar pattern, with Jerome, Cassia, Lincoln and Gooding counties all showing Republican margins of more than 65 percent in the most recent presidential elections. The only consistently Democratic county has been Blaine County, known for its ski resort towns of Sun Valley, Ketchum and Hailey. This pattern continues down the ballot, as Republicans are consistent victors in most contests, except again where Blaine County votes outweigh more rural counties in Legislative District 26, and on the county commission and other local offices.

Only two of Southern Idaho's towns are listed among Idaho's "most conservative" communities, but in practical terms, most of the region skews toward a common-sense, if not strongly ideological, conservative perspective on social and economic issues. Although not a watered-down Republicanism, the region exhibits strong conservative leanings. Still, there's been only one serious effort in 20 years by the hard-right politicos to capture local Republican county central committees, and that effort failed. This is no land of redoubts nor a haven for racial purity, no nullification measures against the

---

(1982-2012). That longevity translated into leadership or chairing committees. Since 2012, Rep. Scott Bedke has served as Speaker of the House. Bruce Newcomb of Burley also served as Speaker from 1998 to 2006. Wikipedia, "Cassia County, Idaho," website, updated Sept. 4, 2018.

376 Hartgen, Stephen. "Southern Idaho Politics," in *Journey West: A Memoir of Journalism and Politics*, Ridenbaugh Press, Carlton, OR, 2014. Some of the discussion of politics in this chapter mirrors this earlier analysis and phrasing.

377 Wikipedia. Twin Falls County Idaho, politics. website 2018. and Idaho Secretary of State, election returns by year. Democrats did about the same in 1912 at 32 percent, with Teddy Roosevelt's Bull Moose Party capturing some 47 percent. In 1916, Democrat Woodrow Wilson carried the county with 52 percent. Since then, it's been Republican except for the Depression years.

federal government, nor the even further right talk of secession of the Northwest from the United States.

On the left, four nearby communities are on a top twenty list of "most liberal" cities in the state, but they're all adjacent to each other in Democratic Blaine County, distant geographically and culturally from the Magic Valley.[378]

But in the Magic Valley, there is still plenty of room for spirited contests within the GOP primaries. These usually pit centrist candidates (usually the incumbent) against more arch-conservative or alt-right individuals whose ideological leanings often override practical considerations. These challengers rarely win in Southern Idaho, where their views are often regarded as outside the mainstream and seem mostly derived from right-wing websites and writings, as well as from arch-conservative blogs.

Among these right-wing conservative groups is the Idaho Freedom Foundation, which is in a more-or-less running feud with more traditional Republican state leadership, which they decry as RINOs, (Republicans in Name Only) and whom they consider to be too moderate on many issues. Funded by both in-state and out-of-state oligarchs, the Idaho Freedom Foundation is more libertarian than Republican, although they latch onto Republican primaries since they lack the numbers to be a viable third party.

The Foundation has offended many in the GOP with its "no prisoners" ratings and rankings of legislator voting records, its blogs which often cherry-pick facts and for its active recruitment of more libertarian challengers to run against incumbents. While they favor transparency in government, their donors try, often unsuccessfully, to remain secret.[379] While active in other counties, the Idaho Freedom Foundation has met with little success in Southern Idaho. Only one local Foundation candidate has ever won. Several of its leading candidates were defeated in primary elections in 2018, suggesting that Idaho voters prefer mainstream Republican candidates.[380]

---

378 Burley and Paul ranked 17th and 18th among most conservative communities. In the most liberal rankings, Ketchum ranked 1st, Hailey 6th, Sun Valley 11th and Bellevue 14th. For both lists, see Blanchard, Nicole. "These are the 20 Most Conservative Places in Idaho," and "These are the 20 Most Liberal Places in Idaho," both in *The Idaho Statesman*, July 27, 2018. Rankings were compiled using voter registration data from the 2018 primary where voters chose which ballot they wanted and thereby showed their political leanings.

379 Russell, Betsy Z. "Lawmakers Call for Crackdown, Fines on Campaign Finance Violators," *Idaho Press*, Nampa, Idaho, Aug. 20, 2018.

380 As Vice-President Thomas Jefferson wrote in a letter to John Taylor, June 4, 1798: "Perhaps this party division is necessary to induce each to watch and debate to the people the proceedings of the other. A little patience and we shall see the reign of the witches pass over, their spells dissolve, and the people recovering their true sight." Quoted in Meacham, Jon. *Thomas Jefferson: The Art of Power*, Random House, 2013.

Magic Valley GOP voters almost invariably chose Republicans with more traditional positions who focus on fiscal responsibility, prudent state funding, keeping taxes low while maintaining essential services, and such national issues as limited welfare programs, anti-abortion, less gun control, strong national defense spending and opposition to drug legalization.

In that sense, local GOP elections are often dominated by more "Establishment" candidates, who may be tagged as too-moderate, but whom voters readily choose. In the 2016 GOP primary, Magic Valley voters chose the more mainstream candidates in all but one contest; the more extreme the candidates' positions, the less likely they were to prevail. None got over 40 percent of the vote, and some were under 30 percent.[381]

This pattern of selecting between centrist candidates and those further to the right seems to offer choice for GOP voters. It's common in other single party dominant states as well.[382] As political scientist V.O. Key explains, politics in areas which are one-party dominant merely shift the choice spectrum. Instead of being left or right between two parties, contests are along a continuum in which the pendulum only moves to one side. That's because the political parties, left and right, are competing for the same pool of middle-class citizens.

Still, local elections do show a gradual shift rightward going back at least to the 1980s. Elections in the 1960s and 1970s were certainly less charged than today, partly due to a more reserved media environment. A pivotal year was 1980, when U.S. Congressman Steve Symms beat incumbent U.S. Senator Frank Church by a narrow margin on the coattails of presidential winner Ronald Reagan.[383] The message to local Republicans was that they too could win with more conservative candidates.

It took a while for this pattern to solidify. Centrist state senators like John Barker, Buhl (1967-1984) and Richard High, Twin Falls (1967-1980), enjoyed broad support across the Republican Party base. Neither ever faced a primary challenge. Barker was succeeded by Darrell McRoberts (1985-1988) and then Joyce McRoberts (1989-1996), both of whom continued in a more centrist strain. Tom Gannon (2003-2008), was also known as a centrist senator. Sen. Laird Noh (1981-2004) followed High in 1980 and served 24 years, again from a more centrist perspective and with only one primary challenge in his long career.

---

381 Idaho Secretary of State, GOP primary returns for Twin Falls, Jerome, Cassia and Minidoka Counties, 2018.

382 Key, V.O. *Southern Politics in State and Nation*, Knopf, 1949.

383 Election 80/The West," *The Washington Post*, Nov. 6, 1980. Symms beat Church by less than 1 percent of the vote, 49.74 percent to 48.78 percent, fewer than 5,000 votes out of more than 400,000 cast.

Sharper differences emerged on the House side. In the 1980s, T.W. Stivers (Twin Falls, 1975-1986), rose to lead the more conservative wing of the party and was elected Speaker of the House after several terms in Boise. His protégé, Donna Scott (1983-1986), also came up from the more conservative side of local politics. So did Celia Gould (1987-2002), who interned with Stivers and then won a House seat of her own. The former chair of the Judiciary & Rules Committee in the House, she now leads the state Department of Agriculture.

Among this right-leaning group, a few moderates – nicknamed "steelheads" because they swam upstream against strong currents – also represented Twin Falls County in the 1980s and early 1990s. Gary Robbins (1985-1990), Doug Jones (1985-2006) and Ron Black (1987-1998), who chaired the House Education Committee, were among this more moderate group, known for their willingness to buck the prevailing philosophy of no-tax increases and socially conservative positions.

But as the 1990s continued, the local legislative delegation did become more conservative. Changes in the support groups (what Key would call interest groups) such as the Republican Women's Club, helped drive the change, electing the club's leader, Sharon Block (2001-2012), to replace conservative Rep. George Swan (2001), who died in office. More centrist groups such as the League of Women Voters faded away, as they have nationally, and more issue-focused groups emerged, such as the county Farm Bureau chapters.[384] The Twin Falls GOP Central Committee remained a more moderate bastion well into the 2000s, but it gradually shifted as well.

In 2008 and 2010, libertarian activists won several precinct chair positions, sparking a new wave of conservatism in the local Republican primary, leaving the Central Committee more conservative than it was a decade ago, after almost 20 Liberty caucus and Tea Party conservatives claimed precinct chair seats. In 2010, for example, City Councilman Lee Heider, with strong support from the Farm Bureau and conservative church goers, picked off the more liberal Chuck Coiner for one of Twin Falls' senate seats by almost 15 percent, in part due to Coiner's support for gay marriage and his support for sharply raising education funding, which would have

384 Wikipedia. "League of Women Voters," updated July 6, 2018. The League's decline can be traced back into the 1970s with the beginnings of modern polarization of politics. Though nominally non-partisan, the League's positions have trended left in recent decades, thus placing it out of step in more conservative communities. All across Idaho, the Farm Bureau Federation has gained in political involvement and influence. The group holds regular candidate forums and supports candidates financially. Locally, they've aligned themselves mostly with Republican candidates and taken an active role in state policy issues." See Idaho Farm Bureau Federation, policy book, 2018.

meant tax increases.[385] In 2012, longtime councilman and former mayor Lance Clow won a House seat after his predecessor, moderate Leon Smith, had barely survived a three-way primary in 2010 and then retired.[386]

From time to time however, tensions still emerged. Prior to the May 2012 primary, some of the precinct seats were challenged by others from the Ron Paul camp, but the libertarians' total shrunk to only a half-dozen precinct positions.[387]

By 2016 and 2018, the right-wing group in the Twin Falls Central Committee seemed more diluted, its members having either left active participation or blended in with their more centrist colleagues.

New state party rules and a new state law effectively closing primaries except to declared party members are in place, but it's uncertain how these will affect either turnout or registration. Idaho voters have long had an independent streak, and we appear to be still in a period of push and pull between the right wing of the local GOP, and a further right group of Ron Paulers, Libertarians, Constitutionalists, and surviving John Birchers of an earlier generation, with the centrist group now more ascendant locally.

Longtime patterns are likely to keep local GOP politics on the right, but perhaps with center-right, right-center oscillations. Local population growth has often come from conservatives fleeing more liberal states and new arrivals often cite the lower cost of living, congestion, crime and the political correctness of their previous home state as reasons they have moved here. When these newcomers get involved in politics, it is usually on the more conservative side.

Democrats have misjudged this influx, thinking that the huge increases in Idaho population over the past 20 years will make the state more liberal, but that's not occurred in Southern Idaho.

One indicator of this is the year-after-year campaign financial support given by a wide array of entities which have broad memberships in the Magic Valley. These include agricultural and commodity groups, and industries like the banking and credit unions, realtors, independent businesses, the Farm Bureau, Idaho Cattle Association, health care groups, insurance, and many of Idaho's leading manufacturing industries.

---

385 Hartgen, p. 191.

386 Hartgen, p. 188.

387 Minutes of the Twin Falls County Republican Central Committee Organizing Assembly, May 23, 2012. The Paul group could muster no more than 8 votes for local party Republican leadership posts, and only 6 for their leading candidate, Rick Martin, versus 27 for his opponent, Joan Hurlock. In delegates to the 2012 June convention, the Paul group got only one alternate post from Twin Falls County among 34 delegates and alternates selected.

It's not unusual for centrist candidates to enter their general election campaigns with significant "war chests" for advertising, events, yard signs, mail cards and sometimes television and radio advertising, billboards and newspaper ads.[388] Since financial resources constitute a significant advantage in messaging and name recognition, the financial differences are often of heightened importance.

Among voters, party affiliation in Idaho is also a good predictor of individual values. A statewide study by the Pew Research Center shows this close alignment. Overall, 49 percent of Idaho adults are Republicans, compared to 32 percent declared Democrats, with 20 percent as neutral. Since the "neutrals" tend to break in elections to the GOP side, Democratic candidates have a steeper wall to get consistent winning margins.[389]

A good share of the state's conservatism plays out in the political arena; there's little disconnect between politics and other values. It's the cultural "linkage" across politics, values and to some extent, religion, which gives Southern Idaho its dominant social features.

A recent survey of Utah Mormons and their Republican leanings is likely the same among Southern Idaho Republicans. While many don't approve of President Donald Trump's personal traits, they're not going to leave the Republican Party over him. Two-thirds (67 percent) of Mormons vote Republican, as do eight of ten Evangelicals and half of Catholics. It's another example of the dominance of Republican politics in the region.[390]

This strong base of support among Republican church goers suggests how difficult it would be to "swing" Southern Idaho elections to the Democrats.

The recent 2018 general election results show a similar pattern, Except for two Twin Falls precincts (# 1 and # 3), every precinct in Southern Idaho (minus Democratic Blaine County) was carried widely by Republicans, from Gov. Brad Little, completely down the ticket.[391]

Beyond Southern Idaho, Little carried 40 of Idaho's 44 counties, losing only in Ada County, the state's most populated, by a margin of less than 2,200 votes, with 92,684 to Democrat Paulette Jordan's 94,772. Little also trailed Jordan in the resort counties Blaine and Teton and in college-dominated Latah County. Otherwise, he swept the state, winning with 59.8

---

388 Idaho Secretary of State, candidate contributions report, May 25, 2018. The three GOP candidates in District 24, Twin Falls, had combined cash available of over $62,000, with two of their candidates uncontested. The one Democratic candidate had a cash balance of $7,880.

389 Pew Research Center, "Political Affiliation Among Adults in Idaho," website, 2018.

390 Fingerhut, Hannah and McCombs, Brady. "AP Exclusive: Most Mormons Back GOP, But Fewer Support Trump," *U.S. News & World Report*, Nov. 29, 2018.

391 Twin Falls County website, Twin Falls County Results, General Election, Nov. 6, 2018.

percent of the vote to Jordan's 38.2 percent, a plurality of over 130,000 votes.[392]

Little's appeal as a common-sense Republican played well virtually everywhere. It's hard to see how any Democrat could have turned the election, even given Democratic strength in Ada and the three other counties.

In short, the dominant politics in Southern Idaho remains decidedly common-sense, not hugely ideological, conservative on issues and Republican in voting. That isn't likely to change much in the years ahead. Newcomers to Idaho line up closely with the Republican/Democratic split already here. Newcomers are likely to reinforce existing leanings rather than undercut or change them.[393] Thirty years from now, it's safe to predict Southern Idaho will be as solidly Republican as it is today.

---

392 Idaho Secretary of State website. Election Returns, 2018.

393 Lyons, Jeffrey. "Don't Californicate My Idaho," *The Blue Review*, Boise State University, Boise, Idaho., Oct. 30, 2017. Lyons, a professor at Boise State University, concludes "Observers of Idaho politics who are expecting changes in the state's partisan composition to come as a result of the people moving to Idaho may be waiting for a very long time. Rather than challenging the dominant political identity in the state, movers to Idaho appear to be reinforcing it, and those hailing from California are no exception. At least with respect to political attitudes, it appears that these concerns about the beliefs of new arrivals and the changes that they bring are not well founded."

16. Southern Idaho Democrats

The Republican Party's domination of Southern Idaho politics goes back to its settlement that laid the groundwork for the conservative values found in the region's social norms, customs and culture. As was discussed in the preceding chapter, this is not by chance, but rather by an alignment of citizens with more conservative candidates for local, state, legislative and national offices. If citizens pick candidates whom they see as best representing their core values, it is not difficult to see why Democrats struggle in Southern Idaho.

Except for recreation-oriented Blaine County, the region has not sent a Democrat to the Legislature in decades. The last local Democrat elected in Twin Falls County was commissioner Dennis Maughan in 1994, who later switched his party affiliation to Republican.[394]

Except for several avowed Democrats on the nonpartisan Twin Falls city council, including Mayor Shawn Barigar and long-time councilman Chris Talkington, Democrats hold few publicly elected seats in the Magic Valley except in Blaine County. A recent proposal at the 2018 Republican State Convention would shut off this hidden Democratic base by encouraging the Legislature to eliminate non-

394 Linked In profile, "Dennis Maughan," 2018. Maughan served until 1999, when he resigned to take a position out of state. Maughan recalls that he switched to the GOP in 1997 "because of my philosophical differences with the Democratic party regarding welfare reform. To this day, I regret having done so, as my deeply help beliefs in most policy areas (are) closer to the Democratic Party." Dennis Maughan, Facebook Message, Aug. 28, 2018.

partisan positions in local government and to require virtually all municipal candidates to run on partisan ballots.[395]

The existing GOP lock on elected positions leaves the local Democrats with virtually no "up and comers." There may be some who eye an elected post, but they turn away from such spirited and often expensive contests in which they are unlikely to prevail. There was only one Democratic candidate on the Twin Falls legislative ballot in District 24 in 2018, with two seats uncontested. No Democrats ran in rural Twin Falls (District 25) or in Districts 23 and 27.[396] This may not be surprising in an area which in 2016 went heavily for President Trump in (three to one, 20,000 votes to 6,000) nor does it auger well for Democratic prospects in the near term.

But it reflects politics in Idaho. Since the middle 1990s, when then-governor Cecil Andrus retired, Democratic representation in the Legislature has shrunk markedly to only 11 seats of 70 in the House and 6 of 35 seats in the Senate in 2016. Democratic strength is now limited to Boise city, Blaine County, two seats in Pocatello and only one House seat elsewhere.

As Republican legislative seats increased, the open primary system in place in the 1990s and 2000s created a window of opportunity for Democratic voters to vote in GOP primary contests, which they did, often picking the more moderate contenders. This "half a loaf is better than none" tactic was overturned in a 2011 federal court ruling, which was followed by a switch to a closed primary system in which only declared party members could vote in the GOP primaries. This change seems to have had the desired effect of discouraging crossover voting.

By the 2018 primary, voting crossover seems to have declined, leaving the GOP with even stronger, if more conservative, representation and the Democratic Party with fewer election options.[397] Legislators still get frequent emails from Democrats and the media asking them to repeal the 2011 closed primary law, but that seems unlikely.

Another potential hurdle facing local Democrats is adding a tie-breaking additional member to today's evenly-split, three-three redistricting commission. Measures to modify the commission's structure, and thus better reflect Idaho's legislative numbers, were introduced in the 2018 session, but were not taken up then. The issue is likely to be revisited by the 2022 election following the 2020 US Census. Twin Falls District 24 is a "donut hole"

---

395 Idaho Republican State Convention, Resolution 16, 2018. "Resolution In Support of Making Municipal Elections Partisan."

396 Idaho Secretary of State, candidate filings, 2018.

397 Blanchard, Nicole. "Are Idaho Democrats Registering Republican to Sway Primaries? Here's What the Data Says," *Idaho Statesman*, Aug. 27, 2018, and Idaho Secretary of State website, 2018, "Primary Elections in Idaho."

district, pointed to by Democrats hoping for local gains by redistricting the city. But that did not materialize and District 24's representation today is as GOP dominated as it ever was.[398]

A further problem for local Democrats is being perceived as a mere extension of both the national Democratic Party and of Blaine County, where recreational activities dominate and the economy turns on tourism. The Wood River Valley is one of America's premier ski and outdoor recreation destinations, with a number of swanky hotels, some very good restaurants, and an airport often packed with out-of-state corporate jets.

That makes the resort towns more expensive places to live than their neighbors to the south. The area is surrounded by federally-managed Sawtooth National Forest lands, as well as some Bureau of Land Management parcels. Over the past 25 years or so, these agencies, supported by local recreational businesses, have shifted land management policies away from multiple use and now almost exclusively focus on recreational uses.

Timber harvest is mostly gone except for fireplace wood and a bit of post-and-pole cutting, resulting in an overgrown and often diseased forest of dead standing trees, a perfect setting for large forest fires, of which there have been a number in recent years. Active mining has long since ended and livestock grazing leases have been curtailed to prevent contact between domestic livestock and wildlife.

Wolf packs and bears abound in the area and there are frequent incidents of depredation. Since recreation and tourism dominate the local economy, it's not surprising that the three Democratic legislators would align with national conservation groups, as well as with the Conservation Voters for Idaho; its website boldly declares its political intent to defeat a local state Republican legislator, Rep. Steven Miller, R-Fairfield, who, it claimed falsely, was trying to "promote a state takeover of our land." That effort was successful in the 2018 general election.[399]

It's a further way in which Southern Idaho Democrats position themselves as a "counterpoint" party to the heavily agricultural neighbors to the south. While some local folks have second homes in the Wood River area and partake in what it has to offer, there are considerable political and cultural differences.

---

398 Kruesi, Kimberly. "Proposal Would Shift Power on State Redistricting Commission to Republicans, from Current Equal Split," *Spokesman Review*, Spokane, Wa., Feb. 26, 2018. Comments on the proposal from Democrats echoed concerns it would further cement GOP control. Former Democratic Senator Ron Beitelspacher wrote, "Power Corrupts and Absolute Power Corrupts Absolutely. Giving one party all the power in reapportionment and congressional redistricting only guarantees that the powerful are going to be represented, not the people."

399 Conservation Voters For Idaho website, 2018.

At a political dinner party in Blaine County some years ago, attended by a number of unsuccessful statewide Democratic candidates,[400] one woman asked what it was like to live in Twin Falls, which she implied, was very different from Blaine County. The response was that the Magic Valley was indeed different, but was a great place to live, an answer which she did not expect.

The basic problem Democrats face across Southern Idaho is the disconnect between their stated positions and the people they seek to represent. As the national Democratic Party has moved to the left on a number of issues, the state party has followed along, adopting a "Bernie Sanders" platform in 2016, which includes free college, single-payer medical insurance for all, legalization of marijuana and support for wider abortion services, repeal of Right-to-Work laws, open immigration and tighter gun controls.

The state Democratic platform also supports gay marriage, eliminating state sales tax exemptions (thus increasing taxes) and continued federal control of public lands.[401] As shown earlier, these positions are opposed by many Southern Idaho voters. While some issues may not address Idaho directly, it's apparent that Democrats here aren't tuned in to local constituencies. Unless that changes, Democrats can expect to remain a minority party in Southern Idaho for the foreseeable future.

---

400 In 2002, Wood River Valley Democrat Alan Blinken lost to GOP incumbent Larry Craig, 65 percent to 32 percent. In the same year, Jerry Brady, of Idaho Falls, lost to GOP Gov. Dirk Kempthorne, 56 percent to 41 percent. In 2006, Brady again ran for governor, losing to GOP candidate C.L. "Butch" Otter, 53 percent to 44 percent. Idaho Secretary of State elections returns website.

401 Idaho Democratic Party platform, website, 2018. See also Moeller, Katy. "Idaho Democrats See A Surge in Interest, But Can That Create a 'Blue Wave' in Red Idaho?," *The Idaho Statesman*, June 20, 2018.

17. Minorities

One of the biggest changes in the Southern Idaho region in the past quarter century has been the beginning of significant ethnic diversity in the Magic Valley. The implications of this trend have rippled down through the valley in many ways, from economics to social services, education, health care and other affected areas.

The changing demographics have inflamed some; others have been emboldened to defend the changing diversity as a positive element in Southern Idaho life. Today, minority relations and impacts are a common topic among coffee shop discussions and are frequently mentioned in local news accounts, as well as in editorial opinions, letters and anonymous blog posts. The comments range from the rational and reasoned to the vitriolic and occasionally defamatory.

Race and ethnicity are among the most volatile public policy discussions across the United States today. Southern Idaho is no different in that regard, even with its relative distance from urban centers and relatively homogeneous population. But while other regions have had these ongoing discussions for many decades, the conversation was muted in Southern Idaho until the 1990s.

That's because the area simply wasn't very diverse. Twenty-five years ago, minority populations in the Magic Valley were almost completely limited to Hispanics, some Asian-Americans and a small number of African-Americans. The 1990 Census showed a statewide population of just over one million people (1,006,748), of which about 53,000 were Hispanic and fewer than 3,400 African-American. The statewide Asian-American population was under 10,000. Virtually all the rest were white.

In Twin Falls County in 1990, the total population was 52,927, with Hispanics making up 5.3 percent (3,200 individuals) compared to 90 percent white. The African-American population was under 70. Asian-Americans totaled 524 individuals, including 48 from Vietnam, 182 from Laos and 92 of Japanese heritage.[402] Some of the Japanese-Americans were multi-generational, stemming from when several thousand were interred at the Hunt Relocation Camp during World War II. The Laotian and Vietnam residents had mostly come through the College of Southern Idaho Refugee Center program, which began receiving refugees in the early 1980s. Minidoka County had the largest Hispanic population at that time, just over 3,700 individuals.

Growth in Hispanic Population. Southern Idaho has absorbed a growing Hispanic population since 1990. This was driven by labor demand in agriculture, particularly dairies. The industry had relied on Hispanic labor for some time, but as demand grew in the 2000s, the local labor supply couldn't keep up. Illegal immigration filled that labor demand.[403]

By 2013, an estimated 8,300 people worked on dairies, many in the Magic Valley, and Congressman Raul Labrador put the number of illegals in that workforce at 90 percent. Idaho Dairy Association director, Bob Naerebout estimated it at 75 to 80 percent, still a large number.[404] Rapid Hispanic population growth has continued in the 2010s with an estimated 3.3 percent growth in 2015-2016 alone, up 18 percent since 2010 to 297,740 statewide.

Twin Falls County's Hispanic population in 2016 was put at over 13,000, about 16 percent of the county's population and an increase of more than 10,000 people in twenty years. Several other Magic Valley counties showed Hispanic populations at or above 30 percent. Overall, the state's Hispanic population has ballooned by more than two percent every year since the early 1980s, three times the rate of U.S. population growth.[405]

These surges are evident throughout the valley. Spanish language can be heard in many public settings, from stores to restaurants. Advertisers announce that Spanish-speaking sales representatives are available to help buyers. Schools have had to search widely to find qualified Spanish-language

---

402 US Census 1990, General Population Characteristics, Idaho.

403 Roeser, Jan. SIEDO Annual Summit, Sept. 25, 2018. The Department of Labor put Idaho's Hispanic agricultural workforce at over 10,000 in 2016, of which fewer than 3,000 were thought to be H2A certified, at an average wage of $11.63/hour.

404 Popkey, Dan. "Most Idaho Dairy Workers Are Not Here Legally," *Idaho Statesman*, May 17, 2013.

405 Idaho Department of Labor, "Idaho Hispanic Population Increases 3.3 Percent for 2015-2016," June 27, 2017. The numbers: Minidoka County, 35%; Jerome County, 34%; Lincoln County, 30%; Gooding County, 29%; Cassia County, 27%.

teachers and aides. Courts routinely provide Spanish-language interpretation, as do health care offices and government agencies.

In a series of articles on the Hispanic population in Jerome County in 2015, the *Times-News* outlined the challenges and impacts of this demographic change.[406] The newspaper editorialized that both Hispanics and non-Hispanics needed to work more closely to overcome language barriers and build a mutually-beneficial community.

Two years later, the Hispanic population continues to grow with no indication of a slowdown, and as it has, there have been changes in the relationship of the Hispanic culture and the larger white community. Hispanic/non-Hispanic marriages are now the most common interracial pairings in America and the Magic Valley is no different. Between 10 and 15 percent of marriages in Idaho are interracial.[407] Closer to home, the author has three such pairings within his own extended family.

Magic Valley Hispanics are now earning more since labor shortages and the need for skilled handling of livestock and crops has raised local wages. It's not unusual to see dairy workers earning over $25,000 annually, which is a high wage indeed compared to work in Central America and Mexico. Depending on the employer, the base wage sometimes comes with free or discounted housing and health insurance, a grocery allowance and sometimes free cable television.

These jobs and benefits have helped Hispanic families join the middle class. It isn't unusual to see second and third generation Hispanic residents buying homes and sending their children to college,[408] an unusual happening just two decades ago.[409] Business startups are another indicator of expanding economic success. The longtime Idaho Hispanic Chamber group in the Boise area expanded into the Magic Valley with a Southern Idaho chapter in 2018. More than 100 people attended the first kickoff lunch, including local leaders in real estate, banking and the hospitality and restaurant industries.[410]

---

406 Brown, Nathan and Wootton, Julie. "As Jerome Lifestyle Draws Hispanic Immigrants, City Government, Schools Scramble to Adjust," *Times-News*, Aug. 30, 2015; and Wootton, Julie and Brown, Nathan. "Young Jerome: Influx of Young Hispanic Families Shapes Community Change," *Times-News*, Oct. 5, 2015.

407 Meckler, Laura. "Dramatic Rise Seen in US Intermarriage Rates Since Landmark Court Ruling," *The Wall Street Journal*, May. 18, 2017.

408 Former College of Southern Idaho interim president Curtis Eaton estimates the CSI's Hispanic student population at 20 percent. Twenty years ago, it was only 6 percent. Curtis Eaton Interview, Jan. 21, 2019.

409 Brown, Nathan. "Jerome Jobs: Immigration Laws Big Deal for Jerome's Dairies," *Times-News*, Nov. 10, 2015.

410 Idaho Hispanic Chamber of Commerce, Southern Idaho chapter kickoff, July 13, 2018.

Hispanic influences are evident in many social institutions. Quinceanera (literally, "fifteen-year-old female") coming-of-age celebrations are common among Hispanic families, as is church attendance.[411] Family ties remain strong among Hispanics and multi-generational family events are common. Political involvement remains under-developed; elected Hispanic leaders remain rare in the Magic Valley, even in counties where they have substantial populations.[412]

That could dramatically change Idaho's future political profile. Hispanics have been elected to the Idaho Legislature, and one has served on the Idaho Court of Appeals. As Hispanic populations get close to or over 30 percent in some counties, political participation is likely to increase. Although traditionally more Democratic in voting patterns, many Hispanics hold conservative perspectives on social issues, which would give them better entry into Idaho's politics, which skews conservative and Republican.[413] As yet, the Trump election of 2016 and the 2018 off-year Congressional campaigns didn't reflect any noticeable uptick in Hispanic political participation locally.

Significant issues remain for Magic Valley Hispanics. A significant percent of this community is not here legally, with many working in agriculture and the dairy sectors. A 2017 announcement by Jerome County that it was considering leasing some space in its new jail for federal immigration deportation prompted a protest by hundreds of local Hispanics. That, in turn, elicited numerous comments on blog sites calling for broader deportation of local illegals, despite the impact on the available workforce and economy. Immigration policies are a much-debated national topic and the local protest and response show that Southern Idaho faces similar divides.[414]

The flashpoint of issues like immigration and the presence of a significant illegal population among area Hispanics suggest an underlying disconnect between the white and Hispanic communities. Social interaction seems limited in non-compelled situations, and even in those, such as schools, the

---

411 Anonymous. "Sweet 15: Rite With Long History Keeps Changing," *Times-News*, Oct. 31, 2008.

412 Brown, Nathan. "Hispanic Political Involvement Still Low Despite Growing Population," *Times-News*, Dec. 13, 2015. See also, Kaufman, Gretel. "Speaking Up: Latinos Seek a Stronger Voice in Idaho politics," *Times-News*, Aug. 22, 2018.

413 Pew Research Center, "The Shifting Religious Identity of Latinos in the United States, May 7, 2014.

414 Brown, Nathan. "Hundreds Pack Jerome Courthouse to Protest ICE Contract," *Times-News*, July 11, 2017. See also, Naerebout, Bob. "Letter to Jerome County Commissioners," July 18, 2017. Naerebout, executive director of the Idaho Dairy Association, wrote "It is time to recognize the value the Hispanic community brings to the Magic Valley! Without them not only would we lack diversity but we also would lack the prosperity we have enjoyed for the last few decades."

groups often separate from each other. This is particularly true when there's a language barrier. Area schools with the highest proportion of Hispanic students seem more likely to reflect these separation patterns.[415]

All in all, Magic Valley Hispanics still face significant hurdles integrating into Southern Idaho life. They have lower high school graduation rates.[416] Their college success rates also tend to be lower and they often need remedial courses at enrollment.[417] Despite these challenges, Southern Idaho's Hispanic community has made considerable strides. With a growing population, Hispanic-Americans are likely to further influence the region in the years ahead.

Refugee Resettlement. Diversity in the Magic Valley was relatively stable between 1990 and 2012. It was then that the mix of nations and immigrants began to change, driven by world displacement patterns. More new arrivals came from Africa, as well as from the war-torn nations of Iraq and Afghanistan, including many refugees of Muslim faith.[418]

This change was noticed locally and nationally. Under a liberal immigration policy of the Obama Administration, refugee allocations rose and states and communities were often told how many new arrivals they could expect, but had little or no say in the settlement process. Widely reported terrorist attacks in many countries, as well as some in the United States, added to rising anxiety over security in the local community.

---

415 Greene, Rich. "Minico Student Arrested for Threatening Violence," *Times-News*, May 9, 2008.

416 Richert, Kevin. "Hitting the '60 percent' goal won't take just take work. It requires a transformation," IdahoEdNews, Nov. 26, 2018. The Idaho Board of Education reports that while 30 percent of white high school students graduate with a 3.5 GPA or better, only 16 percent of Hispanic students do. Among the states, Idaho ranks last in the nation at the percent of Hispanics with a college degree or professional certification at just 13 percent. He writes, "Since Hispanic students make up by far the state's largest ethnic minority, at 18 percent of overall enrollment, their success is interwoven with Idaho's success. It will be virtually impossible for Idaho to reach its 60 percent goal without making major inroads in the Hispanic community." Graduation rates by county reflect the same pattern. Only Blaine County, at 47.6 percent. is over 40 percent. Twin Falls (31 percent) and Cassia County, 29.6 percent, are next. Other Southern Idaho counties are all under 25 percent: Camas, 20.5 percent; Gooding, 22 percent; Jerome, 21.8 percent; Lincoln, 17.1 percent; and Minidoka 24.5 percent. All are below the state average of 40 percent. One school official calls it the "F-150 syndrome," that is, buying a new Ford 150 truck out of high school is perceived as a better investment than continuing on to college or professional training.

417 Idaho Commission on Hispanic Affairs. *The Hispanic Profile Data Book for Idaho*, 4th edition, 2017, using data to 2015. Newer data (2016) shows a similar pattern, with Idaho ranking last among the states in percentage of Latino adults with degrees, at 12.7percent. See Shak, J. Oliver and Nichols, Andrew Howard. "Degree Attainment for Latino Adults: National and State Trends," The Education Trust, Washington, D.C., June 14, 2018.

418 College of Southern Idaho, Refugee Center website, 2018.

Even before this change, there were indications of concern among refugee observers; former CSI Refugee Center director Ron Black noted that the arrival of often-destitute refugees raised concerns about the extent of needed financial support. Other comments along the same line began to show up in anonymous observations in *Times-News* blogs and on social media.[419]

Then, in 2015, a news story brought the issue to a head. It was announced that perhaps hundreds of refugees from war-torn Syria would be relocated to the Magic Valley. The article brought over eighty anonymous responses, almost all of them negative, raising questions about security, national vetting, financial impact, education, language proficiency and both religion and ethnicity.[420]

There were several reasons why these newcomers weren't as readily accepted by the community. One, these proposed arrivals would come from Syria, from which war and terrorism seemed to emanate. In a Post-911 world with almost constant reporting of terrorist incidents in the Middle East, a significant number of locals regarded refugees from that region with suspicion.

Another factor was that locals would have almost no say in the resettlements, which were widely seen as yet another federal intrusion into state and local affairs.

And a third factor, less often stated but clearly evident in anonymous blog comments and elsewhere, was the fact that these new refugees would be predominately Muslim and often people of color.[421]

These circumstances sparked local reactions. Small but vocal groups raised questions about the wisdom of trying to assimilate peoples from such disparate cultures into a mostly homogeneous white population. The debate intensified to the point that federal officials flew in from Washington, D.C. to explain the resettlement program. These officials struggled to answer questions about the wisdom of placing such disparate groups where there was significant opposition.[422]

That didn't do much to quell the local commentary, aided by blogs and national news coverage.[423] By the following spring, discussion of the issue

---

419 Davlin, Melissa. "Public Perspectives on Refugees Aid: Mixed," *Times-News*, Aug. 14, 2011.

420 Wootton, Julie. "CSI Refugee Center Expects Influx of Syrians," April 30, 2015.

421 Hartgen, Rep. Stephen. "Hartgen: Defunding Refugee Center Isn't the Answer," *Times-News*, Aug. 11, 2015.

422 Wootton, Julie. "Hundreds Turn Out for Refugee Forum, *Times-News*, Sept. 24, 2015.

423 Johnson, Kirk. "Idaho City of Refugees Debates Taking In Middle Eastern Refugees," *New York Times*, Oct. 1, 2015 and anonymous comment by "Black Rifle," "Multi culturalism has never worked. That's why nice neighborhoods eventually turn to crap and people move out leaving the immigrants to tear it up and neglect it. Happens time and time

was widespread locally. Rick Martin, leader of the group opposing the CSI Refugee Center, failed to gather enough signatures to put the measure on the ballot, gaining only 894 of some 3,842 needed names, but he nonetheless pushed ahead, putting his own name forward as a candidate for a CSI board seat.[424]

Given the few signatures on the ballot proposal, it was expected that Martin's challenge to board incumbent Laird Stone would fall way short, but in the anonymity of the voting booth, Martin received almost 47 percent of the vote in Twin Falls and Jerome counties.[425]

The vote suggested at least a sizeable minority of voters favored getting CSI out of the refugee center business, which did not escape the attention of the national media. Coverage then spiked following a report of sexual assault on a refugee child by refugee boys. The local police and prosecutor handled the case within state established juvenile case protocols, but these actions provoked accusations of a cover up.[426]

As 2017 turned to 2018, several changes lessened tensions. The Trump Administration put better vetting of refugees in place, and the stream of refugees into Idaho and the Magic Valley declined sharply. Also, the anti-refugee leader Rick Martin moved out of state, and the pro-refugee editor of the *Times-News* left for an editing position elsewhere. With those last two changes, the issue faded from the newspaper's pages, although the current editor continued to claim the paper's role in declaiming bigotry and hate, a common editorial theme previously.[427]

---

again. Foolishness." *Times-News*, Sept. 23, 2015.

424 Brown, Nathan. "Anti-Refugee Measure Doesn't Have Enough Signatures for Ballot," *Times-News*, April 5, 2016.

425 Brown, Nathan. "Stone Keeps CSI Seat," *Times-News*, Nov, 8, 2016. The totals were 19,467 for Stone and 17,126 for Martin.

426 One extremist right-wing outlet, InfoWars, accused local yogurt maker Chobani of intentionally bringing in vetted refugees as employees. Chobani sued and InfoWars settled the case, backing down with an on-air retraction by host Alex Jones. See Riggins, Alex. "Alex Jones retracts accusations linking Chobani to Twin Falls crime," *Times-News*, May 17, 2017. See also Bell, Ryan. "'Fake News" seized an Idaho city. A Local Paper Jumped Right into the Coverage," *Columbia Journalism Review*, Nov. 27, 2017. See also, Dickerson, Caitlin. "How Fake News Turned a Small Town Upside Down," *The New York Times*, Sept. 26, 2017.

427 Smith, Alison Gene. Comment on Bryan Clark's Facebook page, *The Post-Register*, Idaho Falls, Idaho, June 6, 2018, where she wrote: "No one said anything for a long time in Twin Falls when anti-refugee and anti-Muslim people came to town. It created a vacuum where the only ones talking about the issue was a small group of loud, hateful people. The newspaper stood up and said those kinds of people didn't represent us. But it took the city and other community stakeholders joining us to really make a bigger impact. So sometimes what you're saying works. But other times, you have to start a big discussion and be outraged."

By midway through 2018, the refugee resettlement issue seemed in the past. Act Up Twin Falls, aging John Birch Society members and a gun-rights group calling itself the III Percenters, seemed all that was left of the right-wing, anti-refugee movement. These few seem to have retreated to their social media postings and an occasional meeting attended by a few individuals.

Meanwhile, better vetting at the national level further reduced the flow of refugees, down to an estimated 71 locally in 2018,[428] with none from Syria, compared to 300 refugee admittances in previous years.[429] Even then, it took time for local and national media to figure out that Twin Falls was the hard-working, mostly-tolerant place it has always been and remains so today.[430]

African-Americans. The number of African-Americans in Idaho has never been very large, although they have been a presence since before statehood.[431] In the Magic Valley, African-Americans are typically less than

---

428 Wootton-Greener, Julie. "CSI Refugee Center Sees Drop in Federal Funding, Newcomers, But Community Support Up," *Times-News*, Jan. 29, 2019.The center's resettlement numbers have dropped from 328 in 2016 to 91 in 2018, with further dwindling expected in the years ahead. All of the recent refugees have been from Africa; none have come from the Middle East.

429 Kaufman, Gretel. "Fewer Arriving Refugees Means Fewer Workers for Magic Valley Businesses," *Times-News*, Aug. 28, 2018.

430 Wilson, Christopher. "That's Not Who We Are: How A Besieged Heartland Community Rallied Around It's Refugees," Yahoo News, May 14, 2017. See also, Montero, David. "Alex Jones said Refugees Ravaged Idaho Town With Disease and Crime. The Town Says Folks Get Along Just Fine," Los Angeles Times, May 15, 2017. The article drew considerable reaction on the Times' comment section, including this remark by anonymous Idaho Common Tater: "Since unemployment in Idaho is barely 3% and was hardly more even at the depths of the recession, those nativists that were complaining the refugees were robbing them of jobs were usually either only recently unemployed, or had deficiencies in their own abilities or resumes that were keeping them unemployed. But that is something many folks won't admit, looking instead for scapegoats for their own failures. Of course, folks who harbor prejudice are usually also incapable of recognizing the real definition of their collection of reasons for resenting another broad class of human beings. No place is perfect. Twin Falls is not perfect, but it is nice enough. It has always been and still is a very nice place to live, despite the effort of outsiders to come here and attempt to normalize the disgusting and aggressive intolerance of a minority of our residents. I am proud and grateful that a large majority of Twin Falls' citizens have risen above the intensely orchestrated alt-right campaign to distort our community's character, bend its moral compass and, in so doing, sully our reputation among Americans and the rest of the world."

431 The 1870 territorial census listed 60 African-Americans in the territory. That number grew slowly through the decades (201 in 1890; 651 in 1910; 1050 in 1950 and 5456 in 2000). By 2017, the African-American population was estimated at over 10,000 statewide, with 2010 census numbers in the Magic Valley at 309 in Twin Falls County of 77,230, or about .4 percent. Jerome County's numbers were smaller, fewer than 70 African-

one-half percent of the county populations. As with any demographic group, African-Americans are active everywhere. Some are associated with the College of Southern Idaho, others in law, government, real estate and finance. Some individuals are relatively high profile, such as Zeze Rwasama, himself a refugee from the Congo, who heads the College of Southern Idaho's Refugee Center.

In recent years, many refugees from African nations have settled first in the Magic Valley, where many are employed in the food processing industries which dot the region.[432] The 2020 Idaho census is likely to show further increases, reflecting the growing employment opportunities in the area.

African-Americans, including new refugees, find both opportunity and acceptance in Southern Idaho. While their numbers are not large, they are widely represented in such fields as education, health care, government, hospitality outlets and many others. An annual "Refugee Day" highlights traditional foods, dancing and native dress from their homelands.[433]

Like Hispanics, African-Americans are part of a growing number of interracial families. While some may not stay in the Magic Valley after high school, they seem to appreciate their surroundings, at least in none-too-obvious ways.

One common point of intersection is through CSI's well-regarded basketball team, the Golden Eagles, which has recruited promising African-American players from throughout the West and Southwest for many seasons. These young men usually go on to four-year schools, and sometimes to professional leagues. The players are soon well-known across town, where they participate in various civic and community-service roles.[434]

The Hunt Camp. Southern Idaho is commonly regarded as a place from which people depart as they become adults. This out-migration is often cited as a issue of major concern by employers and economic development specialists. But people who once left sometimes return, sometimes to stay and sometimes to capture a sense of their own histories.

Americans or .3 percent of 22,374. total population. See Oliver, Mamie O. "Idaho Ebony: The African-American Presence in Idaho History," *The Journal of African-American Studies*, Winter, 2006; and US Census.2010 and 2017 estimates.

432 College of Southern Idaho, Refugee Center website, 2018.

433 Anonymous. "Magic Valley Refugee Day Highlights Human Experience," KMVT television, June 16, 2017.

434 Pierre Jackson was a CSI player who led the team to a national junior college championship in 2011. He later played with Baylor University and has since played with several professional teams, including the Dallas Mavericks. See "Pierre Jackson," Wikipedia, July 4, 2018.

Every year since 2003, Japanese-Americans have boarded buses in West Coast cities to travel hours to Twin Falls to honor their ancestors.[435] Some haven't been to Southern Idaho before; they come to visit the remnants of the Minidoka Internment Camp where their ancestors spent World War II as detainees and confined farm workers. Many say their parents and grandparents spoke little of the experience but they know it was seared into their memories. Since it's creation in 2001 by outgoing President Bill Clinton, the Hunt Camp Monument, as it is also known, has been on their must visit list.[436]

Following the war, the Hunt Camp internees were released, many returning to their former communities in the Northwest, but often without the businesses and homes left behind. Some stayed in Southern Idaho for work in a sort of reverse diaspora.[437] Their children are now longtime residents, who like most of us are several generations removed from our former homelands.

Basques. The Basque community of Southern Idaho dates back to Idaho's territorial and early statehood days. The Basque people are from Northwest Spain and Southwest France where they left to become some of the first cod fishermen off the Newfoundland Banks of Eastern Canada.[438] Basques found a welcome home in the ranges of the American West. Used to long, lonely stretches of time on the sagebrush plains of Idaho, their independence of spirit and love of life seems to infuse their modern generations as well.

---

435 Watanabe, Ben. "Return to Minidoka: Revisiting the Imprisonment of My Family," Heraldnet, Everett, Wa., June 17, 2018.

436 Clinton, William J. Proclamation 7395, Establishment of the Minidoka Internment National Monument, Jan. 17, 2001, The American Presidency Project, University of California, Santa Barbara, Ca. Clinton used the authority of the 1906 Antiquities Act to establish the 72-acre monument. The Hunt Camp was one of eight relocation centers established in 1942 by President Franklin Roosevelt to hold Japanese-Americans during the course of the war. Roosevelt's confinement order has been frequently disparaged as a violation of civil rights of Japanese-American citizens of the United States. The camp, near Twin Falls, was disbanded in October, 1945 and many of its structures dismantled and/or moved. The remnants of the site, which at its peak held nearly 10,000 people, is managed by the US Park Service.

437 That was the case with the parents of Bryan Matsuoka and his sister, Janet Matsuoka (Keegan) both of whom were born in Twin Falls, where their father returned to work after the war as an air conditioning and heating specialist. Both say their parents spoke little of the Hunt Camp, but say neither of them personally experienced much overt discrimination growing up in the Magic Valley. Janet volunteered many years as a local tour guide for the pilgrimage visitors from the Northwest and Bryan, a former public schools teacher and coach, works at the College of Southern Idaho as director of the Small Business Development Center. Matsuoka Interviews. July 3, 2018.

438 Kurlansky, Mark. *Cod: A Biography of the Fish That Changed the World*, Vintage, 1998.

Some here today are from the "Old Country" and their toughness of spirit and kindness of heart make them the quintessential movie cowboys and in real life, excellent ranch foremen and crew supervisors. They're both physically strong and kind; in the mountains, many carry rifles to protect the herds, yet during lambing, they treat the newborns as the delicate babies they are.[439] Their names reflect their Basque heritage: Aspiri, Aspiazu, Gandiaga, Gusisolo, Guerry, Eiguren, Cenarussa, Oxarango, names which flow as yet more wonderful examples of the American great melting pot.

Many came from the Vizcaya region of the Northern Spanish and French coasts. An estimated 30,000 landed in Idaho, although the precise number is uncertain.[440] A recent survey put Idaho's Basque population and descendants at about 6,600, but that seems a low estimate; in Southern Idaho, cities with some Basque populations include Gooding, 4.1 percent; Shoshone, 3.4 percent; and Homedale, 1.2 percent.[441]

A Basque Museum and Market in Boise have aided visibility of this significant Idaho population and popular festivals and sheep trailing events have added to public awareness.[442] There were Basque boarding houses in many Southern Idaho small towns, including Gooding and Shoshone, as well as regular events in Rupert and into Northern Nevada, also early Basque herding areas.

Yet, as with other immigrant groups, it's been a struggle to keep the Basque heritage alive.[443] Sustaining a culture, its rituals and unique ways, is an uncertain task today and is likely to be even more so in future generations. Yes, we are all Americans, but we are also from other lands, of deep heritage, bequeathed lineage, as Faulkner writes.[444]

A generation or more from now, it seems likely Idaho's Basque culture and memory will be further absorbed into the multi-generational mix of American life in Southern Idaho. Yet, it is being preserved well enough today that it will certainly be part of our known and treasured memories. Perhaps that is enough.

---

439 The author once watched as Ambrosio Aspiazu, foreman for the Noh Sheep Company, lifted a full- sized ewe over a fence and placed her in a loading chute. He didn't need any help.

440 Quitugua, Eric. "Study Attempts to Count Idaho's Basque Immigration," *Times-News*, April 24, 2016.

441 North American Basque Organizations website, 2018. 2000 US Census data.

442 Barnes, Bingo. "A Short Basque History," *Boise Weekly*, July 27, 2005. See also Kurlansky, Mark. *The Basque History of the World*, Penguin, 1999.

443 Quitugua, Eric. "Basque Sunset: Basque Identity Fades as First Generation Immigrants Disappear," *Times-News*, April 24, 2016.

444 Faulkner, William. "The Bear," Random House, 1942.

18. Media

A few decades ago, Southern Idaho citizens lived in what was then a comfortable cocoon when it came to the media. So did most of rural America. Sure, there were daily national news broadcasts and what seems now like quaint local television programming with 6 and 10 p.m. reports. In the morning, the local newspaper (The *Times-News* in this case) gave the overnight national news, the previous day's full range of local news, plus whatever sports updates had come in before the 2 a.m. press run. That was pretty much it.

But times have changed all across America and in Southern Idaho. Today's media landscape is in some ways much broader. There are numerous media outlets on the internet, and hundreds of broadcast channels. Internet delivery has put gigabytes of information at home desktops and now on smartphones. Keeping up is easier than ever, and yet overwhelming. The technologies change rapidly; even early adapters have trouble keeping current. The "Rip Van Winkles" are left behind in the rush forward to, where? No one is exactly sure.

We all know how communications alter both what is said and what is meant. The "Trump tweet" phenomenon didn't begin with "The Donald," and he is unlikely to be the last public official to exploit its enormous reach and power. It is another matter, though, whether the changes have added to the national conversations which underpin our American republic. Henry David Thoreau wondered if the new telegraph of the 1840s connecting Maine and Texas would give either state anything to say to each other.[445] We too should be skeptical of technology's claimed benefits.

An annual report by the Pew Center on the Media[446] gives a good yearly summary of both change and stagnation in the nation's vast communications network which now gives Idaho seemingly unlimited sources of information. Here's an overview on major media entities in the Magic Valley and how they've evolved:

Television. The Magic Valley television area is served by a local station, KMVT, which has been the major local news programming source for many years. The station is owned by Gray Television, which purchased it and a sister Fox station, KSVT, in 2015 for a reported price of $17.5 million.[447] At the time, the station had about 75 employees including what appeared to be a full stable of on-air announcers and reporting staff. Turnover appears to be ongoing, as the property seems a good starting point for young broadcast journalists, but veteran newscasters like Joe Martin add stability to the news broadcasts.

The station has gone through several owners in recent decades, but has kept its coverage of local news more-or less-stable, if not usually groundbreaking. Content is focused on community events brought to its attention. The sensational approach ("If it bleeds, it leads.") found in bigger markets is mostly absent at KMVT; even charged political coverage is low-key, apparently reflecting the station's desire to continue its broad-based dominance across community political perspectives.

General Manager Tim Coles notes that Gray's ownership model is to focus on smaller to mid-sized markets where their stations dominate the local television scene. (KMVT is 189th of 210 television markets in America.[448]) News staff turnover makes it a first job for beginning reporters, who arrive with a college broadcasting degree, a few on-air clips but often with little experience beyond classwork and internships.

The station avoids political slanting of stories and stays away from editorial comment. "We're here to report the facts, not to save the world," Coles says, contrasting the station's mission with the sometimes breathless

---

445 Thoreau, Henry David. *Walden*. 1854. "Our inventions are wont to be pretty toys, which distract our attention from serious things. They are but improved means to an unimproved end, an end which it was already but too easy to arrive at; as railroads lead to Boston or New York. We are in great haste to construct a magnetic telegraph from Maine to Texas, but Maine and Texas, it may be, have nothing important to communicate."

446 Pew Research Center, State of the News Media," 2004-2018, ff.

447 Goodell, Eric. "KMVT, KVST to be sold for $17.5 million," *Times-News*, Mar. 15 2015.

448 Coles, Tim. Interview, Oct. 26, 2018.

"got-ya" journalism in other media and in bigger markets. Audiences seek great content and KMVT tries to consistently to provide it.[449] Through several owners, KMVT has stayed with what seems to be a successful business/news model. That has brought it success and community appreciation. Thus, it maintains a top local position in Nielsen ratings.

In 2018, Gray Television announced another merger, with Raycom, giving it about 57 television stations across the country, most of them the leading station in each of those markets, including KMVT. The merger put Gray in the third largest television group in the country.[450] The company gets high ratings for its financial performance, up almost 19 percent in 2018, with the stock hitting a 52-week high in November, 2018.[451]

Social Media. A particular feature of the media landscape today is the use of social media across virtually all demographic groups. A Pew Research Center report in 2018 found 73 percent of adult Americans used YouTube and 68 percent used Facebook. These are large numbers indeed, since neither platform existed before 2004. Young adults, 18-24, are heavy users, but use by older adults, particularly among those 50-64, is a respectable 65 percent.

There's only a little difference between social media use by suburbanites and rural Americans (67 percent and 58 percent, respectively), suggesting the broad usefulness of these communication tools. Facebook, Twitter and YouTube are the leading platforms. Linked-in is used more by college graduates as a job-seeking tool and for professional connections. Snapchat and Instagram have wider followings among younger people and WhatsApp has stronger numbers among Hispanics.[452]

Although social media use has shown tremendous growth in recent years, it seems likely that as-yet-to-be-developed tools and platforms will supplant some of these current ones. There have been many moments in American history when technology has driven rapid change, sometimes in less than a few years, when a product was widely adopted in a short period of time.

Social media use may well be another example of how seemingly-simple devices change human patterns of life in many ways. Twenty-five years ago, cell phone technology allowed for the first real "car phones." Today, several generations of technology have come and gone, and still more are coming quickly. Smartphones, functioning as hand-held computers, are everywhere.

---

449 Coles, Tim. Interview, Oct. 26, 2018.

450 Associated Press, "Gray TV, Raycom to Merge" June 25, 2018.

451 Zachs Equity Research. "Gray Television (GTN) Soars to 52-week High," Nov. 9, 2018.

452 Smith, Aaron and Anderson, Monica. "Social Media Use in 2018," Pew Research Center, Mar. 1, 2018.

Who can doubt the larger-capacity ones will soon carry even more information, both personal and otherwise?

The rise of social media has had direct effects in Southern Idaho.

As an example, a *New York Times* article on refugee resettlement in Twin Falls and an attack by refugee boys on a young girl shows the power of how hysterical writings at various blog sites turned a basic juvenile crime story into an anti-refugee media field day.

Hundreds of people wrote on the *Times*' comment section, some praising the city's response, others criticizing the reporting, others still critiquing the alt-right group websites which fed the flames.[453]

In another example, social media manipulators with apparent ties to Russia used social media in Southern Idaho to try to impact the 2016 election, but there's no claim, much less proof, that Southern Idaho voters paid any attention.[454] Donald Trump carried Twin Falls County by a 3 to 1 margin over Hillary Clinton, but even extreme conspiratorial theorists haven't claimed that foreign, anti-Clinton messaging had any measurable impact on local voting.[455]

---

453 Dickerson, Caitlin. "How Fake News Turned A Small Town Upside Down," *The New York Times*, Sept. 26, 2017. See also comments section of the *New York Times report*, which includes this comment from "Dicentra," Sept. 17, 2017. "You can say the exact same thing about segments of the population in any town or city in the country. An unfortunate consequence of the computer age is isolation from the broader community. More and more people are living in echo chambers they craft themselves and are assisted in that endeavor by tech company algorithms that feed you more of the same to keep you clicking. Other than purposefully turning your devices off and engaging with all citizens in your community and intentionally seeking out online interactions with others who hold different opinions along with websites posting opposing viewpoints, I don't know how we combat this phenomenon. I do know that we must try something to combat it because the direction we are headed is big trouble." And another comment from "Curtis James," Sept. 26, 2017: "The length of this article highlights the necessary details to showcase the truth. We are currently living in a period where the majority of people are consuming information, often false, all from miniature paragraphs or 140 characters. In the past decade, the availability of broadband internet connection and personal computing has become much more affordable. More people than ever have been given a voice. This is a wonderful opportunity for democracy, but an even more dangerous opportunity for deceivers with a platform of hate and ignorance. The root of these issues can be found in our education system. One can conceivably make it all the way through high school and in many cases, university, without ever being exposed to critical thinking or how to properly decipher between credible and false information."

454 Applebaum, Anne. "If Russia Can Create Fake 'Black Lives Matter' Accounts, Who Will Be Next,?" *The Washington Post*, Oct. 17, 2017. See also, Jalonick, Mary Clare. "Report: Russia Still Using Social Media to Roil American Politics, Associated Press, Dec. 17, 2018.

455 Kennison, Heather. "Update: Locals React to Reported Russian Meddling in Twin Falls Anti-refugee Facebook Rally," *Times-News*, Sept. 13, 2017. See also Shane, Scott. "Purged Facebook Page Tied to the Kremlin Spread Anti-Immigrant Bile," *The New York*

Yet, we can see that, in the years ahead, this kind of participatory journalism will likely become even more commonplace, reminiscent of the press in the post-Revolutionary War period where anonymous writers nearly destroyed the personal and professional reputations of both presidents John Adams and Thomas Jefferson.[456]

Radio. Radio broadcasting in Southern Idaho offers a wide variety of listening choices. As with many small markets today, content is mostly programmed from afar and supplemented by local advertising. National Public Radio, from KBSU in Boise, carries national NPR news and commentary, and KBSU does an occasional "live" story from the Magic Valley, mostly on topics of current interest which tend to follow national topics as well.[457] Short news briefs can be heard on many stations, as well as upcoming community calendar events, and specialized content such as agricultural prices and commodity futures. Spanish language stations are also in the market, as is Christian radio.

The two leading stations in the market are KEZJ-FM, country western, and KLIX-AM, a talk radio format whose local host, Bill Colley, offers a conservative perspective on politics, both local and national.

In the three years or so he has been in the market, Colley has boosted his "Top Story" ratings from 5.1 to 7.3 audience share.[458] Colley came to Idaho from prior talk radio stints in New York and Delaware, where he says he was perceived as more controversial and right-leaning than his markets.

Colley's host station, KLIX-FM, has a long history of offering talk radio, with long-running on-air hosts L. James Koutnik[459] and a more-recent conservative-liberal pairing of Kelly Klass and Jill Skeem. The station also carries a number of national talk radio programs, including Sean Hannity and Rush Limbaugh, well known conservative voices.

Colley stirred up controversy in prior positions, and has done the same in his relatively short time in Idaho, mostly from critics on social issues.[460] He seems particularly attuned to the "alt right" wing of Idaho politics, giving air time to various legislators, almost none of whom represent Southern Idaho. This gives his guest and call-in followers an "Outer Space" flavor of alt-right

---

Times, Sept. 12, 2017.

456 Mattimore, Ryan. "Presidential Feuds with The Media Are Nothing New," History.com. Jan.26, 2018. See also Safire, William. *Scandalmonger*, Harvest, 2001.

457 Nielsen. "Topline Ratings, Twin Falls-Sun Valley, Idaho," July 30, 2018.

458 Nielsen. July 30, 2018.

459 Koutnik had what is said to have been the first call-in talk radio program in the United States. Wikipedia, "Twin Falls, Idaho," updated July 12, 2018.

460 Colley, Bill. "Colley: Potheads. Stay Out of Idaho," *Times-News*, Nov. 29, 2016.

conspiracy theories, anti-United Nations rants and anti-Democrat ramblings and anti-RINO (Republican In Name Only) on most issues.

It is hard to predict how long he might stay in the local radio market. For a time, he was writing a column for the *Times-News*, often from an alt-right perspective. The newspaper quietly dropped it in 2017, replacing him with more measured and more liberal columns from retired state Supreme Court justice, Jim Jones. Nonetheless, Colley's audience has grown, as the Nielsen numbers suggest, so for the short-term, at least, his microphone seems secure.

Another local radio personality with a conservative bent is Zeb Bell, on KBAR radio (1230 AM) in the mornings. Bell has had physical challenges all his life, beginning with childhood polio in the 1950s, but he has overcome them all. He's a popular commentator in the rodeo announcing business and frequently invites political guests onto his show, which is variously critiqued by those on the left politically, but Bell endures nonetheless.[461]

Print. In the super-charged media environment of national politics today, it's not unusual to see a tweet from the President of the United States complaining about how the accomplishments of the administration are routinely ignored by a media which focuses on minutiae. By the time national news filters down to the local level, it is almost wholly anti-administration, as many studies funded by conservative organizations consistently show.[462]

The traditional role of the press of informing citizens of facts and restraint in editorializing has almost been completely pushed aside, replaced with consistently liberal editorials, columns, cartoons and bias in news articles.

The past 15 years or so haven't been kind to the newspaper industry, which has lost revenue and staffing all across the country. With hollowed-out staffs, many important local news events and issues are simply not covered. Reporters may have had formal beats in the past, but now they are frequently pulled off to do general assignment reporting as well.

Here's an example: College of Southern Idaho trustees, a five-member board, are elected in Jerome and Twin Falls counties. In 2018, two trustees retired, yet not a word of their retirements appeared in the *Times-News*. The filing period came and went, again with no notice that seats were even open. Two people filed for the two seats separately, but there was no article about

---

461 Friedman, Cassidy. "Alleged Radio Remarks Irk Democrats," *Times-News*, June 11, 2008. See also ZebBell.com website.

462 Editorial. "Anti-Trump Hatred Shows in 92% Negative Coverage of His Presidency: Study," *Investor's Business Daily*, Oct. 10, 1018. See also, Siegfried, Evan. "Media's Bias Against Conservatives is Real." Think website, July 29, 2018. See also Wikipedia. "Media Bias in the United States," Updated Nov. 10, 2018, for an extensive overview of perceived media bias, both liberal and conservative.

their filings, much less their qualifications, interest areas or previous involvement with the college. Thus, when voters went to the polls in November, they may not have known anything about what was in effect, a perfunctory election.

Although community college boards are officially non-partisan in Idaho, there's some indication of a partisan tilt in both of the candidates; one had run for office before as a Democrat. But there being no publicity, there was no clear way for voters to know. What was even more baffling was that in the prior election cycle, the contest for another CSI Board seat was a spirited one between candidates with very different visions of the college's role.[463]

Once, a daily newspaper in America was a premier community business with many properties operating at over 30 percent profitability EBIDTA (Earnings Before Interest, Depreciation, Taxes, Amortization). Today, margins of one-third that are bragging rights at media conferences.

Newsroom staffs were once filled with reporters covering various beats. Circulations were high, growing on "must read" community content. Today, many newsrooms are virtually empty, with rows of unoccupied desks and few editors or reporters. Many former prominent newspaper buildings around the country have been sold off as the owners downsize to eliminate unneeded space in the new economic realities of the industry.[464]

As a profession, newspaper reporting is now often ranked in the "ten worst jobs" in America, with studies citing low pay,[465] on-call hours, animosity toward the press, deadline pressure and slash-and-burn corporate ownership.[466]

The peak came about 2005, some 30 years after Carl Bernstein and Bob Woodward were portrayed as bringing down President Richard Nixon.[467] Journalists saw the *All The President's Men* film (1976) as granting them further license to critique Republicans and conservatives wherever they were found in national, state or local government.

463 Brown, Nathan. "Stone Keeps CSI Seat," *Times-News*, Nov, 8, 2016. The totals were 19,467 for Laird Stone and 17,126 for Rick Martin.

464 Pristin, Terry. "Struggling Newspapers Sell Off Old Headquarters," *The New York Times*, Oct. 22, 2013. In March, 2018, the *Times-News* began printing *The Idaho Statesman*, Boise, which previously had closed its printing operation. See Kennison, Heather. "The *Times-News* will Soon Print *The Idaho Statesman*," *Times-News*, Jan. 5, 2018.

465 Idaho Department of Labor, Occupational Employment & Wages, South Central Idaho, May, 2017. Reporters had an entry level pay of $30,565 and a mean of $34,741. For comparison, local high school teachers had an entry wage of $37,061 and a mean of $48,025. One local reporter told the author that wages hadn't moved in three years. The reporter soon left.

466 Sass, Erik. "Newspaper Reporter is Worst Job, 3 Years Running," MediaPost, The Daily Blog, May 1, 2017.

467 Noonan, Peggy. "The Legend of Deep Throat," *The Wall Street Journal*, June 2, 2005.

This often led to "got ya" articles on what usually amount to petty mistakes. In the past 15 years or so, The *Times-News*, like newspapers large and small throughout the country, fell into this adversarial role, delving into such topic as urban renewal, college building contracting and claims of racism against local law enforcement. Twin Falls, by the way, was the hometown of Watergate source Mark Felt, better known as Deep Throat from the movie, and an inspiration to many a passing-through journalist.[468]

Newspaper trend data is less reliable than it was 15 years ago, so monitoring revenues, circulation and staffing is more difficult for outside observers. Still, the most recent Pew Center on the Media (2018) reports newspaper revenue in advertising is about $16.5 billion nationwide, a 10 percent drop in one year and off from about $60 billion in 2004, the peak year for newspaper revenue. Circulation revenue rose slightly to about $11 billion in 2017, about a three percent increase and digital revenue in both categories is about 31 percent, again up slightly. Newspaper circulations have fallen sharply since about 2004, continuing a long-term trend in which they peaked in the mid-1940s, more 70 years ago,[469] but publications are now more and more dependent on circulation revenue as advertising revenue has declined so sharply.

Another measure of the industry's change is the decline in newsroom staffing, which is under 40,000 nationwide, down almost 50 percent since 2004.[470] Since reporting is a labor-intensive business, fewer reporters out gathering the news mean fewer news stories, particularly at the local level. Pages are filled instead with wire-service or "canned" copy, bought by the newspaper's parent company on bulk contract, or by running pictures oversized to fill space, filling page "holes" with the publication's self-promotion ads and shrinking the paper's physical size.[471]

Meanwhile, revenue continues to decline as print advertising shrinks and properties use their online sites to beg for subscribers, whose prices rise regularly. Yet, each new rise in subscription rates drives away more paying customers,[472] thereby putting even more of the costs that way.

---

468 Nash, Drew. "#51. Deep Throat's Childhood Home In Twin Falls," *Times-News*, Aug.25, 2014. It was long rumored that Felt, the deputy director of the FBI in the Watergate years, was the "Deep Throat" of *All The President's Men*, but not confirmed until Felt was in his 90s, years later. Felt was born and raised in Twin Falls, and his childhood home, although not exactly a tourism hot spot, is still there at 160 Ninth Ave. N., on a tree-lined street in Twin Falls.

469 Pew Research Center, "State of the Media," Fact Sheet, 2016 data.

470 Pew Research Center, Journalism and Media, "Newspapers Fact Sheet," 2017.

471 Hare, Kristen. "Did We Just Experience The Hardest Decade in Journalism?," Poynter Institute, n.d. (2018).

Today, a *Times-News* combined home delivery and digital subscription runs over $49/month, up from $41/month a couple of years ago and about six times more than what subscribers paid in 2002 for the paper alone, which had more local news.[473]

To many, $588 or more a year is a lot to pay for so little content and biased content at that. Subscriptions are way below 10,000 home delivery, a decline of more than 50 percent in 15 years, with fewer than 5,000 copies delivered in the Twin Falls city zone, despite the growth in city zone households.[474] As parent companies struggle with debt and evaporating print advertising, further regular subscription rate jumps are virtually certain.

Lee Enterprises, the *Times News* parent company, does not break down its public financial reports by property, so it is not always easy to see direct comparisons to how the *Times-News* did under its previous owner, Howard Publications. At its peak in 2002, the *Times-News* had about 135 employees; less than 15 years later, that number had been whittled down to 87, including part-time staff. Payroll dropped from over $4 million annually to about $3 million.[475] Today, the *Times-News* is one of the few Magic Valley business entities which has shrunk since the mid-2000s, despite the enormous economic growth in the valley overall.

In the news department, staffing had gone from about 35 positions to 20 or fewer. Major beats like politics and local government were combined as staff turnover occurred. Some beats, like business and environment reporting, were eliminated entirely, as was editorial writing.[476] Even clerical positions were consolidated and low-cost employees who had worked their entire

472 This section of this chapter draws on the author's previous memoir, *Journey West: A Memoir of Journalism and Politics*, Ridenbaugh Press, 2014, and particularly from a chapter therein, "A Different Newspaper" on changes to the *Times-News* since its purchase by Lee Enterprises in 2002. The author was editor/publisher of the *Times-News* from 1982 to 2004.

473 *Editor & Publisher Yearbook, 2002*. The *Times-News* subscription price in 2002 was $205.40 a year or $ 4.35 weekly. Circulation in 2002 was 23,711 (Sundays.), in a retail trade zone of 104,000 population or about two-thirds of 36,000 trade zone households. Today, the valley population has almost doubled, but circulation has dropped dramatically, as in many newspapers across the country.

474 DataUSA website puts the Twin Falls city households at 16,914 in 2016, an increase of almost 4,600 households or almost 40 percent from 2002. (*Editor & Publisher Yearbook, 2002*). The Alliance for Audited Media report for Sept. 30, 2013 puts the *Times-News* city zone circulation at that time at 4,701. It has undoubtedly slipped further since then, although newspapers now count digital subscriptions along with printed editions.

475 Christensen, Matt. "The Numbers Behind The News," *Times-News*, May 13, 2015.

476 "2018 In Review," *Times-News*, Dec. 30, 2018. The *Times-News* reporting staff at the end of 2018 was 7 reporters, including sports, feature writing and Mini-Cassia news, less than half what it was in 2004.

careers at the newspaper were summarily let go in wave after wave of staff reductions.[477]

Newspapers all over Idaho and in other states, are begging people to subscribe, touting ever-shrinking news staffs while shedding pages or filling them with house ads and other freebies. All while the subscription price goes up and up.[478]

These patterns are widely noticed. It is an industry whose traditional roles have been jettisoned, leaving communities with reduced sources of information, but with more bias.[479]

It is an odd business model indeed in which a product intentionally goes out of its way to alienate subscribers, wrapping itself in self-proclaimed importance.[480] Recent changes locally include an expanded set of columnists from a national syndicate, probably as a cost-savings measure, but with little change in the overall left-tilt of the editorial page. No local conservative voices were added.[481]

Lee Enterprises is known in the newspaper industry as an aggressive cost-cutter, so the reductions in *Times-News* staffing hasn't surprised anyone.[482] The company has had some rough years, with debt-loaded buys of Howard Publications and Pulitzer Inc. newspapers in the early 2000s, which then hobbled the company in successive recessions.

---

477 When a TN news clerk died two months after being let go from the paper, the newspaper lightly related in a news story that she had "wrapped up" years of work at the paper "two months ago," apparently too embarrassed to say they had laid her off in another round of consolidations. See Wootton, Julie. "*Times-News* Remembers Longtime News Clerk," *Times-News*, Aug. 23, 2015.

478 TN website: "We want to deliver news that helps our readers and our community thrive. That means diving deep to find the information important to you - about your safety, your finances, your well-being. Subscribe and join the thousands who support local journalism in our community."

479 Bird, Kenton. "As the Ecosystem of News Changes, will Journalists Adapt Fast Enough?," *High Country News*, Dec. 24, 2018. Bird studies how newspaper competition in Idaho's Treasure Valley between *The Idaho Statesman* and the renamed *Idaho Press* (Nampa) is changing the face of Idaho journalism. See also Abernathy, Penelope Muse. "The Expanding News Desert," Center for Innovation and Sustainability of Local News Media," University of North Carolina, Nov., 2018.

480 Apparently stung by numerous accounts of bias, many newspapers in the summer of 2018 took to their own pages to defend "Freedom of the Press." Many said they don't favor any political party and that part of their role is to provide "balance" through multiple voices. None admitted more than a perfunctory nod to why so many Americans and surveys show such widespread animosity and perception of bias. See Anonymous (Alison Smith). "Our View: A Free Press Is Not the Enemy," *Times-News*, Aug. 16, 2018, and some 20 comments from readers on the topic.

481 Smith, Alison Gene. "New Voices on the Opinion Page," *Times-News*, Dec. 30, 2018.

482 Dool, Greg. "Three Lee Enterprises Execs Tender Resignations," Folio, Sept. 25, 2018.

Lee stock peaked at $49.00/share in 2004, then plunged to $.39/share in 2009. Its recent trade price was $2.65/share on Nov. 9, 2018, a decline of more than 95 percent. Revenue is down from $674 million annually in 2013 to $567 million in 2017, a decline of more than 15 percent. Employee count is under 3,600, down from 4,500, and earnings per share are off more than 26 percent over five years.[483]

Recent consolidations and staff reductions at other Lee newspapers don't bode well for communities in need of consistent, detailed coverage. Continuing hefty bonuses to top company executives and corporate board members while layoffs at local sites have left many rank-and-file "Lee-ites" disappointed and angry. One result has been unionization efforts and then more layoffs, some of which appear targeted at union supporters.[484] Small cities like Twin Falls, Casper, Wy., and Missoula, Mt., have limited employment options for young journalists, so a laid-off staffer has few options but to leave town, or stay and leave newspapering.

The upshot is an overall decline in the community's regard for its newspaper. But even more disappointing in the community is the overt political and socially liberal and partisan bias of the out-of-town "newbies" in the reporting and editing ranks. Turnover among small-community journalists has been an issue for decades, but readers now see it more clearly than before, as they have multiple sources.

While whole economic sectors continue to expand across the Magic Valley region, the newspaper thus lags both as a business and as a voice of the community. Out-of-touch editing and too-liberal editorials can all be fixed, but the paper either won't, or can't do so. Many observers both in and outside the industry can see the results of this we-know-what's-best-for-you bias in many places like Southern Idaho, but whether the industry and press can change remains undetermined.[485]

---

483 *The Wall Street Journal*, "Lee Enterprises" market research, Nov. 11, 2018.

484 Graham, Andrew. "Wyoming's Largest Newspaper Comes to a Crossroad," WyoFile website, Sept. 11, 2018. See also Edmonds, Rick. "Lee Enterprises Still Losing Advertising Revenue but Stays Profitable with Cuts," The Poynter Institute website, Feb.1, 2018.

485 Nelson, Jacob L. "Journalism Needs an Audience to Survive, But Isn't Sure How to Earn Its Loyalty," The Conversation website, Feb. 7, 2019. The author writes: "As the news industry struggles to survive, many within it increasingly believe their best path forward lies with an improved relationship with the public. However, the steps journalists take to do the work of improving that relationship remains an open question."

19. Health Care

There may be some sectors of the Southern Idaho economy which are growing faster than health care, but not many. It's part of a national trend; as the American population ages, more and more communities are finding that a viable health care sector is an important component of a growing and balanced economy.[486]

It's not just hospitals, clinics, physical therapy offices and dental services, as front line as those are. There's additional growth in a wide variety of health care professions too, from nursing to home health aides and specialists, health related social services and nutrition experts.[487]

Nor is it a phenomenon unique to Idaho or even of the Western states. In almost any mid-size community in America, people will tell you how important the health care sector is, how it's become, in effect, the new employment driving force in replacing manufacturing.

In Bangor, Maine, for example, the health care sector accounts for 45 percent of local wages, $4.50 of every $10, about $619 million in

---

486 Kacik, Alex. "Healthcare Industry to Create 4 Million Jobs by 2026," *Modern Healthcare*, Oct. 27, 2017.

487 U.S. Department of Labor, Bureau of Labor Statistics, Employment Projections, 2016-2026, Oct. 17, 2017, says: "Healthcare support occupations (23.6 percent) and healthcare practitioners and technical occupations (15.3 percent) are projected to be among the fastest growing occupational groups during the 2016-26 projections decade. These two occupational groups – which account for 13 of the 30 fastest growing occupations from 2016 to 2026 – are projected to contribute about one fifth of all new jobs by 2026. Factors such as the aging baby-boom population, longer life expectantcies, and growing rates of chronic conditions will drive continued demand for healthcare services."

2017, up from $440 million in 2003.[488] Think about that. Almost half the wages in that community coming from that one sector of the economy.

Bangor, Maine and Twin Falls, Idaho are both relatively isolated small metropolitan communities. There are some similarities, and some differences. The Bangor area has a larger population (153,000) than Twin Falls-Jerome (104,000), but Bangor's population is older (41.6 median age), than the Twin Falls area (34.1). The Bangor area population also is declining, off 0.3 percent in a year, while Twin Falls' is rising, up 1.2 percent. Housing valuations are about the same (Bangor, $137,000 and declining), while Twin Falls is $147,000 and rising. Bangor's workforce is growing, but slowly at 0.92 percent annually, while Twin Falls' is expanding rapidly, at 2.94 percent annually.

In Bangor, manufacturing jobs constitute about five percent of the workforce; in Twin Falls, manufacturing employment is more than double that, almost 12 percent. The numbers reflect, in Bangor, a decline in wood products and paper manufacturing, and in Twin Falls, an increase in food processing. Median household incomes are about the same, $45,000, in both communities.[489]

Looking at workforce data, health care employment in Bangor constitutes 20 percent of workers or 14,500 employees; in Twin Falls, it's 12.9 percent or 6,000 workers in this field. Health care practitioners are the highest paid group in Bangor, and third highest in Twin Falls; Bangor has a higher ratio of primary care physicians (111/100,000 population) compared to 64/100,000 in the Twin Falls area. Medicaid reimbursements in Bangor were $9,287/enrollee, compared with Twin Falls ($9,032).

A closer look at health care employment in Southern Idaho shows how it's grown in recent years. In 2017, health care employment is up about 25 percent since 2007, led only by manufacturing and retail trade. Statewide, five of the top 10 "hot jobs" are in health care, with median pay levels all over $30/hour. Health care wages have risen an average of 4.7 percent annually for the past 10 years.[490]

A 20-year comparison of employment numbers in Southern Idaho shows that overall employment gain of more than 28 percent, 65,457 in 1997

---

488 Fishell, Darren. "How Bangor Became Even More Dependent on Health Care Jobs," *Bangor Daily News*, Sept. 14, 2018. The author grew up in Maine in the 1950s and 1960s and has watched the traditional Maine industries of logging and paper manufacturing decline, now being replaced by health care and other social service jobs.

489 DataUSA website, 2016, comparison of Bangor, Maine and Twin Falls, Idaho.

490 Roeser, Jan. Idaho Department of Labor, SIEDO Annual Report, Sept. 25, 2018. Median pay in the five health care jobs are: nurses, $30.79/hour; nurse practitioners, $48.90/hour; physicians' assistants, $47.89/hour; pharmacist, $58.42/hour and physical therapists, $36.86/hour.

compared to 88,726 in 2017. Agriculture and manufacturing both had modest declines in the recession from 2009-2014, but health care employment rose every year, recession or not, from 1997 to 2017, from 5,778 to 10,191, a 76 percent increase. Measured this way, it's now about 11.5 percent of the labor market.[491]

These sector trends can be seen additionally in other data. As of 2017, St. Luke's Magic Valley Medical Center, along with satellite facilities in Jerome and the Wood River Valley, had about $770 million in revenue. Combined wages and salaries paid were $350 million, with a combined direct and indirect jobs created at almost 7,600.[492] Average annual wages are more than $43,000, making the jobs competitive with most work in Southern Idaho. Health care may not have been always considered great employment, but today, it's the "new manufacturing" in the Magic Valley.

Health care's growth didn't happen overnight, but now seems firmly established in Southern Idaho's economic profile, enough so that competing entities have begun trying to establish footholds and gain competitive market share. St. Alphonsus Health System, which competes with St. Luke's in the Boise market, has looked at a hospital in Southern Idaho, but hasn't announced any definitive plans.[493] In its analysis, St. Al's said the area's rising population and demographics have been factors in the discussions.

Certainly, the area's strong population growth is propelling consideration of additional health services, and that's likely to remain a key factor for the foreseeable future. Virtually every local health care entity is considering expanding or at entering the Southern Idaho market.[494] Even smaller regional facilities are trying to determine how best to find new opportunities.[495]

---

491 Idaho Department of Labor, Southern Idaho Labor Force, 1997-2017. Email from Roeser, Jan, regional economist, Jan. 22, 2019.

492 Peterson, Steven. 2017 Report on Local and Statewide Impact of St. Luke's Community Hospitals, March 27, 2018. Email statistics from Michelle Bartlome, St. Luke's Regional Medical Center, Jan.10, 2019.

493 Wootton, Julie. "Saint Alphonsus Considering New Hospital in Twin Falls" T*imes-News*, Aug. 14, 2017. Ironically, St. Alphonsus once had the opportunity to buy the private Twin Falls Clinic near City Park, but lost out to St. Luke's in the 1990s in a bidding war. St. Luke's then went on to buy the then-county- owned Twin Falls Hospital, and to build its current Pole Line Road facility at a cost of over $250 million. The proposal was approved in an advisory vote by Twin Falls voters in 2006 by more than 80 percent and the new hospital opened in 2011. Full disclosure: The author, then a business consultant, worked with St Luke's on securing the positive advisory vote.

494 Wootton-Greener, Julie. "'Very Significant Growth:' Magic Valley Health Care Providers Get Creative to Serve Booming Population," *Times-News*, Aug. 12, 2018.

495 Wootton-Greener, Julie. "North Canyon Medical Center Plans to Open a Primary Care and Orthopedics Clinic in Twin Falls," Jan. 10, 2019. The following week, St Luke's also

Two other factors are behind the rush to get into the local health care market. One is the increasing seniors population in Idaho generally and in Southern Idaho in particular. An improving national economy is raising housing values in other nearby states and giving opportunity for people there to "cash out" and move to more less-congested communities in the Intermountain region. People elsewhere are doing just that and Southern Idaho is filling up.

The second factor is the likelihood of Medicaid expansion in Idaho, which would add tens of thousands of Idahoans to "insured" status and thus boost health care access and usage. Voter approval of Medicaid expansion was by over 60 percent in the 2018 general election, so some expansion, perhaps with legislative modifications, seems likely going forward.[496] Health care providers in every specialty view this as more business opportunity.

These two underlying changes send a clear message that more health care services are needed, not just in facilities, but also in dental practices, optometry, surgery centers, immediate care clinics, assisted living and in various specialty services like physical therapy, dialysis centers, CPAP centers (Continuous Positive Airway Pressure, for the treatment of sleep apena) and various laboratories and testing facilities. New businesses in these arenas locally are starting up virtually every month.[497]

Another plus is the opening of a Church of Jesus Christ of Latter-Day Saints temple in 2008 in Twin Falls. That, along with the new St Luke's hospital, has made the area more attractive to Mormon medical professionals in many fields, who say they appreciate the valley's outdoors life, good schools and safe neighborhoods and community setting, reasonable closeness to Salt Lake City and central location in the Intermountain region.

The temple and a new medical facility are big attractors to the upcoming generation of health care providers and their families. Southern Idaho is now an up-and-coming small city with expanding amenities and attractive components for new professional families.[498] Spouses want career opportunities as well and the range of these is expanding. That has turned many spouses from reluctant "go alongs" to enthusiastic partners to living in Southern Idaho.[499]

---

opened a Buhl clinic. See Wootton-Greener, Julie. "Why are 2 Medical Centers Building or Expanding in Buhl,?" *Times-News*, March 30, 2018.

496 Idaho Secretary of State, 2018 Election Results, Medicaid Expansion, 365,000 to 238,000.

497 Wright Physical Therapy, for example, has six locations in the Magic Valley, website, 2018.

498 White, Carolyn, executive director, Magic Valley Arts Council, Interview, Jan. 10, 2019.

499 Anonymous, American Medical Association, "Why Doctors Marry Doctors: Exploring Medical Marriages," Jan. 3, 2019.

The growth since 2011 and St. Luke's Medical Center's dominance has put a squeeze on some medical professionals, whose livelihood depends in part on formal association with the hospital. Some don't like St. Luke's corporate model and have felt the need to move on after experiencing some chafing. Others say they would have liked to remain independent but couldn't afford the costs, including malpractice insurance, office expenses, diagnostics and testing.

Yet, there are quite a few examples of independent local health care facilities and practices. For some, it is the right model, both for some patients and medical professionals.[500]

The competition in the medical field caught the attention of both federal and state regulators, including the Federal Trade Commission and the Idaho Attorney General's office. In 2012, the agencies and St Alphonsus Medical Center filed a lawsuit in U.S. District Court alleging unfair pricing and anti-competitive practices by St. Luke's in the Treasure Valley market, but citing health care competition in Southern Idaho as well; it was alleged that there had been a big shift in doctors' employment locally with many more under St. Luke's wings than previously.[501]

---

500 Wootton, Julie. "Twin Falls' Independent Doctors See Growth as Patients Seek Health Care Options," *Times-News*, July 28, 2017. See also Tripp Family Medicine website, 2019. Here's a summary of health care competitive developments in the 1990s and 200s: "A Health Care History," Times-News, July 28, 2017: "Across the nation, younger physicians and specialists are increasingly being employed by growing hospital systems, which are creating under-one-roof, team-based approaches they say will improve health outcomes and lower costs. But some don't agree with that approach. Several government agencies and medical centers including the Federal Trade Commission and Idaho Attorney General filed an anti-trust lawsuit against the St. Luke's Health System in 2012. Regulators cited the Magic Valley as an example of alleged anti-competitive practices. The complaint also alleged rates at St. Luke's Magic Valley are "among the most expensive in the entire state, with rates rising much faster than the national average." U.S. District Court Judge B. Lynn Winmill ruled in 2014 the St. Luke's broke anti-trust laws when it acquired Saltzer Medical Group, based in Nampa. St. Luke's has provided services to the Magic Valley since 2001, when it began managing practices at the Physician Center, formerly run by the Magic Valley Regional Medical Center. In 2002, the medical center – which was owned by Twin Falls County – bought in-town competitor Twin Falls Clinic and Hospital. Proponents of a merger with St. Luke's launched a series of public forums to gather input. During a May 2006 election, 84 percent of Twin Falls County voters approved selling the medical center to St. Luke's. St. Luke's Health System built a new $242 million hospital facility in Twin Falls, which opened in 2011." Full disclosure: the author was a consultant to St. Luke's on the advisory vote in 2006.

501 By 2009, three years after St Luke's won voter approval to buy the county-owned hospital, an estimated 70 percent of local doctors 90 of 130, were St Luke's employees. See Wootton, "St Luke's CEO Responds to Allegations in Anti-Trust Lawsuit," *Times-News*, March 31, 2013.

Although St. Luke's vigorously defended its practices,[502] the judge ultimately ruled in 2014 against St Luke's and that was upheld by the U.S. Ninth Circuit Court of Appeals in 2015.[503]

Comparing prices can be daunting even for medical financial experts, but under Medicare rules in 2018, hospitals are required to post the cost of various procedures. The formats are not particularly user-friendly, but will likely become more so over time. St Luke's and other area hospitals are trying to comply,[504] and it's likely that local medical price transparency will be more common in the future.[505]

Whether health care can convert effectively from the current fee-for-service pricing model to one based on patient outcomes and wellness is an open question, not just locally but throughout American health care generally. Chief executive officer Dr. David Pate says St. Luke's has about a third of its business premised on the value-outcomes approach, mostly from side agreements with insurers and Medicaid.[506] Typical patients may not see it directly. St. Luke's regional administrator Mike Fenello says shifting the health care model will take time and the transition from fee-for-service standard will likely continue at least for a time.

Health Care for the Needy

Getting people to change a lifetime of negative health behaviors is no easy task and isn't likely to be in the future, no matter the cost savings, as long as someone else is paying. People still go to the hospital emergency room, even when lower cost services are available through clinics and family health service centers.

---

502 Dutton, Audrey. "St Luke's Says It's Trying to Fix System, But Has Critics," *The Idaho Statesman*, Aug. 12, 2013.

503 St. Alphonsus Medical Center, et al., v. St Luke's Health Systems, et. al., Ninth Circuit Court of Appeals, 14-35173, Feb. 10, 2015. See also Dutton, Audrey. "Competitive Edge: What We Know from Hospital trial Documents," *The Idaho Statesman*, May 3, 2015.

504 Wootton-Greener, Julie. "Price Transparency? A New Medicare Rule Requires Hospitals to Post Their Standard Charges Online," *Times-News*, Jan. 6, 2019. See also St Luke's Regional Medical Center website, Price Estimates, 2019.

505 Armour, Stephanie, et. al. "Trump Administration Weighs Publicizing Rates Hospitals and Doctors Negotiate with Insurers,"*The Wall Street Journal*, Mar 6, 2019.

506 Wootton-Greener, Julie. "St Luke's State of the System' Focuses on Trying to Improve Patient Outcomes and Lower Costs," *Times-News*, Aug. 30, 2018. Pate said St. Luke's has about 160,000 Idahoans under the value model.

Also, high health care costs are concentrated in a small percent of users, with roughly five percent of patients accounting for 50 percent of the costs. Many of these patients have multiple and chronic health issues. and would benefit by ongoing wellness intervention, but typically they don't participate in that.[507]

Medical services competition is likely to be a part of the health care issue for many years to come, and so are continuing efforts to reduce costs while maintaining quality. Health care in Southern Idaho is probably better positioned to handle these problems than in many other places, but that doesn't mean they will ever entirely go away.[508]

All in all, Southern Idaho is fortunate indeed to have the quality of health care delivery it has.[509] There are many places in the country, and many more in the world, where our array of health care services and expertise would be loudly welcomed. Despite the continuing issues, we should count our community blessings in this area.

An important part of Southern Idaho's health profile is health care for the needy. There are many local low-income people and their expectations for health care are as high as anyone's. Medical providers have extensive programs for charity[510] and the state, working with counties, has a financial

---

507 Fenello, Mike, regional administrator of St Luke's Regional Medical Center, Interview, Dec. 28, 2018. See also Wootton, Julie. "Local Health Care Experts: The Government Isn't Going to Solve Health Care, but Local Hospitals Can," *Times-News*, Sep. 20, 2017.

508 The U.S. government Medicare hospital ratings comparison does not rank St Luke's Magic Valley separately, but St. Luke's in Boise gets an overall 5-star rating. It is ranked above national averages in three categories, safety of care, readmissions and patient experiences, and "same as the national average" in four: mortality rates, effectiveness of care, timeliness of care and efficient use of medical imaging. See Medicare.gov, "Hospital Compare," 2018. Minidoka Memorial Hospital did not have enough measures for a star rating. The hospital was rated above average in readmissions and patient experience; data was not available in the other five categories. Cassia Regional Hospital had a 4.5-star overall rating, and was above national average in two categories, same as national average in four categories, and information unavailable in one category, safety of care. North Canyon Medical Center, Gooding, had an overall rating of 5 star, for inpatient services. It had an above national average ranking in readmissions and patient experience and the same as national average in mortality rate; information was not available in the other four categories.

509 In 2017, St. Luke's had more than 154,000 hospital visits and over 400,000 clinic visits. Since 2006, it has hired 1,152 new physicians and 77 nurse practitioners and physician assistants. Email from Michelle Bartlome, St. Luke's, Jan. 10, 2019. In 2018, St. Luke's was named in the top 15 health care systems in the country for the fifth straight year by IBM Watson Health. See Kissee, Anita. "St. Luke's Blogs," April 23, 2018.

510 St. Luke's provided more than $25 million in charity care service in 2017. Email from Bartlome, Michelle, St. Luke's, Jan. 10, 2019.

assistance program as well.[511] County commissioners decide on requests and eligibility; if a request is denied, the bill goes back to the health care provider, which often has to write it off as a charity contribution.

Minidoka and Jerome counties have the highest uninsured rates in Southern Idaho at 17 and 16 percent of residents. Across the region, every county has a higher uninsured rate than the state; one in four Hispanic adult males in Idaho 18-34 are uninsured.[512]

Another facility is the Wellness Tree Community Clinic, which relies on donations. One of its physicians is Dr. David McClusky, who is semi-retired from St. Luke's. He sees his role as providing medical care and in training new doctors, interns and residents on how the profession is about putting people ahead of other benefits like status and income.[513] Though he's past 70, he continues as a "teaching doctor" at the new Idaho College of Osteopathic Medicine in Meridian.[514]

Another important community asset for low-income health care is the Family Health Services facility in Twin Falls, which operates clinics throughout the valley. Family Health Services offers a sliding scale of costs for patients for a wide array of family health fields, including obstetrics and gynecology, as well as dental care, mental health and pharmaceutical services.

The region is served by the South Central Public Health District, which covers eight counties. The district handles a wide array of public health issues from infectious diseases to restaurant food preparation inspection, as well as tracking teen pregnancy, the prevalence of smoking and drug use.[515] It's not a state agency, but does receive funding from the state as well as from area counties and the federal government.[516] It is governed by a board of county elected officials, plus public health professionals.

South Central Idaho has a long history of public health readiness, dating back to the 1920s when a meningitis outbreak prompted a quarantine for the

---

511 Russell, Betsy. "Idaho's Catastrophic Health Care Program Sees Jump in Cases," Spokane (Wash.) *Spokesman-Review*, Feb. 8, 2018.

512 Brown, Nathan. "Despite Obamacare Growth, Indigent Expenses Still Big for Counties," *Times-News*, April 20, 2016.

513 McClusky, Dr. David. Talk to Twin Falls Republican Women's Club, Jan. 28, 2019. See also Wellness Tree Community Clinic website, 2019. See also Wootton-Greener, Julie. "I'm Just Changing Direction: Dr. David McClusky, A Third-Generation Magic Valley Physician, Is Closing His Practice," *Times-News*, June 17, 2018.

514 Bowen, Patty. "Idaho's First Medical School Nears Opening Date," *Meridian Press*, April 11, 2018.

515 South Central Public Health District website, 2019.

516 Detailed budgets and the South Central Public Health District's strategic plans are available on its website, 2019.

entire city of Twin Falls.[517] Today, it's easy for people to take sanitation and good public health conditions for granted. Yet, public health isn't given the credit it deserves for decades of health improvements all across America.[518]

In South Central Idaho, several ongoing issues continue to be of concern to public health specialists, including adult obesity, teen pregnancy as well as suicide prevention and cancer detection and treatment.[519] Overall, Twin Falls County ranks about in the middle (20th of 44 counties) for overall health outcomes, as do Cassia (24th) and Jerome (28th) counties. Blaine County ranks 3rd while the more rural Magic Valley counties rank lower.[520]

Looking ahead, we're likely to see health improvements in all these areas. Public health issues have become more important in recent years and the consistency of available data has improved as well, trends we would expect to see continue.

---

517 South Central Public Health District website, "Idaho's Public Health Efforts," 2019.

518 Center for Disease Control website, "Ten Great Public Health Achievements - United States, 1900-1999," 2019. American life expectancy was extended by 30 years in the 20th Century, 25 of which was due to public health improvements.

519 South Central Public Health District website, "Community Health Improvement Plan," 2019.

520 Robert Wood Johnson Foundation website, "2016 County Health Rankings - Idaho."

20. Demographics & Families

One feature of Southern Idaho's population is the relatively large percent of young people.[521] As in other states, it's a result of having more young people who, not surprisingly, have the highest rates of childbirth. But if we have more young people here, we also have fewer high-end wage earners as people age.

Compared to both Idaho and the nation, Southern Idaho has a higher proportion of people under 19, almost 30 percent of the population. We're younger here by two years than the state and almost four years younger than the country, with a median age in Southern Idaho of 34.1 years, compared to Idaho's 36.1 years and 37.9 years for the nation.[522]

Yet, with workers, ages 45-64, Southern Idaho lags behind both the state and the nation in wages. The region's seniors, those over 65, constitute about 14 percent of the population, near the state and national averages.[523] This group is likely to increase in the years ahead, as the state's reputation as a retirement-friendly location grows.

One reason for that growth is the relatively lower housing costs. The median property value for the Twin Falls/Jerome micropolitan statistical area is $147,200, compared to $189,400 for Idaho as a whole and $205,000 for the nation. That makes the area attractive to seniors

---

521 Idaho ranks 9th overall in birth rates, at 13.9 births/1,000 population. Utah is first at 17.6; Other high-ranking states include Texas, Louisiana and Oklahoma. The national rate is 12.5. See Friedman, Lauren. "Here Are The States Where People Are Having the Most Babies," *Business Insider*, May 29, 2014.

522 DataUSA, 2016.

523 Roeser, Jan. "Siedo Annual Summit," Sept. 25, 2018. Slides 3, 4.

moving here from elsewhere where they can sell a prior residence and pocket some equity difference in a Southern Idaho purchase.[524]

Similarly, property taxes are lower here compared to either Idaho or the nation. Although they may seem high because they come in a single annual notice that gets people's attention, only 8.6 percent of Twin Falls/Jerome homes have property taxes of more than $3,000 annually, compared to 11.2 percent of Idahoans overall and a large 40 percent of American residences.[525]

Among those Idahoans over 55 but still in the workforce, almost 60 percent are in management, with office occupations among the highest group, but also including trucking and materials handling. That's not surprising. As people age, they gain experience but may also lose physical strength. As experienced workers, they often make good managers; they know the ropes, their way around, in the workplace. Anyone who has ever worked with a group knows how valuable these older workers can be if they're treated with respect and attention, something which younger managers often need to learn.

Idaho workers tend to be younger in fields requiring more physical activity, like food service, health care support and law enforcement.[526] Again, no surprise there.

In education levels, Idaho has traditionally trailed the nation. In STEM jobs (Science, Technology, Engineering, Mathematics), Idaho is projected to catch up with solid growth in the next decade.[527] Still, there's plenty of evidence, real and anecdotal, that bigger places lure away many young Idahoans, many of them not likely to return.[528]

It's been widely observed that much of rural America is emptying out of young people who migrate after high school or college to larger places with more employment.[529] Certainly some of that is related to relatively lower wages in rural communities. But a piece of Idaho good news is that from 1991 to 2017, Idaho's wage growth has grown by more than 105 percent, surpassing the national increase of 80 percent. Most of the gain has occurred since 2009, reflecting the overall pattern of Idaho on a number of fronts.[530]

---

524 DataUSA.com has comparison statistics for cities, counties and micropolitan areas for the United States. The data here is from 2016.

525 DataUSA, 2016.

526 Roeser, Slide 15.

527 Roeser. Jan. Slide 20.

528 Kyle, Zach. "Why Educated Millennials Are Leaving Idaho," *The Idaho Statesman*, Mar. 6, 2016.

529 Anonymous. "Rural America is Losing Young People - Consequences and Solutions," Wharton Public Policy Initiative website, March 23, 2018.

530 Roeser, Jan. Slide 22.

It's an unusual story which cuts against the norms of the Magic Valley, where young people scurry away to college, leave the area and rarely return immediately. They head for bigger places with more neon and things to do in the evenings. But as they age, they may think more about the place they were raised, its pluses and minuses.

Yep, for some, you can go home again. That's what's happened to Rudy and Samantha Ashenbrener, both of whom grew up in Twin Falls and have returned to settle and raise a family. It didn't hurt that both had long family histories in the community. Rudy's grandfather, also named Rudy, was a standout athlete at the University of Idaho and his father, Tom, owns a local cooking store started by the grandfather on Main Street and serves on a local bank board.

Rudy is on the board of the Urban Renewal Agency. He says it's exciting to be in a community that welcomes his input. "It's easier to do in Twin," Rudy says, "to get involved with the community, [to] join specific boards and make the decisions to shape the community. Whereas in Boise – it's so big that it's so much harder."[531] So when the opportunity came to return to Twin Falls, the next generation took it.

Thus is one generation's sense of place transferred to children and then grandchildren. Young people trying to decide how to fit into the world sometimes find familiarity and opportunity and the combination pulls them home.

It's generally known that people in the West are more mobile than elsewhere. The region, after all, was settled by people on the move from elsewhere in America and from overseas, mostly from Europe.

That's reflected in the move in-move out data from census data over time. The typical American today lives less than 20 miles from his or her mother. Family support across generations is a main reason, along with income and education. The more of both, the more likely it is for people to live farther from other family members.

The data also shows that women are more likely to be affected by these patterns. Women have long been the unpaid family caregivers, both up and down generationally. But with more women taking jobs in the workforce in recent generations, family ties for child care and elder care have become more important.

Southern Idaho has a bit higher poverty rate than elsewhere; it's 15.9 percent in the region, compared to 14.1 percent for the state and 14.0 percent for the nation. Also, we have more women in poverty than either the state or

531 Barnhill, Frankie. "Twin Falls Aims for Sustainable Growth as Boise Booms," Boise State Public Radio, June 26, 2018.

nation, 23.5 percent of women 18-44, compared to 13.7 percent for Idaho and 23.1 percent for the nation.[532]

People in the West may be more mobile, but for those with incomes of less than $30,000, they're more likely to live close by family, for both mutual support and family presence. Median household incomes in Southern Idaho are indeed less than elsewhere. For the Twin Falls/Jerome micropolitan area, median household income is $45,297, compared to $51,807 for Idaho as a whole and $57,617 for the nation.[533] In Southern Idaho, 80 percent of households earn less than $75,000 annually, and 33 percent are under $30,000.[534]

To economists, these patterns look like a series of tradeoffs and payments across generations, with some differences among people of different heritage. Hispanic-Americans rely more on generational care; those of European background rely more on financial support, either for day care or elder care, or both.[535] There seems to be stronger family ties among people in Southern Idaho, particularly among churchgoers and our rapidly growing Hispanic population, which is likely to increase in the years ahead.[536]

Still, we're more of European ethnic stock than the nation, less than Idaho. Southern Idaho remains predominately white, including Hispanics, at 77.2 percent, compared to 82.3 percent for Idaho and 61.1 percent for the nation.[537]

Yet, we're more Hispanic in cultural heritage than either Idaho or the U.S. with 19.2 percent of Hispanic heritage, compared to 12.3 percent in Idaho and 17.8 percent of the nation. In citizenship, we're slightly lower in Southern Idaho at 92.5 percent, compared to 96.3 percent for Idaho and 93 percent for the nation.[538]

Non-English speaking residents often need special services to navigate American society, from schools to courts, work to shopping. In Southern Idaho, 16.8 percent are non-English speaking, compared to 10.8 percent in Idaho and 14.0 percent in the nation. Statewide, less than 10 percent of Idaho

532 DataUSA, 2016.

533 DataUSA, 2016.

534 Movoto.com website, Idaho, 2018 survey.

535 Bui, Quotcrung and Miller, Claire. "The Typical American Live only 18 Miles from Mom," *The New York Times*, Dec. 23, 2015.

536 Idaho's Hispanic population has increased almost 25 percent since 2010 and is estimated now at 219,000. The rate of population growth is estimated at over 3 percent per year, twice that of non-Hispanics. Hispanics are also moving into better paying jobs and have an estimated buying power if about $4.5 billion in the state. See Foy, Nicole. "Idaho's Hispanic Population, Economic Impact Continues to Grow," *Idaho Press*, Jan. 4, 2019.

537 DataUSA, 2016.

538 DataUSA, 2016.

residents are non-citizens, with Southern Idaho at 92.8 percent U.S. citizens, compared to 96.4 percent of Idahoans and 93 percent of the nation.[539]

That desire for stronger family ties is reflected in the demographics of the area and how the profiles are changing. People are moving here from elsewhere, for the jobs and the opportunities, and also for the remembrance and familiarity to what they knew in the past. For Samantha Ashenbrener, the return to Southern Idaho with her husband and young son has provided them with family closeness and, not incidentally, some flexibility for their professional lives.[540]

Younger people in their 20s and 30s reflect this pattern. There's Haley, from the rural Central Valley of California, with its vast agricultural fields; Southern Idaho reminds her of home. There's Mandi, from a rural county in Montana whose folks still live there; she located to the Magic Valley area with her husband, who is from Kimberly. She'd like to be closer to her family someday. For now, Southern Idaho is fine. There's Camille, who's expecting she and her husband's first child, a boy, about which they are very excited. Thus does one generation follow another.

They reflect demographic change in the area and diversity of origin, if not of race, or ethnicity, in a community which accepts them. They feel part of the place, at home here. Diversity is often a positive community trait, but if the elasticity of differences is stretched too far, it may simply snap.

That is what has happened in much of America over race, ethnicity, gender, faith, education, money, politics, which side of town you're from, whatever. It is as if the pull of identity politics is overcoming the elasticity of the melting pot which holds the nation together.[541] It used to be we were one people, "one nation, under God, indivisible," but not so much now.

---

539 DataUSA, 2016.

540 Ashenbrener, Samantha. Briefcase 2 Suitcase website, Feb 1, 2019. "I was born and raised in Twin Falls, Idaho. The crazy thing is, this is where I have ended up living! Life does come full circle, and while I have lived in San Diego, Montana, France and Spain, my husband Rudy's job eventually brought us back to Twin Falls. At first we were nervous about the move back to our hometown (because we loved our other location), but after having a baby and living near not one but BOTH sets of grandparents, I couldn't imagine being anywhere better. Built in babysitters are the best! This allows my husband and I plenty of time for date nights and social events, which is amazing!" See also, Barnhill, Frankie. "Our Changing Idaho: Twin Falls for Sustainable Growth As Boise Booms," Boise State Public Radio, June 26, 2018.

541 Yeats, W.B. The Second Coming, 1919. "Things fall apart; the centre cannot hold/ Mere anarchy is loosed upon the world, /The blood-dimmed tide is loosed, /and everywhere the ceremony of innocence is lost /The best lack all conviction, /while the worst are filled with passionate intensity." See also, Tabor, Nick. "No Slouch," *The Paris Review*, April 7, 2015.

Southern Idaho still feels like that melting pot, familiar, comfortable, easier than many places in which to live and thrive. We are held together partly by what Lincoln called the "mystic chords of memory"[542] which bind us together from our common heritage and shared values.

Idaho's population of "move in" Californians has tripled since 1980, due to the lower costs of living and expanding economy here, and is now about 10 percent of the "moved from" population, closely followed by Oregon, Washington and Utah, each just less than 10 percent.

Most other immigrants to Idaho come from the Midwest and some from the South; relatively few from the Northeast or Mid-Atlantic regions. Nearly 60 percent of Idahoans stay within the state, about the same as nationally, and of those who leave Idaho, most are concentrated in nearby Western states. "It's pretty rare to run into a native of Idaho outside the West."[543]

When you ask people what they like or dislike about Southern Idaho, you sometimes get the same answer: Southern Idaho? It's comfortable, quaint, agricultural, parochial, not very diverse, mostly white, isolated. Lots of moms with kids. Lots of seniors. Lots of people going to and from church on Sundays.

Some folks like it that way. Others want to change it into something they're more comfortable with. Something more like where they came from. More urban, more sophisticated, more diverse, less isolated.[544]

The nation may seem like it is spinning further and further into tribalism, fear, resentment. Perhaps that is why Southern Idaho seems so disconnected from the rest of the state and even more so from the nation. Many folks want stability, a less frenetic life, more peace and quiet, and they are finding it in this agricultural valley of the Intermountain West.

---

542 Lincoln, Abraham, First Inaugural Address, March 4, 1861. "The mystic chords of memory, stretching from every battle-field, and patriot grave, to every living heart and hearth-stone, all over this broad land, will yet swell the chorus of the Union, when again touched, as surely they will be, by the better angels of our nature."

543 Aisch, Gregor, et. al., "Where We Came from and Where We Went, State by State," *The New York Times*, Aug. 19, 2014.

544 Kauffman, Gretel. "Stephen Hartgen: A Growing Twin Falls Will Retain Conservative Influence and Values," *Times-News*, Jan. 3, 2019. See also Kennison, Heather. "Syd Havard: It's Time for Diverse Leadership," *Times-News*, Jan. 3, 2019.

21. State & Local Government

Idaho is blessed in many ways when it comes to state governmental structure and practices and these in turn have been of particular benefit to Southern Idaho. It's a broad topic, so we'll discuss just a few specifics here, leaving aside a recitation of civics, agency structure and federal relations, some of the latter which having been already explored in an earlier chapter.

Balanced budget and fiscal prudence. Idaho's Constitution requires an annual balanced budget, and unlike many states, Idaho actually adjusts both spending and revenue to achieve that objective at the turn of new budgeting years on July 1 annually.[545] This helps make for responsible and prudent collection of revenue and expenditure of public funds.

Two-thirds vote required for bond approvals. This provision of the Idaho Constitution is considered too strict by some, who want a lower standard which would be easier to meet.[546] But it reflects the

545 Idaho Constitution, Article VII, Sect. 11, reads: "EXPENDITURE NOT TO EXCEED APPROPRIATION. No appropriation shall be made, nor any expenditure authorized by the legislature, whereby the expenditure of the state during any fiscal year shall exceed the total tax then provided for by law."

546 Idaho Constitution, Article VIII, Sect. 3, reads "No county, city, board of education, or school district, or other subdivision of the state, shall incur any indebtedness, or liability, in any manner, or for any purpose, exceeding in that year, the income and revenue provided for it for such year, without the assent of two-thirds of the qualified electors thereof voting at an election to be held for that purpose."

overall emphasis on prudent fiscal management, particularly when it comes to public debt.[547]

School bond votes generally pass despite the two-thirds threshold and Idaho does allow a lower percentage for some supplemental levies. In the Southern Idaho region, school levies generally succeed, but proponents sometimes need to prune the dollar amount and ask the voters more than once. Taxpayers seem to have a good idea of what they can afford and seem reluctant to go beyond that, particularly in communities with less valuation.[548]

Senate Finance & House Appropriations Committees meet jointly. In many states, proposed budgets are "ping-ponged" back and forth from House to Senate and visa-versa and budget line items are routinely "horse traded." Idaho uses a joint 20-member committee, ten from each body, which hears and votes on agency budgeting proposals. These then go to the main bodies for consideration; most are approved, although hiccups can occur on specifics.

The process doesn't eliminate the give and take of budget allocations, but places it rather in a more defined and transparent process. It also gives extra clout to Joint Finance & Appropriations Committee (JFAC) members who present the individual appropriations measures in the floor debates. Stability in JFAC positions and leadership adds to the credibility of the committee's recommendations.

As key budgeting dates are annually established early in both the House and Senate, the appropriations process keeps the calendar schedule regular and thus assures that most sessions finish by the end of March. Time spent beyond that is considered unwarranted and with the budgeting process pretty much done, there's no need for the Legislature to "cover the clock" before adjourning for the year.

Longevity of legislative leaders. As a state with long-standing dominance by the Republican Party, Idaho's political leadership is more or less reflective of the state's conservative governance principles. Southern Idaho has long contributed to stable legislative leadership through long-serving House and Senate members, who are often in committee chair positions and/or leadership. The Southern Idaho region benefits as these

---

547 Miller, Nick. "School Financing and the Supermajority Requirement," *Idaho Business Review*, Sept. 20, 2017. The article notes that from 2011 to 2017, about half of the bonds votes for Idaho school construction were approved (25 of 53) and the percent would be higher if multiple attempts are excluded. That suggests voters are generally happy with provision and that an attempt to reduce it "would not be a sure thing," the article states. See also, Hartgen, Stephen. "Amendments Would Sidestep Voter Debt Approval," *Times-News*, Oct. 13, 2010.

548 Wootton-Greener, Julie. "After 3 Failed Bond Attempts, Shoshone School District Starting from Scratch," *Times-News*, Sept. 16, 2018.

individuals gain both seniority and experience. Projecting ahead, there's no reason to think Southern Idaho would lose any influence in the coming generation of the Legislature's political leadership.[549]

Yet, no one individual ever strides over the whole, or not for very long. Idaho is an egalitarian state with many civic-minded citizens who put themselves forward for public service, from governor to local government entities. There are always tasks ahead and people are needed to help. It is truly a place, to paraphrase President John F. Kennedy, where folks ask what they can do for their state and take up public roles to make the state better, for our children and grandchildren, and theirs' yet unborn.

Idaho Democrats have not had parity in the Idaho legislature for many years and since 1990 have not won any statewide contest except for Superintendent of Public Instruction. Republicans control more than a veto-proof majority in both houses. This pattern of one-party dominance is the norm in American state politics today and seems unlikely to change in the foreseeable future.[550] Democratic leaders in Idaho, although their caucuses are small, are organized and well-led but their influence remains limited on most votes.[551]

A Citizen Legislature. Idaho's citizen legislature members all serve two-year terms and because they are in session only about three months a year, they are mostly home in their own districts at other times, listening to

549 Kauffman, Gretel. "Stephen Hartgen: A Growing Twin Falls Will Retain Conservative Influence and Values," *Times-News,* Jan. 5, 2019. The Idaho Blue Book lists among long-serving (five or more terms) recent Southern Idaho legislators: Sens. John Barker, 1967-1984; Bert Brackett, 2007-present; Dean Cameron, 1991-2015; Denton Darrington, 1983-2012; John V. Evans, 1953-1958, 1967-1974; Lee Heider, 2011-current; Joyce McRoberts, 1989-1996; Laird Noh, 1981-2004; Jim Patrick, 2013-current; Michelle Stennett, 2011-current; Reps. Maxine Bell, 1989-2018; Scott Bedke, 2001-current; Ronald Black, 1987-1998; Sharon Block, 2001-2012; Celia Gould, 1987-2002; Stephen Hartgen, 2009-2018; Jim Kempton, 1991-2001; Mack Neibaur, 1977-1990; Bruce Newcomb, 1987-2006 and Fred Wood, 2006-current. With the 2019 session underway, Sens. Brackett, Heider, Patrick, and Stennett all held committee or leadership posts in the Senate, with Kelley Anton, R-Rupert, moving to a new role as Senate Republican Caucus chair. On the House side, Speaker of the House Scott Bedke, R-Oakley, is in his fourth term as Speaker, and Rep. Fred Wood chairs the Health & Welfare Committee; Megan Blanksma, R-Hammett, is the new Majority Caucus chair; Lance Clow, R-Twin Falls, R-Twin Falls, is the new chair of the House Education Committee and Clark Kauffman takes a seat on the JFAC committee after being vice-chair of Revenue & Taxation.

550 Greenblatt, Alan. "All or Nothing: In Most States These Days, One Party Holds All The Levers of Power," *Governing*, January, 2019.

551 Idaho Legislature website. The 2019 Idaho Legislature has a 28 to 7 Republican supermajority in the Senate and a 56 to 14 margin in the House. All of the state's constitutional officers were Republican.

constituents and attending legislative-related meetings.[552] This gives them better feel for ongoing local issues than if they were in Boise full time without regular face-to-face contacts with folks back home.[553]

Both bodies experience considerable turnover from one term to the next. There were 30 new House members in the 2013-14 term, and 20 in the 2019-20 term, out of 70. It's uncommon for members to serve beyond five or six terms, since many are in their 60s and 70s when they start. Almost all retire before age 80.

This turnover feature keeps fresh perspectives constantly being added to the mix of people, which gives Idaho's legislative bodies ongoing current points of contact with constituents.

Another plus of the turnover is that Legislative leadership changes occur regularly. Almost no one leads either body for very long and the passage of many bills requires broad consensus and drafting to secure winning margins. There have been very few long-term "bosses" in Idaho's legislative leadership in either body or either party.[554]

Legislative Rules Review. Idaho is one of only a few states in which agency rules arising from statutes are reviewed formally by legislators. Agencies submit proposed rules to implement laws prior to each session and then these are heard in committees much like proposed statutory changes. Most states, as well as the U.S. Congress, have no such "second look" by elected representatives to make sure proposed rules are in conformance with the law's intent.

The rules review process has been in place in various forms for years, and in 1990, the Idaho Supreme Court, in a split decision, affirmed the power of the Legislature to review agency rules, but with limitations.[555] In 2016, Idaho voters approved a constitutional amendment affirming the review power.[556]

---

552 The Twin Falls Chamber of Commerce Public Affairs Committee conducts a weekly conference call with area legislators during the session. Legislators also hold occasional "town hall" meetings where citizens can ask questions and engage their representatives on any issue. Twin Falls Chamber website, 2019.

553 Squire, Peverill and Moncrief, Gary. *State Legislatures Today: Politics Under the Domes*, Rl Publishers, 2015.

554 In the House, Rep. Bruce Newcomb served 10 years as Speaker, 1997-2006; Rep. Lawerence Denney, 2007-2012; and Rep. Scott Bedke, 2013-present. See also, Hartgen, Stephen." Notes on the Legislature," *Journey West: A Memoir of Journalism and Politics*, Ridenbaugh Press, Carlton, OR, 2014.

555 *Mead v. Arnell*, 741 P2nd 410 (Idaho, 1990). The "Mead" in the case was longtime Southern Idaho community leader David Mead, then chairman of the Idaho Board of Health & Welfare.

556 Idaho Secretary of State, 2016 Constitutional Amendment HJR 5 approved on a 55.5 to 44.5 percent vote. The language reads: "Article III, Sect. 29: LEGISLATIVE RESPONSE TO ADMINISTRATIVE RULES. The legislature may review any administrative rule to

The rules review process takes several weeks at the start of every legislative session, but the time spent is considered well worth the effort and sends a clear message that agency rules will get close scrutiny.

Fiscal conservatism, lack of corruption. Many states have experienced runaway costs in recent years by failing to restrain spending. Many of the entreaties to legislative bodies involve either tax breaks for various parties, or adding benefits in such areas as pensions and workforce retention. Idaho has some of this, as the state is growing in both population and gross domestic product, so increases in annual budgets are to be expected, if critiqued in some quarters.[557]

Still, the state generally avoids debt unless there is a clear revenue stream to cover it, as with highway construction anticipation notes, supported by payments from federal gasoline taxes.[558] Thus, the state is often listed in the top group when it comes to low debt to cash flow ratios.[559]

This fiscal prudence is reinforced by a culture of honesty, review of agency operations audits,[560] and established purchasing procedures. Individual conflicts of interest are required to be disclosed by Senate and House rules and legislators get frequent reminders on how disclosure is a critical feature of transparency.[561] Southern Idaho legislators are well aware of these issues; it has been many years, perhaps decades, since allegations of conflict of interest among local legislators has been raised.

---

ensure it is consistent with the legislative intent of the statute that the rule was written to interpret, prescribe, implement or enforce. After that review, the legislature may approve or reject, in whole or in part, any rule as provided by law. Legislative approval or rejection of a rule is not subject to gubernatorial veto under section 10, article IV, of the constitution of the state of Idaho."

557 Idaho Legislature website, Fiscal Facts, 2018. From 2011 to 2017, Idaho's economy grew at a 3.4 percent annual rate, third fastest in the nation. The Idaho Freedom Foundation, a conservative think tank, is a frequent critic of Idaho's government spending. See Birnbaum, Fred. "Five Things to Know about Gov. Little's First Budget," IFF website, Jan. 14, 2019.

558 Engineering News Record, (ENR) website. "Idaho's Garvee Program Completes a Decade of Highway Innovations," Oct 20, 2016.

559 Laffer, Arthur B., et. al. *Rich States, Poor States*. 2018. Idaho ranks number 2 in the nation in economic outlook and number 5 for a low debt service to revenues ratio of 4.5 percent.

560 Idaho Legislature, Audits Division, website, 2019.

561 Idaho House Rule 38 states in part: "A member has the right to vote upon all questions before the House and to participate in the business of the House and its committees and, in so doing, the member is presumed to act in good faith and in the public interest. If a member's personal interest in the issue under consideration conflicts with the public's interest, the member's legislative activities can be subject to limitations, unless such conflicts are disclosed to the presiding officer or to the body. Upon disclosure of any such conflict, the member may vote upon any question or issue to which the conflict relates, unless the member requests to be excused."

Human nature being what it is and the potential for avarice and self-benefitting being constants in government affairs,[562] there have been cases of self-promotion and the "carrying" of bills for financial supporters[563] and personal business interests, but these are relatively rare and usually get at least some media attention.[564]

Internal Party Tensions. Like other one-party dominant states, Idaho exhibits some tensions between competing "wings" of the Republican Party. The common-sense, practical, problem-solving approach is the dominant one, but a more ideological focus prevails among some legislators. This group has little traction among Southern Idaho representatives.

Tensions do arise, however, in the Legislature's relationship with the Idaho Republic Party, whose central committee seems dominated at this time by a more ideological perspective. Resolutions and rules with a decidedly ideological purity intent, including a loyalty oath declaration to the party platform,[565] come up from time to time and these have some resonance among the more ideological legislators.[566] Southern Idaho representatives generally fall on the practical side of governance, but wisely keep an eye on issues which are driven by ideological purity, such as Second Amendment concerns and firearms regulation generally.[567]

All in all, the state seems to reflect a conservative but non-ideological perspective, in proposed legislation. "Hot button" issues come up from time to time, usually brought by the ideologically-inclined legislators, but the overall tone is similar to Southern Idaho's overall patterns of life and governance which befits a fiscally-prudent, down-to-earth and stable representative republic. Overall, it's a model that would benefit other states.

---

562 Former President John Adams to John Taylor, 17 December, 1814, National Archives, Founders Online website, 2019: "It is in vain to Say that Democracy is less vain, less proud, less selfish, less ambitious or less avaricious than Aristocracy or Monarchy. It is not true in Fact and nowhere appears in history. Those Passions are the same in all Men under all forms of Simple Government, and when unchecked, produce the same Effects of Fraud Violence and Cruelty. When clear Prospects are opened before Vanity, Pride, Avarice or Ambition, for their easy gratification, it is hard for the most considerate Philosophers and the most conscientious Moralists to resist the temptation. Individuals have conquered themselves, Nations and large Bodies of Men, never."

563 Russell, Betsy. "E. Idaho Senator Introduced Bill to Benefit Campaign Donor, Collection Agencies," *Idaho Press Tribune,* May 10, 2018. The senator was defeated in the May, 2018 primary.

564 Graf, Gregory. "Nate Email Scandal Rocks East Idaho," Idaho Conservative website, May 14, 2018. Rep. Ron Nate was defeated in the May primary.

565 Idaho Republican Party website, 2019 Rules, Article XIII.

566 Cook, Holly. "Resolutions Debrief," Idaho Conservatives website, Jan. 10, 2019.

567 Idaho Second Amendment Alliance website, 2019.

Cities. Despite restrictions on how much authority Idaho cities have under state law, local municipal governments in Southern Idaho operate with considerable initiative and independence. One example is how Twin Falls utilized a 1988 law to leverage economic development efforts through urban renewal.

A long period of economic stagnation and flat population in the 1980s in Idaho prompted the Legislature to enact new laws to encourage economic growth. Following passage of the Local Economic Development Act,[568] Twin Falls was one of the first communities in the state to see the new law's potential, using the act in the expansion of Universal Frozen Foods, later ConAgra and now Lamb-Weston. The project allowed for a 25-year urban renewal district at a cost of $1.6 million.[569]

That was followed by other projects, including expansion of Henningson Cold Storage, a frozen French fries storage facility adjacent to Universal Frozen Foods; Clear Shield National,[570] a plastic company which made plastic tableware for fast-food restaurants; Seastrom Manufacturing (1994), formerly a California company which makes precision machine parts[571] and Independent Meat Company, a local livestock processing plant. All these projects, and a host of others, resulted in jobs creation and expansion and through them, the city became known as a versatile player in the Idaho manufacturing sector.[572]

An additional impetus for use of the urban renewal law, and a creative way to implement it, came out of the Dell Computer call center project in 2001. The company had its eye on a vacant Albertson's store at Pole Line Road and Blue Lakes Blvd, but it wasn't in an urban renewal district at the time. The city saw a way to make it work by extending a curb-to-curb designation strip some two miles from the downtown out Blue Lakes Blvd. to encompass the proposed new call center. The "spaghetti" strip designation met state law criteria at the time and resulted in Dell coming to the valley center employing more than 500 people with an annual economic impact estimated at more than $27 million.[573]

---

568 Idaho Code, 59-2901.

569 McAlinden, David. Interview, Jan. 3, 2019. McAlinden was the city's economic development director at the time.

570 The author was one member of a city delegation which visited the Clear Shield National headquarters near Chicago, Ill. Upon comparing Idaho's competitive electric rates, the company CEO told the group that Twin Falls would be their new Western expansion site, which occurred in 1998, adding about 85 new jobs in plastics remolding.

571 Seastrom Manufacturing website, 2018.

572 BusinessPlus website, 2018. From 1987 to 2011, this leveraging approach added more than 2,000 jobs to the local economy and over $1 billion in business investment.

573 McAlinden interview. See also BusinessPlusinc.org website, 2018.

The upshot of these and other initiatives has been a broad increase in economic investment, output and overall growth throughout the area as other municipalities, particularly Jerome and Burley, have developed and used the urban renewal law as well.[574] Still, urban renewal is a subject which may pit local officials against state consistency and investment policy. In 2019, for example, legislators considered a change which would require a public vote, and passage with over 55 percent, of public projects and buildings.[575]

With that has come some push-pull with the state, which predates virtually every municipality in the Southern Idaho region. This "home rule"[576] tension has generally played out with mutual respect, but there have been instances in which the municipalities feel they're under the state's thumb.

We see some of this push for independence from state control in the ongoing discussion of local option taxation. As a central economic hub for the area, Twin Falls experiences a workday influx of people from all across the region. City officials have long felt that the strain on roads, police and other municipal services warrants some sort of equity funding from the "outsiders." Not surprisingly, such an "outsiders fee" has been resisted by residents from outside the city, who say such a tax or fee amounts to "taxation without representation"[577] and would lead inevitably to "tax wars" among various municipal governments vying for purchasing dollars.

Local option taxation by municipalities is used in other states, including Colorado and Arizona where it creates a patchwork of tax rates across communities. Citizens often don't know specifically how much the tax is, or how it is used, but they pay it nonetheless.

In Idaho, a few resort communities are allowed to impose local sales tax markups on locally-purchased goods on the theory that recreational communities need additional revenue to handle tourism's influxes of visitors. It's a major source of income for some cities, such as Ketchum.[578] The issue

574 Kennison, Heather. "URA Will Have To Wait On Boundary Adjustment," *Times-News*, Jan. 16, 2019. Changes in the urban renewal law have tightened the standards for creating and administering urban renewal districts.

575 Carmel, Margaret. "Boise Opposes Bill That Would Require Urban Renewal Vote," *Idaho Press*, March 1, 2019.

576 The "Home Rule" concept, also known as the Dillon Rule after the 19th century judge who propounded it, gives states the authority to set the parameters for municipal governmental actions. Idaho is considered a "modified" home rule state, meaning the state gives municipalities some control of their own affairs, but within limits. See Russell, Jon & Bostrom, Aaron. "Federalism, Dillon Rule & Home Rule," White Paper, American City County Exchange website, 2016.

577 The Declaration of Independence specifically accuses England and King George III of "imposing taxes on us without our consent."

578 Ketchum's revenue from local option sales tax (3 percent on room rentals, 2 percent on other sales, except groceries and autos), has varied somewhat over the years, but is now

has been around for many years and the desire for more tax revenue hasn't noticeably been abated by the growth already occurring in Southern Idaho.[579]

The underlying issue seems more about the tension between local government and the state than the revenue itself. Twin Falls assessed valuations have risen sharply in recent years and there are many who feel tax rate increases on sales would only drive business and retail trade away and stifle further growth.

The local option debate seems likely to continue indefinitely. The Legislature's House Revenue & Taxation Committee, in which tax proposals must originate, has 18 members, of which no more than a half dozen seemed likely to approve such a measure.[580] To many members, the proposal seemed yet another effort to raise people's taxes, particularly when the state is growing nicely. Tax increases in such a climate struck many as counter-productive, given Idaho's strong growth rate,[581] and low tax, business-friendly reputation.

Another arena in which the Idaho state and municipal governments are sometimes in conflict is over specific ordinances or proposed resolutions dealing with topics not normally on municipal agendas. Voters in Hailey, for example, approved an ordinance allowing medical marijuana in 2008, but it was struck down by the courts the following year as being contrary to Idaho law and constitution.

In 2016, anticipating an effort by environmentalists to ban plastic bags the Idaho Legislature preemptively outlawed municipal ordinances from imposing restrictions on plastic bags and other "auxiliary containers."[582]

Idaho law also has premptions with respect to firearms. Local governments, for example, cannot impose stricter regulation on permits to carry a concealed weapon, (Idaho Code 46-1008), nor can permit applicants

---

(2017-18) at over $2 million annually. See Ketchum City website, 2018.The adjacent city of Sun Valley raised its local option tax from 1 to 2 percent on building materials" effective **?an. 1?**, 2019. See City of Sun Valley website, 2019.

579 The author has consistently opposed local option sales tax expansion. See Brown, Nathan. "Should Idaho Expand Local Option Taxing Beyond Resort Cities,?" Intermountain Media Pulse, Jan. 15, 2017.

580 The author served on the House Revenue & Taxation Committee from 2013 to 2018. His "nose count" in the committee has been that no more a third of the members would approve local option taxing authority.

581 U.S. Census, "Idaho is Nation's Fastest Growing State, Census Bureau Reports," Dec. 20, 2017, at 2.2 percent per year.

582 Idaho Legislature, HB 372, 2016 session. The measure passed with near unanimous Republican support and unanimous opposition from Democrats. See also "State & Local Plastic Bag legislation," National Conference of State Legislatures, May 17, 2018, and Kauffman, Rep. Clark. "Bag Ban Bill is About Business, Not Local Control," *Times-News*, Feb. 18, 2016.

be required to provide any information beyond what's required in Idaho Code 18-3302 on concealed weapon permits.[583] Idaho law (IC 55-2605) specifically prohibits local governments from imposing restrictions on gun clubs and shooting ranges.[584]

And in 2017, the Twin Falls City Council spent hours discussing a proposed resolution to declare the city a "welcoming" place; the resolution was watered down to read "neighborly community," but still elicited strong response, both pro and con.[585] In 2018, another resolution to condemn family separations at the U.S. borders also elicited strong responses, even though it was not passed and a city diversity committee was formed instead.[586]

Arguably, none of these matters fall within local governmental authority, and in the case of the last two, may be purely in federal constitutional law.[587] Yet, they're examples of how a local council can attempt to exert local control on issues not usually associated with such routine municipal tasks such as fixing roads, providing police and fire protection and handling zoning.

It's unlikely that these kinds of inquiries will diminish in the years ahead. As many observers have noted, American democracy has become more participatory at many levels, and in Southern Idaho, permissive council debates on wider-ranging topics seem more common. The topic may vary, but the base issue is the tension over authority and where it lies. That is an ongoing debate just as likely to be in flux in the future as it is today.

Counties. At the time of statehood, Idaho established a system of creating individual counties out of existing ones as populations increased, and provided that citizens would exercise local control by electing county officials. That structure has endured through the decades and in Southern Idaho, gives the region a pattern of local decision-making on conservative expenditures and overall fiscal prudence.[588]

Idaho law allows for several variations of county structure, but all Southern Idaho counties use the original model which calls for three

583 Giffords Law Center website, 2018. "Local Authority to Regulate Firearms in Idaho."

584 Pember, Matt, County Prosecutor. "Memo to Gooding County Commissioners," *Times-News*, Feb. 15, 2017.

585 Brown, Nathan. "Twin Council Passes 'Neighborly Community' Resolution," May 9, 2017.

586 Kauffman, Gretel. "After Border Resolution Debate, Twin Falls to form Diversity Committee," *Times-News*, Nov. 14, 2018.

587 Article I, Section 8 of the U.S. Constitution gives sole authority over "naturalization" to the federal government.

588 Idaho Association of Counties, "The Idaho County," IAC website, 2019.

commissioners, plus a county clerk, assessor, treasurer, sheriff, prosecuting attorney and coroner, all elected.[589]

Since candidates run as party nominees, the structure allows parties to groom candidates through the local party central committees and appointed offices, such as planning and zoning. There are also a variety of non-partisan positions, including emergency preparedness and response, and veterans' support.

In theory, the two parties would be competitive on the ballot as county issues are generally non-partisan in nature. But in practice, single party dominance is common throughout Southern Idaho, where most county elected officials are Republicans, except in Blaine County, where they are mostly Democrats. The GOP dominance in the region gives the Republican Party a stronger bench from which to draw candidates for other elective offices. Nothing suggests this pattern will change in the immediate future; indeed, some party officials would like to see partisan ballots extended to municipal elections as well.[590]

When it comes to how county government functions, there are arenas in which it reflects overall state directive, such as in the judicial selection and court process, but also arenas in which counties feel regularly chastened by state mandates.

One of those is indigent health care, where the state state caps county responsibility at $ 11,000 with the state picking up the rest. Commissioners often feel these unfunded mandates hamper county government, and regularly make their grievances known on matters of taxation, property valuation and the sideboards often put on state requirements. Twin Falls Commissioner Don Hall, a former Twin Falls mayor, says that as the region grows, younger generations expect more amenities and services, from dog parks to walking paths, bike lanes to fire station upgrades and improved crime prevention. It's a constant struggle to find enough revenue.[591]

Southern Idaho counties generally have a good working relationship with the state, except for ongoing disagreements over funding of programs, particularly new ones. The issues are especially problematic for those counties which are not growing as rapidly as others in assessed valuations; these have a harder time covering ever-rising costs and turn to the state for

---

589 IAC, The Idaho County," p.6-8. From time to time, Southern Idaho counties have considered other forms of county government structure as allowed by law, but have not changed. Jerome County tried a "super commissioner" form in the 1990s, but did not continue it. Cassia County has a professional county administrator, as allowed by law, to handle certain administrative functions.

590 Talerico, Kate. "Idaho Republicans Say You Should Know What Party Your City Counselor Belongs To," *The Idaho Statesman*, Jan. 25, 2019.

591 Hall, Don. Twin Falls County Commissioner, Interview July 27, 2018.

more relief.[592] The state usually tries to be sensitive to such appeals, and helps out as it can, especially when the costs are due to an unanticipated emergency, such as a flood or an unduly harsh winter.[593]

Another arena of county authority is in the assessing and valuation of real property, as well with some personal property in businesses, such as computers and other office equipment.

Property taxes are particularly sensitive, as they are a main source of funding for counties, cities, schools, highway districts, recreation districts and in the case of Southern Idaho, a local levy in both Jerome and Twin Falls counties for the College of Southern Idaho.

Citizens have seen significant increases in recent years, due to both rising valuations, and in some cases, bonding for new facilities which add to the total tax bills.[594] The burden has fallen particularly on farm property, which was previously assessed on the value of crops being grown, and in some cases, on crops not grown.[595] Because property taxes are more visible to citizens, any jump is readily noticed and, if broad enough and fall on enough households, is likely to trigger a tax revolt at the local and state level. Colorado and California have both experienced tax-cap movements brought by citizens and determined tax-limitation interest groups.

Idaho experienced some of this in 2006, when voters in every precinct in the state voted to roll back property taxes by adding a penny to the then five percent sales tax.[596] Now, 12 years later, property taxes again seem to be on citizen's hunting list for flattening or reductions.[597]

By comparison with national county property levies, property taxes in Southern Idaho may not be excessive,[598] but any tax is viewed skeptically.

---

592 Idaho Legislature, Office of Performance Evaluations, "Impact of State Mandates on County Government," Jan., 2019. The report found many county officials cited inadequacy of state support for mandated duties, including courts, judiciary and jail management. See also Kauffman, Gretel. "Counties Want Better Communication," *Times-News*, Feb. 3, 2019.

593 Kennison, Heather. "16 Big-Water Battles: Snowstorm, Flood Recovery Far from Over," Times-News, April 30, 2017.

594 Kennison, Heather. "Assessed Values Are On The Rise," *Times-News*, June 5, 2018.

595 Matthews, Mychel. "Assessor Candidates Debate Farm Valuation Policy," *Times-News*, Dec. 1, 2017.

596 Idaho Secretary of State, 2006 election returns. The property tax rollback proposal passed with almost 73 percent of the vote.

597 Ward, Xavier. "Ada County Property Spiked in 2018, and Residents Are Stuck Footing A Heavy Tax Bill," *Idaho Press Tribune*, Dec. 25, 2018.

598 Russell, Betsy. "Study shows Idaho's Overall Taxes Are Lowest in Region, 48th in the Nation," *Spokesman-Review*, Nov. 24, 2017. The Tax Foundation ranks Idaho 21st in total taxes, but 4th best on property taxes. See Tax Foundation website, "2019 Tax Business Climate Index."

Many taxpayers saw increases of over 15 percent in 2018, on top of increases in prior years as well. And there's discussion among various interest groups and needs assessment committees to soften the new-tax beachhead with talks to civic clubs on how this or that project is essential, with little or no mention of costs.[599] And this would be on top of the three percent annual increases regularly taken by taxing entities as well as a retrieved Twin Falls foregone balance (the difference between what taxing districts are allowed to levy and what they actually levy) in which the city took an additional $770,000 from previous years.[600]

Since these projects are being proposed by different entities, there's no coordination as to which is the highest need, or any ranking of community priorities, or what the cost would be on an average Twin Falls home, which might well be hundreds of dollars a year in additional property taxes per home, or higher.[601]

These kinds of increases could force people out of their homes and surely would drive business and residential development to less costly areas, as has happened in Colorado, California, and to some degree in the Boise area. And they may also spur organized resistance among taxpayers, as is also being seen in the Boise area.[602]

Southern Idaho is growing nicely and is likely to continue to do so, but big projected tax increases are sure to dampen local development. Tax issues are likely to be near the top of citizens' concerns in the years ahead. Proponents might well consider that tax increase proposals could dampen further growth.[603]

---

599 The early back-of-the-envelope calculations would put the project costs at perhaps $250 million, including a new county jail ($44-60m), judicial building ($23m), fire stations ($36m), recreation center ($20m) a special events center at the Twin Falls County Fairgrounds ($10M) and new schools in the next 5-10 years, ($50m). Debt service fees would likely add to those estimates, putting a tax bill of up to $400 million in increased taxes directly onto taxpayers.

600 Kennison, Heather. "Twin Falls Taxable Value is at its Highest Ever at $2.9 Billion," *Times-News*, July 10, 2018.

601 Kauffman, Gretel. "On the cusp of an Outright Emergency," *Times-News*, Dec. 9, 2018; Gretel Kauffman, "Twin Falls City Council Accepts Committee's Fire Station Recommendations," *Times-News*, Dec. 18, 2019; West, Bowen. "Twin Falls Holds Meeting on Proposed Recreation Center," *Times-News*, June 20, 2018; Kennison, Heather. "Back On The Ballot: Twin Falls County Commissioners reconsider bond for event center at the fairground," *Times-News*, Feb. 1, 2018; Wootton-Greener, Julie. "Magic Valley Schools Weigh Options to Deal with Enrollment Growth," *Times-News*, Aug. 2, 2018.

602 Ward, Xavier. Dec. 25, 2018.

603 McCurdy, Terry and Hartgen, Stephen. "Reader Comment: Totaling the Impacts of Proposed Projects," *Times-News*, Feb. 24, 2019. The author and longtime community leader Terry McCurdy analyzed data from the Twin Falls County Assessor's Office which showed a potential tax increase of almost 30 percent on county businesses and homes.

22. Education

College of Southern Idaho. Everyone in Southern Idaho knows the College of Southern Idaho, the tree-lined campus we love to show off to out-of-town visitors, where many of us have taken or taught classes, enrolled our children, attended sports or cultural events, watched high school graduations, benefited in many ways from its presence. "I can't imagine the Magic Valley without the college," says longtime community leader Terry McCurdy. "It moves things forward in education and open-mindedness" in the community.[604]

Indeed, it does. The college would probably appear on every list of important institutions in the Magic Valley, maybe the single most influential community asset. Though it's now more than 50 years old, CSI has demonstrated repeated nimbleness and ingenuity in meeting changing community needs.[605]

Former interim president Curtis Eaton, who also led the school's philanthropic foundation, puts his assessment of the college into three broad contributions: first, economic development, education and the fostering of valley growth; second, its function as a "crucible" for ideas and varied points of view; and third, as an emerging center for the valley's innovations.

The first role, he says, is its traditional one, the development of sound programs in general education and helping grow area businesses and industries, like aquaculture which has had a college technical training component for nearly 40 years.

---

604 McCurdy, Terry. Interview, Jan. 21, 2019.

605 Gentry, James. *50 Years: A History of The College of Southern Idaho*, College of Southern Idaho, 2015.

In fields like agriculture and water management, the school's role is not in pure scientific research, but in the application of research to practical applications to create and expand employment and applied knowledge. It's a role, he says, that the school has been good at for decades and in which it continues to excel.[606]

The varied programs and college offerings reflect this core mission. There are general liberal arts courses for incoming freshmen in English, math, sciences and the social sciences, plus a robust Fine Arts curriculum in music, art and theater. On the vocational side, CSI offers courses in food service and management, wind energy training and food processing, as well as auto and diesel mechanics, aquaculture and agricultural skills.[607] In short, it's a comprehensive community college, filling traditional roles in skilled trades and the general first two years of college education.

The second key role of the college, Eaton says, is to function as a crucible for ideas and trends, a formal setting in which "the community can express views." This role is a more latent one, Eaton says, particularly when it comes to topics like LGBTQ (Lesbian, Gay, Bisexual, Transgender, Queer or Questioning) relationships, religious tolerance and ethnic diversity.

Today, he cites as an example, the Hispanic portion among students is more than 20 percent; two decades ago, it was just six percent. Back then, he says, CSI's students came mostly from local high schools, with many coming from farm backgrounds. They were mostly white with a traditional gender mix and few people of color. Many were entering right out of high school, but there was a mix even then of returning adult students, single parents and people trying to advance in life by obtaining more education.

Today, there's more diversity in every regard, which Eaton sees as a good thing. He points to the college's role in hosting a Refugee Center, which since the 1980s has brought wave after wave of peoples from elsewhere in the world;[608] people proud of their heritage who may feel different, but also comfortable, together in this new land. It's not so much a melting pot of assimilation, but a mosaic of backgrounds and cultures. CSI is a protective cocoon for new arrivals and also an environment in which newcomers and the dominant homogeneous community learn from each other.[609]

In this regard, CSI has been one of the community's leading institutions in the promotion of the arts and culture. As noted in the chapter on the Arts & Entertainment, the college functions as something of a "change agent" in its promotion of artistic expression, but it readily recognizes that there are limits,

---

606 Eaton, Curtis. Interview, Jan. 21, 2019.

607 College of Southern Idaho website, "Catalogs," 2006-2018.

608 College of Southern Idaho, website, 2018, "Refugee Center."

609 Eaton Interview, Jan. 21, 2019.

albeit ill-defined, on community acceptance of classes, programs and the general tone of the institution.

Perhaps because of its close-to-community missions, CSI has been careful not to alienate community groups of any stripe – neither too traditional nor too left-leaning or progressive. In that sense, it is similar to other community entities in Southern Idaho: like the baby bear's dish of pudding, not too hot, not too cold, just right.

The third role of CSI, Eaton says, is fostering innovation. It's evident in CSI's providing support to SIEDO, an economic development group; encouraging practical applications of technologies like wind energy; to creating an expanded program in food processing management in 2019 in conjunction with the state's four-year schools. In all these arenas, CSI is playing a significant if sometimes understated role.[610]

An example of this is in the recent announcement that the school would partner with an Australian/New Zealand company, CropLogic, on a program to train students in the new field of direct specific nutrient inputs management, including herbicides, pesticides and fertilizers.[611] Such partnerships, says Eaton, are likely to be more common in the future. but continue to be based on the valley's needs.

Another example of the college's role in these innovations is the new bachelor's program in food processing technology beginning in fall, 2019. It is the state's first bachelor's degree from a community college, joining a select few community colleges nationwide that offer bachelor's degrees. Not surprisingly, this one has close ties to Southern Idaho's growing dairy industry and workforce.[612]

Yet, as CSI evolves, there are signs of internal tensions. CSI Foundation director Debra Wilson says the academic faculty have traditionally been politically liberal, reflecting the dominant liberal themes of American universities. That's been true of CSI since its formative years, says Wilson.

---

610 Eaton Interview, Jan. 21, 2019.

611 Kennison, Heather. "Ag-Tech company CropLogic to Open Sales Office at CSI," *Times-News*, Oct. 26, 2018. One commentor on the article, AFortiori, asked, "CSI a research institute? That's news to some of us. Move over University of Idaho, Idaho has a new premiere research university.'" See also, CropLogic website, 2019. In a Jan. 21, 2019 press release, CropLogic says it offers "growers of irrigated crops with digital agricultural technology expertise based upon scientific research and delivered with cutting edge technology – science, agronomy and technology interwoven into an expert system for decision support."

612 College of Southern Idaho website, "Food Processing Technology," 2019. See also Vitu, Teya. "College of Southern Idaho to offer Bachelor's Degrees," *Idaho Business Review*, May 2, 2018; and Wootton-Greener, Julie. "The College of Southern Idaho Wants to Offer Two Bachelor's Degrees," *Times-News*, Mar. 23, 2018.

In contrast, the vocational faculty and administrative staff, she says, tends to be local and consequently more politically conservative, which reflects the values of the valley.[613] Wilson, who grew up on a ranch near Bliss and started her CSI career as a secretary, puts herself in this second group; the Foundation Board is regularly sprinkled with Southern Idaho business people, farmers, ranchers and entrepreneurs. "It's our community college," she says of CSI, "the community believes in it; that's why they support it."

The Foundation's annual report is a checklist of hundreds of individual and business donors, most of them local. Wilson says she can relate many instances in which she has had a visit from an area farmer or rancher, whom she didn't previously know, who handed her a six-figure check because, well, it's their local college. That support has boosted CSI's endowment to more than $41 million, one of the largest in the nation for a community college. Most of the proceeds of some $2.1 million in 2018, went to scholarship support.[614]

CSI has been blessed, Wilson says, by having presidents with strong community ties and who understood the college's support derives from the community. She praises all of them – James Taylor, Jerry Meyerhoeffer, Jerry Beck, Curtis Eaton and Jeff Fox – for their deft leadership over CSI's more than 50 years. She hopes the school continues to mirror its unique position as both a community institution and learning center for the changing world ahead.

Current president Jeff Fox has been with CSI for more than 30 years in various capacities. His ancestors came to Southern Idaho in the 1920s and both his parents grew up here. The vagaries of the farm economy in the 1950s forced his family move to the West Coast. He says if the college had been here then, the family might never have left.[615] He came back to CSI in 1987 as an English instructor. He's been here ever since.

A main role of the college, he says, is to help develop the local workforce. Support for the school has been strong since its founding in the 1960s. The relationship is a symbiotic one, in which the community provides the support and the college combines vocational education with two-year general college offerings. That, plus its long-running support for both athletics and the arts,

---

613 Wilson, Debra J. Interview, Jan. 30, 2019.

614 The CSI Foundation has adapted well to the changing Magic Valley. It started in 1984 and under the leadership of executive directors Joan Edwards, Curtis Eaton and Deb Wilson, the foundation has grown assets to over $40 million. At any given time, the Foundation's board makeup seems to reflect an intuitive sense of who are the valley's emerging business leaders and thus maintains a continuing "stream" of donations from various sources. College of Southern Idaho Annual Reports, 2017, 2018.

615 Wootton, Julie. "Jeff Fox Prepares to Step Into Position as CSI President," *Times-News*, Dec. 22, 2013.

give CSI its dominant character. In that sense, Fox says, the school acts as a forum for ideas and discussion.

Over the years, CSI has adjusted its programs to the changing needs of students. In remedial education, for example, CSI has shifted to a more targeted approach which focuses on specific areas where a student might need help rather than a broader full semester of English, math or science.

On the research side, CSI's approach is to focus on the practical application of research in fields like agriculture and aquaculture. The new program in food processing management is an example which derives directly from industry needs: A "workforce degree."[616]

While CSI has many significant pluses compared to many community colleges, it is never likely to be free of challenges. Whether it's adequacy of funding, staff and faculty quality and pay, and how athletics fits the college's mission, the school is likely to face continuing issues.

A particular plus is local governance, in which CSI's five-person Board of Trustees is elected from the two-county CSI taxpaying district, Jerome and Twin Falls. That governance structure has been in place for the school's entire existence and isn't likely to be changed.[617] Although the board isn't immune from partisanship or local parochialism, it's helped keep the school attentive to community needs and aspirations.

CSI's general fund is set annually by the Legislature, which has generally given the school continuing increases to meet the college's needs. The 2019 budget was $43.2 million, of which $14.3 million came from the state and another $6.8 million from the two-county taxing district. CSI prides itself as being the least expensive public college in the state, charging $140/credit hour.[618]

With a thriving local economy, CSI on-campus enrollments have slipped as potential students opt for jobs in the workforce; as with many community colleges, better local economic conditions typically reduce enrollment patterns.[619]

Total enrollment has increased, however, with many high-school students taking "dual credit" classwork, giving them both high school and CSI credits.

---

616 Fox, Jeff. Interview, Feb. 7, 2019.

617 Idaho Code, Title 33, Chapter 21. The governance structure was set out by the Legislature in the 1960s, when both Jerome and Twin Falls voters approved creation of a junior college district. The board representation has been modified in recent years to require at least minimal representation from each of the two counties. (Idaho Code 33-2104A, 2016 session).

618 Wootton-Greener, Julie. "The College of Southern Idaho Has $43.2 Million in its Total Budget," *Times-News*, July 17, 2018.

619 Smith, Ashley A. "No Bottom Yet in Two-Year College Enrollments," InsideHigherEd website, June 21, 2018.

The state has funded the dual-credit program as a way to encourage young people to go on in their educations. Despite the headcounts, a lower reimbursement rate of $65/credit hour, less than half the regular credit hour price, has put the squeeze on CSI's overall budget.[620]

It's just one of many challenges ahead for Southern Idaho's premier college institution. The school's proven and nimble responses over the years to curriculum changes and program development, and its excellent record of listening to the community seem likely to position it well to whatever comes along. Southern Idaho pride in CSI is well-placed.

K-12 Education. Is there any public entity in America which suffers more scrutiny from communities than public education? As in America as a whole, the big picture of public education in Southern Idaho is a mixed one. There are many school districts of various sizes (Eight in Twin Falls County alone), ranging from the almost 10,000-student Twin Falls School District to the handful of students at the modest one-building Three Creek School, some 30 miles west of Rogerson. It has 11 students, grades k-6 and one teacher.[621] The school has been there since 1900, serving the dispersed ranching families of this remote area.[622]

In between are fast growing districts like Kimberly and Jerome, Filer and Buhl, and more remote ones like Richfield, Dietrich and Shoshone. They range in resources from wealthier districts like Blaine County, where teachers make an average of $70,000 annually, and Twin Falls, which is enjoying

---

620 Wootton-Greener, Julie. "The College of Southern Idaho Has Fewer Students, But They're Taking More Classes," *Times-News*, Aug. 19, 2018. See also, Kauffman, Gretel. "As Dual Credit Enrollment Grows, CSI Adapts to Changing Campus, Funding Needs," *Times-News*, Jan. 22, 2019. Comment on this article ranged from critical of CSI (Tumbleweed49: What this article says is that full-time students are going elsewhere. My Son and I went to CSI in the old days, before they became USC-Berkeley. My Daughters and Granddaughters went out of State. They didn't care to become part of a Refugee Center. I suspect, other kids here figure the same. In this day and age, Pocatello or Boise isn't that far."), to supportive of the Dual Credit program. (JA Browne: "This year I am taking over 13 college credits through CSI. Not only is it a great opportunity for me to knock out some of my generals for very little cost, but it's a great opportunity for future students at both high school and college levels.") and (Manicalorbit1: "As a dual credit student who appreciates the local opportunity and would rather not, "go elsewhere for college" due to expenses, the dual credit program is a great advantage.")

621 Public School Review website, "Three Creek Joint Elementary School District," 2019.

622 Brackett, Kimberly Williams. "Three Creek School Celebrates 115 Years," *Times-News*, May 26, 2015. Says former teacher Marilyn Boss: "A one-room school is the best education a student can get because students have one-to-one help, everyone helps each other, and the younger ones are advanced by listening to older ones and older ones review what they learned."

dramatic growth, to smaller and more modest ones where communities are struggling to fund what they have, much less add new offerings.

They also vary widely in ethnic diversity and test scores. Jerome School District has about 3,850 students, more than 50 percent of whom are Hispanic. Its math scores, language proficiency and graduation rates are all below state averages.[623] The same patterns exist for Wendell School District, (1,155 students) and Minidoka County School District (4,175 students).[624]

Blaine County schools tends to have stronger testing results, as do some charter schools, but there are many successful graduates every year from schools rich and poor. Nonetheless, as a region, test scores, proficiencies and graduation rates tend to trail the state as whole.[625] The same is true when Idaho students are compared to national statistics.[626]

Twin Falls Superintendent Brady Dickinson, who's been with the district more than 20 years, says with more of an emphasis today on all young people succeeding, schools are handling a wider range of ethnic groups and special needs students. Earlier refugee groups in the 1980s from Southeast Asia and Eastern Europe were easier to assimilate into Southern Idaho schools; some new arrivals today aren't literate even in their first languages.[627] So a district like Twin Falls, which has numerous languages represented, has an ongoing daily challenge in getting these young people ready for education, work and social assimilation.

This emphasis on making sure every student has an equal chance to succeed in school has tilted more districts to focus on special needs and individual plans for students. That means school staffs have grown beyond traditional classroom teachers. This stretches school budgets and leads to more reliance on levies funded by local property taxes. In Twin Falls, Dickinson says, about 23 percent of revenue comes from such local levies.[628]

There are several alternative high schools in Southern Idaho, the largest being the Magic Valley Alternative High School, which has about 120 students. The alternative schools offer smaller settings than traditional high schools and help students who don't always succeed elsewhere.[629]

As a growing state with expanding student numbers, Idaho has poured tens of millions of dollars into K-12 education in recent years, chiefly for

---

623 Public School Review website," Jerome Joint School District," 2019.

624 Public School Review website, 2019.

625 Idaho Department of Education. "Here are the Magic Valley Schools Idaho considers 'underperforming' and 'top performing,'" *Times-News*, Aug. 16, 2018.

626 IdahoEdNews website, "IdahoEdTrends," 2018.

627 Dickinson, Brady. Interview, Feb. 9, 2019.

628 Dickinson, Interview.

629 Public School Review website, 2019, "Magic Valley Alternative High School."

increasing classroom units, boosting teacher pay and adding to curriculum and transportation budgets. The K-12 school budget gets roughly half of total state general fund revenue, a figure which has wide support among legislators but which pinches other state needs, such as water management, health and welfare and corrections.[630]

There has been consideration of consolidating school districts to gain efficiencies, lower costs and improve student outcomes, but forced consolidation by the state is unlikely. Community identity, including local school sports and individual student attention by teachers who know every student personally are big pluses in small schools. Consolidation may seem compelling for economic reasons, but is unlikely to occur in Idaho except voluntarily.[631]

The changes over a generation or two have also restricted teachers and curriculum, Dickinson says. Today, content is more circumscribed (some might say dictated) and individual teachers have less freedom to teach outside its limits.[632] This is probably a factor in teachers leaving the profession, or finding more favorable settings which fit them better, such as private, alternative or charter schools. The same is likely in districts with high unionization, where social pressure enforces "go along-get along" thinking.[633]

Rapid growth in school enrollments means districts must plan ahead. The Twin Falls district has recently built two new elementary schools and a third junior high school within the past five years, as well as a second high school barely a decade ago. A third high school within another decade, as well as more elementary schools, is already being contemplated.[634] Growth is anticipated to continue at 2-4 percent per year, which for Twin Falls would mean several hundred new students annually.[635]

630 Idaho Legislative Services, 2018 Fiscal Facts, puts public school support for 2019 at $2.462b, of which federal funds are $264m or 10.7 percent, local levies are $322m or 13.1 percent and stated support is $1.8b, or 76.2 percent.

631 Hartgen, Stephen. "Forced School Consolidation In Idaho Unlikely," *Times-News*, Nov. 12, 2009.

632 Dickinson, Interview.

633 Toppo, Greg and Overberg, Paul. "Fewer than Half of Teachers Now Covered by Unions," *USA Today*, Feb. 10, 2015. In Southern Idaho, about the same percent of teachers are union members. Estimate from Twin Falls School District, 2018. Idaho is a Right-to-Work state which prohibits forced union membership.

634 Wootton-Greener, Julie. "Magic Valley Schools Weigh Options to Deal With Enrollment Growth," *Times-News*, Aug. 2, 2018.

635 Wootton-Greener, Julie. "Big Magic Valley School Districts Expect to Gain Students Next Year," *Times-News*, April 17, 2018.

Private, Charter Schools & Home Schooling. The Southern Idaho region has a number of private schools, some of them with religious roots and curriculum, others more secular or offering more "classical" education. Among the first group are Lighthouse Christian, with about 300 students,[636] Twin Falls Christian Academy, a ministry of Grace Baptist Church,[637] and St. Edwards Catholic School, with about 120 students and adjacent to St. Edwards Catholic Church.[638] There are also some smaller religious schools, focusing on early grades, such as Clover Christian School, which goes back more than 100 years to the first settlement of the Clover and Buhl area.[639]

Charter schools make up about seven percent (about 22,000) of Idaho's student enrollment of more than 300,000 students. Charter schools grew by more than 1,100 students per year from 2005-2015; numbers have slowed to about 625 new students each year in the past four years.[640] An estimated 1,500 to 2,000 students are enrolled in private schools across Southern Idaho, with the largest being Xavier Charter School in Twin Falls, with about 700 students and another 360 on the waiting list.[641]

The reasons parents choose a private school vary, but closer teacher attention, better discipline, and a more rigorous academic environment are most often cited. Parents determine that they have few chances to get their youngsters through school successfully and may look for alternatives to traditional public schools. In the case of Xavier, anonymous reviews by students and graduates rate the school highly;[642] they score well on proficiency tests (71 percent reading, 54 percent math, 1170 average SAT, 30 average ACT.)[643]

Charter schools are public schools and are regulated by state law through a charter schools commission. North Valley Academy in Gooding, for

636 Lighthouse Christian School website, 2019.

637 Twin Falls Christian Academy website, 2019.

638 St. Edwards Catholic School website, 2019.

639 Clover Christian School website, 2019.

640 Idaho Legislative Services, Fiscal Facts, 2018.

641 Wootton-Greener, Julie. "Want Your Child to Attend Xavier Charter School? It Could be Tough. There's a 361-Person Waiting List," *Times-News*, Oct. 3, 2018.

642 Niche.com website, Xavier Charter School, 2019. Among the comments: "I love that I am getting a great education at Xavier. It is a more rigorous curriculum that the traditional public schools in this area. It also gives me more opportunities to explore the arts, which I love," and "My grandchildren that attend this school excel where they were not doing well at their other school. I have two grandchildren that live with me and I wouldn't send them anywhere else. Their knowledge base far exceeds other children that I know. The teachers have control of their classes and let their students explore ideas and use hands-on techniques to keep learning exciting."

643 Niche.com website, "Xavier Charter School," 2019. See also Wootton-Greener, Julie. "Charter Schools: Don't Compare Us to Regular Schools," *Times-News*, Feb. 22, 2019.

example, was founded in a "one fell swoop" migration out of the traditional Gooding school district; right from the start, there was an undercurrent of discontent from both those parents and students who left and those who stayed.

The charter school's founders point with pride to their unabashed patriotism which is woven into the school's activities. The drop in enrollment for public Gooding High School sent administrators scurrying to hold staff positions at first; enrollment later rebounded.[644]

There also may have been ethnic and class issues as well behind the split and the move.[645] The North Valley Academy instituted a uniform dress code when it opened in 2008 in an effort have better school discipline; the effect there and at other local schools, has been to reduce gang clothing, inappropriate dress and improved academics.[646] North Valley Academy has a somewhat less ethnic student body (28 percent Hispanic) versus the traditional Gooding School District (32 percent Hispanic), but neither ranks above state averages in proficiency test scores.[647]

When it was founded, some North Valley students were previously home schooled, suggesting that they wanted more structure, but didn't want to re-enter the traditional system.

Idaho is among the most permissive states in the country when it comes to home schooling, with no limits on curriculum, content and virtually no oversight of methods or regulatory authority.[648]

As with private schools and charter schools, there are many reasons parents choose home schooling, but the rapid growth of these alternatives suggests that there may be dissatisfaction with traditional public education in Southern Idaho.

As one home school advocate put it, the way to prevent proliferation of charter schools is to fix perceived inadequacies in the traditional districts, including discipline, patriotism and academic rigor. Doing so would reduce the incentives some now feel to search for alternatives.[649]

---

644 Bonner, Jesse, Associated Press. "Charter School in Gooding Touts Patriotic Focus," *Times-News*, June 2, 2012.

645 Botkin, Ben. "Luna to Gooding: Do Not Become Divided Over Charter School," *Times-News*, Jan. 6, 2009.

646 Wootton, Julie. "Schools Say Uniforms Led to Better Academics, Behavior," *Times-News*, Oct. 3, 2014.

647 Public Schools Review website, North Valley Academy and Gooding School District, 2019.

648 Idaho Coalition of Home School Educators website, "Homeschool Laws," 2019.

649 Botkin, Jan. 6, 2009.

As with other aspects of conservative Southern Idaho life, schools are likely to reflect these undercurrents of both progress and response to change.[650] The response to Common Core standards is seen by some as a further intrusion of federal overreach into school policy.[651] Resistance to such perceived meddling seems closely intertwined with other deeply-held conservative values across Southern Idaho's traits and there's no reason that would be much different in the decades ahead.

650 Albertson Family Foundation website. "Idaho: Ready for Change: What Idahoans Really Think About Education in Idaho," 2016.

651 Corbin, Clark. "House Committee Gets Earful from Out-of-State Common Core Opponent," IdahoEdNews website, Jan. 30, 2017.

23. Fauna, Flora & The Love of the Stream

Although often overlooked and unremarked, there have been many changes in Southern Idaho's plant and wildlife populations, some recent and some dating back the valley's settlement more than a century ago. These dispersions are still going on and there's no reason to think they will ever cease. Plant and animal populations rise and fall depending on many ecosystem changes, of which intensive agricultural production and human presence are but two.

We may think of ecosystem change as something which mostly affects animal and plant species, but there are plenty of studies on how human presence affects the very people who brought "civilization" with them. Latin American ruins show a centuries-long history before the Spanish conquests of the 1500s, of societies rising. falling and reforming under Mayans, Aztecs and Toltecs.

Land use patterns, over-populations in small areas, agricultural mismanagement all combined with cycles of drought and privation to force human adaption and sometimes, societal collapse. Vikings settled Greenland in the 900s, but the settlements failed within 500 years; we still don't know exactly why, but climate cycles, a new "Little Ice Age," over-grazing, resource overuse including the denuding of the sparse Greenland birch, and failure to adapt from European ways to life in the sub-Arctic all seem to have played a part.[652] Patterns like these have

652 Diamond, Jared. *Guns, Germs and Steel: The Fates of Human Societies*, Norton, 1997. See also Brooke, James. "Story of Viking Colonists' Icy Pompeii Unfolds From Ancient Greenland Farm," *The New York Times*, May 8, 2001.

stoked the interests of modern archeologists, bio-ecologists, and now DNA and genetics inquiry.

Southern Idaho represents an American landscape more dramatically changed ecologically than perhaps we realize; we recent human arrivals on an arid and forbidding plain. As our Southern Idaho's physical landscape changes, species give way to one another. Usually, the changes are minute year-to-year, but they are ongoing nonetheless, from mountain forestation to dryland farming, from sagebrush plain and wildland pastures to intensively irrigated farmland. Thirty years from now, the species profile will likely be different. A hundred years from now, there will be yet more changes in the fauna and flora landscapes. It is a process without discernible end.

Fauna. Among the changes in fauna populations is the widespread dispersal of wolf populations since their reintroduction to Idaho in the 1980s. Packs have been identified in virtually all of the state north of the Snake River. Some wildlife biologists think it is just a matter of time before they're in the South Hills as well, given the wolf's great tendency to fan out packs for long distances. As wolves spread, deer and elk populations have shifted, pressured by the predators as well as by human encroachment.[653]

As early as 2002, wolf depredations and packs were being reported regularly in Southern Idaho; one dead wolf was found then in the Glenns Ferry area along Interstate Hwy. 84. suggesting pack dispersal widely in the region. Other dead wolves were found near Carey, Pine and Fairfield, just to the north of Southern Idaho. More recently, an individual wolf was taken by a hunter just ten miles north of Rupert in 2018, way south of the Central Idaho mountain country with which wolves are normally associated.[654]

Other species dispersal, including elk and deer, on which wolves routinely prey, suggest further spreading of wolf packs. Both elk and moose populations are now found in the South Hills near Twin Falls, where they

653 Meyers, Jerry, Idaho Fish & Game Commissioner, Interview, Dec. 10, 2018.

654 Meier, T. (editor) "Rocky Mountain Wolf Recovery, 2002 Annual Report," US Fish & Wildlife Service, et. al, particularly section "USFWS Law Enforcement - Idaho," 2003. By that time, the number of wolves in Idaho was estimated at close to 300 individuals. The number of wolves in Idaho is now estimated at well over 1,000 animals and dispersal of wolves to form new packs is widely reported. Fish & Game reports the wolf killed near Rupert in 2018 was from the Corn Creek pack, North of Boise, and before that, from the Yellowstone Park area.

once thrived but were rooted out by the mid-20th century.[655] Populations also seem to be expanding for species like raccoons and pronghorn antelope.[656]

Fish & Game officers recently documented two live collard ringtails in the Southern Idaho region; the secretive, nocturnal animal is a member of the raccoon family and the local captures, in 2014 and 2015, are the first live examples of the mammal in Idaho. Little is known of its range, but ringtails are more common in Nevada and Southwestern states, suggesting a drier climate in Idaho may be expanding their range northward.[657] There are previous hints of the animal's existence in Idaho going back to the 1960s. The research isn't yet definitive.[658]

Other species have also come into Idaho's wildlife picture, including the European Collard Dove, a larger relative to the common American Mourning Dove, which originated in Asia, then to the Bahamas in the 1970s and then to Florida in 1982. Since then, it's exploding population has covered the United States and Southern Canada all the way from Newfoundland to Alaska, reaching Southern Idaho between 2007 and 2009. The bird's dramatic increases may be due to landscapes which are "highly modified by human activity" since the bird can "readily adapt to suburban life."[659]

---

655 White, Craig. White, regional director for Idaho Fish & Game, has said the agency is considering expanding the elk hunt in the South Hills to include antlerless (female) elk due to increasing populations there. Twin Falls Kiwanis Club presentation, Jan. 3, 2019.

656 Matthews, Mychel. "Idaho Fish and Game officers: Let 'em Be. Wildlife Need Space," *Times-News*, June 21 2018.

657 Hutchins, Virginia. "Collard Ringtail Released at Big Cottonwood," Times-News, Mar. 9, 2015. See also Hutchins, Virginia. "Radio-collard Ringtail is a First For Idaho Science," Times-News, April 6, 2014.

658 See comment by "TrapperR" in comments section of the previous citation, who writes "I can understand the skepticism associated with the recent ringtail in southern Idaho. But in fact, ringtails are not new to Idaho and are a native species. Albeit rare, there are records going back to the 1960s. While ringtails are commonly thought of as desert species associated with steep rocky terrain, they occur in many different habitat types including forests, such as those found in southern Idaho. With southern Idaho being the northern extent of their range (with the exception of Oregon, where they occur further north in primarily forest habitat), they would be expected to occur in relatively low abundance. This, combined with the fact that they are nocturnal and highly elusive (even where they occur in high abundance, they are rarely seen), would make detections of ringtails rare, at best. Habitat models for ringtails developed for the southwest predict southern Idaho as suitable habitat (see Southwest Regional Gap analysis map at http://swregap.nmsu.edu/habitatreview/Range/180577.pdf) and some older range maps include south-central Idaho near the border with Utah and Nevada, as well as the southeast corner of Idaho and some of Wyoming. Ringtails are not threatened anywhere across their range and ringtail pelts are not highly desired by trappers."

659 Bonter, D. N., et. al., "Invasive birds in a novel landscape: habitat associations and effects on established species," Ecography, 2010. See also Cornell Laboratory of Ornithology, "Eurasian Collard Doves Conquering America," Project FeederWatch, Jan. 17, 2011.

Unlike many invasive species which negatively impact existing habitats, the Collard Dove doesn't appear to have reduced common Mourning Dove populations. But it's well-documented that ecosystem changes, from forestation practices to "ditch bank" agriculture, have affected many species. We shouldn't be surprised to see that such changes which accompany American agriculture should impact wild species too.

Hunting of Chinese Ringneck Pheasants was a common after-school activity in Southern Idaho during the mid-20th Century. But loss of habitat, increased predation and fewer weedy ditch banks have all diminished pheasant populations since that time. Their sweet, early-morning cackles can be heard occasionally in the countryside, but it's not like the "good ole' days."[660]

Efforts to establish Bighorn Sheep herds in Southern Idaho have not been particularly successful either. The habitat may not be a preferable one, and ranchers there have repeatedly clashed with environmentalists seeking to eliminate domestic sheep grazing on public lands in the West. Begun in the mid-1980s, the Big Horn sheep reintroduction efforts by 2017 were deemed "impractical due to the proximity of domestic sheep and goats, motorized recreation, and habitat issues such as juniper encroachment."[661]

More common species seem to be changing in numbers as well, and some are increasing. Thirty or 40 years ago, one would see an occasional Mule Deer near Twin Falls, sometimes on the links at the Blue Lakes Country Club, or in the Russian Olive and Teasel thickets along Rock Creek. Today herds of 20 animals or more are routinely seen close to town, where an expanding city brushes up against farm ground, providing both cover and food. Milder winters and less near-town hunting pressure are likely to further increase their numbers.

The snapping turtle is another invasive species found occasionally in Idaho. A specimen estimated at 30 pounds or more was recently found on his farm field by state legislator Rep. Mike Moyle along the Boise River west of Boise. Snapping turtles aren't native to Idaho, but are found in rivers and lakes throughout the Eastern United States and Southern Canada. The

---

660 Nellis, Carl, retired regional Fish & Game director, says earlier irrigated agricultural practices gave pheasants plenty of cover in Southern Idaho in the 1950s to about the 1970s, but changes since then have reduced cover, habitat and nesting patterns. Crops are now planted "right to the roadway" of highways; pivot irrigation and frequent cuts of alfalfa give pheasants less habitat in which to nest and thrive. As a general rule, he says, the presence of humans has impacted wildlife negatively across the area. Interview, Jan. 14. 2019.

661 Christensen, Matt. "Battle over Bighorns," *Times-News*, Jan. 24, 2008. See also McDonald, Mike. "Hunter Expectations for Bighorn Sheep in Unit 54," Magic Valley Region 4 Report," Idaho Department of Fish & Game, April 5, 2018.

incident suggests they may be more widespread than previously thought in Idaho.

Another species directly affected by humans is the Barn Owl, a common nighttime hunter of farmland often found roosting in agricultural buildings and in the canyon walls of the area. These agile predators glide above the fields and roads from twilight 'til dawn. Many are killed along highways, where they apparently are attracted to rodents along the roadways, but not agile enough to avoid being struck by fast-moving vehicles. It is estimated that thousands are killed annually along the Interstate 84-86 highways from Boise to the Utah state line. The development of agricultural land through Southern Idaho has both given them food in the form of many mice and voles, but also has caused high mortality rates as well along busy roads.[662]

One major impact on Southern Idaho's animal and bird population has been the increased use of all-terrain vehicles, which allow more access to the backcountry. These versatile off-road vehicles are common in the area, says Idaho Fish & Wildlife biologist Mike McDonald and have put virtually all of the non-designated wilderness areas within easy access of humans. Although hunting is technically prohibited from any vehicle, McDonald says it occurs nonetheless. Snowmobile use has turned even the winter backcountry into recreational playgrounds.[663]

Another change which affects wildlife populations is the buying up of larger tracts of ranch and rangelands by wealthy individuals and sometimes non-profit entities, and then closing off some or all of it to public access. This creates protected tracts for species, but makes for limited public use and more difficult wildlife management decisions, say both McDonald and retired regional director Carl Nellis. The issue looms large in Idaho wildlife management, says Fish & Game Commissioner Jerry Meyers. Deep-pocket buyers, often from other states, are buying up large tracts of Idaho private land and limiting access to places which previously were open. "When people have had access to lands for 30 years, they feel they have a right to it," he says.[664] In Southern Idaho, this process affects sections like the Bennett Hills north of Glenns Ferry, and other tracts in Gooding, Camas and Blaine counties.[665]

---

662 Boves, Than and Belthoff, James Robert. "Roadway Mortality of Barn Owls in Idaho, USA," *Journal of Wildlife Management*, Sept., 2012. See also Glazar, Ed. "Owls Killed Along I-84 Could Number 1,500 Per Year," Times-News, Jan. 30, 2014.

663 McDonald, Mike, regional Fish & Game biologist, Interview, Jan. 14, 2019.

664 Meyers, Interview, Dec. 10, 2018.

665 Wildlife migration corridors along Hwy. 20 from Mountain Home to the Timmerman Hill junction have resulted in many vehicle-wildlife collisions. Nellis and McDonald Interviews, Jan. 14, 2019.

Flora. The American philosopher Henry David Thoreau, author of *Walden* on the merits of simplicity, was a discerning naturalist as well, particularly on the dispersion of plant seeds by wind, water and other means. He never visited the West, but he would not have been surprised to see, as the Southern Idaho region became populated, that foreign species of plants would soon arrive.[666] The coming of various weed and noxious plants to the West is well documented. Species like Canada Thistle, Cheatgrass, Chinese Elm, Kochia, Russian Olive, Salt Cedar and others have been part of Southern Idaho as far back as when the farms were first plowed.[667]

There are dozens of species of plants which have come into the West by various means. Some are waterborne and windborne; others stick to animal furs and hides; some are deposited from animal and bird droppings and gnawings. What child of the rural Magic Valley hasn't examined a lava rock crevice under a boulder and wondered where the gathered seeds have come from, each with a tiny hole through which the kernel has been taken?

Lewis and Clark weren't just explorers; they were biologists and botanists as well, taking detailed journal notes with detailed descriptions of plants and animals then new to science. Their records, and those of others, give a very good overview of what the West looked like before intensive settlement.[668]

---

666 Thoreau, Henry David. *Faith In A Seed*, Island Press, 1993.Thoreau's manuscripts have many pages on the dispersion of seeds and how plant species spread across the landscape. The manuscript, from the 1840s and 1850s, was unpublished until 150 years later.

667 Kochia is native to Europe. Russian Olive was first grown as an ornamental plant in Germany in the 1600s and was brought to the United States in the late 1900s, where it has spread widely in the West. Chinese Elm is another import, from Asia, in the 19th and 20th centuries as an ornamental tree. Cheatgrass or Downy Brome, is a native plant of the Eurasian steppes. It was first found in the United States in the 1860s and is particularly adept in drier, Intermountain plant zones. Canada thistle isn't native to Canada but to Eurasia. It has spread widely throughout North American as a contaminant in feeds. Salt Cedar is an ornamental bush native to the Middle East, where it is called tamarisk in many ancient sources, including the Bible. Introduced and widespread in the Great Plains and the Southwest to prevent soil erosion, salt cedar often displaces willows and cottonwoods along riparian habitats and irrigation canals. It appears to be expanding its range north and west in the United States.

668 Cutright, Paul Russell. *Lewis & Clark: Pioneering Naturalists*, University of Nebraska Press, 1969. The explorers sent numerous plant specimens back to President Thomas Jefferson from the Corps of Discovery. One magpie and a prairie dog survived the journey down the Missouri and Mississippi rivers to New Orleans, and then to Jefferson on the USS Comet, a trip which took four months of over 4,000 miles (p. 379.) Many plant and animal specimens were later lost in a P.T. Barnum fire in 1865, but others may be seen today in various museum collections. In his book, Cutright says he examined one specimen of the Mission Bells plant that "is in such superlative condition that it might have been collected only yesterday" rather than in 1806 from an island on the lower Columbia River. (p. 368.)

Now, many species are distributed by human activity, vehicle transport, feed production and outdoor recreation activities like hiking, hunting and fishing, anything which brings people in contact with outdoor plants.[669]

The spread of human recreation in the past two decades has certainly expanded the range of many plants, limited perhaps only by extent of human wandering. If every part of the West has been trod upon by humans, it's likely there's a seed carried there or away from that spot by the same human or another. Thus, as Southern Idaho and the rest of the West give up their empty quarters, we can expect further dispersions far and near, sometimes with unintended consequences.[670]

This process has been going on a very long time. Ethnobiologists and archeologists can now use plant identification as a way of dating archeological remains and sites; Native American specialists can trace the trade routes of Indian peoples by obsidian chips and plant basket fragments found far from their source locations.

These emergent inquiries have changed the nature of wildlife biology and transformed Idaho's Department of Fish & Game to an agency with broader concerns and pressure to play more roles for more people.

Deer and elk hunters don't necessarily share the same use of the outdoors as bird watchers, yet it is the former which carries the department's budget through licensing. As in other states, resistance is strong by trail walkers and bird watchers to "pay" for a "game" license of any kind. Even campground fees elicit frequent public grumbling. Changing this pattern is likely to take years, if not decades. Meanwhile, the natural and human world of Southern Idaho continues to evolve and change.[671]

The Love of the Stream. It is past dawn on a clear June morning and down on the slicks and eddies of Silver Creek, trout are slurping the cloud of the trico[672] hatch, now just coming off the sliding current. In a nearby thicket

---

669 Whitson, Thomas D, et al. *Weeds of the West*, University of Wyoming Press, 1979.

670 The introduction of the Japanese yew shrub as an ornamental bush in yards and landscape settings has made the toxic shrub available to elk and deer, which come close to homes at night and nibble on available bushes. See Cripe, Chad. "Poisonous yew plants have killed elk in Southern Idaho again," *The Idaho Statesman*, Jan. 11, 2019.

671 Nellis, Carl: "People believe nature is in balance, but it's not. It's constantly changing." Interview, Jan. 14, 2019.

672 *Tricorythodes* (tri-cor-y-tho-des) is a small (2-3 mm) aquatic insect in the Mayfly genus. It's an important trout food insect on many Western rivers, but its small size (24-26 hook) makes it a difficult pattern to present. See Neuswanger, Jason. "Mayfly Genus Tricorythodes (Tricos)," Troutnut.com website, 2019, who says "Their widespread, reliable, heavy hatches draw impressive rises of ultra-selective trout which demand the most of a technical dry-fly angler's skills."

of willows, a deer stirs uneasily. Chats and warbler calls fill the air, mixing with the raucous clatter of Red Wings and Magpies. A light breeze rustles the cattails and Great Basin Ryegrass. A sparse carpet of Gentian Violet flowers hugs the streambank, brilliant spots of color as if from a Monet painting. This spot, part of Southern Idaho's outdoors, is so pristine, so very beautiful, treasured.[673] The fishing is almost incidental; the stream is one endless flow of solitude and beauty.

A half mile or so from the parking lot and there are only the sounds of the natural world except for an occasional overhead jet. Other human noises are generally absent. It is just the rustle of the wind in branches, the hum of a nearby insect, the drumming of a woodpecker. When these suddenly stop in mid-sound, it is usually because they have sensed a human presence.[674]

In his wonderful story of wildness and civilization, "The Bear," William Faulkner describes how Ike McCaslin, deep in November's dank, Southern woods on a hunting trip, notices the bear track in the mud, so fresh it is filling with water even as he watches. Only then, does he see the bear, "Old Ben," watching him, "fixed in the green and windless noon's hot dappling," before it eases back into the forest across a clearing. It is a moment in which the boy comes face to face with the essence of the natural world.[675]

So it is at Silver Creek. A day on a stream is usually in an unspoiled setting, untrammeled by human intrusion. Trout thrive best in clean water with abundant aquatic insect life and these are not found when pollution and sediment cloud the trout's environment. An observant intruder will often spot examples, large and small, of nature's beauty. A blown-down warbler nest, delicate and woven of fine grass and bits of leaf; a wash of rounded stones, glistening wet, just below the surface, left behind by the spring's high water; a few tracks in the mud from a muskrat dragging bits of grass to an undercut bank; a twist of bark, curled and bleached by the sun beneath a black birch shrub.

---

673 The Nature Conservancy, Silver Creek Preserve, website, 2018. The Silver Creek Preserve encompasses nearly 900 acres of the lower Wood River Valley. Silver Creek, a spring fed stream, winds slowly through the area. Its stable, year-round temperature helps produce wave after wave of aquatic insects, thus giving the trout a daily smorgasbord of various insects. It's one of the most renowned trout rivers in the country, indeed in the world, with fly fishermen coming from everywhere. The trout are finicky, and the glass-like water surface makes dry-fly presentation a singular challenge. The stream well deserves its reputation as a "Master's Degree in Fly Fishing."

674 The remainder of this chapter draws on the phrasing and language of the "The Love of the Stream," chapter in Hartgen, Stephen. *Journey West: A Memoir of Journalism and Politics*, Ridenbaugh Press, 2014.

675 Utley, Francis Lee, et. al., eds. *Bear, Man and God: Seven Approaches to William Faulkner's The Bear*, Random House, 1964.

It is a life-mission to fish every trout stream in North America, a goal probably no one has accomplished, and won't, as the number of fishable trout waters surely is in the hundreds of thousands, if not more. No matter, every single one is a joyful and new experience.

Even below the canyon wall and cliffs of Rock Creek Canyon near Twin Falls, the riparian stream banks today are mostly untouched. A hundred years ago, this shallow canyon would have been barely visited in Twin Falls' first years, except for an occasional hunter and flint gatherer near the natural caves crevassed into either wall.

A long period of ignorance and desecration followed, evident from the many scraps of metal and car bodies thrown carelessly over the side, now rusting away; the detritus of 20th century consumerism, from early cans and bottles, to old toasters from the 1920s, to car fenders, milk cans and farmyard hand water pumps, to more recent washing machines and now, even some electronic debris of the early computer age.

It will surely be decades before that evidence is completely gone, but a new ethic in the past generation has begun the recovery of this decidedly "town stream" to something more like its condition at the time of permanent settlement.[676] The water quality of the creek is slowly improving. Irrigation return flow clouds the water in the farming season, but that is much reduced by better practices, small holding ponds at the ends of fields, to catch the sediment.

But otherwise, Rock Creek generally runs clear, particularly in the fall and winter, and insect life abounds. Turn over any stone from under the surface, and there is a myriad of caddis cases, baetis pupae and mayfly eggs and nymphs. A bright spring day brings a boil of trout to feed on this bounty; a nymph pattern fished in the runs and pools invariably brings up dozens of rainbows and a few browns. So does a dry pattern fished on the surface, or just beneath as an emerger.

An early short book on fishing, and likely one of the first books in English written by a woman, is Dame Juliana Berners' *A Treatyse of Fyssynge Wyth An Angle* (1496). One fishes, she says, not for the sport alone, but for the "health of the soul," a statement no less true today than centuries ago when she wrote it. In our pressured world of work and sometimes play in modern America, simpler pleasures rise in importance. "If there be nought in the water," she writes, "yet as the least he has his wholesome walk and merry at his ease, sweet air of the sweet savor of the meadow flowers that makes him hungry. And if the angler take fish, surely then is there no man merrier than he is in his spirit."

---

676 Matthews, Mychel. "The Rock Creek Canyon Recovery: How Can Residents Reverse Decades of Disrepair,?" *Times-News*, May 20, 2018.

"Thus have I proved in my intent," the prioress continues, "that the (sport) and game of angling is the very mean and cause that induces a man into a merry spirit – and therefore to you that be virtuous, gentle and free-born, I write and make this simple treatise following by which you may have the full craft of angling to disport you at your lust to the intent that your age may the more flower and the more longer endure."[677]

Virtuous. Gentle. Free-born. Odd words to our modern ears, but in the Middle Ages, these defined upper-class society of which leisure was a part. There have been many examples of the beauty of angling in outdoors literature, but there are few as simple and forthright as this short and eloquent reflection from Medieval times.

It seems likely that decades or more from now, there will be plenty of Americans who cherish the natural world, who are, in short, virtuous, gentle and free-born. An ethic of respect for nature will likely be an even bigger part of our American way of life, and while it may be extreme at times in the political arena, it is likely to be a dominant feature of public discourse in Southern Idaho.

Yes, the debates may change and the human population will surely grow. But the streams, bluffs and mountains are as clean and pristine as they have been in generations, and getting better through the stewardship of many. We may not have "world enough and time," to accomplish it all, but there will surely be others to carry those causes forward; they are too important to be set aside. The conditions may change, but the love of the stream and the natural world of Southern Idaho will endure.

677 Encyclopedia Britannica's Facts Matter website says Dame Juliana Berners was the prioress of an English nunnery in the mid-1400s, at St. Albans. It continues, "Various accounts of the history of fishing literature describe her as a woman of keen intellect and an accomplished practitioner and avid devotee of outdoor sports, including angling and hunting. Despite its antiquity, Treatyse remains a remarkable work for its detail and vision. A comprehensive guide for the anglers of its time, the book contains substantial information on fishing destinations, rod and line construction, and selection of natural baits and preferred artificial fly dressings categorized by the season of their optimum utility. Perhaps most remarkable are the essays on the virtues of conservation, respecting the rights of streamside landowners, and angler's etiquette. These concepts would not come to be commonly accepted and advocated in the angling world until 400 years after the publication of the Treatyse." Other sources say the good nun is a myth, as there is virtually no evidence to support her existence beyond the oblique reference in the Treatyse itself.

24. Energy & Environment

Energy

It's a clear, slightly hazy morning in 1996 outside the tinted glass of Clear Shield National's corporate headquarters in suburban Chicago. Inside, at a large square of tables in a non-descript conference room, a delegation of Twin Falls city officials and local business leaders is nervously flipping through the sections of prepared notebooks, looking at the information they've brought. Each has a different topic, ranging from availability and quality of water, to school performance, to recreational opportunities in the Southern Idaho region.

Clear Shield is a national manufacturer of plastic forks, knives and spoons for schools, institutions and the fast food industry. Millions of the wrapped packages are distributed nationwide every year. The company is considering a western location to better serve coastal markets. Southern Idaho is getting a detailed look.

Dave McAlinden, Twin Falls' economic development director, and city manager Tom Courtney are leading the discussion. They've put together a group of community representatives to fly to Chicago as a team "tactical force" to seal the Clear Shield initiative.

The next tab is on electric rates and energy supply. They all turn to it as Dan Olmstead, Idaho Power's regional representative in the Magic Valley, takes everyone through the numbers on megawatt availability, peak loads, backup supply. Then he gets to pricing.

Clear Shield's rate in Twin Falls would be at or below 2.5 cents per kilowatt hour, he tells them. Ears perk up. Eyes lift. Olmstead holds up a single sheet with big type on it: less than 2.5 cents per kilowatt hour. "I think we can save you $300,000 a year," he says,[678] referring to a comparison he has made from Clear Shield's own costs at another plant.[679]

Company officials look up from their notebooks. They already know a lot about Twin Falls. Western location. Right-to-Work state. Land provided. Available rail to bring in plastic raw product from petrochemical plants elsewhere. Twin Falls is already on the short list; that's why we're here, to perhaps close the deal.

One company leader asks Olmstead, "Did you say under 2.5 cents/kilowatt hour? That's several times less than what we pay anywhere else. How can you do that?" Olmstead says it's because Idaho Power is an almost all-hydro generating system, a series of dams along the Snake River, a run-of-river system, as well as a vertical company which owns its own transmission lines and sells direct to customers. Small, as electric utilities go, but sizeable enough to meet demand and expansion and new industry.

"Ok," he says, closing the briefing book. "We're coming to Twin Falls." McAlinden says he later learned the company's side-by-side comparison of Twin Falls to the next ranked community gave Twin Falls an eight percent advantage.[680]

Southern Idaho has many pluses when it comes to economic development, but towards the top is the low cost and reliability of electric rates. In 1996, when Clear Shield made the decision to come to Twin Falls, several economic development reports identified the low cost of power as a key business recruitment advantage for Southern Idaho. Clear Shield was only one of a number of opportunities in the plastics extrusion industry, where electric costs are key.[681]

Even today, more than 20 years later, Idaho still ranks well on national electric rate comparisons, third-lowest in the nation at 9.58c/kwh, behind

---

678 Olmstead, Dan. Interview, Feb. 8, 2019.

679 McAlinden says he often would ask an economic development prospect for a recent one-month electric bill, from which could be calculated an estimated comparison bill in the Magic Valley for similar usage. Almost always, he says, it was substantially lower. Interview, Feb. 7, 2019.

680 McAlinden Interview, Feb. 7, 2019.

681 Business Plus, Inc. grant to Clear Shield was $65,000, helping to secure the company's 85 new jobs and economic impact of $7.6 million. Twin Falls also used tax increment financing to build a rail spur to the company's location, says David McAlinden, economic director at the time. (Interview, Feb. 7, 2019). The business community also raised the money, in an effort led by former mayor Doug Vollmer, to buy the land for the plant. Twenty years later, the company has been sold twice and now operates under a new owner, Dart Container, but still makes plastic dinnerware here. See BusinessPlusInc website, 2019; See also, Carlson, Nikki. "Dart Container Buys Red Solo Cup Maker for $1B," *USA Today*, March 22, 2012; See also Dart Container website, 2019.

only Washington (9.46), another state with significant hydro generation and Louisiana (9.09), a state with significant petroleum refining. Hawaii, Alaska and the New England states have the highest rates, from Maine (16.38) to Hawaii (33.82).[682] Idaho's average commercial rate is 9.63c/kwh, fourth lowest in the nation (November, 2018).

In November, 2018, Idaho produced about 1.334 megawatts hours of electricity, but only about one tenth of one percent was from coal, 54 percent (3rd nationally) coming from hydro, 23 percent from natural gas, 2.2 percent from solar (9th nationally) and 16 percent from wind (10th nationally) but none from commercial nuclear power. Those contribution pieces have changed over the years,[683] as Idaho Power has converted from coal to gas-fired plants and a growing portfolio of renewables in addition to its hydro-dominated overall system.[684]

Idaho Power's peak loads generally occur in the summer months, with a daily peak of roughly 3,300 megawatts, when Southern Idaho's irrigation crop watering is in full swing and home and business air conditioning is running hard.[685]

For much of the rest of the year, the company generates a surplus of 300 to 500 megawatts daily ("long" is the term electric company people use, as in "long" on supply.) This "long" or surplus energy is sold to out-of-state systems on the transmission grid, says Olmstead.[686]

In recent years, the company has moved away from coal-fired electricity. It now relies more heavily on both its long-standing hydroelectric dams and on natural gas. A major natural gas pipeline runs underground across Southern Idaho which Idaho Power taps with gas-fired generating plants at Middleton and Mountain Home.[687]

Until recently, Idaho was not a commercial fossil fuels producing state, although oil seeps had been known in Payette County for decades. But in recent years, improved drilling techniques and better deposit mapping have

---

682 ChooseEnergy website, Jan. 29, 2019.

683 Magic Valley electric generation comes from more than 40 generating facilities, including Idaho Power's 7 large dams on the Mid-Snake reach of the Snake River, plus numerous "small-head" hydro plants on canals, streams and ditches, as well as some wind and biomass generation from livestock and dairy operations. Information from Buhidar, Balthasar. "Hydropower and Non-Hydropower Facilities in The Mid-Snake River Area," Idaho Department of Environmental Quality, June 12, 2018.

684 ChooseEnergy website, "How Is Your Electricity Generated,?" Feb. 5, 2019.

685 Idaho Power Company website, "Idaho Power Sets New Peak Demand Record," July 18, 2017. The demand that day was 3,422 megawatts; the previous high was 3,407 megawatts, back in 2013.

686 Olmstead interview, Feb. 8, 2019.

687 Williams Northwest Pipeline website, 2019. The pipeline is about 4,000 miles in length.

brought previously-unrecoverable gas deposits into production.[688] No fossil fuels deposits are known in Southern Idaho, although various locations have been identified for wind, bio-mass (manure), solar and geothermal energy production.[689]

Electricity in Southern Idaho is generated at more than 40 sites, including Idaho Power's string of hydro-electric plants on the Snake River, as well as numerous "small head" hydro-electric sites,[690] wind farms, biomass, solar, natural gas and geothermal. The Idaho Power facilities include 17 sites directly on the river and its tributaries, with generating capacity from 9 to 75 megawatts each.[691]

Partnering with Rocky Mountain Power, Idaho Power is building a major transmission line from Wyoming through Southern Idaho. The Gateway West project of about 1,000 miles will carry electricity across the Intermountain grid to better serve the region. The line would cut across several Southern Idaho counties but is expected to mostly skirt private ranch and farmland.[692]

LS Power, a national electric and transmission line company, is working on a proposed Southwest Intertie Project North (SWIP) 500-kilovolt line from the Midpoint station North of Twin Falls to the Ely, Nevada, area. The project may include reconsideration of the China Mountain wind project, scuttled in 2012 due to resistance by environmental groups and the federal Bureau of Land Management.[693]

---

688 Dunnahoe, Tayvis. "Idaho Enters Ranks of Hydrocarbon Producing States," *Oil & Gas Journal*, Feb. 6, 2017.

689 West, Bowen. "Harnessing the Power in Cow Pies. Can dairy digesters turn cow poop into profit,?" *Times-News*, March 12, 2019. There are five dairy anaerobic digesters in Southern Idaho, says Idaho Power, producing about 14.5 megawatts of power, but they're economically viable only on larger dairy operations.

690 The Northside Canal Company, Jerome, has a 1.2 mgw plant in its system at "Head of the U" drop, using 8 micro turbines., *Irrigation Leader*, Feb., 2019. These small-head hydro plants help their owners defray other costs through the sale of the energy.

691 Buhidar, Balthasar "Sonny." Idaho Department of Environmental Quality, "Hydropower and Non-Hydropower Facilities in the Mid-Snake Area," June 12, 2018, which states: "Virtually all of the water used is non-consumptive, that is passes through the facilities."

692 Olmstead Interview, Feb. 8, 2019. See also Gateway West Transmission Project website, 2019.

693 LSPower website, 2019. The company says of the project: "SWIP North is a 275-mile 500 kV transmission line under development in Idaho and Nevada. SWIP North will provide new transmission capability to deliver renewable wind, geothermal and solar energy resources north and south by resolving a significant missing link in the western grid. In addition, the project will enable bulk reliability enhancements, congestion relief, economic energy exchange, and energy imbalance market opportunities through connectivity of the Northwest and Mountain West electricity markets to the Desert Southwest and California ISO." See also Barker, Rocky. "Utility Pulls Out of Idaho Wind Project," Likely Killing It," *The Idaho Statesman*, April 23, 2012. Full disclosure: The author was a business

While hydroelectric remains the dominant source of Idaho Power's generation, wind, bio-mass, geothermal and solar generation also play expanding roles. Today, U.S. Geothermal operates a geothermal generating plant at Raft River, on the far eastern side of the Magic Valley.[694] There are also various wind and "low-head" hydro generation sites, mostly less than three megawatts capacity, throughout the valley and solar sites are being considered as well.[695] Additionally, there are various small hydro generators on canal drops and minor waterfalls throughout the region.[696]

Whether these renewable sources will eventually compete with fossil fuels and hydroelectric systems, or with nuclear power, remains an open question. Idaho Power estimates its peak hour load will increase about 50 megawatts (mw) annually for the next 20 years. The peak hour load grew from 2.164 mw in 1992, with 306,000 customers, to 3,400 mw in 2013 with 534,000 customers.[697] It almost reached that level again in 2015. With conservation, as well as further development of hydro and other renewables, Idaho Power says it is well positioned to meet current demand and expected growth.[698]

Environment

It's not on everyone's radar. nor is it everyone's inconvenient truth, but environmental protection in Southern Idaho has made significant improvements over the past three decades.

There's more work to be done; the Mid-Snake River is still a "working river," as it has been described, and non-point issues, meaning they have no specific point of origin, including nitrates and phosphorous loading are significant challenges. But in other arenas, there's been considerable improvement.

---

consultant to the China Mountain's earlier developer, RES Industries, from 2006-2008.

694 Future Power Technology website, "The Raft River Geothermal Project, Southern Idaho, USA," 2019.

695 Kennison, Heather. "Renewables Are Vital to Idaho's Energy Production," *USA Today*, June 23, 2018.

696 Both the Twin Falls Canal Company and the North Side Canal Company have small head hydro generating plants on their canal systems. See Matthews, Mychel. "North Side Canal Company Touts New Hydroelectric Plant," *Times-News*, June 2, 2015.

697 *Idaho Power Today*, 2017 Integrated Resource Plan. Email from Dan Olmstead, Feb. 26, 2019.

698 Olmstead Interview, Feb. 8, 2019.

Silt from field soil runoff is being addressed by better holding pond collections. Field burning of crop residue is much reduced and occurs under better guidelines, brought about by agreed-to rules and laws from both users and regulators.

Water quality for domestic use has improved with better filtration, inspection of septic drain fields and better monitoring for contaminants like benzynes, inks and oils. Discharges into the Snake River from both industry and municipalities have decreased markedly. Farm and livestock nutrient management has further to go, but is improving as well. So is field application of chemical herbicides and insecticides. Mercury in fish is monitored regularly.

Arsenic traces in wells have also declined, both naturally occurring and introduced on fruit orchards decades ago to control coddling moths. Arsenic abatement is expensive, as some municipalities have sadly learned.[699] Overall, farm management practices are better with the help of 21st century technologies and bio-chemistry.

On the processing side, consumer demand for purer products is leading to upticks in organics and environmentally sound products. Point-source discharging from processing plants is undergoing closer monitoring and municipalities are making regular improvements in discharge standards.

These improvements don't get much media attention. Yet, in almost every environmental arena in Southern Idaho, progress is real and continuing. It's another example of how the region sets aside posturing and works to find and implement practical solutions.

Idaho operates under what is known as a primacy rule; that is, federal law allows the state to monitor and regulate environmental quality standards, provided these are at least as strict as federal standards. State law generally directs the agency to implement a no-less-than, no-more-than standard, which allows Idaho to keep its own oversight of environmental issues, a real plus when it comes regulation.

It's a clear choice, says state Department of Environmental Quality director John Tippetts, when Idahoans consider whether they'd rather be regulated at the local and state level or from afar by the Environmental Protection Agency from Washington, D.C.[700]

---

699 Buhl found it had to install a new filtration system to reduce arsenic levels, but the effort raised peoples' water/utility bills significantly. The effect was to make the community more expensive for homeowners and renters. See Brown, Nathan. Report: Rep. Simpson Blocked Tighter EPA Standards, *Times-News*, July 9, 2014. See also: Kennison, Heather. "Magic Valley Cities Face Big Water, Waste Water Challenges," *Times-News*, July 10, 2016. Buhl Mayor Tom McCauley says the improvements have positioned Buhl well for growth due to increased capacity.

A major change in EPA/state relations has resulted from the 2016 election of President Donald Trump and the subsequent rollback of proposed EPA rules offered by the previous administration. An example is pulling back a definition of intermittent "waters of the United States" which would have affected many Western water interests by defining even intermittent waters and seeps to be under regulation. These and similar changes at the federal level, including personnel changes at various federal land management agencies, appear to have broad support in Idaho, particularly in the natural resources sectors.[701]

Here's a brief overview of environmental issues today in Southern Idaho:

Air Quality. "Southern Idaho has some of the best air quality in the entire country," says Bobby Dye, the regional air quality manager for DEQ. That's due in part to the geography of the region, a flat terrain with decent winds and no "bowls" to trap stagnant air. Even Ketchum has good quality air, unlike many mountain communities in America. There are times when harvest dust roils the landscape, particularly in Mini-Cassia area, but those periods are usually of short duration.[702] Field burning regulations in recent years have pretty much eliminated complaints.[703]

The major air quality issue affecting the region is smoke from rangeland and forest fires, sometimes hundreds of miles away, which may drift into the area.[704] But for most of the year and under most conditions, Southern Idaho's air quality is good to excellent. From 2014 to 2018, the Twin Falls monitoring station had no fewer than 313 days of "good" air quality, except during the smoky summer and fall of 2017. There were no days of either "very unhealthy" or "hazardous" local air quality through the entire five-year period.[705]

---

700 Tippetts, John. Interview, Feb. 22, 2019. See also "Idaho Pollutant Discharge Elimination Program," Idaho Department of Environmental Quality website, 2019.

701 Russell, Betsy. "Risch, Crapo Praise Trump EPA Water Rule Rollback," *Idaho Press*, Dec. 11, 2018.

702 Dye, Bobby. Interview, Feb. 28, 2019.

703 Department of Environmental Quality website, 2019. "Crop Residue Burning." The DEQ's annual report for crop burning for 2017 recorded about 37,000 acres of crop burning, down from more than 67,000 acres in 2012. The report concludes that "No health concerns were reported resulting from any approved crop residue burning in 2017."

704 Wildfire airborne particulates in Idaho in 2017 totaled over 111,000 tons, ten times the particulates over three years from all the state's vehicles. Particulate emissions from Idaho industries in 2017 were 3 percent of wildfire particulates. See "2017 Idaho Wildfire Emissions Compared to Other Emission Sources in Idaho," Department of Environmental Quality, Healthy Forests website, Jan. 9, 2018.

705 Department of Environmental Quality, "Twin Falls AQI Summary, 2014-2018." Email from Bobby Dye, regional air quality manager, March 19, 2019.

Waste Water Quality. The days are past when communities along the Snake River discharged waste directly into the river, a common practice into the 1970s, says state DEQ scientist Balthasar "Sonny" Buhidar. Municipal treatment, higher permitting regulations on all point-source discharging industries and better technologies have all contributed to improved water quality discharging.

In Twin Falls, the municipal waste-water treatment plant has been routinely upgraded, and pre-treatment by industries like Chobani Yogurt is now required before plants can come on line.[706]

The discharges from Twin Falls facility have higher quality water than the river itself, Buhidar says.[707] Improvements like these have attracted other businesses committed to environmental sustainability, such the energy-bar company, Clif Bar, which chose Twin Falls for a plant partly for those reasons.[708]

Southern Idaho soils are known for their poor drainage characteristics, so the placement of drain fields for individual septic tank systems is often a challenge. Drain field regulation falls to public health districts and would-be homeowners occasionally run into placement issues they didn't expect when a lot is purchased. Better technologies and planning have reduced complaints.

Drinking Water Quality. Time was when drinking water in Southern Idaho was scooped right out of an irrigation ditch or a roof-drained cistern and consumed without treatment. That and an occasional artesian well or spring creek were all that was available in this high desert climate. Today, groundwater wells and aquifer pumping are the most common sources.

Chlorine is added to municipal systems as a disinfectant for microbe control. Disinfection is considered one of the most important public health advances of the 20th century and is widely used in the United States. The city publishes an annual report on water quality; the 2018 report shows arsenic parts per billion (ppb) at 6.5 compared 10.0 maximum contaminant level;

---

706 Wastewater Discharge Agreement, City of Twin Falls and Chobani, Sept. 1, 2015.

707 Buhidar, Balthasar "Sonny." Interview, Feb. 28, 2019.

708 Jarvis, Ben. "Clif Bar, Twin Falls Recognized for Pollution Prevention Achievements," Department of Environmental Quality, News Archive, Sept. 19, 2018: "Among its achievements, Clif Bar can tout a substantially more efficient building and bakery due to the use of hybrid cooling towers that reduce water use by over 30 percent, LED light fixtures and a reflective roof that reduce energy use by 20 percent, and process equipment that result in emission reductions of over 40 percent. The facility is also on track to achieve a zero-waste certification, which it anticipates completing by the year 2020. Efforts currently underway to achieve zero-waste certification include heavy investment in recycling of wood, cardboard, and plastic and supplying over 2,000 tons of feed to local dairy farmers."

2.31 parts/million of nitrates, compared to a contaminant level of 10 ppm; and fluoride at .97 compared to a standard of 4.[709]

Mercury Accumulation. The presence in seafood of mercury and other injurious elements such as selenium has been of concern to health scientists worldwide. Mercury concentrations have been found in Southern Idaho, specifically in fish from the Salmon Falls Creek Reservoir, which has the highest concentrations in the state, resulting in consumption advisories for fish taken from the reservoir.[710]

Nitrate Concentrations. One area of continuing concern is nitrate contamination in Southern Idaho. Nitrates are typically present from septic fields, animal feedlots, and fertilizer applications. Some of these sources are considered "non-point," meaning they have no specific point of origin, but are widely used.[711] In Southern Idaho, Twin Falls, Bliss, Glenns Ferry and Minidoka are among 34 sites in Idaho listed as Nitrate Priority Areas. In the Twin Falls area, some 540 of 618 sites showed concentrations of over two milligrams/liter, of which 35 sites were over 10mg/liter, the state and federal drinking water standard.[712]

The U.S. Geological Service report identifies the Paul and Minidoka areas as having the highest concentrations.[713] Agricultural leaders dispute the accuracy of these reports, saying they fail to look at other potential sources of the problem.[714]

Idaho's nutrient management plans for livestock and dairy operations are handled by the state Department of Agriculture, an oversight authority some environmentalists fought as not providing enough regulation. Confined animal feedlot operations (CAFOs) are generally better-sited today and early complaints about location of CAFOs have been mostly resolved.[715]

---

709 City of Twin Falls website. "Consumer Confidence Report, 2018."

710 "Wet Deposition of Mercury in Idaho," Department of Environmental Quality website, March 2013: "The spatial distribution of mercury wet deposition in Idaho follows regional climatic, latitudinal, and terrain-based factors. No major anomalies that could be attributed to local sources are detectable. Most wet deposition in Idaho appears to come from the global pool." The report downplays a perception that mercury in Idaho comes from Nevada mines.

711 Department of Environmental Quality website, 2019, "Nitrate in Ground Water."

712 DEQ nitrates report, 2014.

713 Skinner, Ken. US Geological Service, quoted by Cotterell, Adam. "Pollution Increasing in Idaho's Snake River Aquifer," Boise State Public Radio, Jan 29, 2015: "The areas where we found the greatest nitrate concentrations is around the Paul and Minidoka area: There's a lot of nitrogen inputs coming in that area, but the ground water there is just moving along slowly. So those nitrogen inputs have time to hit the ground water table, and start working their way down into depth were the pumps are for people."

714 Ellis, Sean. "Ag Leaders Reject USGS Nitrate Study," *Capital Press*, Feb. 13, 2013.

Looking ahead, says DEQ director Tippetts, point-source pollution issues to water bodies and rivers are being addressed, but there needs to be more effort, and money, put into programs to enhance best management practices for non-point agricultural operations. That's likely to be a continuing challenge in the years ahead.[716]

Phosphorous Loading. Another environmental concern is the level of phosphorus in the Middle Snake River. Phosphorus is a commonly-used fertilizer in many non-point agriculture operations, as well as on lawns and gardens. Reduced flows in the Mid-Snake through the Magic Valley mean less dilution; the result is an increase in phosphorus loading in the river which leads to aggressive algae growth, reduced fish habitat and sluggish river conditions generally.[717]

DEQ reports and other studies of the phosphorus accumulation issue suggest multiple potential causes. Going back to studies in the 1980s and 1990s, phosphorus loading appears linked to increased manure from livestock operations and other sources.[718] A comprehensive 2014 study for the Environmental Protection Agency also identified phosphorus levels as a potential major issue for the river's water quality.[719]

Buhidar says non-point management practices need to be monitored and implemented year-round, not just intermittently. Half of the river from Milner Dam to King Hill, he says, now tests at .08 mg/l, higher than the .075 mg/l standard.[720]

Increased pressure from regulatory authorities has prompted review of how to reduce phosphorus levels and setting new standards for total maximum daily loads (TMDL) with which industry and municipalities would need to comply, at high estimated costs.[721]

Environmental Politics. Nutrient management remains a specific concern for many in agriculture that won't be resolved anytime soon. An ongoing issue is how environmental issues are politicized. Objectively,

---

715 Idaho Department of Agriculture website, 2019. "Environmental/Nutrient Management Program."

716 Tippetts Interview, Feb. 22, 2019.

717 Buhidar, Balthazar "Sonny" and Woodhead, Sean. Idaho Department of Environmental Quality, Interview, Feb. 28, 2019.

718 Carey, Anna, et. al. "BUL 877 Phosphorus In The Calcareous Soils of Southern Idaho," *University of Idaho Extension Bulletin*, April, 2011.

719 Tetra Tech. Reevaluation of Mid-Snake/Upper Snake-Rock Sub-basin in TMDL (Total Maximum Daily Load), US Environmental Protection, Agency, Sept., 2014.

720 Buhidar, Interview, Feb. 28, 2019.

721 Sunquist, Cassie and Jeszke, Chris. "Reopening of the Mid-Snake TMDL," US. Fish & Wildlife Service, Power Point Presentation, May 4, 2018.

Tippetts says, decisions would be based on science, but for many, environmental issues are emotional and spill over into policy choices.[722]

Today, various environmental groups are active voices and lobbyists on a host of environmental issues affecting Idaho. Idaho Rivers United, for example, works on water quality issues and opposes mining development. Like other environment groups, it posts donation appeals throughout its website. It even has a "brewshed" link for local microbreweries to get involved in water quality issues "Simply put: Great beer begins with clean water."[723]

The Conservation Voters For Idaho is a politically-active group which says its mission includes "elect(ing) candidates to public office who will protect Idaho's clean air and water, natural places, wildlife and human health." It has become involved in various Southern Idaho political contests, usually but not always, on the Democratic side.[724]

The Idaho Chapter of the Sierra Club advocates for dam removal on the lower Snake River, as well as the return of wild salmon runs. It is also involved in various national conservation issues.[725] The Nature Conservancy of Idaho, led by former DEQ director Toni Hardesty, is involved in many state conservation efforts, including easements and purchases. It manages the Silver Creek Preserve in Blaine County, one of the premier trout streams in the state and nation.[726]

Another active group is the Idaho Conservation League which like others, is engaged in lobbying on state conservation issues, as well as on broader concerns like climate change and its impact on Idaho.[727]

One of the best-known groups on Idaho's environmental scene is Western Watersheds Project, founded in 1993 by Hailey activist and architect Jon Marvel. He's since retired, but in his more than 20 years of environmental activism, he focused on removal of cattle and sheep ranching on Western public lands. The group's mission is now broader in scope, but anti-grazing on public lands remains a key focus.[728]

---

722 Tippetts Interview, Feb. 22, 2019.

723 Idaho Rivers United website, 2019.

724 Conservation Voters for Idaho website, 2019. See also Idaho Secretary of State, campaign finance reports, 2018.

725 Idaho Chapter, Sierra Club website, 2019.

726 Nature Conservancy of Idaho website, 2019, "Annual Report, 2018."

727 Bunch, Riley. "Climate change hearing shows lack of data on potential impacts on Idaho," *Idaho State Journal*, March 7, 2019.

728 Western Watersheds Project website, 2019. See also Barker, Rocky. "Idaho's Anti-Grazing Activist Jon Marvel Has Retired," *The Idaho Statesman*, May 7, 2015.

The Snake River Alliance focuses on anti-nuclear issues and has opposed nuclear research and development at the Idaho National Laboratory site near Idaho Falls for decades. A 1995 waste cleanup agreement between the Department of Energy and the state has not been completely met, thus giving the Alliance further anti-nuclear arguments.[729]

DEQ director Tippets says the state maintains good leverage on INL's nuclear waste issues. Federal financial support is important to INL's future with development of small-scale nuclear generation prototypes.[730]

While acknowledging that progress is being made on a number of fronts, Southern Idaho is likely to see environmental issues two or three decades from now. Given the widespread issues of agriculture and environmental protection, we could hardly expect otherwise.

---

729 Snake River Alliance website, 2019. See also Idaho Department of Environmental Quality, "INL Oversight Program" website, 2019, which publishes annual reports from the DEQ on INL waste issues. The issue flared again in the 2018 governor's campaign with winning GOP candidate Brad Little saying he would support allowing small amounts of spent nuclear fuel into Idaho for research purposes. See nuclear-news.net website, "Idaho politics – differences between governor candidates on nuclear issues," Feb 8, 2018.

730 Tippets Interview, Feb. 22, 2019.

25. Recreation & Tourism: Where Are The Falls?

When visitors enter the Twin Falls Visitor's Center, perched as it is on the rim of a 486-foot-deep canyon looking out on a high bridge spanning 1,500 feet, rim to rim, the first questions they are likely to ask are: "Where are the falls?" and second, "Where did Evel Knievel jump?"

Directions to Shoshone Falls, dubbed the "Niagara of the West," are easily given. An out-of-town road to the east and a couple of tight turns down the canyon lead visitors to a viewing platform very close to the precise spot where the artist Thomas Moran painted the rushing cataract in 1900.[731] If the time of year is right and the water is running, visitors can see the plunging falls of more than 200 feet to the mist-shrouded pool below.[732]

The Evel Knievel jump site can be seen from the Visitor's Center, but it's on private land and not accessible to the public. Although Knievel's attempt failed in 1974, the location has an almost cult-like status among the motorcycle bikers who were there by the thousands and the estimated millions who watched it on television.

Knievel was a self-promoter of the first order, having begun his motorcycle jumping career by wheeling over a 20-foot box of

---

731 "Shoshone Falls on the Snake River" is at the Gilcrease Museum, Tulsa, Ok. The Moran painting on full display is 6 by 12 feet. It is considered one of Moran's best Western landscapes. A nice copy is on display at Twin Falls City Hall.

732 Twin Falls city-managed Shoshone Falls overlook logged more than 100,000 vehicles halfway through 2017, with revenue over $300,000. Kennison, Heather. "High Water Lifts Magic Valley Tourism," *Times-News*, Aug. 27, 2017.

rattlesnakes and two live cougars.[733] The jump attempt event drew a crowd estimated at between 5,000 and 10,000 people but estimates vary up to 40,000. No one really knows. As the time neared, boisterous spectators rampaged two full beer trucks, emptying them of their contents. Photos show the crowd passing a near-naked woman hand-over-hand at shoulder height above the throng. Police struggled to restore normalcy, and it's something of a badge of honor today to say "I was there" on that September afternoon.

It was our own little Woodstock, an event *The Times-News* called the "put on of the century" that was thankfully over.[734] Evel left town owing debts but in a 1999, 25-year anniversary visit, he said he had cleared all bills presented to him. Locals say angry bikers smashed and torched some 200 new wooden outhouses and on his 1999 return, he was presented with one bill for $9,591.71, plus interest running for 25 years. He claimed to have made Twin Falls the "Center of the Universe for just one day."[735]

It's a good bet people remember this event more than another on the same day, Sept. 8, 1974; that was the day President Gerald Ford pardoned his disgraced predecessor, Richard Nixon, but it's not likely anyone at the visitor's center today remembers that. Evel Knievel? Now him, they remember.

Tourism and recreational sports have come of age in Southern Idaho since that rowdy afternoon. The Visitor's Center, which wasn't there at the time, now handles more than 13,000 sign-in visitors from all over the world during peak months.[736] The Idaho Department of Commerce lists tourism as the state's third largest industry, behind agriculture and technology, employing more than 13,000 people and generating about $1.4 billion in annual revenue. For South-Central Idaho, the department lists the region as generating over $184 million and employing 2,600 people. Four in 10 visitors are from elsewhere in Idaho, to visit family and friends, tour the area and "experience the outdoors."[737]

---

733 Wikipedia, "Evel Knievel," Updated, Sept. 26, 2018. See also Kennison, Heather. "Tourism Boom: Increased Lodging Sales Highlight South-Central Idaho's Successes," *Times-News*, Sept. 11, 2016.

734 Wrote the *Times-News* editorial board, "Evel was surely correct when he said the jump would place Twin Falls squarely on the map. But to be known as the host city of the put-on of the century is hardly the kind of fame this community wants or deserved. Thank heaven it's over." N.D., quoted in Smith, Brian. "Retracing Knievel's Jump Through *Times-News* Coverage," *Times-News*, Sept. 7, 2014.

735 Friedman, Cassidy, et. al. "Locals Recall Evel's Circus of '74," *Times-News*, Dec. 1, 2007.

736 Twin Falls Chamber of Commerce, Visitor's Center statistics show 2017 numbers at 62,185 signed-in visitors compared to 53,569 for 2016, a 16 percent increase, and nearly 2.5 times the visitor count in 2014 (18,087) at the tail end of the Recession. Email from Shawn Barigar, Chamber executive director, Oct. 8, 2018.

737 Idaho Department of Commerce, Idaho Tourism website, 2015 statistics.

As tourism has grown, so have different ways of enjoying what the region has to offer. Sports like BASE (Bridge, Antennae, Structure, Earth) jumping, rafting, kayaking, rock climbing, cycling and just walking a fitness trail have increased in popularity along with the more traditional activities associated with outdoor recreation in the Intermountain West.

There was a time, not too many decades ago, when outdoor recreation meant hunting, fishing and maybe a little camping, but the range of activities has created robust industries and benefitted their purveyors and suppliers.[738] Political groups have sprouted up as well, which often oppose multiple land uses and extractive industries. These groups often base their funding appeals on exaggerated claims of how ranching, cattle grazing and other traditional uses are damaging public lands and pitch their fund-raising messages accordingly.

When recreational users and tourists get to town, they often choose to stay in a hotel or motel, and Idaho has seen a huge building boom in this sector in the past two decades. The state has almost 23,000 hotel rooms and new facilities are being added at a quickened rate. Burley has two new motels, as does Twin Falls, and more are being developed in Ketchum and Hailey.[739]

There are about 1,200 hotel and motel rooms in the immediate Southern Idaho area, many of which have been built since 2000. More are on the way.[740] Most are about 75-120 rooms each, including LaQuinta (101 rooms), Hilton Garden Inn (107), Holiday Inn Express (91) Fairfield Inn (92) and Hampton Inn (75).[741] Occupancy rates vary by season.

There are numerous golf courses as well the premier membership course, Blue Lakes Country Club in the canyon below the Perrine Bridge. Many others, including municipal and other golf venues with varying degrees of difficulty and vistas, are close by, as well as assorted driving ranges, putting tees and clubhouses. Many are open most of the year, given the area's late fall and early spring weather.

---

738 Pew Center of the States. "Idaho: The Economic Contributions of Hunting, Fishing and Wildlife-watching on BLM Lands," Oct. 4, 2018. This report puts the statewide economic value of these activities at $85 million in salaries and another $295 million in sales on the 11.9 million acres of BLM land in the state.

739 Vitu, Teya. "For Idaho: The Year of the Hotel," *Idaho Business Review*, June 13, 2017.

740 Kennison, Heather. "Rooms with A View: Four-story Hotel Planned for Canyon Rim," *Times-News*, Jan. 8, 2019. The hotel announcement brought numerous comments about Twin Falls' growth and planning decisions, most of them negative. See Woods, Steve. "Planned Hotel Is an Attack on Twin Falls," *Times-News*, Jan.13, 2019 and comments following.

741 Email from Barry, Melissa, Southern Idaho Tourism director, Oct. 18, 2018. See also Kennison, Heather. "No Room At The Inn," *Times-News*, Feb. 8, 2019.

A common local complaint is the lack of a large convention center, but a private-sector center, Canyon Crest, already exists on a dramatic canyon rim property, and there is little evidence that residents want to pay more taxes for a public facility.[742]

Two participation sports, BASE jumping and rock climbing, illustrate how additional venues have added to the Southern Idaho recreation profile. BASE jumping from the I.B. Perrine Bridge began in the 1980s. but expanded dramatically when the Visitor's Center opened just a short walk from the bridge. On almost any nice day except in winter, jumpers can be seen in the visitor parking lot, folding their parachutes and checking their equipment. Jumps are generally to the east, where a landing zone is established on the river's south shore.

The bridge is one of the few places in the country where BASE jumping is legal and encouraged, so it draws jumpers from all over the country and world. There are a number of "jump training" businesses in town, and some jumpers have made multiple jumps in a single day.[743] A one-time Chamber of Commerce director, J. Kent Just, had a sign along Interstate 84 which appealed to jumpers directly, as well as to general tourists and Knievel fans. "Evel jumped here," it said, with a picture of the bridge in the background, "but you can take the bridge." Why, yes you can, unless you only want to jump off, halfway across.[744]

A premier rock-climbing site in Cassia County, the City of Rocks National Reserve, was formally created in the 1994 and has been a climbing destination ever since. Its granite spires are along the original route of the California Trail, just a few miles upstream on the Raft River cutoff from the main Oregon Trail. Hand-carved inscriptions can be seen on many of the rocks where trail pioneers rested and grazed their teams.[745] The site is remote, but not isolated; it lies in a picturesque valley of the Albion Mountains and offers, along with nearby Castle Rocks State Park, some spectacular scenery, challenging climbing sites, cheap camping, a visitor's center, and in the

---

742 Small city convention centers rarely bring in the hoped-for revenue and are often expensive to build and expensive to maintain; they rapidly become "white elephants" from long periods of vacancy. See Hood, Nathaniel. "Convention Centers: It's a Race to the Bottom," Strong Towns website, July 11, 2012.

743 Glazer, Ed. "Twin Falls Man Makes Leap Jumping BASE Accessories," *Times-News*, June 10, 2014.

744 Kennison, Heather. "BASE jumper sets record in South Idaho," *Idaho State Journal*, June 25, 2017.

745 An estimated 52,000 people traveled this route by covered wagon to the California gold mines in the single year of 1852. We know who some of them were from the inscriptions they left more than 150 years ago and there are even photos of some from later in their lives. See National Park Service, "City of Rocks," updated May 25, 2017. See also, Stone, Beverly and Gary. *Stone By Stone On The Oregon Trail*, Stone Studios, 1993.

hamlet of Almo, a restaurant and country store.[746] A close-by state park, Castle Rock, has excellent beginners' climbs and offers limited "bunkhouse" style accommodations, including campsites and yurts.[747]

With so much public lands nearby, it's not surprising that Southern Idaho would blossom as a recreation mecca. Numerous trails, riding paths and hiking sites abound in the area, offering outdoor recreation of all kinds. Off-road recreational vehicle use is common in all seasons, with various groups like the Magic Valley Trail Machine Association[748] providing riding and snowmobile routes through nearby hills and high desert landscapes.

As a high-desert region, Southern Idaho may not be perceived as having much water sports, but numerous reservoirs, rivers, streams and natural lakes provide many opportunities. Redfish Lake in the Stanley Basin, has crystalline waters and the nearby high Sawtooth Range remind visitors of Canadian lakes and parks.[749] Jet-skiing, boating, water skiing and riverfront beaches also offer opportunities for water enthusiasts.

Nearby snow-skiing hills are well used in the winter months. Magic Mountain, just south of Twin Falls, is a family-friendly and lower-cost ski hill, as is the Soldier Mountain ski area, north of Fairfield. Pomerelle Ski Area, on Mt. Harrison in Cassia County, often has annual spring skiing second to none in the region.

And of course, there's the glitzy Sun Valley/Ketchum area with its world-famous Mount Baldy ski area, swanky accommodations, fancy restaurants and world-class entertainment and ice-skating shows.[750] Like the rest of the industry, the Sun Valley area has gone out of its way to promote the area as a year-round destination, with various promotions including arts, in-town saloons and bars, summer antique fairs, fall "trailing of the sheep" festivals and an array of activities available in the adjacent Sawtooth National Forest. The nearby Frank Church River of No Return Wilderness offers multi-day trips on the Salmon River, one of the Northwest's remaining free-flow drainages.

This wide assortment of activities inevitably puts recreational pursuits in regular conflict with traditional resource industries. As was noted in the previous chapter on multiple use, industries like mining and timber have mostly faded, and yearly pressure on grazing allotments is diminishing livestock operations. How these competing uses – indeed, competing values

---

746 MacDonald, Dougald. "Welcome to Paradise City," *Climbing*, Sept. 25, 2013.

747 Idaho Department of Parks and Recreation, "Castle Rocks State Park," website, N.D.

748 Magic Valley Trail Machine Association website, 2019.

749 US Forest Service, Department of Agriculture, "Redfish Lake" website.

750 Sun Valley Resort website and VisitSunValley.com., 2018.

– will play out in the West is one of the great unknown policy issues today, and is likely to be so in the future.

One new and positive development is the location of recreational manufacturing in the area. Smith ski goggles and Scott ski poles and goggles merged in the 1970s, with Smith, of Ketchum, turning out 200,000 goggles a year.[751] But the sector was relatively undeveloped until recently. Then, ClifBar, an energy food bar company, opened a bakery and production plant in Twin Falls. The company focuses on recreation and sustainability in its marketing and its presence here could lead to further development of recreational/foods manufacturing.[752]

Numerous studies and reports on the state's recreation industries quantify the sector's direct and indirect economic impacts[753] and a state tourism fee on motel accommodations and similar properties helps spread the word on Idaho's many tourism attractions.[754]

A Twin Falls Recreation Center?

As the Southern Idaho region grows in population, some think the community needs more recreational public venues. There's a recreation center in Jerome, gifted to the community when Tupperware closed and the buyer of that facility didn't want the adjoining center and pool. But there are costs associated with running a public recreational center and Jerome County has some of the highest property taxes in the area, a likely sore point in any discussion.

An ad hoc committee is studying the idea, but how to fund it remains a significant unknown.[755] There are many potential needs in the community, including schools, jail expansion, road and street development, fire stations,

751 Shapiro, T. Rees. "Bob Smith, inventor of ski goggles, dies at 78," *The Washington Post*, April 28, 2012.

752 Matthews, Mychel, "Twin Falls ClifBar Bakery Begins Shipping Bars," *Times-News*, June15, 2016. The company said it selected Twin Falls because in "all Five Bottom lines - sustaining our business, brands, people, community and planet – Twin Falls really stood out." ClifBar & Company website, 2018. "Twin Falls FAQS."

753 Longwoods international, Idaho 2017 Regional Visitor Research, 2016-17 Travel Years, website. South Central Region, p 176 ff.

754 Idaho Department of Commerce, Office of Tourism Development website. The hotel/motel fee is a 2 percent surcharge. Annual lodging tax receipts are over $12 million, with part of the money being returned to local tourism entities.

755 Kennison, Heather. "Does Twin Falls Need a Recreation Center? The City Hopes to Find Out," *Times-News*, May 15, 2018.

maybe even a larger convention center, so it's not clear how a recreation center would fit into all that.

Then there's the likely opposition from various fitness centers in the community whose businesses would be hurt. A city pool, taken over from the YMCA in 2017, is losing money, and there's no immediate solution to that either.[756]

All in all, it's a good bet that there will be more recreational pressure on resources, costs and choices of amenities. Parks and recreation thinking today embodies community pride and envy, so an area like Southern Idaho, already known for its recreation, isn't going to want to be "second baseball diamond" to anyone.

756 Kennison, Heather. "City Pool Reports Overall Loss in First 11 Months," *Times-News*, Mar. 18, 2018.

26. Generosity & Volunteerism

As in many smaller American communities, life in Southern Idaho is marked by much civic pride, volunteerism, out-of-pocket giving and support for many charitable organizations. Idaho has generally ranked well on "giving ratio" rankings; a 2012 study found Idaho ranked No. 2 in the country, behind Utah, in tax reported charitable giving at 4.09 percent, with the national average about 3.5 percent of income.

As across the nation, Idahoans of more modest means gave a higher proportion of income, nearly 10 percent, than wealthier individuals. Overall, charitable giving in Idaho came back strongly after the recession and passed $860 million in 2012.

There were differences among Idaho regions. The more generous regions were Southern and Eastern Idaho counties, typically higher than, say, Ada County (3.39 percent) which was closer to the national norm and lower than either Southern or Eastern Idaho.[757]

Other studies also rank Idaho highly on charitable giving, but more than one survey notes that the high numbers for Utah and Idaho may be due the higher proportion of Church of Jesus Christ of Latter-Day Saints members, which encourages members to tithe 10 percent of their incomes. Since churches are considered charities for tax purposes, surveys which include church charities may have an additional advantage when measured this way.[758]

---

757 Wright, Samantha. "Idahoans Give More Than People in Most States", Boise State Public Radio, KBSU, Oct.n14, 2014. and see *Chronicle of Philanthropy*, "How America Gives", Oct. 3, 2017.

Even without church donations, Idaho giving has expanded greatly in recent years with the establishing or expanding of several major statewide foundations, including the Albertson Foundation ($28 million) the Idaho Community Foundation ($5.3m) the Laura Moore Cunningham Foundation ($4.1m)[759] and the Micron Foundation ($3.4m)

This has given rise to a new industry in the state of grant writing, grant administration and charitable giving entrepreneurship. Many communities, including Twin Falls, have dozens of specialists whose work usually involves significant fund-raising.

Additionally, many broad-based charities operate in the state including nationally-known entities like the American Cancer Society, the Humane Society, as well as politically-active ones like the Sierra Club, the Nature Conservancy. and Conservation Voters of Idaho. Some of these are outwardly engaged in public policy debates and may take positions assisting or trying to defeat political candidates. Additionally, government entities have expanded their support role for a long list of civic causes and programs, a practice which is now coming under closer scrutiny.[760]

Many local charitable groups are particularly active during the holiday season, which some rely on for a good share of their annual budgets. "Festival of Giving" tree and wreath purchasing events are held in both Twin Falls and Burley. Auction dinners for the College of Southern Idaho Foundation and celebration nights for groups like the Boys and Girls Club of Twin Falls[761] are common events, as are various golf tournaments, gun club turkey shoots, fun runs and all sorts of open houses for social service-oriented groups and clubs. These are typically given some attention in the media and most also have Facebook pages and events calendars.[762]

Community giving in places like Southern Idaho has been studied extensively and researchers often find that being generous often has specific, if non-monetary, rewards for givers as well as recipients. It's well-known that giving helps people feel good about themselves, as well as helping the less-

758 Bever, Lindsey. "Which States Give the Most to Charity? The Ones with Church-goers," *The Washington Post*, Oct. 6, 2014

759 The Grantsmanship Center, "Top Giving Foundations: Idaho," 2006-2018.

760 Kennison, Heather. "Twin Falls Has Given More Than $1.5 Million to Non-Profits," *Times-News*, Sept. 10, 2018.

761 The Boys and Girls Club of Twin Falls raised more than $60,000 for the building project at a dinner in November, 2018.

762 Wootton-Greener, Julie. "Here's How 4 Magic Valley Non-Profits Prepare for the Holiday Season," *Times-News*, Nov 22, 2018. The 2018 "Festival of Giving" raised over $300,000, a 50 percent increase from the previous year. *Times-News*, Dec. 20, 2018.

fortunate.[763] That seems particularly so in a place like the Magic Valley, where giving and volunteerism are so widespread.

Foundations. Prior to the 2000s, charitable contributions from larger groups consisted of long-established local sources, but new groups have widened the scale and added new participants since. In 2006, St. Luke's Regional Medical Center, in a bid to take over an aging Twin Falls County hospital, put $15 million into a community health care fund, which disperses local annual grants.[764] Since 2008, the fund has distributed $2.9 million in local grants; 16 recipients got a combined $250,000 in 2017, ranging from $4,962 to $20,000.[765]

The College of Southern Idaho Foundation is one of the largest community college foundations in the country with assets of almost $41 million and gave out more than $2 million in scholarships help in 2017; its goal in the coming years is to provide scholarships to cover half the school's students.[766]

A third large charity established in recent years is the Chobani Foundation, established by the company's CEO, Hamdi Ylukaya, which is known for its Greek yogurt, and its one-million square-foot plant in Twin Falls. The self-made entrepreneur and Turkish immigrant, has an estimated personal worth of more than $1 billion and has said he plans to give a good share of that to charity. Since establishing Chobani in Twin Falls, the company has made numerous donations to civic projects, charities and other local causes, including dairy industry scholarships, non-profit creative grants, the Twin Falls downtown plaza, and holiday food projects to help the needy.[767]

All three of these entities are relatively new to the Southern Idaho charities scene. The CSI Foundation dates to the 1980s; the other two are less than 20 years old. Yet, all are making significant contributions to the charities picture in the Magic Valley.

They supplement entities like the Salvation Army, the Glanbia Charities Challenge ($2.1m given to area 501(c)3 entities since 1993), the Twin Falls School District Education Foundation ($1 million-plus in assets in 2018), the

763 Anon. "Giving Rewards the Giver with Happiness," *Healthy Women*, Aug. 15, 2017.

764 Twin Falls Health Initiatives Trust website, 2018.

765 Wootton-Greener, Julie. "Twin Falls County Nonprofit Received an Early Christmas Present: a Grant for 2018, *Times-News*, Dec. 22, 2017.

766 College of Southern Idaho Foundation Annual Reports, 2017, 2018. website. See also 2005 Annual Report, assets, $20m, $640k scholarships; 2010 Report, $26m assets, $1,147m scholarships; 2013 Report, assets, $33m, $ 1.295m scholarships.

767 Kennison, Heather. "Chobani Foundation Is Offering $100k Grants for "Big Ideas" in the Magic Valley," *Times-News*, Oct. 3, 2018.

Twin Falls Library Foundation, First Federal Savings Foundation, the Florence Gardner Trust and the Janice Seagraves Family Foundation, founded in 2001 by Ms. Seagraves, who had won a sizeable lottery drawing.[768]

Looking ahead, it's likely the expanding wealth of Southern Idaho people will lead to more foundation support for local projects and causes. We can expect to see more sizeable donations in the coming decades. A broad and expanding support for charitable giving is a good indicator of community financial health. By that measure, Southern Idaho is coming of age as an expanding group of local individuals in the Magic Valley routinely give back to their communities.[769]

Civic Clubs. Twin Falls has a long-established record of civic clubs, including three Rotary Club chapters, Kiwanis, P.E.O., Optimists and Lions. Some, like the Twentieth Century Club, have faded with time and the passing of their members. Rotary and other traditional organizations have also seen dwindling membership over the decades, but remain active.[770]

They sponsor numerous fund-raising events and take on occasional special projects like Rotary's Roy and Verna Marie Raymond Centennial Memorial Pavilion at Waterfront Centennial Park and the CSI Fitness Trail which winds along the Perrine Coulee through the CSI campus.[771] Kiwanis hosts an annual Octoberfest traditional German dinner of sausage and sauerkraut to raise money for youth projects.[772] Rotarians sponsor a "Death

---

768 Janice Seagraves Family Foundation website, 2018. The website says Ms..Seagraves won a Powerball Lottery on Christmas Day, 1996, and established the foundation "hoping to make a lasting impact in the community, Ms. Seagraves used her winnings to set up the Janice Seagraves Family Foundation to help future generations. Since 2001, the Foundation has awarded grants to a variety of organizations around the Magic Valley. Although Ms. Seagraves passed away, her legacy lives on through the Foundation and its governing Board of Directors."

769 Welch, Laurie. "King's to Close all Stores," *Times-News*, Feb. 21, 2017. Herman King gave $1 million to the Burley community for the new King Performing Arts Center. In Twin Falls, the Kyle family gave $600,000 for a new addition on the YMCA building. See Brown, Nathan. "McDonalds Owners Donate 600k to YMCA," Times-News, June 21, 2014. Retailer Earl Faulkner gave $6 million to CSI for a planetarium. Longtime Twin Falls retailer, John Roper, is honored by the Twin Falls High School Roper Auditorium.

770 Wootton, Julie. "Clubs Need Influx of Youth to Keep Service Legacy Rolling," *Times-News*, Nov. 27, 2016.

771 The Twin Falls Rotary Club alone has raised and donated nearly $1 million in various projects since the 1980s, including CSI Fitness Trail, $100k; Waterfront Centennial Park, $120k; Roy and Verna Marie Raymond Centennial Memorial Pavilion, $90k; Downtown Plaza and Splash Park, $120,000; Death By Chocolate, $375k; Rotary Foundation since 1950s, $299k. Email From Kevin Bradshaw, club secretary, Nov. 29, 2018.

772 The Twin Falls Kiwanis Club has raised and allocated about $167,000 from 2002 to 2018. Email from Zach Anderson, Kiwanis Treasurer, Dec. 13, 2018.

by Chocolate" sweets-sampling evening and an ice cream social at City Park; Kiwanis members have added a horse-therapy support effort for children[773] and Optimists sponsor a "Lost Wages" evening fundraiser.

The clubs may be smaller than they once were, but they've reached out in recent years for members to once-overlooked groups like women and minorities. Kiwanis in the 1980s had female members (Shawna Fuller), and this author sponsored the first woman (Morgan Jeno) to the Twin Falls Rotary Club, following a 1987 U.S. Supreme Court ruling that women could not be denied membership in civic clubs based on gender. A few men quit the club over the issue, and in Buhl, a number left Rotary to form a "West End Men's Club," which continues today.[774] It was another decade until Twin Falls Rotary had its first female president, accountant Ruth Stevens Pierce. Today, perhaps a third of the Twin Falls Rotarians are women and they've taken the lead in many projects and fundraisers. Most are professional women with important roles in the community, which is better indeed for their involvement.

Another long-term practice, that of black-balling prospective members, has been wisely discarded. Black-balling was done out of personal animosity, business competition or affiliation with a controversial group like a union. It was common practice in the 1980s, but again wisely, it's been years since this practice occurred.

With the crunch of many commitments on people's time, it's been widely noticed nationally that civic clubs struggle for both new members and missions. Twin Falls, following examples in Boise and Idaho Falls, has attempted to form an ongoing City Club of Twin Falls, sponsoring local forums on topics like health care, court reform and a forum of gubernatorial candidates. It remains to be seen if this will stick in the community, although the initial forums have a wide array of topics have attracted younger audiences.[775]

Volunteerism. It's not easy to gauge the dollar contributions in civic involvement in the Magic Valley over the past three decades or so, but a good guess might be well over $100 million. Whatever that number, it's probably long since been surpassed by the number of hours Southern Idaho people have put in civic affairs and charitable pursuits.

---

773 Matthews, Mychel. "Children and Horses Bond at Rising Stars Therapeutic Riding Center," *Times-News*, Nov. 22, 2018.

774 The author writes about this in his memoir, *Journey West: A Memoir of Journalism and Politics*, 2014.

775 Wootton-Greener, Julie. "New City Club Plans Republican Governor Forum," *Times-News*, Dec. 17, 2017.

There's an opportunity for every level of skill and participation. Volunteers build homes for Habitat for Humanity, drive seniors to medical appointments and serve meals at Senior Centers, collect winter coats for KMVT's Christmas for kids, lead Scouting programs and field trips, watch children in a Kid Zone after school program at Filer First Baptist Church Others rake gravel to maintain fitness trails, serve at Salvation Army food dispensaries, volunteer time at the LDS' Deseret Industries and Relief Society programs, and serve in more formal roles like child advocacy in courts, maintaining the front desk at the Twin Falls Visitor Center and helping patients at St. Luke's Regional Medical Center. Valley House Homeless Shelter helps people in homeless situations get through those trying circumstances.[776]

The list of volunteer-based contributing organizations is considerable and if not listed here, it's due to space constraints only. All are appreciated and help make Southern Idaho the generous community that it is.

Looking ahead, it seems likely that civic participation will continue to evolve in Southern Idaho, with yet more donations and perhaps large projects funded both locally and from out-of-valley interests.

There may be changes in groups and clubs, but a future visitor is still likely to find a wide array of charitable giving opportunities. Southern Idahoans have always been generous in their giving habits which the valley's increasing prosperity is likely to expand in the years ahead.

776 Dunlap, Tetonia. "Shelter Plans Expansion as Homeless People Stream into Valley House," *Times-News*, Feb. 19, 2017.

27. Public Safety & The Law

Public safety and the administration of justice in Southern Idaho remains commensurate to necessity; we are neither underserved by law enforcement nor is it an excessive presence. Unlike many larger communities, those with sharper ethnic divisions, and alt-right places where anti-government views abound, there is less of a "us versus them" mentality toward police, or vice versa.[777]

Most law enforcement agencies in Southern Idaho are relatively small in numbers; the largest are the Twin Falls County Sheriff's office, which oversees the more-than 7,000 square-mile county, manages the county jail and provides local court security, as well as handling firearms permitting, sex offender registration and drivers' licensing.[778] The Twin Falls city Police Department has more than 100 employees.[779] Smaller counties employ fewer and small municipalities often have less than a dozen personnel.[780]

---

777 The only discernable exception to this may be in how the Hispanic community views federal immigration enforcement by the Immigration and Customs Enforcement (ICE) agency. See Brown, Nathan., "Hundreds Pack Jerome Courthouse to Protest ICE Contract," *Times-News*, July 10, 2017. The issue dissipated somewhat when no ICE contract was signed, and the county began filling available beds with general prisoners from other counties, but not from deportation holds. See Kauffman, Gretel. "With No ICE Contract, Jerome County Turns To Less Controversial Ways to Fill Its New Jail," *Times-News*, Dec. 21, 2017.

778 Twin Falls County Sheriff's Office website, "Overview," 2019.

779 City of Twin Falls website, "Twin Falls Police Department," 2019.

Since county sheriffs are elected officials going back to statehood in 1890 and also run on a party slate, incumbent sheriffs often invite public scrutiny of their work and/or personalities. It's not unusual for a sheriff to face a challenge from someone who wants to succeed him and promises to do a better job. Since sheriffs accumulate critics through thr actions of their subordinates, a challenge and occasional ouster is not unusual.[781]

They undergo considerable scrutiny when there is a botched investigation or incident involving office personnel, drug and property seizures or jail management. For better or worse, the scrutiny usually falls directly on the sheriff.[782]

Overall, the law enforcement training and professionalism has improved with time in Southern Idaho. Occasionally, there is talk of making sheriffs a non-elected position hired by county commissioners, but it doesn't seem likely. Once again, Southern Idaho citizens seem to like keeping their government entities simple and easy to understand. An elected, responsive sheriff meets that need.

City agencies range broadly in professionalism. Like other professions, there appears to be a pecking order in local law enforcement, which in Southern Idaho means deputies in small departments and small community policing, up to larger entities which may pay more and have better benefits.[783] As a result, staff "raiding" from one agency on another is quite prevalent.[784]

Officers also may leave the Twin Falls Police Department for more urban departments in the Boise area, to the Idaho State Police or federal agencies. Reasons vary, but and benefits often figure into the mix.[785]

---

780 Kauffman, Gretel. "Booming Populations and Stagnant Resources: Small Police Departments Make Available Resources Work," *Times-News*, July 19, 2018.

781 Jackson, Andrea. "Taking the Oath: New County Leaders Sworn in Monday," *Times-News*, Jan. 12, 2009.

782 Friedman, Cassidy. "Weaver Era Ending in Jerome County," *Times-News*, March 21, 2008. Weaver served three terms from 1997-2008 but then retired. He was severely criticized, but later absolved, for a botched drug arrest in Eden in 2001 in which two Jerome County deputies were shot and killed as well as the suspect.

783 Idaho Department of Labor, Occupational Employment & Wage Survey, 2018, lists the following mean and entry wages for these occupations in South-Central Idaho: Protective Services, $37,728 and $21,144; First Line Police Supervisors, $61,290 and $55,132; Fire Fighters First Line Supervisors, $49,708 and $34,723; Police and Sheriff Patrol Officers, $45,459 and $34,421. An estimated 2,000 people or more are employed locally in these careers.

784 Brown, Nathan. "Twin Falls Commissioners Vote to Switch to PERSI," *Times-News*, April 25, 2015, and Smith, Alison Gene. "Sheriff: Lack of PERSI Sends Experienced Deputies Packing," *Times-News*, April 24, 2015.

785 Kennison, Heather. "Council Approves Raises for Cops, Firefighters," *Times-News*, Jan. 31, 2017.

Training for law enforcement personnel usually includes seminars and field work at the Idaho POST Academy, (Peace Officer Standards & Training) but many agencies look for candidates with more experience.[786] POST certification in a variety of protective service work is often considered a prerequisite for advancement. The College of Southern Idaho also offers a law enforcement program and certification which allow officers to train locally.[787]

As in many other fields, women have entered law enforcement in increasing numbers in recent years in Southern Idaho. It is no longer unusual to see female officers in these professions. Female firefighters are now coming onto federal rangelands fire crews and have begun to be hired on city crews elsewhere in Idaho.[788] From time to time, claims of harassment, discrimination and inappropriate comments are brought and may result in substantial awards or in negotiated settlements, which then result in higher county liability premiums.[789]

A major issue in many Idaho counties is the costs of incarcerations. The state has a relatively high proportion of inmates to population, 13th in the nation,[790] and there is almost constant pressure to find space. Some state inmates are housed in other states' prisons,[791] and some are kept in county jails, which are not ideal circumstances. Jerome County recently built a new jail facility[792] and Twin Falls County is considering one as well, despite the estimated cost of more than $60 million.[793]

Partly in response to such pressures, the Idaho Legislature is considering revamping state sentencing standards which could lower costs by diverting offenders to halfway houses, non-incarcerated probation and parole and lighter sentencing for drug and alcohol related violations.[794] But with a long history of public support for harsh sentencing, it remains to be seen if Idaho

786 Idaho POST Academy website, 2019.

787 College of Southern Idaho website, Law Enforcement Program, 2019.

788 Boise Mobile Equipment website, "Women in Fire Fighting Leadership Roles," Feb. 28, 2018.

789 Matthews, Mychel. "Gender-based Lawsuits Now More than Half TF County's Settlements," *Times-News*, Aug. 2, 2016.

790 Council of State Governments, Justice Center, "Cost of Incarceration Rising In Idaho," Oct. 10, 2018.

791 Russell, Betsy. "With Idaho's Inmate Population Skyrocketing, Idaho Mulls $439m Prison Expansion," *Idaho State Journal*, June 12, 2018.

792 Kauffman, Gretel. "Jerome County Looks to Fill Jail with Local Prisoners," *Times-News*, Feb. 1, 2018.

793 McCurdy, Terry and Hartgen, Stephen. "Reader Comment: Totaling the Impacts of Proposed Projects," *Times-News*, Feb. 24, 2019.

794 Brown, Nathan. "Even with Prison Expansion, New Lockup Could Be on Horizon," *Post-Register*, Jan. 24, 2019.

can both secure public safety and meet future needs with these changes. "Idaho's the mirror image of the nation," on these issues says Idaho Chief Justice Roger Burdick. Other states face similar problems, without obvious good solutions.[795]

Another point of pressure is within the prosecution offices and public defender. These costs traditionally have fallen to individual counties, but small counties have difficulty paying for them. Twin Falls County has been fortunate in having a longtime prosecutor, Grant Loebs,[796] and professional public defense services under Marilyn Paul, but many other counties find these positions hard to fill and maintain.

One group which has gained credibility and political clout in recent years is the Professional Fire Fighters of Idaho, a union which has chapters in many of Idaho's larger communities. The PFFI negotiates contracts with municipalities and lobbies at the state level on issues such as safety and health and workers' compensation benefits.[797]

The Judiciary. Idaho's judicial system is a third branch of government under the Idaho Constitution, but derives its annual appropriation through the Legislature as a state agency. The annual hat-in-hand money requests chafe some in judicial circles, but there is little likelihood this would change in the immediate future.

As the state has grown in population, there have been additional increases in caseloads, courtrooms (which counties provide) and court-overseen services such as pre-trial diversions and problem-solving courts dealing with drugs, alcohol, domestic violence and veterans' services.[798]

The state's judicial administrative office is under the purview of the State Supreme Court; the state court director makes regular presentations to legislators and the Governor's office on court needs, staffing, technology and training.

Idaho has a modified "Missouri" judicial selection system in which judicial candidates run on a non-partisan ballot. Magistrate judges are selected by regional commissions comprised of county commissioners, mayors, attorneys and public at large who interview candidates and select magistrate judges. District Court, Appeals Court and Supreme Court

---

795 Burdick, Chief Justice Roger. "Criminal Justice – For Who,?" City Club of Southern Idaho, Feb. 25, 2019.

796 Loebs, Grant, et. al. "Correcting the Record on Idaho's Prison Population," *Times-News*, Sept. 16, 2018.

797 Professional Fire Fighters of Idaho website, 2019.

798 Full disclosure: the author's spouse, Linda, was the trial court administrator for the Southern Idaho region from 1992 until her retirement in 2015.

appointments are made by the governor with pre-screening by a statewide Judicial Council. Judges at all levels stand for election or retention and while not common, ousters have been known to occur. Roughly 27 percent of Idaho's judges today are female,[799] including Supreme Court Justice Robyn Brody.

While nominally non-partisan, it's usually well known in the legal community what party a prospective judge identifies with. Some were previously-elected prosecutors in the community, a partisan position, and others were active in local politics earlier in their careers.[800] It's not uncommon either for inquiries to be made into the prospective judge's background, associations and general suitability for the bench.

Yet, partisanship is rarely evident in Idaho judicial rulings. The state's judiciary is well regarded by the legal community as well as by legislators who set their salaries.[801] The Chief Justice gives an annual "State of the Judiciary" report to the Legislature[802] and the court's administrative office pays close attention to legislative concerns. Case decisions are rendered in a timely fashion and anticipated high-profile rulings are handled vigorously.[803]

Judicial disciplinary actions are all handled through the Judicial Council, which may find the complaint is not valid, or render a proscribed action, usually taken in private. It is the rare disciplinary case which appears anywhere in the public record and thus receives media attention. When an individual is deemed unsuitable, resignation is the usual outcome.

Judicial officials frequently make the case to legislators that they are underpaid and overworked compared to judges in other states and that the pay is a barrier to recruitment. Depending on the area, most judicial vacancies draw multiple applications suggesting that judicial quality is fine in Idaho. Furthermore, district judges, appeals court judges and Supreme Court justices receive an excellent retirement plan covering both themselves and spouses which the state has needed to shore up.[804]

---

799 Burdick, City Club of Southern Idaho, Feb. 25, 2019.

800 Justice Brody, for example, was active in Republican Party politics in the Magic Valley before running for a seat on the Supreme Court; Justice Richard Bevan, also on the Supreme Court, was a Twin Falls County Republican prosecutor early in his career.

801 Russell, Betsy. "New Bill Would Bump Judges' Pay 3%," *Idaho Press*, Feb. 27, 2019.

802 Russell, Betsy. "Idaho Chief Justice: Better Ways to Deal with Criminality than Bigger Prisons," *Idaho Press*, Jan. 20, 2019.

803 The Supreme Court heard oral arguments on a Medicaid expansion case on Jan. 29, 2019 and issued a ruling a week later on Feb. 6, 2019. See Russell, Betsy. "Idaho Supreme Court Upholds Medicaid Expansion Initiative, Rejects Legal Challenge," *Idaho Press*, Feb. 6, 2019.

804 Hurst, Dustin. "Panel Approves Plan to Plow More Taxpayer Cash Into Judicial Pensions," Idaho Reporter, Jan. 23, 2017. While in the Legislature, the author served on an ad hoc legislative committee examining judicial compensation, retention and benefits.

Generally, Idaho's judiciary and that of the Southern Idaho region has done a good job of administering justice in local communities. A growing population will continue to pressure courts and staffing, but the basics of Idaho's judicial system remain on sound footings.

Part IV: Fuller Lives

Rocks & Water/Vincent Andrew Hartgen, 1984.

28. Arts & Entertainment

The Arts

While Southern Idaho may not be a cutting-edge arts community, there's plenty to do around the Magic Valley, and plenty of nearby venues in Ketchum, Boise and Salt Lake City. Arts events and overall appreciation has growth appreciably in the past 25 years. There's the Magic Valley Arts Council,[805] the CSI Arts on Tour series,[806] Jazz On The Canyon,[807] drama productions at both the College of Southern Idaho and the off-beat Orpheum Theater,[808] the Dilletantes[809] musicals productions, the Magic Valley Symphony[810] and occasional chorale and vocal performances.

On the visual arts side, the Herrett Museum[811] on the CSI campus regularly features works by local artists in many mediums, and in the past few years, public sculpture has begun to appear on business plazas, at the new Twin Falls City Hall plaza and on the Snake River Canyon

---

805 Magic Valley Arts Council, website, 2018.

806 "Do You Hear The Music," Arts on Tour 2018-2019 Season," at CSI.edu., 2018.

807 KMVT television. "Jazz On The Canyon Event to Raise Money for Local Music Programs," June 29, 2016.

808 Orpheum Theater website. 2018.

809 Dunlap, Tetonia. "Six Decades of Dilletantes," *Times-News*, March 19, 2017. The Dilletantes group was founded in 1959 by David and Martha Mead and others and has continued to do numerous popular shows through the years.

810 Magic Valley Symphony website, 2018.

811 Herrett Center for the Arts & Science, College of Southern Idaho website, 2018.

rim near the I.B. Perrine bridge.[812] Regular pottery shows, often before holidays, offer ceramics in many styles, glazes and firings.[813]

The CSI Fine Arts program[814] gives budding artists a chance to learn basics and show their works. High schools sponsor regular drama productions. There's a long list of dance troupes. An arts community scholarship program initiated by longtime entertainer Danny Marona encourages young people to consider arts careers.[815]

Church groups regularly give religious-themed productions, often during the holiday season, and the King Performing Arts Center in Burley offers an extended array of travelling concerts, musical productions and dance groups, some from overseas.

There were several efforts decades ago to widen arts appreciation in the community. David and Marty Mead helped establish the Dilletantes performance group in 1959 along with Roger and Margaret Vincent. These efforts were soon followed by the Magic Valley Symphony (1960), Magic Valley Little Theater (1965) and the Magic Valley Chorale (1973). and Jump Company (1984).[816] The Twin Falls Municipal Band dates from the city's earliest years and performs popular City Park concerts weekly in the summer months.[817] It's one of the community's signature summer arts series.[818]

---

812 Jackson, Andrea. "Twin Falls Twins: Artist Unveils Sculpture on Canyon Rim," *Times-News*, April 8, 2008. The sculpture of early Twin Falls surveyor John Hayes, on the plaza at Twin Falls City hall, was funded partly from urban renewal money, as well as from private sources. The total URA money in the public art was $47,702, with $20,000 going for the statue, $20,000 for lighting and signs and $7,700 for other art, including wall and utility boxes. Email from Rothweiler, Travis. Twin Falls city manager, Jan. 11, 2019. See also Matthews, Mychel. "How an Unsung Twin Falls Pioneer Is Finally Getting His Due," *Times-News*, Feb. 15, 2017.

813 "Magic Mud Pottery Sale Comes to CSI," *Times-News*, Nov. 29, 2018.

814 CSI Art Department website, 2018.

815 Koch, Blair. "Encore," *Southern Idaho Living*, Jan. 1, 2008.

816 Dunlap, Tetonia. "Six Decades of Dilletantes," *Times-News*, May 19, 2017.

817 The Municipal Band once had a famous guest conductor, John Phillip Sousa, who led the group on a stop during one of his Western tours. See Wootton, Julie. "5 Tidbits of Magic Valley Music History," *Times-News*, Nov. 7, 2013.

818 Hartgen, Stephen. *Journey West: A Memoir of Journalism and Politics*, Ridenbaugh Press, Carlton., Or., 2014 and Hartgen, Stephen. "Music At City Park Is A Magic Doorway," *Times-News*, Aug. 7, 1988: "It is said that of magic doorways there is this, "you do not see them even as you are passing through. And some routes, reflecting the circular nature of experience, return to the place from which they began, crossing both distance and generations. Knowing this is perhaps why, family upon family, we bring our children and grandchildren to City Park summer after summer, to launch them on carpets of flat evening light and the melodies of familiar tunes. By doing so, we pass on to them a bit of our community, our country, our love and ourselves. If they are lucky, they will be able to do the same someday for children of their own. Oh, you can take the kids out of the small towns, sending them off to colleges, work and life's great choices. But there is something

Two entities have done much to foster this wide range of the arts in the Magic Valley: CSI and the Magic Valley Arts Council.

The Fine Arts Center was the first building on the new CSI campus in 1968 and has hosted thousands of performances, concerts, forums, theater, dance, music and community productions. Without the center, and the college's many arts programs, arts in the region would be far less developed today.[819]

Recognizing the importance of that emerging role, then-president James "Doc" Taylor hired Lavar Steel as the college's first arts faculty member in 1966. It was a prescient move. Over more than 30 years at CSI, Steel and others added steadily to the central position of the CSI arts program on campus and in the community.[820] Key faculty, such as Tony Mannen in theater, Fran Tanner in drama, speech and debate, and Carson Wong and Ted Hadley in music, added professionalism and stability.[821]

The result can be seen and heard all over campus in the course of typical year. The center is used many evenings for practices and productions; expansion in a recent remodel has added to its versatility. With the Herrett Museum and Faulkner Planetarium, and nearby Lavar Steel art complex, the college is truly the valley's arts centerpiece.

One feature of the arts locally is that it generally sticks pretty closely to traditional artistic norms. Artistic expression may leave some uncomfortable, if it's edgy in a personal sense, and not many productions over the years have tilted that way. This is common for smaller cities. When they do, they elicit considerable discussion, often anonymously. For example, a 2017 performance of "The Vagina Monologues" found numerous pro and con comments on both the play and its underling conflicts of values.[822]

---

about a summer evening listening to a medley of songs – which stays fresh and crisp on the memory forever. Years from now, they will still recall the smell of the green grass with perfect clarity as if transported back to that same spot on the lawn under a shading maple, before a freshly painted bandshell."

819 Gentry, James. *50 Years – A History of CSI, College of Southern Idaho*, 2015.

820 Lavar Steel Art website. 2018.

821 Mannen, Tony. "50 Years in the Footlights," *Times-News*, Sept. 15, 2015. See also Magic Valley Symphony website, 2018. See also "Fran Averett Tanner," obituary, *Times-News*, Dec. 12, 2012.

822 Dunlap, Tetonia. "The Vagina Monologues Returns to Spotlight Women's Issues," *Times-News*, Mar. 17, 2017. Among the posted comments were from Jarrik Varizen, "My Angry Vagina"? Oh brother. Image all this garbage in man text. "My Angry Test-icle!" Or "My Penis Is My Village!" So laughably liberal these things are. Thank you to the classy, real world, hard working women who don't support this crap. Please know that the real men of America notice and respect you even more for it;" from West Coast, "My guess as to why anyone would take time out of their lives to participate in something like this, is because they are quite inept at anything actually productive in life;" from 0527, "You go Ladies.

The range of responses suggests that some arts expression in Southern Idaho remains an area of potential controversy. But having the arts take the lead role in presentation of "edgy" material is hardly new in America, and Southern Idaho isn't the first rural community in which this has occurred.

Yet, there's little doubt that Twin Falls is adding new perspectives in the arts, and in unexpected ways. Partly, it's due to changing demographics and lifestyle choices, particularly among younger people. A summer mid-week music concert series regularly draws hundreds of people; it's new within the past decade. An article on some of the new trends even included comments on how gay-rights issues were being addressed in the local arts scene,[823] a topic which would not have been openly discussed in the not-too-distant past.

In Blaine County, the arts scene includes a number of galleries featuring weavings, glass works, paintings and sculpture. Regular performances grace the Sun Valley Symphony stage and national "name" artists regularly perform to enthusiastic, often sold out-crowds.

A nice reproduction of Thomas Moran's Shoshone Falls on the Snake River (1900), graces Twin Falls City Hall, a newly-purchased item in 2018.[824] The original Western painting is owned by the Gilcrease Museum, Tulsa, Ok. After the artist's death, Moran's family offered to sell it to for $10,000 in the 1930s, but the city of Twin Falls and the state both declined during those Depression years.[825]

Private collections of fine arts aren't common locally, but occasional pieces do grace some homes.[826] Local galleries typically veer to the popular and representational rather than the abstract or even the semi-abstract. Themes often include landscapes and mountain scenes, with a mixture of Native Americans, hunters and trappers and explorers. But there's nothing

---

Ignore the exploding heads and keep doing the good work;" and from Ramsey, "I saw the show. It was fantastic. You righties sure are scared of some odd stuff."

823 West, Bowen. "Growing Up: Cultures Develop but Challenges Persist in Twin Falls Entertainment Scene," *Times-News*, Sept. 7, 2018.

824 The Moran painting reproduction, one of a limited print edition, was purchased by the city for $7,900 from the previous owner, the Greater Yellowstone Region Geotourism Center, Jackson, Wy. See also Twin Falls City Council minutes, Sept. 5, 2018, with payment from the city's arts purchase fund.

825 Boag, Peter. "Thomas Moran in Idaho, 1871-1900," *Idaho Yesterdays*, Fall, 1998. Moran's daughter, Ruth, contacted a number of Idaho officials after her father's death, including the governor, Congressman Addison Smith, who was from Twin Falls, and I.B. Perrine, but to no avail. Though Moran himself considered the painting one of his finest works and the family was willing to sell it, the asking price was apparently thought too high for those difficult times. Thus, what the historian Boag calls "a renowned masterpiece at a bargain-basement price" was allowed to slip away from Idaho's potential grasp.

826 The author remembers seeing a magnificent, early folio edition of an Audubon bird print in a Twin Falls home in the 1980s.

here like the dramatic Remingtons and Russells of Montana or the Georgia O'Keefes of New Mexico.

One prolific artist, Archie Teater, known for his scenes of the Tetons and the Jackson Hole, Wy., area,[827] owned a dramatic Frank Lloyd Wright studio home in Hagerman; it is still in private hands but is occasionally open for the public.[828] It is the only Frank Lloyd Wright structure in Idaho.

Popular arts seem to proliferate everywhere, from regular Art In The Park summer displays to the Arts Building at the Twin Falls County Fair. A Thousand Spring Arts Festival on Ritter Island in the Snake River near Hagerman draws dozens of artists and thousands of visitors annually. An "Art & Soul" showing every summer gives artists a chance to display their work, as well as giving businesses an opportunity to draw viewers who then vote their favorites.[829]

One particularly popular artist is Gary Stone, whose Oregon trail and windswept routes grace many private businesses as well as a multi-paneled depiction of the valley at the Magic Valley Regional Airport.[830] Stone has been drawing, painting and wood engraving for many decades and his work is just as much in demand as ever as he nears age 80. His works are a featured at the Oregon Trail Interpretative Center at Montpelier, Idaho.[831] With his wife, Beverly, they've produced a fascinating book using Oregon Trail dairies and Stone's depictions of the trail's great use in the 1840s and 1850s.[832]

On the literary side, the Ketchum/Sun Valley area has the Ernest Hemingway home, tucked away obscurely on a Ketchum side street; it's not open to the public, but may be visited if someone has the right connections.

---

827 Ridler, Keith. "Idaho Museum Hopes to Renew Interest in Forgotten Painter Archie Teater," Associated Press, Aug. 28, 2017.

828 Wright, Samantha. "Idaho Man to Talk About the Only Frank Lloyd Wright House in the Gem State," BSU Public Radio, Mar. 8, 2016. The author toured the house in 1987. See Hartgen, Stephen. "Teater's Knoll," *The Times-News*, Dec.18, 1987.

829 Art & Soul of the Magic Valley, Magic Valley Arts Council, website, 2018. New categories are added from time to time, says Carolyn White of the Magic Valley Arts Council, including a "quilting arts" category for 2019. Carolyn White Interview, Jan. 10, 2019.

830 Art & Soul of the Magic Valley, Magic Valley Arts Council, website, 2018. New categories are added from time to time, says Carolyn White of the Magic Valley Arts Council, including a "quilting arts" category for 2019. Carolyn White Interview, Jan. 10, 2019.

805 City of Twin Falls website, 2019. Magic Valley Regional Airport, "Historical Mural Project" video.

831 The National Oregon/California Trail Center, Montpelier, has some 44 Oregon Trail paintings by Gary Stone, given by J.R. and Esther Simplot. See website, 2018.

832 Stone, Beverly and Gary. *Stone by Stone on the Oregon Trail*, Stone Studios, 1993.

Hemingway died there by his own hand in 1961. He's buried in the Ketchum cemetery under a simple slab marker and a serene monument to him may be seen West of Ketchum along Trail Creek Road.[833]

Occasional "Hemingway conferences" are held in the resort community and draw scholars and followers from around the world. The writer himself has been endless studied and written about as one of the most important authors of the 20th Century, and his Idaho connections and death continue to spark literary interest.

The Idaho Commission on the Arts and the Idaho Humanities Commission both play important roles in advancing the arts across the state, through local grants, regular newsletters and program information. These include projects and programs throughout the Magic Valley. Other support comes from both individuals and corporate sponsorships; Twin Falls was recently featured in the Zions Bank community newsletter on city arts improvements.[834]

As for other local literary figures, the list is short. Vardis Fisher, who wrote *Mountain Man* (later the movie *Jeremiah Johnson*, 1972, starring Robert Redford) could be found signing books in Twin Falls in the 1960s.[835] Bill Studebaker,[836] a CSI professor, produced a good body of poetry until his kayaking death in 2008. But most other work has focused on fantasy, crime, mystery, children's books and popular short novels.[837] Twin Falls native Kelly Jones, who lives in Boise, recently has published a fictional account of the Evel Knievel jump in 1974, but the remainder of her mystery novels are set elsewhere.[838]

---

833 Seminara, David. "Trespassing at Ernest Hemingway's House," Literary Hub website, Oct., 2017. The author toured the house in the 1990s; it was virtually unchanged then from the time of Hemingway's death almost 40 years earlier. See also, "The Ernest and Mary Hemingway House and Preserve," The Community Library, Ketchum, Idaho website, May, 2017.

834 Hollingshead, Natalie. "5 Art-inspiring Cities in Idaho," Zionsbank,com, Sept. 12, 2018.

835 Gentry, James. *In The Middle and On the Edge: The Twin Falls Region of Idaho*, College of Southern Idaho, 2003.

836 Darr, Deanna. "An Idaho Poet: A Look at William Studebaker Through His Own Words," *Boise Weekly*, July 23, 2008. See also, Casella, Marissa. "An Independent Spirit: Remembering Idaho Poet William Studebaker," Boise Weekly, July 3, 2018.

837 Probably the best known is a local doctor, Dr. Jane Bennett-Munro, who is a pathologist at St. Luke's Regional Medical Center and the author of a half dozen mystery tales which, not surprisingly, sometimes involve pathology investigations and other themes. See Bartlome, Michelle. "St. Luke's Pathologist Writing Sixth Book In a Series – a Toni Day Mystery," St. Luke's Blogs, Feb. 12, 2018. See also, Marcantonio, Patricia Santos, whose *Red Ridin' In the Hood and other Cuentos* (2005) is listed among Amazon's Latino's children's books best sellers.

838 Kelly Jones website page, 2018. See also Jones, Kelly. *Evel Knievel Jumps the Snake River Canyon and Other Stories Close to Home*, Ninth Avenue Press, 2014.

There's no Ivan Doig, no Larry McMurtry, no A.B. Guthrie, no Wallace Stegner to yet emerge from Southern Idaho. No identifiable, recognized literary "voice" of the region, as William Faulkner was for the rural South. No Laura Wilder's *Little House on the Prairie*, (1932), no Sinclair Lewis' *Main Street*, (1920) or Ole Rolvaag's *Giants in the Earth*. (1927).

"It's a meat and potatoes place" says Beverly Stone in a recent interview, along with her artist husband Gary. Art and cultural affairs here reflect a more-middle America setting than an urban one. It's something they've always respected about Southern Idaho and it's given them a long list of followers and admirers.

"Archie Teater told me artists can't make a living in Idaho," says Gary, "but I have, and you can too." That was back in the 1970s.[839] Fortuitous path-crossings with people like Carl Hayden from Cactus Pete's in Jackpot, Nv.; Robert and Barnee Erkins, Bliss area aquaculture entrepreneurs; and potato magnate J.R. and Esther Simplot helped along the way, but it was mostly the Stones' hard work, as well as some luck. He recounts taking his paintings to many community art fairs and displays, from which he often brought them home unsold for the next exhibit. But little by little, he kept at it and sales increased.

Their 1993 book on the Oregon Trail printed 10,000 copies and they're almost sold out, 25 years later. On his painting style, Stone says he paints for himself. "It's hard to paint for others. I enjoy just letting it fall out of the end of the brush, whatever is in my head.All I ever wanted to do was to paint pictures that people wanted to buy."[840]

Stone seems a good example of both Idaho talent and a practical outlook. He's perfected an artistic style that keeps people knocking on his door. Those who encouraged him early on would certainly be proud.

As Southern Idaho grows and artistic expression blossoms with it, there will certainly be more venues, more organizations, more buyers and admirers of the arts' many examples. That's the joy of living in an area where arts are expanding every year.

A commenter on the Magic Valley Arts Council's posted Facebook page once referred to the arts council as an "oasis in the cultural desert of Southern Idaho," which seems to have been meant as a compliment to the council and a put-down to the region it serves.

If the region ever was a "cultural desert," it's no longer so and the Arts Council is another important reason. In the past few years, it's become the

839 Stone, Beverly and Gary. Interview, Dec. 6, 2018.

840 Stone interview. See also Dunlap, Tetonia. "Your Neighbor: The Man Who Took to Art Like a Duck in Water," *Times-News*, Oct. 20, 2013.

lead sponsor of many programs, productions, shows, festivals and gallery exhibits.[841]

The English novelist and essayist D.H. Lawrence writes that "through art, we may be brought to live many lives and each may have so many fields of life to wander as to never feel wretched and empty."[842] That seems a fitting definition of the role the arts plays in Southern Idaho. We have our own literal fields in which to wander in this beautiful, stunning place. Art gives the community an opening on how to have "so many fields of life" in which to do the same.[843]

The Arts Council executive director, Carolyn White, says awareness in the community continues to expand, but that there are limits to what's considered acceptable. What she calls a "moral compass" guides the choices and a long history of arts exhibitions and performances in the valley provide a good idea as to what is acceptable and likely to draw good crowds.[844]

Developments in other arenas, she says, have bolstered Southern Idaho's beginning emergence as an arts arena. The new St Luke's Regional Medical Center and its growing professional staff, as well as the growth of research divisions in the agricultural sectors have attracted people here who have an appreciation of art molded in other places, and their arrival has added to Southern Idaho's art awareness.[845] People seem to want more of what they experienced elsewhere, but with ill-defined boundaries as to taste and subject matter.[846]

Local high school productions now often have an "improv" theater tone to them,[847] as do the various independent films and theater performances showing occasionally at the renovated Orpheum Theater. As in other aspects

---

841 Magic Valley Arts Council website, 2018. Using a widely-regarded "Arts & Economic Prosperity" calculation, the Magic Valley Arts Council has gone from $204,000 support expenditures in 2005 to $493,000 in 2011 and $827,000 in 2017. Information from Carolyn White, executive director, Jan. 10, 2019.

842 Lawrence, D.H. *Art and the Individual*, 1908.

843 The author's father was a well-known Maine artist from the 1940s until his death in 2002.

844 White is a Twin Falls native who worked with Warner Brothers Studios in California before returning to her hometown in 2005. Interview.

845 White, Interview.

846 A tour show from Second City, a Chicago-based comedy and diversity group, wasn't successful here, White says. White, Interview. See also The Second City website 2019, which says its mission includes "fostering community with cultural sensitivity." The group focuses on "pioneering improv groups in the LGBTQI, Asian American, African American, and Latinx communities."

847 Xavier Charter School, Twin Falls, focuses on a classical education for students including theater, dance, literature and logic. See Xavier Charter School website, 2018. Many area schools include arts education in their curricula, including theater, music, chorale and bands.

of Southern Idaho life, the arts are showing both growth and increased outlets and opportunity. And that's just up to 2019.

Looking ahead, it's likely the arts in Southern Idaho will continue to grow and expand. Not every effort will succeed, but the overall impetus is toward more awareness. It's a wider world out there to which Southern Idahoans have been exposed and we shouldn't expect that to contract, but rather to expand.[848]

Entertainment

There's no clear division, nor should there be, between art and entertainment. The one is an expression of creativity; the other, venues in which others can enjoy that creativity. Southern Idaho offers a wide range of entertainment options, from traditional classical music to rock groups and country music fests, from local bands to touring groups, from Christmas dance performances to stage shows at Jackpot, Nv., Cactus Pete's casino.

The mix leans toward the popular but shies away from groups and themes which aren't popular draws locally, such as rap, hip-hop, and on the other end, classical opera. This emphasis on the popular is likely to remain, reinforced by radio formats and an endless range of television and cable programming. Cactus Pete's is a good example. Its dinner/stage shows draw good crowds, particularly if the performers are well known. The same is true for the Twin Falls County Fair; the better known the country music group, the larger the crowd.

On the non-concert evenings, the Fair offers other entertainment acts, including rodeo, stand-up comedy and monster truck competitions. The fair is one stop on the Professional Rodeo Cowboys Association regional circuit and there's always a good crowd for steer wrestling, saddle bronco and busting, bull riding and barrel racing.[849] The CSI rodeo team has a full schedule and more than 7,500 followers on its team website.[850]

For motor enthusiasts, the Magic Valley Speedway offers a series of races during a spring-fall schedule. It's close to the Twin Falls Regional Airport

---

848 West, Bowen. "Let's Dance: Local Dance Studios Grow," *Times-News*, Jan. 27, 2019.

849 The 2018 Magic Valley Stampede, Aug.31-Sept 1, had a total payout of over $107,000 in 7 events. See "Full Rodeo Results - Magic Valley Stampede," Professional Rodeo Cowboys Association website, 2018.

850 CSI's rodeo team website, 2018. There's also an Idaho High School Rodeo Association which gets young people started in the sport.

and is one of only a handful of stocks car tracks in Idaho.[851] There are boat races at the Idaho Regatta at Burley on the Snake River and snowmobile and all-terrain vehicle groups throughout the area.

As good as these venues and opportunities are, they're likely to expand in the future. Recreation, tourism and a long list of both organized and personal uses dominate Southern Idaho's entertainment scene; we're an outdoors area after all, and many of the activities here are outdoor-focused.

Additionally, the "plaza-i-zation" of Twin Falls' downtown is likely to spur further venues. Specialty bars and small eateries are beginning to proliferate, following an influx of urban renewal money, and weekday evening concerts draw crowds of people, many of them younger. Given Idaho's somewhat unique laws on liquor licensing,[852] we're not likely to see these venues explode in number, but further growth is certainly likely, even if some of it comes with the usual rowdiness.[853]

The danger, of course, is that in "painting up" the town to make it more of an entertainment venue, communities often lose the very traits they wanted to display in the first place. This kind of transformation can be found in once-undiscovered communities all over the country and enhanced entertainment is usually a feature of the local revival. Most of the jobs created this way are just moved-around positions which would be with the establishments regardless of where they located.[854]

Some economic development promoters consider downtown recreation/tourism venues to be a major positive step in the city's future, but more realistically, it's a collection of establishments which would have likely gone elsewhere in town, not the creating of new jobs, but a reshuffling of existing ones to new locations.

This vision of Twin Falls is a series of bars, sidewalk seating cafes, weeknight music fests, loud bands and parking lots filled with young people looking to meet someone. They've all been to places like that in their travels and they had fun there, so why not come home and create the same thing here?

---

851 Magic Valley Speedway, Facebook.com page, 2018.

852 Kennison, Heather. "Olive Garden Buys Liquor License, Plans to Hire a least 150 in Twin Falls," *Times-News*, Dec. 20, 2018. Idaho's Constitution, Article III, Sect.24 says "The first concern of all good government is the virtue and sobriety of the people, and the purity of the home. The legislature should further all wise and well directed efforts for the promotion of temperance and morality." It is hard to see how an expansion of liquor accessibility would be squared with this constitutional provision.

853 Kennison, Heather. "Commission Cuts Back on Hours for Bumpin' Bernie's," *Times-News*, Oct. 10, 2018.

854 Renn, Aaron. "The Next Big Challenge For Small Downtowns," CityLab website, July 30, 2017.

At the end of 2018, the city was named to a "Ten Most Underrated U.S. Cities" list, where it joined Camden, Maine, an ocean town on Penobscot Bay; Beaufort, SC., Bentonville, Ak., home of Wal-Mart; Springdale, Utah and Taos, NM. The descriptive note on Twin Falls focused entirely on recreational opportunities.[855] This kind of discovery seems to be precisely what the industry wants. Whether that's a good thing or not for Twin Falls is an open question.

---

855 The Discoverer Blog website, December, 2018. "Who needs Niagara when you have a taller waterfall in Southern Idaho. Shoshone Falls is the highlight of a visit to Twin Falls, but there's abundant other things to see and do. The Snake River Canyon Rim Trails is 10 miles (16 kilometers) of walking and biking routes in the city and along the river. Get active by kayaking on the river or relax with a picnic at the river parks. Perrine Bridge is a favorite spot for base jumpers."

29. A Shared Love of Country

Since the 1960s, an openly patriotic love of country is sneered at in liberal circles in America. It's that way today on many college campuses, during the Obama Administration, and among some so-called liberation and social justice churches. It's common in so-called intellectual magazines and among columnists, editors and reporters of many newspapers, big and small, as well on many national broadcast media outlets, cable television and virtually all late-night television's snarky programming. It's a staple of Hollywood films, many independent films as well, and a long list of progressive political figures.[856]

But in Southern Idaho, love of country is alive and well. Its outward expression can be found in every-day civic events, from the Rotary and Kiwanis Clubs, to the Chambers of Commerce, to city councils, school boards and county commissions, to the American Legion posts and their auxiliaries, to sporting events, churches and prayer breakfasts, Memorial Day services and Veterans' Day ceremonies.

These events often begin with a patriotic song, the Pledge of Allegiance and an invocation. Flags fly proudly in front of homes and on porches as reminders of the freedoms we all share. On Veterans Day and Memorial Day, our cemeteries are festooned with bunting, flags and decorated graves of the veterans who served. At the monthly meetings of the Twin Falls County Republican Central Committee and

856 Author's note: Hartgen, Stephen. *Journey West: A Memoir of Journalism and Politics*, Ridenbaugh Press, 2014. This chapter echoes the section in Journey West on this topic, and sometimes includes similar language and phrasing.

the Republican Women's Club, members listen to short Constitutional moments on the importance of a section or amendment. On the Fourth of July, crowds gather at the College of Southern Idaho for patriotic concerts by the Twin Falls Municipal Band and fireworks show at twilight.[857]

It is a real pleasure of life in Southern Idaho that these patterns of patriotism are everywhere. The critics and naysayers have it backwards: people do not listen to conservative talk radio and follow Fox News out of prejudice, racism or anger. Rather, they listen for the echo of patriotism they hear in themselves, the unabashed love of country which is so widely discounted in the broader culture.

Critics of America routinely complain about the so-called oppression they see from corporations, social conservatives, business people and many more. These critics and naysayers occupy public squares and blog sites, but they do not occupy Southern Idahoans' hearts. That space is left for our love of our blessed nation.[858]

It's not surprising that this appreciation abounds in an agricultural region like Southern Idaho, where crops turn from green in the spring to the golden brown of harvest in late summer. All around us is the bounty of our nation's fruitful land; you need not have traveled very much in the world to know this is not the same in many other places.

Many senior citizens retain this love of country from their childhood schooling. They may now be the last generation to have learned in school about our nation's heroes, men like Nathan Hale and Patrick Henry, women like Florence Nightingale, Abigail Adams and Mary Ludwig Hays, better known as Molly Pitcher.

These heroes' eloquence and courage were part of the school culture in the American past which was mostly swept aside in the 1960s in the name of political correctness, the stories replaced with messages tied to the inequality, national shortcomings and various expressions of failure, as if these define us as a people.

Most Southern Idahoans know better. Every legislative day in Boise, the House chaplain opens the floor session with a prayer, invoking guidance to do our best as the representatives of our communities, state and nation. He often alludes to the fact that our nation and civil government cannot endure without the Providence of our Creator. Providence is a word not much used today, meaning "coming from the One who provides." Yet it captures the ongoing blessings of liberty, freedom and representative government. In this,

857 Dunlap, Tetonia. "Twin Fall Band Gets Set For 108th Summer Concert Series," *Times-News*, May 31, 2013.

858 Jackson, E.W. "The Liberal Lie That America Is Hateful and Bigoted," *American Thinker*, Feb. 21, 2019.

we are all receivers of an enduring American exceptionalism which our Founding Fathers understood to be a special gift from the Creator to all mankind.[859]

Southern Idaho may seem a quaint pocket of such expression, perhaps because it is somewhat isolated. The disrespect for our country seen so frequently elsewhere has less weight here, less dominance. Why is that? Westerners have no monopoly on love of country; the Southern states have long been noted for the patriotism of their region, born of self-determination, individualism and courage.[860]

The West, it seems, has something of the same heritage. Idaho wasn't the only place Civil War veterans landed, but it was one, particularly in the mining camp towns.[861]

But by the time of Southern Idaho's settlement after 1900, Civil War memories were fading and reconciliations among veterans of North and South were common. Aging veterans of Gettysburg, for example, met yearly on that battlefield to pledge allegiance to an America already much changed but joined again.[862]

So while Southern Idaho today has strong skepticism of federal reach and power, the region is not infected by an incipient nullification movement, much less a secessionist bent, both of which can heard in locations more radicalized than this one.[863] Once again, tolerance and practical approaches to

---

859 Pease, Donald J. "American Exceptionalism," Oxford Bibliographies website, updated June 27, 2018.

860 Cash, Wilbur. *Mind of the South*, 1941: "Proud, brave, honorable by its lights, courteous, personally generous, loyal, swift to act, often too swift, but signally effective, sometimes terrible, in its acts, the South at its best. And such at its best it remains today, despite the great falling away in some of its virtues. Violence, intolerance, aversion and suspicion toward new ideas, an incapacity for analysis, an inclination to act from feeling rather than from thought, an exaggerated individualism and too narrow concept of social responsibility, attachment to fictions and false values, above all too great attachment to racial values and a tendency to justify cruelty and injustice in the name of those values, sentimentality and a lack of realism -- these have been its characteristic vices in the past. And, despite changes for the better, they remain its characteristic vices today."

861 Barnhill, Frankie. "Legacy of Hate: Idaho's Confederate Connection," Boise State University Public Radio, Oct. 3, 2017. The article quotes BSU history professor Todd Shallat as saying Idaho has been "a northern satellite of the South" since the Civil War period.

862 Both the 1888 Gettysburg Reunion (25th Anniversary) and the 1913 Reunion (50th Anniversary) were widely reported and both seen as expressions of national reconciliation across America's regions. See Allen, Scott. "Gettysburg at 50: The Great Reunion of 1913," MentalFloss.com website, 2018 (2011), and Smith, Karlton. "The Grand Reunion of 1888," The Blog of Gettysburg National Military Park, Oct. 16, 2015.

863 Legislature.Idaho.gov. website. House Bill 461, 20128 session, defeated on a 40-29 vote. All but one Magic Valley legislator, including the author, voted against the measure which

solving real problems have overridden the ideological excesses seen elsewhere.[864]

In Southern Idaho's recent history, there are very few points at which locals struck an ideological course when a more practical one was available, even if it relied on closer harmony with federal authority. We may have different takes on how to push back against perceived federal encroachment. But that does not open the door here for the alt-right extremism found in North and Central Idaho where federal/state relations are testier, the rhetoric sharper, the government more broadly attacked.

Patriotism is love of the whole country, not just part of it. It is hard to see how this would change dramatically, unless a small splinter group of alt-rightists were able to gain control of the local GOP central committees, as has happened elsewhere in the state.[865]

The fanatics there imposed their will on others after centrist, common-sense citizens retreated and left the field to the alt-right radicals. Southern Idaho has gone through local convulsions of this stripe, but only in neighboring Elmore County have they been successful. Here, our love of country runs deep; not many would want to tear our community, state and nation apart for such thin, divisive porridge.

Thomas Jefferson writes that the tree of liberty must be occasionally watered with the blood of patriots. But equally important is the commitment of spirit in daily lives by remembering how this great nation came into being and an appreciation of liberty and freedom which sustains us in every generation. This, said Abraham Lincoln, is the great task remaining before us.

Patriotism here seems to rest on two pillars: one is the outward display of love of country through veterans' holidays, patriotic music, rituals of civil participation and a community in which flags fly proudly, including the author's home.

The other pillar is the deeper carrying in the heart of love for the country, its values, form of government and history going back to the Revolutionary War. It incorporates the Bill of Rights and those freedoms spelled out therein, freedoms of expression, the right to own firearms, statements of government' limits on citizens, a free people. These might the best indicators of love of country, duty and honor; they are found clearly in many of our nation's founding documents and seminal tracts.[866]

---

would have allowed the state to nullify federal measures with which it disagreed.

864 Hartgen, Stephen. "A Republican Perspective: Nullification: An Old Debate Resurfaces In Idaho," *Times-News*, Feb. 25, 2018.

865 Petersen, Anne Helen. "Here's What Happens When Republicans Have No One To Fight," Buzzfeed, Oct. 22, 2017.

866 Bennett, William J. *Our Sacred Honor*, Simon & Shuster, 1997.

It is thus another positive trait of Southern Idaho that these strains of patriotism are so intertwined in our lives. The first is readily apparent, the other, not so much, but there nonetheless.

Veterans. A major contributing factor to this outlook is the steady presence in Southern Idaho of modern veterans and their various organizations. American Legion Posts, Legion Auxiliary units, Veterans of Foreign Wars chapters can be found in many Southern Idaho communities. These are our children, our colleagues and comrades, men and women who have taken time in their lives to serve our country.

In Southern Idaho, 10-12 percent of the population are military veterans. World War II veterans are passing away and now constitute only about 6 percent of local veterans; Korean War vets, about 13 percent; the Gulf Wars of the 1990s and since 2000, about 46 percent. The single largest group is Vietnam War era veterans, roughly 37 percent.[867]

We all know how the Vietnam War and its aftermath have rippled through many aspects of American life, and the impacts in Southern Idaho were just as far-reaching. Many of today's local veterans went through that trying time and more than a few were lost on those distant fields. The local memorial lists 17 Twin Falls individuals who gave their lives; the names are listed on a City Park plaque which simply says, "They Served Us Wisely, Well, Honorably."[868] Similar memorials can be found in other Southern Idaho communities and designated markers can be seen as well on highways.

Honoring returning veterans and those lost in conflict has a history dating to ancient times. Funeral vessels from Greek and Roman times give much information about the participants, as do major monuments like Emperor Trajan's column, completed in 113 AD to glorify his military victories. Numerous tombstones from ancient times record the names, length of service and military units or legions in which the individual served, not unlike our military markers today in cemeteries nationwide.

Southern Idaho has many such individual markers to our fallen men and women, in town plots as well as in rural graveyards, where families, military groups and others lovingly maintain them in perpetuity.[869]

867 DataUSA, "Twin Falls, Idaho, Military Veterans," 2016.

868 Matthews, Mychel. "Hidden History: The Vietnam Memorial In City Park," *Times-News*, June 8, 2016.

869 The author occasionally visits the grave of Marine Maj. Alan Blake Rowe, a Gooding High School graduate who was killed in 2004 in the Iraq War, where he rests now and forever at the Mountain View Cemetery near Fairfield. See Perry, Tom. "Marine's Widow Looks to the Future, Can't Forget the Past," *Los Angeles Times*, Dec. 19, 2005. The author's cousin, William Clayton Hartgen, was killed in the Vietnam War in 1967; his name is on the Vietnam War Memorial in Washington, D.C., Panel 24E, Line 27.

Local military recruitment is high and our own National Guard unit, the 116th Combat Battalion, was deployed to Iraq in 2010.[870] They returned home in 2011 to their proud loved ones. That gives people here direct connections to military service which helps advance a national perspective, not a regional one, on how we view the federal government. It is not a state they chose to serve, but the nation.[871]

In 2017, Idaho was ranked No. 3 in the country, behind only Georgia and South Carolina, for the highest percent per 1,000 population of "military enlistees".[872] earlier data also shows Idaho ranking highly.[873] That's a tangible manifestation of a love of country.

From time to time, citizens have raised questions about nearby military facilities at Mountain Home Air Force Base, which uses nearby rangelands for training missions. The questioning was more common during the Gulf War, but potential conflicts of use with ranchers and other civilians were resolved with modifications.[874]

More recent proposals to conduct urban training flight missions over Idaho communities, including Jerome in Southern Idaho, have also raised concerns, as well as support.[875] A recent proposal to combine Magic Valley National Guard armories at a new location near the Interstate Highway 84 and the Highway 93 interchange also seems to have community support, particularly if some of the costs would come from federal coffers.[876]

Veterans health care is an issue across the country, as well as in Idaho, but at least currently, there isn't any plan to expand the Veterans' Health Clinic,

---

870 Wootton, Julie. "Welcome Home: Members of the 116th Reunite With Their Families," *Times-News*, Sept.3, 2011.

871 In 2017, Idaho had more than 10,000 active duty military personnel, reserves and military civilian employees, not including Idahoans serving overseas. See "Military Active-duty Personnel, Civilians, by State," Governing.org website, 2018.

872 Clark, James. "These States Have the Highest (And Lowest) Enlistment Rates in America," taskandpurpose.com website, June 27, 2017. Idaho had an enlistment rate of . 61/1000 population in 2013. See SCRIDB website, 2019, "Non-Prior Service Active Comprehensive Enlistment Accession, 2013." As of September 2017, Idaho had nearly 4,000 people serving in the armed forces.

873 U.S. Census data puts most of Southern Idaho counties at 8-12 percent veterans. See Vizual Statistix website, "Normalized Military Veteran Population in the United States", 2018. Elmore County, home to Mountain Home AFB, is listed at one of the highest percentages in the nation, over 25 percent of county population being veterans.

874 Anonymous. "Environmentalists Try To Stop Plan to Expand Bombing Range," *The New York Times*, Aug. 17, 1997.

875 Katz, Michael. "Air Force's Proposed Urban Warfare Training Raises Questions for Some Idaho Residents," *The Idaho Statesman*, May 4, 2018.

876 Matthews, Mychel. "Guard Proposes Fewer, Larger Armories Across State, Starting in Magic Valley," Times-News, Oct. 16, 2015 and Brown, Nathan. "Snake River Bridge, Magic Valley Armory on State's Infrastructure Wish List," *Times-News*, May 13, 2017.

in Twin Falls.[877] The VA, however, has picked a Buhl site for a national veterans' cemetery, the first one in Idaho.[878] Some states have reduced taxes for veterans as a way of attracting more to the state; Idaho has considered such a measure, but not passed it.[879]

Over the years, there have been many veterans' events and patriotic celebrations which reflect the resilience and courage of foreign war veterans. Many have an air of quiet dignity about them for they share a special bond.

We have also seen many veterans of the Vietnam War and now of the Gulf War and Afghanistan War who have sacrificed much and have huge difficulties establishing their lives back home.

Have we treated them fairly? Certainly not in the 1970s when many came home only to be called baby killers and murderers. No one now condones the lack of respect to which they were subjected.

Sure, there are gaps today in how veterans are treated, but in Southern Idaho, veterans' programs seem generally appropriate to the needs and resources available. Certainly, the love of country and admiration of our veterans is widespread, displaying the respect we all feel.

---

877 Brown, Nathan. "VA Won't Expand in Twin Falls," *Times-News*, June 7, 2017.

878 Matthews, Mychel. "VA Purchases Land for New National Cemetery in Buhl, First In Idaho," *Times-News*, Oct. 4, 2016. An estimated 14,000 veterans live within 75 miles of Twin Falls.

879 Idaho Legislature, 2014 Session, HB 420. Failed on a 35-31 vote in the House on Feb. 24, 2014.

30. Sports

In addition to many recreational opportunities, Southern Idaho offers a wide range of school sports, but the relative isolation and low population of the region acts as a barrier to dominance by any one college or professional team.[880] That was certainly the pattern 30 years ago, with people's allegiances to college programs showing a broad mix between Idaho schools, religious institutions and others across the West. It's the same broad pattern today of Southern Idaho sports, but with some qualifications.

People identify with college programs by their own leanings, family and heritage and sometimes due just to the success of the school's programs. For example, there are many Southern Idaho graduates of the University of Idaho, and multi-generational "Vandal Booster" families, although the school is more than 400 miles away. The same pattern is evident in allegiance to Brigham Young University, particularly among Mormon sports-enthusiasts. BYU's continued competitiveness in sports like football and basketball gives it long-standing allegiance among Southern Idaho followers.[881]

The same pattern of dispersed allegiances can be seen at the professional sports level. Southern Idaho is geographically a long drive from bigger cities, so professional team allegiances are widely

---

880 A Slate website survey in 2013 couldn't come up with a single sport with which Idaho is identified. Tongue in check, it identified whitewater rafting as a leading activity since Idaho has "more whitewater river miles than anywhere in the lower 48 states. Way to go, Idaho." See Levin, Josh. "United Sports of America," Slate, Oct. 7, 2013.

881 The Cougars won the national football championship in 1984 and have been competitive in a number of other sports in the decades since. See Brigham Young University website, "National Champions," 2018.

diversified here, in several directions. Some people follow Denver teams, others track Portland, Seattle and San Francisco, and there are more than a few followers of teams in Dallas, Minneapolis and Chicago. The Utah Jazz basketball team draws allegiances as well; it's one of the only major professional sports teams across most of the Intermountain West.[882]

This dispersal of college and professional sports allegiance cascades to alumni association meetings and financial support. Not surprisingly, the bigger and more successful college programs draw the widest support among their fans, as well as donations and facility development.[883]

Several changes have modified this overall dispersal pattern and could alter significantly the profile of sports allegiance in Southern Idaho in the future. These other factors include:

Continued progress for the Boise State University football program. With its growth and national visibility, BSU is now the leading school in Idaho for incoming students from within the state.[884] BSU has already proven itself as a major "second tier" football program under several coaches, and has won a number of high-profile games, including a Fiesta Bowl victory over favored Oklahoma in 2007. Although the game was more than a decade ago, it put BSU on the football national radar, where it remains today.[885]

BSU's rising visibility has brought it much national attention and has arguably brought a positive "rub off" effect on Idaho as a whole. Long-time University of Idaho followers may grumble enviously at BSU's dominance, but the Broncos record speaks for itself. The football program gives the school and the state more cachet than either probably would have occurred otherwise.[886]

While BSU has enjoyed success and visibility in the Football Bowl Subdivision, formerly called Division I-A, sports at the University of Idaho and Idaho State University have had more difficulty. Both play in the Football Championship Subdivision, formerly called Division I-AA, in the Big Sky Conference, against similar smaller programs. The Vandals move

---

882 Google.com Map of Geography of Professional Sports Affiliation in Western States, website, 2018.

883 Smith, John. "Boise State: Doing More with Less For Two Decades and Counting," BroncoCountry, July 19, 2018. The BS U overall athletic department brought in over $45 million in 2017, mostly from football.

884 Richert, Kevin. "Idahoans' Many Paths to College," IdahoEdNews.org, Sept. 24, 2013.

885 Tramel, Barry. "Epic Fiesta Bowl Win Did Wonders for Boise State and its Home City," NewsOK, Sept. 9, 2018. See also, NCAA website, Finances, 2016-2017 where Boise State ranks 69th in the country in athletics revenue. The University of Idaho was 127th with close to $24 million revenuers and Idaho State University was 191st with $13 million.

886 Cotterell, Adam. "How Winning Football Games Can Impact Academics at Boise State," BSU Public Radio Apr. 7, 2015.

down from the FBS in 2018 was opposed by many, including alumni, and may have contributed to the president leaving the school.[887] In the case of Idaho State University, overall enrollment stagnation has hampered the Bengal's ability to recruit and build on past successes in the FCS.[888]

Sports Media. It's a cutthroat world in media visibility, sponsorships, advertising, ratings and money. Schools all over the country have had to learn to tell their stories better, but that isn't as easy as it once was. Media attention is 24-7, pervasive and is often either overly positive or negative, including ongoing issues like funding sources, off-the-field troubles for athletes and ongoing relations with state and federal programs and officials.

Even without a four-year school, Southern Idaho has more than its expected share of media attention. Local television news, as with many other smaller market stations, devotes a third of its daily half-hour newscasts to sports, mostly high school and the two-year College of Southern Idaho (CSI). The *Times-News* usually has at least two to three pages daily as a sports section and sometimes more. The mix is decidedly local in content with roundups of national sports teams and standings.

Local sports photos often run large, thus encouraging individual copy sales and providing a ready "clip service" for athletes and their families. A multitude of high schools and the growth of women's sports contests have further added to the media volume.

As is the case elsewhere, the traditional sports dominate the coverage, for both boys and girls. For boys, football, basketball and baseball get the most attention, with lesser coverage of track, cross country, wrestling, soccer and golf. For girls, basketball and volleyball dominate the coverage, with occasional reporting on gymnastics, track, softball and cross country as well as golf.

The media attention may make it seem like Southern Idaho is a "sports crazy" place, but that's not the case compared to other parts of the country, particularly in the Southeastern states. There's little "Friday Night Lights"[889] intensity here, no huge stadiums, not even much rah-rah.

A few players go onto colleges on athletic scholarships, but mostly, they're headed to smaller schools. Only a handful of players across the Southern Idaho in the past few decades, for example, have gone on to major

887 Sun, Rachel. "U of I President to Leave After Next School Year," *Spokesman-Review*, May 25, 2018.

888 Harris, Shelbie. "We Want to Be Loud: ISU Signs Nearly $1 M Contract to Promote University," *Idaho State Journal*, Oct. 27, 2018.

889 H.G. Bisssinger's *Friday Night Lights*, an account of high school football mania in Texas was first published in 1992 and made into a movie in 2004.

college programs, and an even smaller number have advanced from there to professional sports.[890]

Despite long odds, many young people still grow up dreaming of a college or professional sports career, and that's no different in Southern Idaho. One of life's early lessons for many teens is to realize that going on with a sports scholarship isn't a realistic possibility, so they usually focus on other things like an education, work and family.

It's common to see many parents and grandparents in the stands at school sports events as they watch their youngsters compete in these healthy pursuits. It's a healthy transition to life and these young people often vicariously relive their sports years when their own children begin competing.

In many smaller communities, school sports are a popular local entertainment and help give small schools and communities a local identity. Thus, resistance to school district consolidation, which might improve educational resources for smaller districts, isn't likely to recede. School consolidation hasn't occurred in Southern Idaho in many decades. Sports seems to be one important reason.[891]

School districts know that sports are often a main draw in town, so proposed bond elections often include upgrades to gyms, fields, bleachers, locker rooms and other sports-related facilities. Most of these bond proposals pass, although they may take a second or third time at the polls.[892]

Many school leaders say that including athletics in bond proposals helps get the two-thirds margin needed for passage. Some citizens may grumble on how local property taxpayers are "stuck" with paying for overly-emphasized school sports, and there's usually a significant number who vote no," often 30 percent or slightly more. But the pattern is not likely to change anytime soon in Southern Idaho.

College of Southern Idaho. Another development has been the success of the College of Southern Idaho's sports programs, particularly men's basketball and baseball and women's basketball and volleyball and other teams. As a community college with limited resources when it began in the 1960s, CSI has specialized in only a few sports, one of which was basketball.

---

890 Two such successful players from Southern Idaho are Andy Toolson, a Twin Falls basketball standout (1984) who later played for Brigham Young University and then the Utah Jazz (1995-96), and Korey Hall, a football player from Glenns Ferry (2001) who had a successful career with Boise State University and then with the Green Bay Packers where he was on the SuperBowl XLV winning team in 2011.

891 Hartgen, Stephen. "Reader Comment: Forced School Consolidation in Idaho Unlikely," *Times-News*, Nov. 12, 2009.

892 Richert, Kevin. "Why Did So Many Bonds and Levies Pass So Easily Last Week?," IdahoEdNews, March 21, 2017.

The school has the largest indoor venue in the valley (3,500 capacity) and the gym was part of the original construction plan for the CSI campus in 1967. The size and convenience makes it an ideal venue for CSI's team sports, which often draw capacity crowds.[893]

National junior college competitiveness and regular national championships have helped CSI's visibility as well, giving it a long line of out-of-state players who have then gone on to four-year programs and occasionally the pros. Their successes in turn have given the college and region increased visibility, both in and out of Idaho; the school's first president, James "Doc" Taylor, often laced his legislative requests with sports related stories and was something of a legend when it came to promoting CSI and its sports successes. His first basketball coach was Eddie Sutton who led CSI to national success and later coached at Kentucky and Oklahoma State.[894]

The teams recruit from far and wide, as well as among prominent local prospects. Out-of-state players sometimes come from other countries and varied urban communities elsewhere in America and thus add to the community's diversity.[895]

As at almost every level, there are some who feel CSI's sports programs are emphasized too much in the community. But these criticisms seem out-of-step with both the community and the college. The many tournament banners in the CSI gym show a positive trail of successful sports programs going back many years, and one likely to continue in the years ahead.

Women's Sports. A big change at both the high school and college level has been the development of women's teams, leagues and offerings. Spurred by both legal challenges (Title IX laws)[896] and rising equity concerns, most schools now provide a modicum of equality when it comes to women's athletics. Southern Idaho schools have readily adapted to the changes. It is routine now to see women's sports get much-enhanced coverage in local sports reporting.

As new opportunities emerged, most have been "added on" to existing athletic departments; men's sports generally haven't been discontinued locally to make room for the women's programs. There have been many studies on how the rise of women's sports has affected colleges and high schools, and Southern Idaho is no different on this topic. Promising local women routinely get offers to compete at the college level, and many do.

---

893 College of Southern Idaho Athletics Department website, 2018.

894 Gentry, James. *CSI – 50 Years – A History of the College of Southern Idaho*, College of Southern Idaho, 2015

895 Gentry, James. CSI.

896 Wikipedia. "Title IX," Updated Dec. 15, 2018.

Some then continue their interests as coaches, mentors and community sports enthusiasts where they often make big and welcome differences in young lives.[897]

A Baseball Stadium In Our Future? In the 1950s and 1960s, Twin Falls had a Pioneer League minor-league baseball team which played at Harmon Park. The league went through several changes and the team was known as the Magic Valley Cowboys in the 1960s[898] until it was discontinued in 1971. From time to time, as the region has grown, there have been proposals from various baseball interests to bring a minor league baseball franchise back to the region, where there are short-season Single-A Pioneer League teams today in Idaho Falls, Ogden and Orem, Utah.

These ideas come with high costs to the community, such as building a Minor League Baseball-approved stadium, etc., and without substantial funds or exit guarantees by the outside owners.[899] The projects haven't borne fruit, and the Magic Valley remains a large geographic area without locally-based professional sports except for the semi-professional Sun Valley Suns hockey club.[900]

In the case of baseball, the idea of a minor league team in Twin Falls is a dream of some, but they're realistic enough to know it wouldn't be an easy sell if it involved public funds. A viable proposal along those lines hasn't emerged, but can't be ruled out in the coming years and decades. There are many who remember the 1960s games at Harmon Park for whom the cry "Play Ball" would be a sweet return.[901]

---

897 Flores, Victor. "CSI Head Volleyball Coach Dead At 44," *Times-News*, Dec. 19, 2017.

898 "Twin Falls Cowboys" and "Magic Valley Cowboys," Wikipedia, 2018 website.

899 The author attended one such meeting in the late 1990s, at which the prospective team owners, who had a team in Canada, proposed to secretly move the team to the Magic Valley if the community paid for a new stadium and gave over other revenue sources, including naming rights, "free to leave" exit clauses and a piece of concession revenue as well as ticket sales. Asked how the community would benefit, they said the community would see increased overall traffic and community "pride." Finding a subdued and cautious response among local community leaders, they did not further pursue it.

900 Cordes, Jeff. "Suns Anchor the New Black Diamond Hockey League," *Idaho Mountain Express*, June 6, 2014.

901 Flores, Victor. "All The Right Players: Growth May Bring New Teams, Facilities to the Magic Valley," *Times-News*, Sept. 8, 2018.

31. Libraries & Broadband

It's common for people to think of libraries today as musty, aging buildings packed with decaying printed items once known as books, inhabited by immense silence enforced by a frowning, cardigan-clad staff.

But that's a picture from the past, if ever. Today, it would be hard to name another long-lived Idaho institution which has contributed more to the development of the state. Today libraries are evolving rapidly to embrace new technologies, audiences and standards of operation. Today, Idaho library use has never been higher, even in a competitive internet world, with more than 8.6 million library visits in 2014 and the fifth highest circulation of children's materials in the nation.[902]

Idaho libraries have a long history. In the late 1800s and early 1900s, library books were carried by wagons to mining camps and small settlements, an early version of the bookmobile. By 1904, when Southern Idaho was first settled, more than 100 communities were already receiving books. By the 1920s, there were libraries in all of Idaho's cities and in many small towns as well.[903]

---

902 University of Idaho, McClure Center for Public Policy Research, "Idaho Libraries," April, 2017. The report concludes: "Idaho libraries play a critical role in supporting the state's education and workforce development priorities. Ever-increasing use levels suggest patrons appreciate and support this system. With state-of-the art online resources rapidly joining traditional library buildings and book collections, Idaho public libraries now receive more than 8 million visits per year. Collaborations between library administrators, librarians, and policy makers at the local and state level are increasingly important to maintaining and expanding library services to all 1.6 million residents of Idaho."

903 Idaho Commission for Libraries website, 2019.

Today, libraries throughout Idaho wrestle with dizzying change on issues like accessibility for the disabled, freedom of access to many expressions of opinion, to balancing open access to the internet to policies on controversial materials. They're as much about continuing education, research, wide-ranging resources on many varied topics, community involvement and leadership as they are as a book distribution center. Despite many new roles, libraries continue as a core repository of knowledge and information, from which an endless line of patrons check out books and examine documents.

In some libraries, the new roles have taken on seemingly bizarre twists. In Salt Lake County, Utah[904] for example, the library system has been giving away donated gun locks in an effort to reduce accidents and encourage suicide prevention. In Pennsylvania, one library offers a tool-lending service, allowing people to borrow tools for home projects they might not need more than once. It's one of some 50 libraries nationwide which offer such "renter center" services.[905]

Why are libraries branching out in these ways? Why are they offering gun locks and hand tools to patrons who once asked only to see a particular book or magazine?

The answer lies in how libraries are now defining themselves as centers for resources inquiries of all kinds, no longer limited to books and magazines and newspapers, or even to the printed word, but to finding ways to help communities and citizens with whatever tasks they confront.[906]

Twin Falls Public Library director Tara Bartley is a native of Southern Idaho who worked in a small library in Pennsylvania before returning about four years ago. She sees libraries today as "Keepers of Discovery," not just keepers of books. Like other libraries, the Twin Falls facility is branching out to fill a wider variety of community needs by becoming more of a community center in which traditional library functions are just a part. That means constantly looking for ways to "give people a reason to walk in," she says.[907]

It's a view more broadly held among Idaho librarians than one might suppose. Ann Joslin, director of the Idaho Commission for Libraries, cites an

---

904 Wahlberg, Rebekah. "Salt Lake County Gives Away Free Gun Locks in an Effort to Promote Gun Safety, Suicide Prevention," *The Salt Lake Tribune*, Jan. 3, 2019.

905 Cebzanov, Erica. "Millvale Library Launches Tool Lending Program," LiveTrib.com, June 20, 2018.

906 The author's daughter, Tiffany Paisley, is the manager of the Cheyenne Mountain branch of the Pikes Peak Library District in Colorado Springs, Colo., and her husband Joseph Paisley is at the Old Colorado City branch, a Carnegie library from the early 20th Century. The author is grateful to both for their insights into how libraries today are broader in both content and community development.

907 Bartley, Tara. Interview, Jan. 28, 2019.

example from Glenns Ferry where a new librarian asked questions, "wasn't afraid to make the library the center of the community," got the library involved with a nearby state park, and raised its visibility and usefulness for more citizens.[908] It's not the size of the library or its budget,[909] Joslin says, but the enthusiasm, energy and commitment which make the difference.

To be successful, dynamic libraries need to connect with citizens in numerous ways, as learning is a life-long process, open for all, for education and discovery. "We need to do a better job of making those connections," says Twin Falls' Bartley.

So libraries add free, albeit taxpayer supported services beyond traditional roles. One can now do 3-D printing at the Twin Falls Public Library, do copying, take computer classes, search genealogical records in the internet, participate in a "good yarn night" for knitters and weavers, use a meeting room, participate in a "board games" evening to sharpen one's Monopoly skills, or listen to "human books" of citizens telling life stories as part of the Human Library program, which is held at more than 700 locations worldwide.[910]

For kids, there's a program for making things like a bee hotel, churning butter or raising goats. For families, there's a family-friendly film each week, and a "Random Fandom" group for followers of Harry Potter and Doctor Who, as well as technology group gabs for the science and computer inclined.[911]

The new expansiveness has left library professionals scurrying to make sure their offerings meet community needs and standards, since many Idaho libraries today are funded publicly as part of municipal budgets which go

---

908 Joslin, Ann. Interview, Jan. 29. 2019.

909 Library revenues in Southern Idaho vary greatly in 2017 by the size of the community, from the Oakley Library District at $21,000 (9th smallest) to the Twin Falls Public Library at $1.645m (9th largest). Email from Joslin, Ann, Jan. 28, 2019.

910 Twin Falls Public Library website, 2019. The Jan. 4, 2019 "Humans of the Magic Valley" post on the library's Facebook page raised some comment when it said one of the participants would present herself as a "post-Mormon." Others then commented. Amanda Cutler Derricott wrote "I don't see a post-Catholic, or post-Muslim. Why single out one religion? We should promote the good about different cultures, religions and backgrounds. I love the library programs because they are positive and uplifting. Allowing this seems to go against all that and it makes me sad. On the other hand, America is a land of free speech and we are all free to do just that. I hope the discussion involving the post Mormon is a positive, not hateful experience for those who are there." The library responded that "The volunteer shares whatever they'd like about their experience. So far, all of the conversations our volunteers have had have been respectful and inciteful." It's evidence yet again that libraries aren't immune from sensitive topics of discussion and how the library provides a discussion forum on community issues.

911 "Things to do at the Library," Twin Falls Public Library website, 2019.

before elected council members for approval. Sometimes, there's a library board and in many cases, a separate foundation to raise additional funds.[912]

Smaller libraries in Southern Idaho aren't typically as comprehensive in their programs, but do what they can with the resources and within standards of freedom of information availability. The Burley Public Library, for example, has a lengthy mission statement on its website which covers standards for resources and use of materials.[913] Many other libraries in Southern Idaho specialize in materials related to their own geographic areas and can offer outside materials through the Libraries Linking Idaho website, LiLI.org.

The new approach of openness and accessibility can be disconcerting to longtime patrons who used libraries in a different way in years past, having gone from "gatekeepers of information" to a "learn together" model, reflecting what the community says it wants and needs. Entities like the Idaho Commission for Libraries and the American Library Association maintain websites and other tools to help library staff stay up on current trends and ideas.[914]

Education standards for library professionals are changing too as more libraries expand their outreach efforts and community involvement. Online graduate courses are now offered at more universities, which may include on-campus time, and professional information services graduate degrees are expanding.[915]

In these ways, libraries are likely to evolve in Southern Idaho as elsewhere and may place even more emphasis on community space, while providing myriad resources for a growing Southern Idaho population. Their

---

912 City of Twin Falls website, 2019.

913 Burley Public Library, "Resource Selection Policy, 2016."

914 American Library Association, Library of the Future, "Trends," website, 2019. Among topics listed are "Data Everywhere;" "Digital Natives,"(Children who grew up in a digital world as opposed to "digital immigrants," we older adults of even a generation before); "Gamification" ("application of game elements and digital game design techniques to non-game settings, and game-based learning, or game playing that has defined learning outcomes);" and "Haptic Technology." "Haptic technology, haptic feedback, or simply haptics, is technology that incorporates tactile experience or feedback as part of its user interface, creating a sense of touch through vibrations, motion, or other forces."

915 Joslin Interview, Jan. 29, 2019. Interest in the online program has prompted one school, Emporia (Kan.) State University, to offer graduate classes in Boise beginning in fall, 2019. See Emporia State University, School of Library Science and Information Management website, 2019. San Jose State (Calif.) University, offers a similar graduate program in Library and Information Science. SJSU website, 2019. Both programs are accredited by the American Library Association.

role is becoming more about meeting community needs beyond providing books.[916]

Broadband Access. Partly due to isolation of some rural communities and the low density of population in scattered farms and ranches, Idaho has been behind the curve on broadband and internet access in rural areas. The issue was brought up by new Gov. Brad Little his "State of the State" address on Jan. 7, 2019, so it appears there may be new efforts to "close the gaps" in rural broadband service.[917]

Overall Idaho connectivity ranks 37th out of the 50 states with 82 percent coverage and an average speed of 25.6 megabytes/second, just above the federal 25 mg/s standard used to count as connected.[918] Urban areas are reasonably well served in Idaho, often with more than one provider, but other areas are not.

Since reliable, high speed access to the internet is essential to economic development, rural areas and communities have a distinct disadvantage if their access is limited. Even a 37th ranking is a show of improvement. In 2017, Idaho was ranked last in the nation, about 13 megabytes/second, and that was a 10 percent improvement from the year prior.[919]

On the plus side, Idaho's urban areas are about 98 percent internet capable, and even in rural communities, the state average is almost 70 percent. It's the large stretches in between which aren't yet connected.

These include much of rural Lincoln, Gooding, Camas, and lower Blaine Counties, as well as scattered parts of Minidoka, Jerome, lower Twin Falls and lower Cassia Counties. and adjacent Elmore County.[920] The high percentage of broadband coverage may also be exaggerated by how providers

---

916 Paisley, Tiffany. Comments, Jan. 20, 2019. "We're trying to get people out of their comfort zone, to see the library as a place of continued use, all through life."

917 Little, Idaho Governor Brad. "State of the State and Budget Address," Jan. 7, 2019. On broadband connectivity, Gov. Little said: "In my travels, I constantly hear how the absence of adequate broadband infrastructure is a deterrent to growth and economic development...To ensure Idaho can adapt to the rapidly evolving digital world, we must actively work to improve Idaho's broadband access, pursuing all options to increase broadband connectivity. I will work with the Legislature to ensure both rural and urban Idaho are connected and well-positioned to attract and create maximum success." See also McCurry, Cheyenne. "Gov. Little Pushes Rural Broadband Improvements," *The Owyhee Avalanche*, Jan. 16, 2018.

918 "Internet Connectivity in U.S. States," BroadbandNow website, Aug. 14, 2018. See also, U.S. Federal Communications Commission, "2018 Broadband Deployment Report," Feb. 2, 2018.

919 Molla, Rani. "These Are the States with the Fastest – and the Slowest Internet Speeds," Recode.com., June 7, 2017.

920 BroadbandNow website, "Internet Providers in Twin Falls, Idaho," 2018. The city is largely served by two wired providers, CableOne and CenturyLink.

define coverage; a single hookup in a census tract gives it covered status, even if it is the only connection in the entire tract.[921]

Given how rapidly change occurs in internet technology, it would seem that two or three decades from now, internet connectivity would be available pretty much everywhere, even in remote rural Idaho. In contrast, rural electrification and telephone connection took many decades to be commonplace in America.[922]

Internet access, even given its now-common presence in most communities, is still a relatively new technology that is still evolving. It didn't exist before 1990, just three decades back, and no, Al Gore didn't "invent" it then.[923]

New wireless versions may reduce or eliminate the need for hard-line capacity, just as smart phones can now send and receive information at rapid rates. It's uncertain in this rapidly-changing field how remote places in Idaho will be served in the future, but it's a good bet they will be connected better than they are today.

---

921 "Broadband Competition in Idaho," Institute for Local Self Reliance, Mar. 12, 2018. The report states: "While about 1 million people in Idaho have access to two or more options, nearly half a million people are not nearly as lucky. Approximately 327,000 of the state's 1.683 million people have only one option for broadband service, and 169,000 still do not have access to broadband."

922 Anderson, Paul E. "Sam Rayburn and the Rural Electrification Act," East Texas History website, Jan., 2019. Rayburn, then a powerful chairman and Speaker of the House, said that from the 1930s to 1959, over almost 30 years, the percent of rural farms served by electricity grew from 3 to 90 percent.

923 Kessler, Glenn. "A Cautionary Tale for Politicians: Al Gore and the 'Invention' of the Internet," *The Washington Post*, Nov. 4, 2013.

32. Local History: Preserved, Interpreted

While Southern Idaho's development hasn't received a great deal of national historical attention, that's likely to change in the years ahead as an appreciation of the region's past finds wider expression and more local preservation efforts. As the Southern Idaho region has grown in the past quarter century, so has a new respect for who we are and how we have come this way.

Perhaps it is the maturing of the community, the increase in thoughtfulness, civic pride and celebration. Perhaps too, it's due to increasing wealth. With higher revenues coming in, endeavors like public art and historic restoration are now seen as more affordable than in the not-too-distant past.[924]

Another factor may be the state's Centennial year in 1990, the Twin Falls Centennial in 2004 and restoration of Idaho's capitol which reopened in 2010 after a $120 million restoration project.[925] These milestones seemed to say, "Look, We've Come of Age" and opened the way for further respect for Idaho's and the Magic Valley's past. The 2018 complete remodel of the Idaho State History Museum in Boise,

---

924 Anonymous. "Twin Falls Council to Consider Buying $7,900 Shoshone Falls Painting for City," *Times-News*, Sept. 5, 2017. The city reported it had close to $16,000 set aside for public art.

925 Idaho Public Television. "Capitol of Light," website, 2018. The author served on the Idaho Capitol Commission from 1998 to 2016, which oversaw the restoration project. The renovated capitol has been widely praised for its stately grandeur and for the project being completed on time and under budget.

with its stunning interactive displays and a whole section on Idaho agriculture, is likely to spur further interest and appreciation.[926]

These milestones have spun off more attention to local history, restoration and refurbishing of historic properties, sites and overall public awareness. Groups like the Idaho Historical Society, the Idaho Centennial Commission, capitol restoration and Centennial license plate programs, The Idaho Heritage Trust, the Twin Falls Historical Commission and the Twin Falls County Historical Museum have all helped spread the importance of history in the area.[927] Local history groups can be found in smaller communities as well, sometimes with public funding support.[928]

Professor James Gentry's book on the area, *In The Middle and On The Edge: The Twin Falls Region of Idaho*,[929] is one of only a handful of specific accounts of Southern Idaho history.[930] It was an ambitious undertaking, supported by the College of Southern Idaho, and well done indeed. But it stands virtually alone as a comprehensive treatment of the Southern Idaho past down to about 1990.

Mostly, the Southern Idaho region is seen as part of Idaho history generally,[931] or as a specific topic of inquiry, such as studies on the irrigation systems of the West.[932] Sure, there have been focused reports on Idaho's pre-history, which include Native-American archeological sites,[933] Chinese mining works,[934] and specific sites like Caldron Linn of the Wilson Price Hunt Party in 1811,[935] the Stricker Ranch waystation on the Oregon Trail on

---

926 Carmel, Margaret. "Idaho State History Museum Will Open This Fall," *Idaho Press*, Aug. 3, 2018.

927 Matthews, Mychel. "Stricker Ranch: Pioneer Graves and an Opium Den," *Times-News*, July 23, 2017.

928 Matthews, Mychel. "Local museums preserve history that's uniquely ours. But how long can they do it without money or manpower,?" *Times-News*, July 23, 2017.

929 College of Southern Idaho, 2003. Although now retired, Gentry is by all accounts the "Dean of Southern Idaho History." He taught for many years at CSI and gives frequent presentations on many aspects of local history, trends and patterns.

930 See also Quinn, Larry. *A History of the Magic Valley*, Publishing West, 1996.

931 Arrington, Leonard J. *History of Idaho*, University of Idaho Press, 1994; Schwantes, Carlos A. *In Mountain Shadows, A History of Idaho*, University of Nebraska Press, 1991

932 Fiege, Mark. *Irrigated Eden: The Making of an Irrigated Landscape in the American West*, Weyerhaeuser Books, 2000.

933 Gruhn, Ruth. "New Excavations at Wilson Butte Cave," Idaho Museum of Natural History, 2006 (1961).

934 James, Ronald L. and Lytle, John C. Ruins of a World: Chinese Gold Mining at the Mon-Tung site in the Snake River Canyon, Bureau of Land Management, Idaho State Office, 1995.

935 Irving, Washington. *Astoria*. 1836.

Rock Creek,[936] the Hagerman Fossil Beds along the Snake River,[937] the Castle Rocks National Preserve and Castle Rocks State Park[938] at Almo and the Minidoka Japanese Internment Camp (Hunt Camp) near Jerome.[939]

All of these, and quite a few more, have received scholarly and popular attention. But American historiography has traditionally treated much of Western history as lacking the sweep-of-events narratives like the American Revolution or the Civil War or the convulsing social movements of our own time. It seems almost as if there's no definitive battle fought in an area, either actual or otherwise, the area gets less notice.

Idaho's most recognized historian is Leonard Arrington whose contributions touch many topics. The Twin Falls native rose rapidly in academic circles for his many studies on Western history, Church of Jesus Christ of Latter-Day Saints history and, in his final years, a comprehensive two-volume *History of Idaho* (1994), the go-to reference on the state.

Although he didn't focus on Southern Idaho directly, his works are infused with an appreciation of the region's settlement, agricultural history, culture and norms. A book by him on his native region would have added greatly to our understanding of Southern Idaho.[940]

Arrington was something of an anomaly for his time, a professional historian working on controversial topics like LDS history and the lives of early church leaders. He served for a time as LDS church historian, but was squeezed out in the late 1970s for his more iconoclastic views. Although a devout Mormon, Arrington drew a line at how LDS history should be vetted by church authorities. He once said "I do not think we could determine the truth of what had happened in history by having the Quorum of the Twelve vote on it."[941]

Recent historical approaches to Southern Idaho have mostly avoided controversial subjects, such as those involving the church, its settlements and its own historical perspectives. History professors James Gentry, Russell Tremayne, Ronald James and Larry Quinn have all been connected to the College of Southern Idaho, a public institution which gives controversial topics considerable open-forum range and expression. Arrington, on the other hand, was closely associated in much of his career with LDS church-

936 Idaho Historical Society, Stricker/Rock Creek, website 2018.

937 National Park Service, Hagerman Fossil Beds National Monument, website, 2017.

938 Idaho Department of Parks & Recreation, website. Castle Rocks State Park, 2018.

939 Tremayne, Russell M. and Shallat, Todd. *Surviving Minidoka: The Legacy of World War II Japanese-American Incarceration*, Boise State University, 2013.

940 Arrington, 1994. See also, "Leonard J. Arrington,". Wikipedia, updated 2018.

941 Quoted in Topping, Gary. *Leonard J. Arrington: A Historian's Life*, University of Oklahoma, 2008.

supported Brigham Young University; it wasn't surprising even then that his studies put him in occasional conflicts of interpretation with church authorities.

Examination of local historical topics has been supplemented by several good local historians, whose own curiosity has led to solid vignettes of earlier times. Writers like Virginia Ricketts, Donna Scott, ZoeAnn Shaub, Lorayne Orton Smith and Bessie Wright have all explored pieces of Southern Idaho history with enthusiasm and attention to detail. Still more recent and continuing good work is being done by columnists Kimberly Williams Brackett and Mychel Matthews regularly in the *Times-News*.

But since there was no "Battle of Little Bighorn" here, there's no George Armstrong Custer to intrigue generations of historians. The Idaho Nez Perce War happened hundreds of miles to the north. The Lewis and Clark Corps of Discovery route also was north of the Southern Idaho region. Many Oregon Trail accounts treat Southern Idaho as a barren, dusty place to be traversed and then left behind on the way to a green and lush Oregon.[942] Southern Idaho? "Move along, Folks – Nothing to See Here."

So, with a few exceptions such as Gentry's definitive book on the region, Southern Idaho history has been mostly the purview of local historians, community history followers and traditional media accounts. Much of this material is well-researched and well-written and certainly adds to an overall account of the area.

There are also useful accounts on such activities as the beginnings of cattle ranching,[943] the building of the Oregon Short Line Railroad[944] and the rise and then decline of the sheep industry,[945] as well as numerous town histories and even a new account on early Southern Idaho newspapering.[946] Local studies on various topics come out from time to time, and historical columns regularly appear in the *Times-News*.[947]

---

942 Stone, Beverly and Stone, Gary. *Stone By Stone on The Oregon Trail*, Stone Studios, 1993. This account contains many direct quotations from original Oregon Trail pioneers and many observations from them on the trail's course and difficulties. The Southern Idaho region was considered the most difficult stretch.

943 Brackett, Gus and Kimberly, et. al., eds. The *71': A Century of Bettering Conditions on the Range*, The 71 Livestock Association, 2017. See also Young, James A. and Sparks, B. Abbott. *Cattle in the Cold Desert*, University of Nevada Press, 1985.

944 Revolvy.com. Oregon Short Line Railroad, website. 2018.

945 National Academies of Science, Engineering & Medicine." Changes in the Sheep Industry in the United States" 2008. See also, Soward, Adam. "Why Sheep Started So Many Wars in the American West," Zocalo website, Oct. 5, 2017.

946 Brackett, Kimberly Williams. *Keepers of the Record*, Kindle Direct Publishing, 2019.

947 Kimberly Brackett and Mychel Matthews, both local journalists, often focus on local historical events and personalities. Ms. Brackett's column runs under the title "Curious Mind" and Ms. Matthews' column is called "Hidden History." See also Ricketts, Virginia.

But it feels, historically speaking, as if there's little to say about the region, except in the context of these other inquiries. Some of this may be due to the changes in how history is researched and written. Sine the 1960s, writes historian David Hackett Fischer, there's been a disconnect between "professional history and popular memory."[948] As much of Southern Idaho's story is rooted in the second, taking a broad pen to the region's history seems to lack wider consideration.

That's true generally of Western American history. There are individual state histories, such as T.A. Larson's *History of Wyoming* (1978) and accounts of the early explorers such as Bernard DeVoto's *Across the Wide Missouri* (1947), but comparatively few comprehensive accounts of the settlement of the West and the region's impact on how Americans see themselves.

Leo Marx's *The Machine In The Garden: Technology and the Pastoral Ideal In America* (1964) drew on the then-emerging field of American Studies for this multi-dimensional work exploring history, literature, technology and sociology. Other observers have explored the West's impact on national myths and symbols.[949]

Even today, more than a half-century after Marx's challenging book, Western American history seems to get "second shelf space" in American historiography, compared to say, the nation's wars and a long list of movement history from Progressivism to Prohibition, Women's Suffrage to Civil Rights, the Vietnam War to the Reagan years. Despite its narrow subject matter, Native-American Studies is probably more broadly taught by college history departments nationwide; gender studies programs have proliferated and various "cultural studies" offerings are in the catalogs to show how "with it" the departments are today.

It's as if professors know that if they can't fill the seats, they'll soon be marginalized and nothing disses history like plain, old vanilla lectures on events involving land settlement, farming and canal building by just another group of European settlers, true accounts though they be.

Frederick Jackson Turner's "Frontier Thesis," dating from the 1890s, is as far back as the frontier closing itself, an historical speck just ahead of settlement of Southern Idaho itself. Today, the notion that the existence of

---

Then and Now in Southern Idaho, Falls City Pub., 1998; Wright. Bessie M. Kimberly, Idaho History, 1990; *Hunt For Idaho: Evacuees 1942-1945*, 1994; Milner, Murtaugh, Murtaugh Lake, 1998; and *Oakley, Idaho: Pioneer Town*, 1987; and Scott, Donna and Schaub, ZoeAnn. *Gifts of Heritage, Pioneer Portraits*, Twin Falls Centennial Commission, 2004.

948 Fischer, David Hackett. *Paul Revere's Ride*, Oxford University Press, 1994.

949 Marx, Leo. *The Machine In The Garden*, Oxford, 1964. See also, Smith, Henry Nash. *Virgin Land: The American West as Symbol and Myth*, World, 1971 and Limerick, Patricia Nelson. *The Legacy of Conquest: The Unbroken Past of the American West*, Norton, 1986.

open land helped shape the American experience seems quaint, even archaic.[950]

So it's not surprising that the account of Southern Idaho's settlement would be given, at best, short-shrift by historians. One modern website describes the Turner Thesis as the purview of a dead past, fraught with error, a tilt toward "enduring romanticization of the West," with many omissions, particularly of modern sensibilities toward minorities and various social movements.[951]

As with many other aspects of Southern Idaho's past, present and future, there's both challenge and opportunity with respect to local history. It's similar to how other regions of the country have come to appreciate what they have, to set about preserving their history and telling the story of settlement here in new and compelling ways.

Given today's charged political climate in which places like Southern Idaho are dismissed as "fly over country" by coastal and academic elites, it isn't likely to be a story immediately given wide visibility. But so-called "popular" historical accounts have a way of exciting popular appreciation, as we have seen with Stephen Ambrose's *Undaunted Courage* on the Lewis and Clark expedition (1996) and in an earlier generation, Bruce Catton's *Centennial History of the Civil War* (1961-1965). While the settlement of Southern Idaho may lack the dramatic flourish of those events, historical writing on the region is likely to further come of age in the coming decades.

Beyond the narratives, local historical groups throughout the valley, some more active than others, now work lovingly on preservation efforts for historical buildings and town districts. The Rupert City Square and its premier historic building, the Wilson Theater, are good examples of what can be accomplished over time by devoted citizens who care about their special place.[952]

Until about 25 years ago, such efforts were mostly low-key, but when it comes to local history, times have indeed changed in Southern Idaho. There's

---

950 Turner, Frederick Jackson. *The Significance of the Frontier in American History*, American Historical Association, 1893.

951 Brand, Lauren, et. al, eds. Lumen: "US History II. The West As History: the Turner Thesis," website, 2018."The history of the West was many-sided and it was made by many persons and peoples. Turner's thesis was rife with faults, not only its bald Anglo-Saxon chauvinism in which non-whites fell before the march of "civilization" and Chinese and Mexican immigrants were invisible but in its utter inability to appreciate the impact of technology and government subsidies and large-scale economic enterprises alongside the work of hardy pioneers. Still, Turner's thesis held an almost canonical position among historians for much of the twentieth century and, more importantly, captured Americans' enduring romanticization of the West and the simplification of a long and complicated story into a march of progress."

952 Welch, Laurie. "Wilson Theater: A Cornerstone of Rupert," *Times-News*, Jan. 22, 2013.

a new appreciation of the region's past, and concentrated efforts to preserve it. Public arts and architecture seem to be improving and even Twin Falls City Hall has a nice reproduction of Thomas Moran's historic painting of Shoshone Falls (1900) and a new and inviting plaza with a statue of Twin Falls' first surveyor, John Hayes.[953]

Other historical pieces have come into place in recent years. The Twin Falls Public Library maintains an excellent "Idaho and Pacific Northwest History Room" of special materials related to the valley's origins and development.[954] The Twin Falls Visitor Center, which gets thousands of tourists a month, has a magnificently-restored late-1800s stagecoach once owned by I.B. Perrine, and a prominent statue of Perrine himself surveys the canyon's sweep.[955] Local preservation efforts have drawn both interest and results in Twin Falls through the work of dedicated individuals like attorney Paul Smith and city historic preservation chair Nancy Taylor.[956]

In Twin Falls City Park, a stone monument and horse-drawn plow commemorates the valley's founding with engraved quotations reflecting the valley's origins, fitting reminders of the hard labor needed to shape the early valley. At the Twin Falls Regional Airport, a multi-panel display shows off the valley and honors Southern Idaho's soldiers lost in recent conflicts.[957] Though of the more recent past, it too reflects on our heritage, and the sacrifices of our lost service members.

It seems true enough, as historian David Fischer writes, that modern historical writing is often consumed with trivia. Perhaps this is so, he says, due to the modern emphasis in many fields of political correctness and multi-culturalism. This focus on "social structures, intellectual systems and material processes" has led to a slighting of "contingent events" around which things really happened.[958]

The surveying and settling of Southern Idaho was one such seminal occurrence, one of the last large Western land settlements under the Carey Act and its predecessors. In just 15 years, the region went from near zero

---

953 West, Bowen. "The Heart of the City: Twin Falls Downtown Commons Almost Ready To Open," *Times-News*, June 12, 2018.

954 Twin Falls Public Library.org. website, 2018. "Idaho and Pacific Northwest History Room."

955 Wootton, Julie. "Stagecoach has New Home in Visitor Center," *Times-News*, April 26, 2015.

956 Matthews, Mychel. "Twin Falls Attorney Receives Award for Decades of Historical Work," *Times-News*, Feb. 14, 2019.

957 Knopp, Bill. "Artist Gary Stone Commended by Military for Creating Veterans' Mural," *Mountain Home News*, Jan. 1, 2010.

958 Fischer, Paul Revere's Ride.

human population to 65,000 people, virtually all of them immigrants and their children.

It was a huge in-migration which transformed the valley and created the patterns of life we see around us, more than a century later.

Historians know "what really happened" isn't reducible to a series of events, facts and quotations. "We can never be certain that we have recaptured it as it really was," writes historian Barbara Tuchman. "But the least we can do is to stay within the evidence."[959] Writing vividly at the end of the Civil War, Walt Whitman, who tended the wounded in field hospitals, wrote that "the real war will never get in the books." The courage, suffering and dignity on both sides were simply too overwhelming to be conveyed.

Yet, there are perhaps 75,000 books on the Civil War, something like one and a half written for every day since Appomattox.[960] That war remains emblazoned in our American memory, seared into our national reminiscence of generations, race, equality and migration.

By its very nature, history looks back at the past from the present. But it also looks forward. It may be sometimes predictive, sometimes not, but we can surely learn from either. Its study opens us to insights into how our own paths have unfolded.

Southern Idaho's history has a wealth of insights into American life and particularly into how our values were formed and now retained. Surely that is a story worth telling and worth telling well. As with many other aspects of life here, future historians will surely be equal to the task.

---

959 Tuchman, Barbara. *Practicing History,* Penguin, 1982.

960 University of Iowa, graduate college, international writing program, "Whitman and the Civil War," website. 2018.

33. Funerals & Obituaries

Another early spring is upon us in Southern Idaho and the landscape abounds with flowering Lilac, Forsythia, Apple and Cherry blossoms, all signifying the renewal of life, and with it, enduring faith. We are blessed in this beautiful valley every year as winter finally gives way to the rich greening of fields of wintered-over alfalfa, wheat and barley. At community cemeteries all across the region, family members place flowers and fresh mementos on their loved ones' graves, lilacs last in a dooryard bloom'd,[961] memories of those passed on.

We don't take as much time as we should to ponder eternal truths. We relegate them to funerals and obituaries, but in this still reverent and respectful valley, these events are the chords of family structure and community. On weekday or weekend afternoons, people steer their cars to the side of the road to let funeral processions pass, lights on, to nearby final rests.

We may not even know the family or the deceased, but we make this small gesture out of honor. It is yet another feature of Magic Valley life

---

961 Whitman, Walt. When Lilacs Last In The Dooryard Bloom'd. (1865): "In the dooryard fronting an old farm-house/ Near the white-wash'd palings,/Stands the lilac-bush tall-growing with heart-shaped leaves of rich green,/With many a pointed blossom rising delicate,/With the perfume strong I love,/With every leaf a miracle – and from this bush in the dooryard,/With delicate-color'd blossoms and heart-shaped leaves of rich green,/A sprig with its flower I break."

and generational passage. Try participating in a funeral procession in a big city, cars whizzing by, some honks, nothing else. Didn't know him or her.

Sometimes here, in cases of someone killed in military service to our country, or as a first responder here at home, citizens line streets to show pride and respect. It's a tradition we hope is never lost.

Such simple expressions have been in place locally for generations, and despite changes, they are mostly still here, and in at least one way, obituaries, they are writ larger than in the past. Indeed, they are part of the cultural "glue" which holds Southern Idaho together, which cement our community history, myth and legend.

By myth here, we don't mean untrue stories of false narrative. Nor do we mean by legend any sort of false reporting. Rather, we mean the ordering accounts of past events which Joseph Campbell says are the root elements in all societies, the continuing story of mankind across generations.[962]

Sometimes, there's a direct remembrance in funeral processions to a person's past and that of the valley, for example, the use of a horse-drawn funeral wagon for an elderly farmer or a rousing rendition of "The Saints Go Marching In" for someone in the media or entertainment field.

More likely, there's a recitation at the funeral itself of the deceased's personal faith, accomplishments, his or her help to others, to making our community, state and nation a better place for having been here.

If there are warts in the deceased's life, they are passed over or mentioned humorously or only in brief. These often elicit a chuckle from the audience and family, which is their intent; humor in remembrance lessens the pain of loss, as any preacher or chaplain can attest.

We see the same patterns in modern obituaries as they appear on funeral home websites and in printed form in newspapers. It wasn't always that way. Twenty-five or thirty years ago, most Idaho newspapers followed a rigid, pre-set style for obituaries, as outlined in the annual Associated Press style guide for writing. There was little variation, and the obituaries weren't very informative, nor satisfying to family members who wanted their loved ones memorialized more completely.

But then, as society became more "personal," families asked why they couldn't write the obituaries themselves. Well, why not? And thus, another formalism gave way. By the year 2000, there was a new normal.[963]

---

962 Campbell, Joseph. *The Power of Myth*. (1988).

963 Author's note: *The Times-News*, of which the author was publisher at the time, wasn't the first Idaho newspaper to adopt this new approach, but it quickly caught on locally and has been used ever since. Obituary placement was treated as an advertisement since the deceased's family controlled the content. At first, the fees were small; with most placements costing only $50 to $100. Now, the obituaries are generally much longer and,

The result is that, even in an age in which people prize their privacy, modern local obituaries are quite complete, often covering the deceased's early life, education, marriage (sometimes more than one), children and step-children, life accomplishments, work, military service, hobbies and community involvements, pets, sports, outdoor hunting or fishing pictures, as well as statements of endearment, family love, thanks for care from medical and hospice personnel and professions of faith and remembrance.

Given the growing acceptance of gay marriages, it's no longer unusual to see a person's survivors include a same-sex life partner, or when the deceased has been married more than once, there is the simple matter-of-fact statement, that he or she divorced and later remarried. There's no false reporting in that, though the breakup isn't usually detailed.

Obituaries often contain statements of the deceased's personal character, incidents of how his or her values were formed by hard work or other experiences; there are sometimes unusual funeral requests, such as college football colors for funeral clothing.

Sometimes, though still not common, a person will pen out his or her own obituary or statement of personal faith or testament, thus giving others insight into how the individual sees himself or herself. When written, these are particularly instructive, often containing "life lessons" for children and grandchildren, shortened memoirs which rightly find their way into ancestry inquiries, searches and future generational research.

All of these personal details reflect a deeper meaning, that of community linkages. Even with different religious affiliations or none at all, these patterns hold with both church attendees and non church goers. The particulars change, but the expressions are constants.

They're now spread even further by blog and social media postings, which in turn elicit expressions of sympathy and condolences, somewhat like a previously mailed sympathy card, but with wider audiences. Funeral homes routinely provide places for postings, and these are often "recycled" in years following as "keepers of memory" notices, sometimes with a convenient link to continual posting for a fee, or to a nearby floral shop which offers memorial flowers as well.

A cynic might observe that it's just another form of modern capitalism finding yet more unexploited niches in an online age, but the underlying

---

with rate increases, have become more expensive. But since they're part of lasting remembrance, the costs are rarely questioned. Rarely, different sides of a family want the person remembered differently, resulting in separate versions of the obituary with different accounts of the deceased's "life history," usually having to do with different marriages or personal struggles which the deceased encountered. Sadly, these battles may extend in families beyond a person's passing.

reason is, of course, the continuance of human experience, across place, generations and cultures. That they are common in Southern Idaho shouldn't surprise anyone, as they are yet another way in which heritage and rituals entwine our daily lives and passings.

Modern life and the dangers of political incorrectness have long excluded expressions of faith and remembrance in many settings, but we still readily accept these in the context of someone's passing. Collectively, they're an anthology of the past, a path of stones stretching back in time, yet leading, on a path forward as well. That's the nature of Southern Idaho community history, its threads linking us, one to the other.

Part V: A Partially Known Future

Four Western Scenes, Vincent Andrew Hartgen, 1983, 1984

34. The Spirit of Place, Revisited

This book began with a question, "Who are we then, we people of Southern Idaho?" An initial answer would be, we are first "people of the land" whose ancestors then, and we now, have taken up this place and transformed it by opportunity and toil into the verdant landscape we see around us.

Slowly at first, then more rapidly and now seemingly at a frenetic pace, we have grown and prospered. We have done this by individual effort and common endeavor, through both strength of character and determination. We have done this in numerous arenas, from agriculture to education, politics to generosity, government to the arts. We have transformed it all into a bustling valley of specialized commerce and an agricultural plain of bounty and prosperity.

Our ancestors would be proud indeed. They would marvel at the physical transformation wrought in only a few decades, but they would also remark on how we have kept our cultural values of hard work, faith and egalitarian roots. They would ask, "How did you keep those so intact?" "How did you manage to both transform place and yet hold to remembrance?"

The short answer is, we came here with those values and never set them aside. That's why, in whatever chosen topic, one still hears echoes:

- Constants? The Earth as it was and yet shall be again, eons ahead.

- Growth? All around us, but it has not altered our character.
- Agriculture? Still individualistic, yet with common endeavor.
- Land ownership? Larger farms, but still of human scale.
- Faith? Currents of change, as elsewhere, yet resilient and adapting.
- Politics? Conservative, but not overly ideological.
- Education? We should count our blessings.
- Generosity? It's in our community DNA to help others.
- Government? Simple, representative, participatory. Citizens all.
- Patriotism? Love of community, state, nation.
- Diversity? Not as much as in many places, but changing too.
- Isolation? Yes, but there are pluses in that. It's a long way to anywhere.
- Natural Beauty? All around us, writ large and small.
- The Information Age? In our libraries, homes, schools, businesses.
- Local History? We're still writing that.

At the end of *The Great Gatsby*, the narrator Nick Carraway wonders how the then-forested island of Manhattan must have seemed to those first Dutch sailors, seeing for perhaps the last time in human history, a continent, a pristine land "commensurate with their capacity for wonder."

Early Magic Valley settlers must have been struck by the same vastness of this place, yet determined to overcome the tasks ahead. It must have seemed endless in possibility, spread out before them in each successive generation.

Today, we look back on the frenetic years of growth and change, privileged to have been here at turn the state's centennial, the valley's centennial, the onrush of events and progress. Every day, it seems, brings accounts of new projects, new uses, new initiatives. new research, new employment.

We'll end with a single issue of the *Times-News*, Tuesday, Feb. 26, 2019, a "nothing special" day, except with the bustling of local progress. A new milk processing plant will employ more than 100 people. A proposal to replace older facilities with three new fire stations in the city is on the May ballot. A new veterinary sciences building may come to the CSI campus. A committee is forming to welcome newcomers, foster diversity and continue tolerance.

These all illustrate a region coming of age. It is said that sometimes we do not see how momentous a time is, even as we are passing through it.

Pause for a moment and consider Southern Idaho.

Now think of the towns and cities you know elsewhere. Would we trade what we have for any of them? Each place has its own spirit, says D.H. Lawrence, its own character and identity, moment in history. This is Southern Idaho's.

Index

About the Author

Stephen Hartgen has been an Idaho resident for almost 40 years. He's served as editor and publisher of *The Times-News*, 1982-2005, and on numerous boards and commissions, including the Idaho Capitol Commission from 1998-2016. He's been a business and economic development consultant as executive director of Business Plus which has helped create thousands of jobs and more than $2 billion in capital investment to Southern Idaho.

Beginning in 2008, Hartgen was elected to serve five terms in the Idaho House of Representatives until his retirement in 2018. He chaired the House Commerce & Human Resources Committee and served on the Revenue & Taxation Committee, the Energy, Environment & Technology Committee, the Millennium Fund Committee and as the House's representative to the Permanent Building Advisory Council.

Hartgen holds a Ph.D. in American History (1976) from the University of Minnesota and taught journalism and media history at both Minnesota and Ohio State University. Before coming to Twin Falls as editor in 1982, he was a reporter at *The Minneapolis Star* and editor of the *Casper* (Wyo.) *Star-Tribune*.

Hartgen is an author, co-author and editor of several books including *New Strategies for Public Affairs Reporting* (1976), *Idaho Media Law Handbook* (1984), *Vincent Andrew Hartgen: His Art and, Legacy* (2008), *Frances Caroline Hartgen, Maine Passage* (2006) and a personal memoir, *Journey West: A Memoir of Journalism and Politics*, also from Ridenbaugh Press (2014).

He lives in Twin Falls with his spouse, Idaho House of Representatives member Linda Wright Hartgen, who was elected to the same seat, District 24B, in 2018. They have five children. In his spare time, he enjoys writing, historical reading and fly fishing Western waters.

In 2019, Hartgen became a contributing columnist for Idahopoliticsweekly.com. on current Southern Idaho issues. He may be reached at 208-733-5790, through his email, Stephen_Hartgen@hotmail.com or followed on his Facebook page, www.facebook.com/stephenhartgen.

Made in the USA
Columbia, SC
07 August 2019